D0870461

Champagne Tony Lema: Triumph to Tragedy

An inside look at the career of one of
golf's most popular champions

Bill Roland

ROLAND Golf Services LLC   2014   Columbus, OH

ROLAND Golf Services LLC

Champagne Tony Lema: Triumph to Tragedy

Bill Roland

Copyright © 2014 by Bill Roland

All Rights Reserved

Copy Editor: Sandy Roland

Cover Design: Bill Roland, Jacob Samblanet, and Beau Filing

Interior Design: Jacob Samblanet

Published in the United States by ROLAND Golf Services LLC

First Edition

ISBN 978-0-9911293-1-7

This book is dedicated to Tony Lema's only sister, Bernice, his two brothers, Harry and Walter, and Harry's wife Judi. Shortly before publication, Harry joined Tony in the eternal heavens. May they rest in peace.

I would also like to dedicate this book to all young golfers, both male and female, who have been introduced to the game and like it from the get-go. May they enjoy reading about Tony Lema and learn from him many of the life's lessons that can be found in this biography. I think Tony would be happy to know that other people could "pick up some pearls" from the wayward shots he experienced. After all, from his early days as a caddy until his final days as a pro, he was always looking for the lush fairways of life.

Contents

Prologue

During the last round of the 1966 PGA Championship at Firestone C.C., Al Geiberger had just made the turn and was munching on a peanut butter sandwich. He was prepared to take a bite of his first major championship. It was a different story for Tony Lema, who stood on the 18th tee and would eventually finish 34th. He was the last in his threesome to hit his tee shot and he absolutely crunched a drive down the center of the fairway on the long par-4 finishing hole. Two young boys, about ten years old, began arguing about who would own the golden tee Tony had just used and had landed at their feet. "Hold on boys," Tony said. He calmly reached into his pocket and slowly dropped about a dozen golden tees into the outstretched hands of these youngsters. It was as if those small fingers were clutching solid gold. Tony patted them both on the head and began to walk down the fairway. For several years I had been an ardent fan of his and on that given day I had watched Tony play quite a few holes. I was no more than a few yards away and said, "That was nice, Tony." "Hey," he smiled as he glanced towards me, "they're only kids. Besides, this is my last hole." I wished him luck. He said, "Thank you." With his head held high, he strolled down the fairway. I stood there on the 18th tee wondering when and where I would see my favorite golfer play next time. Little did we know just how special that gesture was to those two youngsters. Little did he know it was his last fairway. Within fours hours of that simple but thoughtful act, Tony Lema, his wife Betty and the two pilots would perish in a horrific plane crash some 380 miles away. The twin-engine Beechcraft Bonanza piloted by Doris Mullen and co-pilot Dr. George Bard lost power as both engines cut out briefly near the Lansing Airport located close to the Indiana-Illinois border and eventually crashed near the seventh green of the Lansing Sportsman's Club. The 32-year-old Californian had risen to the top echelon of golfers throughout the world. Suddenly his dream career had come to an end and the exciting life of Champagne Tony Lema had been snuffed out.

Education at Lake Chabot

This is a story about Anthony David Lema, born on February 25, 1934 in Oakland, California to parents of Portuguese ancestry. He was the youngest of four children. The oldest was his sister Bernice, followed by two brothers, Harry and Walter. When Tony was three years old his father died of pneumonia. His mother, Clotilda, known to family members as Cleo, raised the four children by working at Hale Brothers Department Store and the Washington Pharmacy. The family lived on 105th Avenue. At the time of her husband's passing, Cleo was 27 years old with the four children. She was beside herself. A friend told her, the best thing she could do would be to put the kids in a Catholic school. She replied, "Where do you think I'm going to get the money for a Catholic school?"

"I don't know, talk to the priest."

So she went to see Father Silva and told him she had four kids and that someone told her to put them in Catholic school. "But Father, I don't have the money."

"Ok" he said, "I'll pay for it. They will go to St. Bernard's Grammar School on 62nd Avenue."

Bernice was in the fifth grade, Harry in the third grade, Walter in the second grade and Tony was still pre-school. Father Silva paid for all four of the Lema children to attend grammar school. Years later, Monsignor Silva built St. Louis Bertrand School on 100th Avenue. He knocked on Cleo's door and said, "I need some help." And she said, "Of course. You helped me then. Now it's my turn."

Tony was the only one of the four children born in the

hospital. His mother wanted a girl because she already had two sons. Bernice was six years old when he was born. "It was pretty exciting," she remembers. "Mother told me years later that it was much easier giving birth in a hospital compared to the home birth with mid-wives that she experienced with the three of us."

Bernice recalled Tony's early years. "Because he was my baby brother," she said, "I took him everywhere I went. We would go to the movies every Saturday and he always wanted to sit on the aisle. He was four or five and he would slip out to the lobby and play with the water fountains or whatever looked like fun. Finally, the manager said you are going to have to keep an eye on him so we made him sit in between us. He was just a character.

"The thing that always comes to my mind, Tony was very active. Some kids are moving all the time; have to have something to do. Mother complained to the doctor, 'This boy is very active, how do I handle him?' One of my fondest memories was that we had a big driveway and plenty of room to skate back and forth. When he came home from school, Mom would say, 'Let's go skating.' 'Oh, ok, Mom,' he replied. They would skate up and down the driveway. He always has so much energy.

"When he was about ten years old, we were coming out of the movies and saw some high school friends. I said, 'This is my baby brother Anthony.' Afterwards on the way home, he said, 'I think I need to talk with you.' 'What's the matter?' 'Number one, I would rather you call me Tony. Don't call me baby brother Anthony. And your baby brother! Have you looked at how tall I am and how small you are and how dumb it sounds calling me your baby brother?' 'Oh, I didn't think about that.' 'Well' he said, 'you don't have to do the baby brother stuff anymore. OK?' "

Tony played basketball all the time. The family lived within walking distance of St. Louis Bertrand Church and all three Lema boys were active in the church. Cleo would make oatmeal cookies every day. The boys would race home, scarf down the cookies and head back to the church and play basketball. Tony was a very good player and since he had such a high energy level, Cleo and Bernice were always trying to make sure that he was on the straight and narrow path. It was the basketball at the church that was the saving grace for the boys. Every night at 6 o'clock, the church bells rang and the boys came home for dinner. When they were in high school they played high school sports. Bernice's husband Art, had a basketball team that played in an industrial league. Tony played on that team with all of his high school friends, and they remained friends forever. He was very sports-minded from the start.

"Smoking got him in trouble," Bernice recalled. "He started smoking when he was about 13 or 14. He tried to hide it, but mother knew what he was up to even though he always denied it. During his freshman year at St. Joseph's, he was caught smoking in the bathroom and they suspended him. He came home, told his mother about it, and added, 'You know I'm not going back.' 'Where are you going?' 'I am going to St. Elizabeth's' 'What makes you think you are going to St. Elizabeth's?' 'I am going to go and talk with them.' He did just that and they told him you couldn't smoke in the bathroom there either. And he didn't and he loved St. Elizabeth's. They understood him, and they knew in his senior year when he was not in class, he was at the golf course. I would say that three quarters of his senior year he spent at the golf course. When it came time to graduate, his diploma was not signed. They said to him, 'You know you have to go to summer school.' And he did. The courses at night went so smoothly, he said later on, 'If I knew high school was that easy, I would have gone to class.' They finally gave him the diploma; they met him half way. He had two different report cards and my mother did not know the one she saw was filled out by a friend. The one the school gave him, well, only Tony knew where that was hidden. The school has treated him pretty well; they have a tournament for him every year.

"One time, when he was about 15 or 16, he and a friend were out fooling around. They were in a convertible or whatever they had, and in front of them was this beer truck. They looked and on the back of this truck was a case of beer. One of them said, 'I bet you we could get one of those and that guy would never know the difference.' They slowed down and one of them jumped out of the car and secured the case of beer. Meanwhile, right in back of them sat a police officer. They never even looked behind them to see if anybody was watching. So of course the cop stopped them and said, 'I've never seen such dumb kids in all of my life. Didn't you see me in back of you?' 'No, all we saw was the beer.' 'And you're going to take that beer back, aren't you?' They immediately said, 'Yeah,' 'And you're never going to do that again, are you?' 'No, we're never going to do that again. Believe me, we're never going to do that again.' So, the cop got the attention of the beer truck driver and said, 'These kids have something to give you.' He went home and told his mother, 'You won't believe what happened to me today?' He told her the story and she said, 'You are a very lucky young man and I hope you realize that.' And he said, 'Yeah Mom, we won't do anything that dumb again.' And of course they didn't. In today's media, there would have been a big to-do and whatever but back then they said, forget it kids and don't let it happen again. It really taught them a lesson. It shook them to their shoes, but it helped Tony learn to respect the law."

Bernice reflected on how Tony first became acquainted with golf. "He loved all athletics," she explained. "Uncle Charlie played golf all the time and he also caddied at several golf courses in the Oakland area. When Tony was about 12, he tagged along with Uncle Charlie. Around the same time, his older brother, Walter, advised him to come with him and caddy. He said, 'You're tall and nobody is going to know how old you are. Come with me and we'll caddy together.' "

Shortly after he started looping at Lake Chabot, he was assigned to carry the bag for Clarence Jones, a comptroller by trade. They hit it off from the very first round. "I took a liking to him immediately," Jones recalled. "It wasn't long before he was the only caddy I used." And the player-caddy relationship was a two-way street. Tony caddied for Clarence from 1946 until he joined the Marines in 1953. Coincidentally, Clarence Jones was transferred to Flint, Michigan about the same time. As fate would have it, a wonderful reunion occurred in 1958, Tony's first year on the tour. In a story filed by a reporter for the *Flint Journal*, it seems that a few weeks before the Buick Open, Clarence and some friends went down to watch the pros in the Western Open played at the Red Run Golf Club in Royal Oak, Michigan. "That was funny," Jones said. "We decided to follow Sam Snead for a few holes and I couldn't believe my eyes when I saw Tony playing in the same threesome. I knew he had turned pro, but I never thought about running into him in Detroit."

Tony ended up staying with the Joneses while he played in the Buick Open and told the reporter about the days he was caddying for Clarence Jones at Lake Chabot. "He is the most considerate person I ever met," Tony said. "He used to go out of his way to pick me up and take me to the course and then he started letting me play a few holes with him when we got out of sight of the clubhouse. That's the way I learned this game. When he took a bag of balls out on the practice tee I would shag half the time and then he let me hit the other half. A lot of times we'd be out there practicing long after dark, using the headlights on his car to keep track of the balls."

When Tony was 13, Mrs. Jones let him use her clubs to compete in junior tournaments. At 15 he won his first caddy tournament with the borrowed set. Four years later he won the City Amateur championship in Oakland. "By then I had my own clubs," Tony added.

"Tony was a good boy," said his Mother Cleo. "A little hot headed when he was very young, but a good boy. Many times Tony took my last dollar for green fees. Most of the time, though, he was working at odd jobs or caddying. He'd always try to arrange his hours so he could get out to play golf. At first, I thought it was only because he loved the outdoors so much. He couldn't stay at any job inside, he had to get outside. He worked the early shift at Pacific Cannery and he worked the night shift at Gerber's, but he always got back to the golf course. He used to cut school, I know. And he was always hungry. Don't know how a boy that slim could eat that much. He'd come home and Bernice would say, 'Lock up the refrigerator.' He could eat two good steaks. Of course, he loved music and dancing, too. We had a stereo and Tony always put it on—and when he was home he was on the go every minute."

In his book, *Golfers' Gold*, published in 1964,Tony talked about those years when he growing up and getting in and out of trouble. "My father had died when I was three years old," he wrote. "Leaving no insurance and three boys and a girl for my mother to raise in the industrial section of Oakland. Everyone in the family had to work pretty hard through the years to help make ends meet, and though I did everything I could to carry my share of the breadwinning burden I also did a little bit of hell-raising on the side.

"I was pretty tough to handle in high school, ran with a rough crowd, and though we got into trouble quite a bit we were lucky enough to stay out of the local lockup. Those are years I would love to have the chance to do over. We got into trouble because we would sit around and booze it up from time to time, then start talking big and pump ourselves full of a lot of false courage. Phew! Talk about close calls! Thank goodness for golf. I began to caddy when I was 12 at the nearby Lake Chabot municipal golf course because I could pick up a couple of bucks a day that way. Then I began to play. How I loved to play! When I hit a good shot I got a strong thrill out of watching the ball hanging in the air and then the slow way it floated down to earth. The excitement of sinking a long putt was almost physical. I loved to play basketball, but that was a team sport, and the most important kick I got out of golf was the individual challenge. I didn't have to rely on anyone else. There was no team to blame for losing or to blame me for losing. A bad score was entirely my fault and a good one was entirely to my credit. Everything was right there in front of me and I could see it happening and know why it happened. By the time I was in my teens I loved the game so much that I would play hooky from school to be able to play golf. In the summers I would work the night shift at the cannery so that I could play golf during the day. The thought of making golf my life's work, however, had never occurred to me."

There was a driving range and par-3 course in Oakland along the shore of San Francisco Bay called Airways Fairways. It was owned by Rig Ballard, who recognized the talents of a black man named Lucius Bateman. Bateman ran the driving range and he became one of the nation's very best teachers after realizing in 1942 that the game was not ready to accept African Americans as playing professionals. Originally from Biloxi, MS, Lucius served in the Air Force and after he was discharged he moved to California and took a job in a San Francisco shipyard, still with an eye on a golf-playing career. While he was there he visited the old Alameda municipal course to recapture his swing and promptly attracted considerable attention. Lucius' first round was a 66! In one exceptional period of a few weeks, Bateman tied the Alameda course record with a 63, registered 66's at Crystal Springs in San Mateo municipal course, 67 at Tilden and Hayward, and 68 at Chabot and 69 at San Jose's Hillview.

The pro at Alameda, Earl Fry, liked Bateman and asked him if he would mind giving some of the many juniors hanging around the course some instruction. Fry himself had a heavy junior workload. Bateman soon built an enthusiastic following as a teacher. After four and half years at the shipyard, he decided to return to golf on a full-time basis. Rig Ballard, owner of the Airways Fairways, recognized Batemans talents and gave the gentle black man a job at the driving range. After he became head pro at the range, Bateman received many offers of professional positions from good Bay Area clubs. When asked why he did not accept any of those lucrative offers, Bateman replied, "I'm not a rolling stone. Besides, Rig Ballard gave me a job here when none of the others were interested."

In 1947, when Tony was 13 he met "Loosh" and caddied for him in several tournaments. Lucius took him under his wings. "Tony was a scraggly little kid who loved golf," Bateman recalls. "At first I didn't think he was going to be a very good golfer. He didn't seem to have much talent, but he was a fighter. I've seen some of the other kind, boys with all the talent in the world but without the competitive drive." Bateman got Tony a job at the Airways Fairways and the two spent quite a bit of time on the practice tee. Tony's game came around quickly.

"I would take Tony to the toughest East Bay courses and we would challenge anyone in a best-ball match, " Bateman said. "Tony didn't look too strong with a golf club in his hands and we appeared to be pushovers. But he was impressive in those money matches. He would always come through in the clutch on key holes to help us win. Before every one of those matches I'd tell Tony, 'Know what you've got, play up to it and when the chips are down, don't choke.' He seldom failed."

Some nights, he would tell his Mother that he was going down to Lucius Bateman's to hit balls and he was out with his friends. On one occasion, Cleo called Lucius because Tony was late and asked him to send Tony home. Lucius said, "He's not here tonight, did he tell you he was coming down here?" She said "Yes" and that she would take care of things when he got home. After that, whenever he didn't show up, Lucius would call Cleo and say, "Is he supposed to be here tonight, because he's not here?" After that, Tony knew that if he said was going down to Lucius' place, that's exactly where he would go or Lucius would be after him big time. Lucius was a Southern gentleman.

Tony recognized Bateman's other virtues as being even more important than his considerable teaching ability. "Many kids might have made jails instead of pars and birdies if it hadn't been for Loosh," Tony said. "He knows kids—how they think, how to talk to them and what to do for them. As long as I've known him he's always been willing to help kids for nothing in return."

Perhaps the lone sore spot in Bateman's career is that he has not been able to interest any sizable number of African-American boys in golf. "Colored boys don't think it's their sport," he explained. "When Joe Louis was heavyweight champion all of the colored youngsters wanted to be fighters. It would be the same with golf if an African American pro came up who could rival Arnold Palmer for headlines."

Nevertheless, Bateman was confident that one of these days a Negro boy will make links history. Possibly, only the fate of being born too early kept Loosh himself from fulfilling this role. But he was not bitter. "My mother taught me that everything happens for the best," Bateman said. "What may seem like a tough break often works out the other way. I have no complaints."

Who helped Tony the most with developing his game as a junior golfer? It's hard to say, because Fry took him under his wing and Tony spent so much time at Lake Chabot. On the other hand, he spent so much time with Lucius; it's probably a toss up. Golf was part of Tony's every day life. In a *Sports Illustrated* article, Tony gave credit to some of those who helped him... to Lucius Bateman of Rig Ballard's Airways Fairways, the late Ralph Hall, an Oakland police officer who taught him course tactics, and to Lake Chabot Muni professional Dick Fry and his son, John; John Geertsen, John Fennelly and Bill Burch. "One time I took my young son Marc to go watch Tony play in a local tournament," Bernice recalled. "He didn't know we were there. All of a sudden he spotted us and said, 'You came out here to watch me play?' Of course we did. Tony was a home person. He loved his family. There wasn't enough he could do for us. Because we weren't wealthy, we had to be one for all and all for one. I went to work. Harry went to work. Walt went to work. Tony went to work. And Mother went to work."

One of Tony's first victories was in late December of 1951 when he captured the first Olympic Club Junior championship held at the San Francisco Golf Club. On the first day, the 17 year-old fired a brilliant 70 which put him atop the leader board. The final round was played in miserable rain as Tony stumbled to a nine-over 44 on the front, but steadied himself on the back nine with a 39 for a total of 83. Coupled with the first round, his 153 was good enough to edge out his friend John Fry, son of the Lake Chabot's head pro, Dick Fry, who carded a 76-78—154. In addition to the Junior championship, there was an exhibition division comprised of amateur golfers played simultaneously over the same layout and that was won by a 20-year-old Bay Area golfer named Ken Venturi. Despite the inclement weather, Ken posted 18 consecutive pars over the San Francisco layout and edged John Geersten Jr., son of the San Francisco pro who shot a 73 and the National Public Links titlist, Tommy Jacobs, who shot a 74. Readers of the San Francisco area newspapers were informed about this crop of junior golfers, but who could have predicted these talented youngsters would make such an impact on the PGA Tour?

Perhaps Tony's most memorable victory before he joined the Marines in October 1953 was the Oakland City Golf Championship contested at the Lake Chabot Municipal golf course where he narrowly defeated his archrival Johnny Fry by two shots in the 36-hole event. Both boys, playing companions at Lake Chabot since they were no taller than a golf bag, put on a great exhibition for the hometown crowd. The *Oakland Tribune* noted that it was the first all teen-age final in city championship tournament history with both boys playing steady golf. Neither golfer became flustered by a gallery estimated to be 1,000 who made full use of automobiles and strategic points to the watch the boys unravel Chabot's famed high hills and low dales. If a 36-hole contest can turn into a single shot, the shot came on the 17th hole of the final 18 with the boys all even. Johnny Fry's three-iron was hit to left of the 193 yard par three and slid down the slope to the hollow guarded by Sager's Fence. Tony also missed the green, but went one-up with one to go as he chipped within 7 feet of the cup and made the putt. Johnny flipped his ball onto the green but needed two putts.

Tony coasted home the winner when he reached the 667-yard par-6 eighteenth hole in three and two putted for his unique birdie five. Fully aware that he was one shot down, Johnny attempted to spin a wedge close to the pin that was cut in the front part of the green. His gamble failed when the ball dropped short of the green and he settled for a par-6.

Some years later Johnny recalled that he noticed how Tony's eyes glistened when he was presented the set of sterling silverware. By then Tony had already collected an assortment of (to him) useless trophies. This was beautiful and real. He grabbed the silverware and literally ran all the way home to present it to his mother. "Tony was grateful to mother for the job she did as breadwinner during those early years," his brother Harry said.

Bateman believed Tony gained much of his self-confidence in his game when he won the Oakland City Championship. "After that tournament he told me he wanted to be a touring pro," Bateman recalled in 1965. "Not many people believed he had the game to succeed, but look at him today."

Johnny eventually became the assistant pro to his father at Lake Chabot. In 1963, a local scribe for the *Oakland Tribune*, asked the elder Fry his recollection of Tony's early days at Chabot. "He was the skinniest string bean you ever saw," Dick recalled. "And he was always broke. I didn't like some of his associates, especially one sharp real estate agent from Los Angeles. Tony was overawed, I guess. He went into the Marines, and it did a lot for him. He came back stronger and taller. Since then, too, he has worked out with weights to develop his forearms. "He was always a 'hungry player—a winner,' Dick remembered. "He was always a good golfer, and had a marvelous short game for a youngster... He was also a good practicer and I was always chasing him off areas where he wasn't supposed to be hitting balls... His main strength now seems to be his driving, something he's gained through physical development...He doesn't seem to be successful now when he has to scramble."

Upon getting out of school, he didn't know what he wanted to do. He always had a job. He worked in shipyards, drugstores, car factories, canneries, gas stations, and grocery stores, any possible way he could make a buck. One year he had so many employers; he didn't have enough room on the income tax form. He always had a job, didn't stay very long. But of course, you know why? Because he would go out and play golf. Typically, he reserved a portion of his earnings as his stake in money matches among fellow caddies.

In 1953, when he was 19, Tony enlisted in the Marines "on the spur of the moment." Bernice recalled, "He loved the Marine Corps. Tony was a Marine. I mean a Marine. My husband Art was a Marine. They never get over being a Marine. For Tony it came around at the right time. He loved being in the Marine Corps, but he played a lot of golf. He kept saying, 'I want to go to Korea. I want to fight the war, I want to fight the war.' That was in him, he wanted to fight that war. They found out that he could play golf so he represented the Marine Corps all over the United States. He played in the All-Marine Championship at Parris Island and in the All-Service Championship at Langley Air Force Base in Virginia. So after about a year, they sent him to Korea. He served in Korea as an observer with the artillery Corps, but the fighting was over and he never got into any combat."

In 1955, when Tony was 21 years old and a Corporal in the Marines, he came home from Korea and secured a month's leave from Camp Pendleton. Tony led the field of over 200 qualifiers for the 63 places open for the Oakland City Championship as he toured the Lake Chabot course in 35-35—70, two under par. Tony, who won the Lake Chabot caddy championship in 1947 was a winner of the Oakland city title in 1953, but unable to defend that honor in 1954 because he was in Korea.

Imperial Valley Open

In October of 1955, Tony had just been discharged from the Marine Corps and his second hand Chevrolet was purring along smoothly on a clear and balmy California afternoon. Suddenly the sounds of music from his car radio were interrupted by the shrill and unmistakable sound of a police siren. Tony was cruising along the highway near Hayward, CA, just east of San Francisco. He pulled over to the side and a police car from the county sheriff's office pulled over in front of him. Tony was thinking this was one hell of a way to get back into civilian life. The police officer climbed out of the car and turned out to be an old golfing companion, Jerry Kroeckel of Oakland. Tony and Jerry had played a lot of golf together before he had joined the Marine Corps and both had won the Oakland City Amateur Championship. Jerry described how this coincidental meeting took place. "I think it was a Thursday, and I was patrolling Foothill in the vicinity of 167th Avenue," he recollected. "I was doing about 35 or 40 when suddenly this car flashes by me. I figure I'd better slow this guy down so I hit the red light and siren. Still in uniform, he pulls over and I tell him, 'Say, you're going a little fast,' before we recognized each other.

"We shot the breeze for about 10 or 15 minutes. Finally, I asked him what his plans were and he said he didn't know yet, but that he might go back to the cannery. That's when I told him about the assistant position available at the San Francisco Golf Club. John Geertsen, the head professional there, had mentioned to me about ten days earlier during a pro-am at Silverado, that he was interviewing applicants."

Jerry reflected on those days when he and Tony played and practiced together. "He was like a lot of young fellows—he'd joke and he'd wisecrack, and he had a temperament as bad as mine on the golf course. But most everybody liked him. He had ability and liked to practice; we'd stay until dark at Chabot, chipping to the 18th green for nickels." Tony thanked his friend for the tip and as he drove on home to San Leandro, he realized they never did get around to discussing the fact that he had been going seventy in a fifty-five mph zone.

There were 12 applicants for the position, but John Geertsen was impressed by the presentation made by Tony. He was at the right place at the right time with the right credentials. He became a golf professional but the job wasn't much. He worked around the golf shop selling equipment and clothing, cleaning the members clubs, and sweeping floors. He made $225 a month, but if the job wasn't much to talk about the club certainly was. At that time, the San Francisco Golf Club was one of the poshest in the Bay Area and its membership was comprised of some of San Francisco's most successful businessmen and the area's most prominent and wealthy families. According to *Oakland Tribune* golf reporter Ray Haywood, "San Francisco Golf Club is a nonworking man's club where members sometimes turn in their Cadillac because it's easier than emptying the ashtrays." Working there proved to be quite an experience for Tony. In short, he learned how to dress, how to behave in polite society and how to play golf with a professional flair. Former USGA president and San Francisco native Frank "Sandy" Tatum said it best. "I think coming from where he came, exposure to somebody such as Geersten in a setting such as the San Francisco Golf Club had a huge influence on how Tony developed, as a person and as a player." Years later, Tony mentioned in an interview with a *Chattanooga News-Free Press* reporter that he "regarded John Geertsen to be the finest club pro in golf."

Tony had the opportunity to play quite a bit of golf at the San Francisco Golf Club. The 6,828-yard course, designed by one of the best golf course architects, A. W. Tillinghast, featured 200 bunkers which no doubt gave Tony the chance to practice every sand shot imaginable. And of course, he found time to get into some good matches. "I hustled the assistant pros around San Francisco pretty well," he said. "I'm afraid I fleeced them. I always seemed to offer them one stroke less handicap than they needed."

In an article for *Golf World* in July 2004, Jim Moriarty brought to mind that Ken Venturi and Harvie Ward were hanging around at the San Francisco Golf Club at the same time. "When Byron Nelson took me under his wing, while I was practicing, I'd say aloud what Nelson was telling me," said Venturi. "He (Lema) would pick my brains on what to do." Tony, at 6-foot 1, was taller than most golfers at that time and leaned over the ball. He had a little loop but a graceful tempo. "He would come out of his swing a lot," says Jackie Burke, "and that would pull him off the ball. But he was a very creative player, always inquisitive."

At the other end of the range was a boyish Johnny Miller, also being taught by John Geertsen. "I saw Tony working on his game when I was out there getting my lessons when I was seven, eight, nine," said Miller. "He played a high draw a lot with a very rhythmic swing. Basically, in the 70s I had three swings. I played (Lee) Trevino on my cuts, I imitated Lema on my draws, and I hit the ball straight with my own swing. So, I would use his swing hitting into greens probably six times a round, maybe Trevino three or four and Johnny Miller the rest of the time. Basically, I won all those tournaments with Lema hitting a third of my shots. I was always thinking, 'OK, Tony, this is your shot. Back-left pin. Nice little lazy draw in there.' Nobody used Lema more than I did. Nobody."

In late May of 1956, the sectional qualifying rounds for the U.S. Open were being held in San Francisco at the California Country Club. Eddie Lowery, who became famous as the 10-year old caddy for Francis Ouimet in the 1913 U. S. Open at Brookline, had moved west and became owner of a Lincoln-Mercury dealership. In addition, he was a big man on a USGA Board of Directors and he encouraged a lot of young assistant pros to sign up and try to qualify. His purpose was to swell the size of the local qualifying field, and therefore earn for the area more qualifying spots. Sure enough, despite his limited experience in professional golf tournaments, Tony was one of the six or seven qualifiers who made it to the U.S. Open at Oak Hill CC in Rochester, New York.

It was Tony's first major tournament and he was a rookie when it came to registering at the club, finding his locker, securing his caddy, obtaining the coupon books that entitled participants to eat at the club for half price and all the other incidentals of getting around the tournament site. For the first time, he had the opportunity to meet some of the famous headliners in the world of golf. Before his arrival as a participant in the U.S. Open, he had read about many of them in magazines and newspapers. Suddenly, he was sitting in the men's grill room at a long table having lunch with the likes of Sam Snead, Ben Hogan, Tommy Bolt, Doug Ford, the 1955 PGA Champion, Jack Burke, the current Masters champion and Cary Middlecoff, the eventual winner of the Open that year. "I thought it was such a big thing," he said later. "I didn't dare open my mouth." Tony was so impressed and wanted to avoid being embarrassed so he crept over the hill to Oak Hill's adjoining 18-hole course to do his practicing away from the big names. In addition, it was Tony's first trip to the Northeast and he was awed by the magnificent tree-shaded fairways and the unbelievable condition of the Oak Hill golf course. He said upon returning to the west coast that it was the finest course he had ever seen.

Despite the excitement, the pressure of playing in his first major, the pairing he had with a nervous young amateur, he played fairly well. As one might imagine, in the first round he was among the dew sweepers who teed off shortly after sun up. In the second round, he was sent out so late he thought maybe he was supposed to pick up the sandwich wrappers or collect the flagsticks as he went along. Nevertheless, on the eighteenth hole of his second round, he hit a terrific 5-iron shot within three feet of the cup and made the birdie for a 71 to go along with a 77 in his opening round. He had no idea there was a 36-hole cut at the Open and that the field would be reduced to the low 50 and ties. After dinner that Friday night he was in the hotel lobby and overheard someone talking about what score would qualify for the final two rounds on Saturday. "What's this?" Tony asked one of them. "Doesn't everyone play tomorrow?" "No," was the reply. "There's a cutoff and it looks like 149 will make it."

He realized his 148 was good enough to make the cut, but as he made his way back up to his room he thought about how important that 5-iron was on his last hole. A bogey instead of a birdie and he would have gone to the course expecting to play and would have been embarrassed to find out about the 36-hole cut. Fortunately, he would gain more experience by playing 36-holes on the final day of the U.S. Open. Tony recalled in his book, *Golfers' Gold*, the impact of playing that day. "There was a mob of about 10,000 people around the first tee," he described. "Waiting for the leaders like Peter Thomson, Middlecoff, Ted Kroll, Julius Boros, Hogan, etc., to go off, and I was so nervous I almost missed my drive completely." He finished with a 79 and an 81 for a tournament total of 308, a score that beat one amateur but netted him a check of $200. He explained later that the experience of playing in the Open came a little too fast and was so overwhelming he was determined that becoming a tournament golfer was something that he could do without.

Later that year, Tony was still working at the San Francisco Golf Club, but the Western Open was being held at the nearby Presidio Golf Course. He decided to play in it. His first three rounds were a 76, 71, and a 72. For the final round he was paired in a threesome with Bob Rosburg and Dow Finsterwald. Tony was familiar with Rosburg since he was from the Bay Area, but they had never met. Bob had recently won the San Diego Open and Dow was well known, having won a few tournaments. Tony discussed the experience of playing with a couple of golfers well established on the Tour. "There I was," he said, "nothing but a shop assistant, paired with two of the top players in the game. Finsterwald put on an exhibition of golf the likes of which I had never seen. He drove the ball perfectly and practically hit the hole with every iron shot he hit into the greens. Here was where I really got that idea that I did not want to make touring golf my livelihood. He shot a 66 on the par 72 Presidio course and I said to myself, 'If this is the way I have to play golf before I can make it on the tour, then the tour is no place for me.' Finsterwald's virtually flawless round of golf gave him a 66 and put him into fifth place. My final total of 291 for 72 holes placed me in a tie for twenty-second place and earned me $185. The U.S. Open and the Western Open had given me my first taste of tournaments with the big timers. I felt very inferior. I just wanted to pick up my meager little check, go back to the San Francisco Golf Club and happily clean the clubs that the members would use that day.

"In another way, however, the experience has been valuable. The first time you do anything it is difficult, but now at least I knew how to pick my way through the confusion that surrounds a big tournament, how to go about checking in and of course, where the practice areas were located. Basically, I figured out how to find my way around. But as far as I was concerned, the tour seemed about as far off as the foreign legion. I was simply not good enough and never would be good enough to play on it. It took a rather astonishing tournament, played only three months later in the tiny town of El Centro, near the California-Mexico border, to begin to convince me otherwise."

Tony had come to El Centro, about 100 miles east of San Diego, in late January 1957 as a part of a tournament golf vacation. In a few weeks he would be starting as head professional at a nine-hole municipal course in the gambling resort of Elko, Nevada. Eddie Lowery had lent Tony $500 towards his expenses at three or four tournaments that he wanted to play in between leaving his job at San Francisco and starting at Elko. The first week he had played in the Bing Crosby pro-am and had not done very well. The following week he played at the Caliente Open in Tijuana and had not even made the cut.

While some well-known players such as Ken Venturi, Cary Middlecoff and Jimmy Demaret were making the headlines at Palm Springs, in the featured tournament of the week, the others, the has-beens and the wanna-bes, were at El Centro. Despite the purse of only $5,000, there were some credible golfers in the field. Lionel Hebert, the chubby member of the Hebert brother golfing twosome, who would go on to win the PGA championship later that year was on hand. So was Al Balding, the tall former truck driver from Canada who had already won a tour tournament and would win three more in 1957. Paul Harney, the slender but long hitting Holy Cross

College graduate was also in the field. Other prominent players included previous winners of the event, Bob Toski and Bob Rosburg.

Tony had learned a fairly good lesson as the week progressed. "I thought it would be glamorous. But it isn't. In the first place there is the constant traveling and practice until it becomes hard work. Also, it's expensive. They were having a two-day pro-amateur tournament and I wasn't in the field, so I couldn't play. I only had $60 in my pocket and I didn't know if I should try to go on or head back home."

After missing the cut at the Caliente Open in Tijuana, Tony was practicing next to Jay Hebert, who had recently won the Bing Crosby Pro-Am tournament on the Monterey Peninsula. Tony was complaining loudly about not making the cut and Jay strolled over to have a few words with this newcomer to the tour. Hebert asked him how things were going. "I told him I was discouraged." "How long have you been on the tour?" Herbert asked. "Four weeks," Tony answered. "Four weeks!" said the surprised Hebert. "You shouldn't be discouraged. I've been on tour for more years than I'd like to remember and I didn't win my first one until the Crosby."

Hebert's consideration cheered Tony to the point where he decided to stay and eat hamburgers on the chance of earning steak money. Jay said missing the cut was something that happened frequently to even the most experienced and talented players and that he should not let it discourage him in the slightest. Tony said later that the chat with Jay was not only good for his morale, but it also convinced him that these guys out on the tour were actually human and not just high powered golfing machines. The Imperial Valley tournament was the sixth major event in Tony's pro career. Despite lack of experience, he had missed the money only once. He had survived the cut in the 1956 U.S. Open and won $200. He had earned $185 in the Western Open at San Francisco, $150 in the Northern California Open and $66.66 in the Crosby tournament.

Tony decided to stay over in Tijuana an extra couple of days to practice and didn't arrive at the Barbara Worth Golf Course until late Monday afternoon, in time for nine-hole practice round. That was all he was able to play before the tournament started since the two-day Pro-Am tournament was held on Tuesday and Wednesday. The course was closed to those who were not included in the Pro-Am. So, for two days, instead of being able to learn something about the golf course, Tony was part of the group who were obliged to sit on their hands or at the club bar and they were all furious. Tony told about the night that he went downtown in a tee-shirt and Levi's, found a dingy little joint in a side alley where a game of lowball was in progress and he sat in.

Having had a few drinks and some headstrong betting along with some exceptionally good cards he was able to stay ahead and finally had a chance to win a really big pot. The house rules specified that a perfect low was an ace—two—three—four—five, and that was exactly what he held in his hand. The group of guys that he was playing with looked mean enough to slit his throat for two bits, but another player in the game held what he thought was a pretty good hand an ace—two—three—four—six. He kept betting the pot up and up until it reached well over $100. With a sure hand, Tony kept betting and the other fellow kept raising and pretty soon Tony began to get a little scared. He knew he had him beat, but he figured that if he cleaned him too badly that guy might decide to cause some trouble. Tony finally called. When he showed his unbeatable hand everyone looked pretty sullen. Tony decided he has had enough cards for one night because he didn't want it to be his last night. He grabbed his winnings in the pot and walked smartly out the door into the alley with the bills still in his hand. He said if anyone jumped him with a knife he was going to hand over the cash and say, "It's yours. With my compliments." Tony figured his life was worth more than $150, but he said he ran so fast no one had a chance to catch him. He jumped into his car, sped right back to the hotel and told friends he got to his room before his knees had started to shake.

Tony admitted that he spent most of his low-ball winnings at the clubhouse bar during the week—don't forget, he wasn't allowed on the golf course and he had spells in those days when he could lush it up with the best of them. Consequently, his first two rounds were mediocre as he opened with a 71-73. However, on the third round he shot a very respectable 67 and went into the final round tied for fifth place, six shots behind the leader Paul Harney. He didn't think he had a chance to win, but he was determined to fight for a sizeable chunk of the prize money.

The Barbara Worth Golf Course was flat with tall trees lining the narrow fairways. The desert course had grass on the fairways that were as brown as straw while the well-watered putting surfaces were lush and emerald green. For the first eight holes, Tony remained even par for the day despite the fact that his drives were not accurate and he was in and out of trees. It was his sheer determination and a few long putts that kept him in the tournament. On the ninth hole his game began to jell. On the short par four he hit his tee shot to the edge of the green and then chipped in from 45-feet for an eagle two. He birdied the tenth hole, sank long putts for pars on the eleventh and twelfth and found himself four under for the day on the sixteenth tee. At that point he was hoping that he might earn a check of about $500 or $600.

He glanced through the trees bordering the sixteenth tee and saw the two leaders—Paul Harney and Bob Inma—using irons off the thirteenth tee. The fairway on the thirteenth was narrow and they were being cautious in an effort to keep their drives in the fairway. Tony had used a driver on that hole and thought, "That's pretty good. Here are those two cautiously dillydallying around. They might just out choke each other over there and I might just slip in and win this tournament."

Later on he said he didn't really think that would happen. He finished his round by sinking a long putt for a birdie on the seventeenth hole and he drained a putt of least 60 feet on the eighteenth hole for another birdie to finish with a 65 and a four-round total of 276. At that point, Tony thought Harney could easily shoot a 70 on this course and beat him by at least one shot. With that in mind, he returned to his favorite place, the bar, and drank down three scotch and waters. He was reaching for his fourth drink when someone came running in and said that Harney would have to get up and down from in front of the eighteenth just to tie him. Tony pushed the drink away and floundered outside in time to see Harney chip his ball within seven feet and make the putt.

The two were summoned to the first tee for a sudden-death playoff and Tony was slightly peeved at himself for belting down those scotch and waters instead of anticipating the situation. But maybe, he said later, the drinks took his mind off the pressure. First prize for the Imperial Valley Open was $1,000 while runner-up netted $700. As they prepared to hit off an official suggested they split the difference in prize money, a common practice in playoffs, and play only for the honor of winning the tournament. Harney had been on the tour for a couple of years and had made some high finishes in important tournaments, but Tony wasn't about to split anything with anyone. The official was furious with Tony when he said, even before Harney had a chance to express himself on the subject, that he would have nothing to do with such an arrangement. "Who the hell do you think you are, anyway?" the official asked. "I'm the guy in this blasted play-off," Tony said in no uncertain terms.

Tony had the honor on the first hole and hit a pretty good drive on the short par-4 opening hole. Harney, considered pound-for-pound the longest hitter on the tour, stepped up and ripped one about 40 yards past Tony and ended up nearly pin high to the right of the green. Tony hit a wedge into the middle of the green, but it didn't stop quick enough and rolled to the back edge of the green about 20 feet above the hole. Harney chipped his ball about four feet below the cup and a birdie looked certain for the tall New Englander. Tony repeated what he had done all afternoon. His putt rolled down the green straight into the cup for a birdie. Tony said later that it was about the tenth long putt he had made that day and it jarred Paul so much that he barely made his four-foot putt to tie the hole.

The next hole was another rather short par-4, but the fairway curved to the right around a clump of trees and a pond guarded the left side of the green. The best way to play the hole is to aim down the left side of the fairway so the approach shot comes in from a relatively safe angle. So Tony did the expected. He pushed his drive into the trees on the right side. Fortunately it hit a tree and kicked back to the edge of the fairway. Paul then laced another perfect drive down the left side of the fairway in perfect position for his approach shot. Tony described the shot he faced on the second hole of the playoff. "If I hadn't still been feeling the effects of my visit at the bar I would have known that this was the end for me. I was partially stymied by a tree and would have to hit a fantastic shot to get the ball on the green. I finally decided to use a seven-iron and aim the ball right at the pond to the left and try to hit the shot in such a way that it would fade into the green along a left to right trajectory. I hit the ball firmly and it flew toward the pond. Then, just as it seemed that the ball was heading toward a watery end, it reacted to the spin I had given it and faded right in about 10 or 12 feet from the hole. Harney must have figured by this time that he was contending with a freak that used black magic. His nine-iron shot left him 25 feet short of the hole and his first putt was still short. I then got over my ball and using still more of that black magic putted it straight into the cup to win the playoff and the tournament."

The 22 year-old from San Leandro had made four consecutive birdies on holes number 17, 18, 1, and 2 that enabled him to defeat Paul Harney and capture the Imperial Valley Open. His statement to the press after his victory displayed his unselfish attitude. "Any success I've had in golf, I owe to the prayers of my friends. This is the happiest day of my life."

According to *Arizona Republic's* Sports Editor, Frank Gianelli, Tony was one of the up-and-coming youngsters in the world of golf. "Lema, particularly, represents one of the more promising of the new faces," he reported. "He won the El Centro Open on Sunday in a dramatic playoff with power-hitting Paul Harney. Lema, former assistant pro at San Francisco CC, shot a last round 65 and then birdied both holes in the playoff to defeat Paul Harney. He credits his victory to a new putter— one of the Phoenician Johnny Reuter's—which he bought just before the tournament started. 'I guess that putter's paid for itself many times over,' " Tony said. It was undoubtedly a Bull's Eye putter. What an appropriate name for the putter he used to can putts of 8, 20, 5, 18, 60, 20, and 11 feet on that memorable Sunday afternoon.

When asked to describe the 60-foot putt that he made on the eighteenth green, Tony shared his thoughts. "I didn't think I had a chance in the world of holing it," he said. "I was just trying to get it close and the thing went in." He also mentioned some other thoughts, which indicated he knew early in his career what it takes to win tournaments. "I've learned par golf is no good. Doesn't mean a thing if you hit 17 greens but score 72. This tour is like learning to play all over again. You've got to learn how to score and to do that you have to think out your shots. There are 150 guys out here who hit the ball perfectly. To win you have to know how to get it in the hole."

Looking back at his experience in the 1957 Imperial Valley Open, Tony reflected on the impact that week had made on his career. "All of a sudden," he recalled, "I had won the tournament and a check for $1000, which looked like an awfully big paycheck to me. I didn't think that I had played particularly well, but at least I fooled people into thinking I could. When I heard my name coming over the radio and read it in the local newspapers, I had even begun to fool myself. This was a vital little push, and it is the push that has tumbled many, many players—pro or amateur—out onto the tour. I wasn't completely conscious of it at the time, but it was then that I decided how I really wanted to make my living. That little tournament was also valuable in another respect. I had won it even though I had started so badly. I had kept working hard, even though I was not playing well, and when suddenly things began to break my way I was able to take advantage of the breaks. In the depression years of 1959 in 1960, when I was throwing clubs, losing my temper and giving up at the first sign of bad luck, I forgot the lesson I should have learned at El Centro. It was when I finally began to reflect back on what had happened there, and what could happen again if I kept working to save every stroke I could, even when strokes didn't seem to be worth saving, that I began to play golf again the way it should be played."

Tony's victory in the Imperial Valley Open was reported in such sensational fashion that he immediately attracted national attention. He played the last 10 holes of the tournament and the two holes he needed to defeat Paul Harney in a play-off in eight-under par. "Yes," Tony recalled, "I was playing just so-so until my putter began clicking on those last few holes. In fact, I was seven-strokes behind when I began reeling off the birdies. I tied Harney, then had to shoot two more birdies to beat him in the play-off."

With that check for $1,000 tucked away in his wallet, Tony would probably have gone right out on the tour right then and there. But he had signed a contract to start work as the head professional at the nine-hole Ruby View Golf Course at Elko, Nevada commencing March 1. And Tony took care of one more detail as he headed for the small gambling town in northeastern Nevada. He sent a $500 check to the Lincoln-Mercury dealership and reimbursed Eddie Lowery for the money he had lent him before his meaningful experience in the Imperial Valley Open.

Rookie Season

Tony described Elko, Nevada as the poor man's Las Vegas. There were about six thousand residents in this small town in the northeast corner of Nevada. In addition to the Ruby View nine-hole golf course there were three casinos, a couple of nightclubs, and a few restaurants. Most of the out-of-state visitors were from Idaho and Utah, but occasionally high rollers would arrive from the west coast. Tony described his year in Elko with no exaggeration and brute honesty. "There is not much to do in Elko," he explained, "except drink and gamble. Any visitor with a little energy left over could play golf."

Tony's responsibilities were to run the pro shop, set up tournaments for the men and women who played there and occasionally give a few lessons. It gave him plenty of time to practice and play golf. His routine after work was nearly the same every evening. He would have a few martinis with friends before dinner—sometimes no dinner at all—then walk over to one of the gambling casinos for the remainder of the evening. Sure Tony won a few hands, but he lost a few too. He let it be known that he never established a savings account at the local bank in Elko.

Tony was sharpening his competitive skills and some good things happened on the golf course. The Nevada Open was held right there at Ruby View in 1957 and after two rounds Tony was at 138, seven strokes behind Bill Johnston from Provo, Utah. Tony held nothing back in the third round when he fired a sensational 61 for a course record, including a 29 for the best nine holes ever turned in since the course opened. His putter was no doubt hot in the desert sun as he had 11 birdies in his round. His record-breaking performance enabled him to gain nine strokes on Johnston and a two-shot cushion after 54 holes. On Sunday's final round he shot a 70 and Billy Johnston got back on top with a 65 and first place. Prior to his 29, the nine-hole record was 30 shared by Vince Holian, Cliff Whittle and Ernie Schneiter, Jr.

In August of that year Tony won the $3,650 Montana Open by shooting a final round 66 to wind up with a 12-under par 272. The tournament outcome was in doubt until Tony parred the final hole and edged Smiley Quick of Los Angeles by one stroke. Quick three-putted the last green and Tony won the $750 first prize. He finished runner-up in the Idaho Open to Dick Kramer of Salt Lake City. His 276 at the new Hillcrest Country Club in Boise was three strokes off the winning pace. A few years later Tony explained that he was creating an imaginary little drama in his head. He wasn't playing in the Montana Open or the Idaho Open. He would say to himself, "It's the Western Open. And I'm not playing with Walt Harris, or Dick Kramer or Cliff Whittle. These guys against me are Finsterwald, Rosburg and Middlecoff. And the year was never 1957. It was always in the future: 1962 or '63 or '64 or '65 or '66. This activity sounds childish, but if you are the pro at a nine-hole course in a backwater of Nevada it's surprising the number of things you will do to put a bit of juice in the daily routine." He also described how he would go out for a nine-hole practice round and play two balls—one his, the other Ben Hogan's. He candidly said, "Hogan never had a chance." And of course when he got to the practice putting green, he would throw three balls down. One was Hogan's, another was Sam Snead's and of course the other was Tony Lema's. For some reason, regardless of the distance, the first two putts would graze the cup, but the third putter, guess who, would always bang his ball right in the middle of the cup.

During that year in Elko, Tony had become familiar with a pudgy young playboy who lived in Portland, Oregon and owned a house at Sun Valley. Jim Malarkey had a plywood business in Portland along with major real estate holdings in Sun Valley. He dropped in from Sun Valley occasionally and became a familiar face at Ruby View. He played a little golf, gambled, and enjoyed cocktails while he was in town. Malarkey had a delightful personality and became interested in Tony's career. Cliff Whittle, another pro from the area who had become friends with Tony, had a plane and the two pros flew up to Sun Valley to play in a pro-am event. Tony and Cliff stayed at Malarkey's house during the tournament and while having cocktails after a round one evening Cliff Whittle suddenly asked Malarkey a rather pointed question. "Jim," Whittle suggested, "why don't you put Tony on the tour?" Malarkey was well past his first drink, but without changing the expression on his face, he replied. "Fine, I'll do it."

Suddenly Tony realized he had a sponsor so he could follow his dreams and play on the PGA Tour. He shook hands on an oral agreement that called for Jim Malarkey to advance Tony $200 a week. Tony would pay that money back out of his prize winnings and, in addition give him one-third of anything he made over that. Malarkey also agreed to help make payments on a new Plymouth, which Tony took with him on the tour. Obviously, Tony was a rookie in the business end of things as well as playing on the tour, but he was so elated to have this opportunity. All he could think of was the excitement of teeing it up with the big boys.

The first big tournament on the 1958 PGA Tour was the Los Angeles Open. Nearly every touring pro and most club pros throughout California have their eyes set on being part of that field. It's prestigious and many Hollywood stars were seen at Rancho Park Golf Course, where the Los Angeles was played from 1956-1972. There was only one small problem and Tony addressed it from the get-go. About 350 golfers must pre-qualify in order to get one of the twenty or thirty spots available. But there was another option. All golfers who finished in the money at the preceding tournament automatically qualified for the next tournament. Many players make a special trip to play in the last event each year with the hope that they will finish in the money—meaning the top 60 and qualify to play in Los Angeles.

This was the route Tony decided to take but there was another small problem. The last tournament on the 1957 schedule was the Mayfair Inn Open in Sanford, Florida on December 12–15. It was a long trip and he estimated it would cost about $500, but if he finished thirtieth or better he would

make the field for the Los Angeles Open. Having spent a season
in Nevada, Tony showed that he wasn't afraid to take the gamble
of traveling across the country in order to secure a position
in the field at the Los Angeles Open. After a moderately slow
start in his first round at Sanford, Tony played well and shot
66-69-67 for the last three rounds and finished in a tie for sixth
place. His share of the purse was $725 and he made the field for
the Los Angeles Open. Shortly afterwards, Tony discussed his
thoughts about making the transition from playing in local state
tournaments to going on the tour. "Some of the professionals
out west," he explained, "Smiley Quick, Jimmy Clark, Willie
Goggin and Billy Johnston, convinced me that I should try the
tour. My play at Sanford was very encouraging and did a lot for
my morale."

Tony learned a valuable lesson following his third round at
Sanford and he talked about it years later. "I was through early
in the day," he explained. "So I went out to follow some of the
better players in case they were any secrets to championship
golf that I didn't know about. I watched Bob Toski and Jay
Herbert play some of the holes I had played earlier. I was
surprised to find that they had no secret at all. Outside of the
fact that they seemed to be knocking their approach shots
consistently closer to the flagstick, they played each hole
almost exactly as I had. They had consistency, I saw, but that
was something I would pick up as I gained experience. The trick
I had overlooked—and did not really learn for four years—was
that something very vital and very important was going on in
their heads. On the surface there was no indication that this
consistency of theirs—and of every fine player—stems from an
emotional and mental discipline that keeps him working hard
over every shot no matter how badly he may want to give up,
no matter how badly he may want to wrap his clubs around
the handiest tree, no matter how heartily he may be cursing
the ill luck that caused a bad bounce. These veteran players
seemed, however, to be hitting the ball the same way I was. I
said to myself, 'what the hell, I can do the same thing. It's just a
question of a little time.'

"It took me more than a little time. I was to survive a
checkbook full of fines and a lot of temper tantrums before

I realized that playing golf was 30 percent physical and 70 percent mental. A player who wanted to win, therefore, had to be mentally tough enough to keep bearing down for every stroke of every hole of every round of every tournament... Emotional stability under pressure is not something that comes easily to all of us. Some are lucky enough to be born with it. The rest simply must practice it until it becomes second nature. There is no other way to be a truly successful golfer."

Those first half-dozen or so tournaments represented a giant learning curve for Tony. Not all rookies on the PGA Tour get the royal treatment similar to the one received by Tiger Woods at the Milwaukee Open in 1996. "Welcome world," were Tiger's first comments as a $40 million check was being deposited in his bank account on behalf of Nike. Not quite the same in 1958 when Tony Lema was greeted by absolutely nobody when he arrived in Los Angeles, Arizona, Texas and on to Louisiana and Florida. The registration desk never could seem to get his name right and the locker room attendant was always too busy to assign him a locker. He learned quickly that there was a caste system involved in pairings and tee times. The rookies started extremely early in round one and very late for the second round or the other way around. In those days, Doc Giffin was working as the PGA publicity man traveling with the tour. Basically, there were four groups: in the first were all the previous tournament winners; the second group consisted of players who were non-winners, but had picked up big checks lately; group three were players who had not been atop the leader board but were consistently making cuts and getting checks; group four consisted of everybody else— including the local pros and amateurs who had qualified to get into the tournament. So the names from each group were put into a separate hat and were picked out accordingly. The first two rounds were threesomes, but after the 36-hole cut the pairings were based on scores. Those who barely made the cut teed off earlier on Saturday while the players with lower scores teed off later.

At that time, players trying to become established on the tour were considered members of the Ghost Squadron, the Dew Sweepers or the Litter Brigade. If they played exceptionally well in the first two rounds they would be paired on the weekend with some well-known players. Not only did that have an impact on their confidence, but the rookies would soon feel as though the veterans on the PGA Tour were accepting them. After the rookies proved the validity of their game, the veterans would be more cordial and include them as partners during practice rounds as well as invite them to social functions. Tony explained that a rookie does not go out to the practice range and ask Julius Boros, Sam Snead or Arnold Palmer if they could scoot over just a little so I can practice right here. Nor did rookies walk into the grillroom, see an empty chair at someone's table and ask if they could join them for lunch. Like any other fraternal organization, all members pass some sort of "pledging period" where they earn their stripes. On the PGA Tour, a rookie's credentials consisted primarily of his position on the money list.

Consequently, Tony played most of his practice rounds with players of his own caste. He had more in common with other rookies or players who had been around just a bit longer. He considered himself extremely fortunate to fall in with three very congenial men; Johnny Pott had played golf for Louisiana State University and went straight to the tour in 1957; Tommy Jacobs had won the National Junior championship in 1951 and had joined the tour in 1957; and Jim Ferree, a lively, personable North Carolinian who had been on the tour since 1956. For most of 1958, these four golfers traveled together, lived together, ate, and played most of their practice rounds together. Their friendship served as a sort of buffer to help each of them withstand the pressure and inconvenience of living as a nomad from one golf tournament to the next.

After six weeks on the tour in the winter of 1958, Tony's game began to come together at the Tucson Open played at the El Rio Country Club. It was basically a flat desert course with many desert palms and scrub pines lining the fairways. It was a fairly good layout but short and not too difficult. Tony shot a 63 to capture second in the pro-am and followed that with a 66 in the first round and a 65 in the second. His 131 after two rounds put him in a tie for first place with his nemesis from the Nevada Open, Bill Johnston of Provo, Utah. Carl Porter, sports writer for The *Arizona Daily Star* reported that the third round at El Rio Country Club would get under way "with two jittery unknowns" all alone in the spotlight. But Tony Lema and Bill Johnston could find nothing new about each other. They've been carrying on a friendly version of the old Hatfield-McCoy feud for some time now. And while neither has ever captured a tournament of major import, the pair has been trading strokes in state tourney finals for several seasons.

"What do I know about Tony," laughed the genial Johnston after his 67 in the second round. "We've been fighting over championships for a while. I was defending champ in both the Montana and Nevada State Opens last year. Tony beat me at Montana but I won in Nevada. Of course, he turned around and won my own tournament at Provo. I even got him a date with a girl named Leslie and he still won the tournament!"

Before Johnston had finished his round, Tony had the solitary lead and was besieged by photographers, newspapermen and radio and TV representatives. In the locker room afterwards Lema sighed, "I hope they want to talk to me when the tournament's over."

Lema credited his high school basketball and baseball play with building his physical endurance. Now his whole life was wrapped up in pro golf and he had his eyes set for the top of the ladder. In three days of golf at El Rio, including the pro-am, Lema shot rounds of 63–66–65. Asked if he liked the El Rio course, his mouth split into a wide grin. "Like it? That's an understatement."

When asked about leading a PGA tournament after two rounds, Tony added, "This is pretty fast company. And I'll admit it makes me a little nervous. But I'm not scared of them. I've got a lot of respect for them and some day I hope to be up there."

The third round produced the lack of consistency that haunted Tony for the first few years on the tour. He always seemed to have one bad round per tournament, which kept him from having at least a chance to finish high on the leaderboard. At El Rio Country Club on Saturday he scrubbed it around in even par 70 while most of the leaders were in the 60's. Tony finished with a 12-foot birdie putt on the last hole to register an even-par round but he told Art Rosenbaum of *The Chronicle*

Sporting Green that he had played his "worst round of the tournament. I was lousy. I drove bad a couple of times and I three-putted once from 18 feet—on the same hole where I nearly made a hole-in-one yesterday." Despite a poor round, he was in a tie for third place, only three shots behind leader Don January. Later he explained what he was telling himself at that time, "You played poorly and still shot a 70. You have an excellent chance to win."

At this point, Tony had played in 10 tournaments on the tour, not counting the Imperial Valley Open, which he had won a year earlier. He had done pretty well in a couple of them, but this was the first time that he felt he had a real chance to win. It was also the first time he experienced the terrors of real pressure and how it can affect a man. He found himself in a situation he had never been in before and he simply did not know how to react to it. Despite going to bed early he had a fitful night and he found himself lying awake worrying about the oddest thing. He was trying to figure out what he would say at the presentation ceremony.

It didn't take long for the pressure to hit Tony in that final round as he was paired with the leader, Don January, and an old-timer named John Barnum. On the first hole, he hit a nice drive down the fairway and had nothing but a short 9-iron left to the green. He didn't quite catch the approach shot solidly and left the ball about 20 feet short of the pin. He putted first and rolled it within two feet of the cup. He marked his ball and stepped back to let the other players hit their putts. As he stood there waiting he later said he could feel himself tightening up. His knees were feeling a little wobbly and his breath coming in fast, quick spurts, the way it does when you jump into a very cold lake or the ocean. By the time he got over the ball he really had the shakes and his two-foot putt didn't roll anywhere near the cup.

After that he felt he didn't have a chance. Suddenly, the fairways became narrow, every hazard on the course jumped out on him, and his swing felt unnatural. He began to play with sheer abandon, not caring whether he made a bogey or a birdie and usually getting one or the other. He birdied the last hole for a 75, wound up with a tournament score of 276 and finished in a tie for fourteenth place, 11 shots behind the winner Lionel Hebert.

It was his first experience with choking and he began to wonder if that kind of physical reaction would happen every time he was in contention. He worried whether his nerves would explode like firecrackers every time he was in the hunt or would the fear of choking prevent him from being able to put himself in contention at all. He explained later what he was going through as both alternatives seemed pretty dismal. "It was an experience," he said, "that stayed with me for a long, long time. Winning that first tournament began to seem like finding the pot of gold at the end of the rainbow. It is not much consolation to think that this kind of emotional upheaval has bothered other players as well. Don January summed it up very well after he lost the 1961 PGA Championship in a playoff with Jerry Barber. The winner had caught him on the last three regulation holes with putts of 20, 40, and 60 feet, but January had a couple of chances to wrap it up, in spite of Barber's phenomenal putting, and had missed them both. 'I guess I was just plain scared to win from that dude,' was his unique and colorful way of expressing a pretty common state of mind."

Despite the rough weekend that Tony brought upon himself, there were others that could see a great deal of potential in his game. In his column entitled "Overheard" Art Rosenbaum of *The Chronicle Sporting Green* said, "Tony Lema is a name to be reckoned with in professional tournament golf. He made a fine showing in the Tucson Open last week finishing with a 276 and winning $327.50. Lema was described by *United Press* as a 'young fellow, 23, who is built like Ken Venturi, swings like Venturi and even looks like Venturi.' The facial resemblance is not so noticeable, but Lema is definitely 'another Venturi' in confirmation and gyration. Only a few who have followed the young man's progress realize how good he really is—or can be. He came out of San Leandro ...and soon he was playing in tournaments and he came to the attention of the gallery at the Harding Park San Francisco City golf tournament...Young Tony rose to some local prominence, winning the Richmond City tournament and placing well elsewhere. A small sum was raised, more or less off record, to help him hit the road. In the

National Open (1956) of two years ago, the USGA measured drives of the leading golfers on one long fairway. Mike Souchak, George Bayer, Sam Snead, Ben Hogan and other power boys were up there. Near the top, well over 280 yards, was then 21-year-old Tony Lema.

"On the tour, he now represents Napa's Silverado Club. Whether he has a personal sponsor at this time is something of a secret; undoubtedly a few bucks have been raised to keep him in hash-and-eggs while on tour. As he admitted the other day in Arizona, 'I eat according to my score. If I shoot a 66, it's steak. If I shoot a 76, I starve.' "

Rosenbaum wrote another interesting story of an odd occurrence, which took place on the famously beautiful eighth-hole at Pebble Beach. "In the recent Bing Crosby tournament," he reported, "Lema came to public notice in a perverse way. He was rolling along rather well, with 144 for two days, and was beating up Pebble Beach when he reached the eighth hole. His amateur partner, Marty Welch, described the horror. 'He never missed a shot,' said Welch. 'His drive was straight but it hit a rock on the fairway, bounced high in the air and over the cliff. Instead of going into the water, it stuck in some ice plant. Tony tried to play it out and only those who have had a ball in this stuff know how tough it is. He walloped the ball up to the top, but it hit a clump and then rolled down again…Oh, well… anyway, he took a ten on the par four hole.' On his final round at Pebble Beach, Lema improved his score from 80 to 70, and took away $175 as tournament winnings."

By the time the tour had reached the southeastern part of the country in the spring of 1958, Tony had recharged his game and was playing well although he came upon another physical hazard. After two rounds in the Azalea Open in March, Tony was in sixth place but he completed the weekend shooting 76-76. Was it another case of the nerves? No, this time it was a bad case of the flu. But that didn't stop the 24-year old, as he got well and headed for Greensboro in April.

Tony had some interesting comments to say to a reporter for the *Oakland Journal* before the tournament started, "I'm not on this tour just for a fling," he insisted. "If I didn't think I had the game to win with, I would go back to my club job. I've been playing with the best in the business now since last winter, and I know I can beat any of them. I don't want to sound cocky, but I just haven't been playing the kind of golf I am capable of yet. Playing ordinary golf and the way they play it on this tour is as different as night and day. Par just doesn't mean anything to these guys. They'll tear any course apart. This is a good test here, but they'll rip it up too. I look for someone to win with about 275. It could be lower. But I still think I can win in this league. I'm going to stick with it until I do even if I half to hock my car and clubs to keep going in the meantime."

He played his most consistent tournament over the Starmount Forest Country Club layout as he shot 69-69-70-69 for a 277 and finished in a tie for second. Another rookie, Bob Goalby, finished strong with a 66 in the final round and posted a 275. Goalby had been a reserve quarterback for the University of Illinois before he returned to his first love, playing golf.

Bob Goalby's first prize was $2,000 and the $1,080 check Tony received for finishing in a five-way tie for second was his biggest payday on the tour up until that time. But something must be said about the players surrounding Tony on the leaderboard. The golfers included in the tie for second with Tony were: Sam Snead, who was gunning for his seventh victory in the Greater Greensboro Open; Don January, who would win ten tour events including the 1967 PGA Championship; Dow Finsterwald, who would go on to win the 1958 PGA Championship; and Art Wall Jr., who would win the Masters in 1959. Not only that, but third place was comprised of Al Balding from Ontario, Canada, Gary Player and the long-hitting Mike Souchak. Tony must have realized the high caliber of golf he was playing at the time and it's amazing to think he was fearlessly banging heads with these great players despite the fact that he had only been on the tour for four months.

The next stop on the PGA Tour was Louisville, Kentucky, site of the Kentucky Derby Open played at the rock-hard and exceptionally hilly Seneca Country Club. Actually, the Kentucky Derby would not take place for another couple of weeks when Calumet Farm's Tim Tam with Ismael Valenzuela in the irons won that year's "most exciting two minutes in sports" in a relatively slow time of 2:05:00. But it was an exciting year in thoroughbred racing as Tim Tam was considered to have a strong chance to capture the Triple Crown after winning the Preakness Stakes. However, in the Belmont Stakes, coming down the home stretch toward the lead that seemed to assure victory, Tim Tam fractured a sesamoid bone and hobbled the last yards across the finish line in second place. His injury ended his career but he went on to be a successful sire.

Tony might have been considered the "thoroughbred of the field" as he got off to a great start at Seneca CC with a pair of 67's and shared the lead at the halfway mark with Paul Harney and Bill Collins. His round was highlighted by a hole-in-one on the 138-yard, par 3 thirteenth hole as he hit the perfect 9-iron shot. Unfortunately, Tony's play on the weekend was sub-standard as he shot a 75 and a 70 for a 72-hole total of 279, five shots behind Gary Player's wining score of 274. It turns out that Tony and Gary were driving back and forth from the hotel to the course each day and Gary kept up a stream of amusing talk about how grateful he was to be able to play on the U.S. tour, and what he hoped to learn from the U.S. players and how much he enjoyed the whole experience. Sounds like Gary could have been in the role of the teacher as all four of his rounds were in the 60's.

Naturally Tony enjoyed sharing the lead after 36-holes and he said that leading a tournament could be fun as well as tense. "You are up there on top," he explained, "the newspapers are full of you, and the other players have always got the friendly needle out. 'Hail Our Leader,' they are likely to say. 'Feel like choking a little bit today?' "

But this time it was not about Tony choking over the final 36 holes. He and his friend Johnny Pott had been paired together for the first two rounds and after the second round, which they had finished early in the afternoon, they picked up lunch at a drive-thru restaurant and headed back to the motel where they spent about three hours at the swimming pool. While Johnny lounged around the side of the pool eying the girls pretty carefully, Tony decided to put on a long and vigorous exhibition of swimming and diving. He wasn't sore immediately but the next morning he woke up and his arms felt like two bags of sand. He said that he wasn't in a state of brutal pain, but his arms felt like they belonged to some other player in the tournament. He scrapped it around in 75 on Saturday and had to birdie three of the final four holes on Sunday to post a 70. Afterwards Tony said the moral of the whole experience was simple. "Swimming is for beach boys, not for golfers!"

Long before he became known as "Champagne Tony", the word was out that Tony liked the fairer sex and from all the stories that were told, the fairer sex liked him too. So who could blame him if he stepped out here and there? Let's face it, he was a tall, handsome man, and as the years rolled by, the galleries he played in front of increased and the number of women in those galleries increased likewise. John Brodie, the popular quarterback for the San Francisco 49ers was an excellent golfer and gave the tour a try in the late 1950's. He roomed with Tony much of the time he was on the tour and was asked about the high cost of following the golf sun. "Of course, it costs Tony a little more," he explained. "He's a goer that one. He's single. He has to fight off the girls."

An interesting experience took place in June of 1958 when Tony was visiting New York City for the first time and was playing in the $50,000 Pepsi-Cola Open on Long Island. It seems there was a girl that he had been fond of out west, but had moved to New York and become a successful model. Tony called her when he hit town and it turns out the golf tournament was just a place he was forced to spend four or five hours a day away from "this beautifully built female." He added in his book, "My scores were even higher than the tabs I was picking up each night and I finally finished 17 shots back of winner Arnold Palmer. I was lucky and placed well enough to earn $150, but my check didn't even cover two nights on the town."

Shortly after, the U.S. Open was held at the always-tough Southern Hills CC in Tulsa, Oklahoma where Tommy Bolt won and survived by shooting a 283, three over par. Tony did not make the Open that year nor did he qualify for the PGA Championship at Lianerch CC in Havertown, Pennsylvania. That was the first year the PGA adopted the 72-hole stroke-play format after it had been strictly match play since its inception in 1916. Dow Finsterwald won at the Lianerch CC layout, just outside of Philadelphia, with a four-under par 276. A year earlier, he had been runner-up to Lionel Hebert 2 & 1, when the

PGA was played at the Miami Valley Golf Club in Dayton, Ohio.

The reason the switch was made to 72-hole medal play was primarily due to the popularity that golf was beginning to have on the television market. Arnold Palmer had won the 1958 Masters for the first time and more and more golfers were watching the live telecasts. The folks at CBS felt that match play didn't have the grandeur of showing an array of popular golfers playing those final three or four holes on Saturday and Sunday. If the quarterfinals and the semi-finals of match play were shown on Saturday, that's eight golfers at the most that would be seen over the weekend. The morning round would have to be taped and the technology wasn't developed yet. In addition, if some of those players were not household names, the ratings would be low and that's always a problem. What would happen if Johnny Fairway and Lucky Putter made it fair and square to the finals but nobody had heard of either golfer? We must realize that in the late 1950's we did not have the technology regarding cameras on towers or the cranes used in modern day telecasts. There was always one more thorn about scheduling match play events on live television. A favorite golfer plays out of his mind, makes every putt he looks at, and when the golf tournament comes on the air, the announcer tells us that Tommy Terrific was seven-under par on the first 11 holes and crucified Bobby Shortdriver 8 & 7. Bottom line—change the PGA to medal play and expose more golfers on national television so golf will continue to grow while networks and sponsors will benefit as well.

As the season progressed Tony continued to gain experience and play well, but he did not capture a tour victory. In September, his traveling friends Jim Ferree and Tommy Jacobs won their first PGA tournament. Jim won the $40,000 Vancouver Open primarily on the strength of firing a fantastic 61 in the second round. Professional sports were not allowed on Sunday in Canada so Jim Ferree had to sit on a lead from Saturday evening until Monday. "The players were taken on a pleasure cruise up the Strait of Georgia after the third round," Tony recalled. "This put a lot of pressure on Jim, sitting on his lead all day like that with nothing to do but ride around in a boat. The rest of us were afraid he might blow the tournament, but Jim is such an easy-going, extroverted fellow that the pressure never really did get to him until he had such a big lead it didn't matter. Jim made a huge hit with the galleries and the tournament sponsors in Vancouver. Throughout the tournament he had worn a tiny, crazy looking straw hat. The club kept the hat after he had left and made a bronze replica of it for display in their trophy case."

Two weeks later Tommy Jacobs won his first tournament, the Denver Centennial, in the town he was raised in. Tom shot a 65 the first day and took the lead he held right to the end of the tournament. Tony was his roommate that week and protocol has it that you show special consideration when your roomie is atop the leaderboard. If he wants a Coke or a favor, you don't ask questions, you just do it. If he acts a little nervous, you tell him he has nothing to worry about, just keep doing the things he has been doing. Often, it's stuff he doesn't believe or even want to hear, but it seemed to work pretty well. Tony finished in a tie for fifth in this tournament but that's not the story he was telling the press.

Tony talked about something that happened that Saturday night. "The night before the last round," he recalled, "Tommy and I went out to dinner with some Denver friends of his and on the way back to our motel the car broke down. It was about 11 o'clock at night and here we were climbing all over that stubborn automobile. The fan belt or something had busted. Tommy was down under the hood and I was lying on the engine as if the car had swallowed me up. We were hammering away at this blasted car with the wrenches, hammers and screwdrivers and we were both covered with grease and dirt just as if we didn't have to go out the next day and play in a golf tournament that Tommy had such a great chance to win. We finally got the thing fixed and went to bed about 1:00 am. We talked a little bit before dropping off to sleep and I was surprised to see how little Tommy was reacting to the pressure. Then the next morning I woke up early and looked over at him. The ashtray on the side of his bed was so crammed with cigarette butts it looked like a plate full of noodles! So he had been feeling the pressure, however, his nerves were terrific. A bunch of guys the final day were shooting 64's and 65's, but Tom fired his third straight 67 and won by a shot. Now he too was gone from the Dew Sweepers and Litter Brigade."

As the 1958 season drew to a close, Tony had come a long way and many thought despite not winning a tournament he should have been named the PGA Rookie-of-the-Year. His best performances were the tie for second at Greensboro, fourth in the Havana Invitational, a tie for fifth at Denver and a tie for sixth at Louisville and the Havana International. According to the PGA Field Secretary Jim Gaquin, "If tall and talented Tony Lema doesn't win a PGA co-sponsored tournament pretty soon, a lot of people who follow golf closely are going to be very surprised, for here is a young fellow with everything except experience. Tony actually won nearly $2000 more than fellow circuit freshman Bob Goalby, but in late August, Goalby was unanimously voted "freshman of the year" by leading money winners on the tour." Many felt that Goalby's win at Greensboro was the difference maker.

Tony's Official PGA earnings for the year amounted to $10,282 and that placed him 35th on the tour. After including at least a half dozen non-sponsored events, Tony's total earnings amounted to $15,000. He won the Idaho Open in Twin Falls, ID by firing a blistering 257 for the 72-hole event highlighted by a 63-65 in the final two rounds. He clipped his friend Cliff Whittle by six shots in that tournament and took home a first place check for $500.

The PGA reported that Tony had been one of the more active players on the circuit as he played 150 rounds. Based on four rounds per tournament, that's more than 37 tournaments. He was in the 60's in 32 rounds and under par in 62. He averaged 71.80 strokes per round.

Tony talked about his rookie year on the PGA Tour and his goals for the following season. "My year ended well enough. I was among the top 40 money winners and therefore was invited to play in two rich tournaments in Havana during November. I finished fourth and sixth in the two events, and all of us were given the red carpet treatment—free rooms at the best hotels, chauffeured limousines, cocktail parties at private haciendas. I was getting a taste of being an international playboy and it's seem pretty intoxicating to a rookie on the pro tour. It was a long way from the canneries of Oakland, the pro shop at the San Francisco Golf Club or the little nine-hole municipal golf course in Elko, Nevada. When I returned home for the Christmas holidays I was pretty pleased with myself. I had won over $10,000 in official money, a few thousand more in unofficial money at pro-ams, and I was looking forward to a much better year in 1959. I felt that all I needed to do was make a few minor alterations in my game and I would not only win my first tournament, I would win a lot of tournaments. Jacobs and Ferree had done it. Now I would do it."

About five years later, Tony looked back at the swing alterations he considered at the time and their consequences. "The changes I wanted to make were simple ones," he explained. "I decided that I needed to hit the ball on a higher trajectory and with a left-to-right fade. I felt this was necessary because we played so many elevated and heavily trapped greens that I wanted to bring the ball into them with a high flight. The ball would thus clear the danger in front of the green and also land with the soft impact that a fading ball achieves. I had the right idea, but I was going about it in the wrong way. I had a good swing and a good grip, but to develop the new trajectory I tried to change my grip. What I should have done was simply move the ball further to the left at address and stay down with the shot longer at impact. These adjustments were going to make me a big winner, a top star, a rich man. As it turned out they almost put me out of business entirely."

The Professional Golfer's Association of America
OFFICIAL MONEY WINNERS - 1958

1	Arnold Palmer	$42,607.50	25	Don January	13,373.75
2	Bill Casper	41,232.75	26	Ed Oliver	13,311.11
3	Ken Venturi	36,267.75	27	Gene Littler	12,897.29
4	Dow Finsterwald	35,393.00	28	Don Fairfield	12,809.61
5	Art Wall, Jr.	29,841.45	29	Tommy Jacobs	11,682.10
6	Julius Boros	29,817.15	30	Paul Harney	11,563.93
7	Tommy Bolt	26,940.62	31	Bob Goalby	11,052.48
8	Jay Hebert	26,384.83	32	Jim Ferree	10,940.79
9	Bob Rosburg	25,170.67	33	Marty Furgol	10,659.45
10	Doug Ford	21,874.87	34	Stan Leonard	10,438.92
11	Fred Hawkins	19,664.09	35	Tony Lema	10,282.18
12	Mike Souchak	18,137.94	36	Chick Harbert	9,956.14
13	Billy Maxwell	17,993.46	37	Bill Collins	9,918.71
14	Jack Burke, Jr.	16,870.05	38	Al Balding	9,251.20
15	Frank Stranahan	16,642.48	39	Tom Nieporte	9,012.76
16	Ted Kroll	16,409.61	40	Walter Burkemo	8,948.34
17	Cary Middlecoff	16,050.02	41	Howie Johnson	8,505.62
18	Sam Snead	15,905.00	42	John McMullin	8,325.24
19	Ernie Vossler	15,410.32	43	Dave Ragan	8,239.17
20	Bo Wininger	15,398.74	44	Gay Brewer, Jr.	7,770.29
21	Wes Ellis, Jr.	15,377.97	45	Don Whitt	7,328.83
22	Lionel Hebert	15,236.23	46	Robt. De Vicenzo	6,873.67
23	Doug Sanders	13,739.75	47	E. J. Harrison	6,693.33
24	George Bayer	13,592.97	48	Bill Johnston	6,648.33

49	J. C. Goosie	6,084.77	75	Mike Krak	1,921.67
50	Jimmy Demaret	5,788.33	76	Paul O'Leary	1,779.44
51	Bert Weaver	5,784.85	77	Earl Stewart, Jr.	1,642.50
52	Mike Fetchick	6,675.92	78	Bill Nary	1,585.00
53	Johnny Pott	5,137.48	79	Bill Parker	1,525.00
54	Dave Marr	4,873.66	80	Milon Marusic	1,520.00
55	G. Dickinson	4,645.17	81	Bob Toski	1,491.00
56	Dick Mayer	4,448.01	82	Bob Keller	1,488.61
57	Jim Turnesa	4,374.43	83	Bill Ezinicki	1,421.11
58	Leo Biagetti	4,275.02	84	Bill Ogden	1,404.77
59	Fred Haas	4,087.50	85	Otto Greiner	1,357.00
60	Pete Cooper	3,970.00	86	Bob Watson	1,345.00
61	Jerry Barber	3,867.51	87	Shelley Mayfield	1,318.93
62	Al Besselink	3,855.27	88	Buster Cupit	1,300.00
63	Lloyd Mangrum	3,710.34	89	Zell Eaton	1,205.00
64	Jack Fleck	3,673.44	90	Bob Hill	1,162.50
65	Bob Harris	3,585.83	91	George Fazio	1,116.66
66	Al Mengert	3,530.62	92	Gordon Jones	1,106.43
67	Joe Conrad	3,453.09	93	Mike Dietz	1,098.11
68	Ben Hogan	3,033.32	94	Bob Duden	1,070.00
69	John Barnum	2,675.00	95	Buddy Sullivan	1,062.00
70	Henry Ransom	2,574.75	96	Byron Nelson	1,056.25
71	Claude Harmon	2,407.63	97	Walker Inman	1,024.06
72	Bob Goetz	2,367.00	98	Dick Metz	1,016.67
73	Jerry Magee	2,254.44	99	Everett Vinzant	997.92
74	Max Evans	2,110.18	100	Bill Bisdorf	980.00

The Learning Curve

A fter such a solid rookie year on the Tour, Tony had intentions of doubling his winnings for the 1959 season. He had come close to victory and thought with all the experience he had acquired, this season was the time to break through and win a tournament. His sponsor, Jim Malarkey, was on the same page. He drew up a written contract and advanced Tony $14,000 for the year to cover expenses. He would not have to start sharing his earnings with Malarkey—two-thirds for Tony, one-third for him—until Tony had reached the $14,000 level. It all sounded good and he thought with the financial problem out of the way, he could concentrate on his game.

Fans who followed the PGA Tour with a watchful eye probably could not figure out the year Tony Lema had in 1959. The tall, talented Californian came onto the tour like a lion in 1958, but seemingly became a lamb in 1959. Some suggested that Tony was the victim of the sophomore jinx. Some consider the jinx just part of the maturation process on the Tour, while others don't consider an off-season any sort of jinx at all. But to Tony, who was becoming popular and attracting larger galleries, the jinx was real enough. In 1959, he won only $7,466 or about $5,000 less than he had the year before. He dropped to 55th on the money list in 1959 and to 77th in 1960 ($3,060). His best performances in 1959 were a tie for fifth in the Portland Open, tenth in the Texas Open, and twelfth in the Milwaukee Open. At the Centennial Open in Portland, Oregon, Tony grabbed the opening round lead with a seven-under par 65. He followed that with a 68 and shared the lead at the midway point with Billy

Casper, the U.S. Open champ that year. Eventually, he settled for fifth place and won $1,000 in his best performance of the year. In 37 tournaments, Tony finished in the money in only 15. That's quite a few missed cuts, unhappy Friday evenings, and long weekends.

"I didn't know what was happening," Tony recalled later, "but I guess I started worrying when I didn't win a tournament. I became confused and depressed. I felt I had no friends. I even started to try some major experiments with my game." When a touring pro begins to tinker and make changes, it usually leads to inconsistency, doubt, and more lost shots than saved ones. But at the same time, here is a 25 year-old young man, on the PGA Tour with a sponsor. Did we really expect that he wouldn't experiment if he wasn't shooting the scores that would make him happy?

As the winter tour got underway at the Los Angeles Open in 1959, Tony had a respectable 17th place finish and won $680 while Ken Venturi edged Art Wall by shooting a 63 in the final round at Rancho Park Golf Course and picked up the first-place check of $5,300. Tony went on up to Pebble Beach to play in the Crosby, but unfortunately he wrenched a disc in his back and had to withdraw. After a few weeks of healing, he caught back up with the tour for the San Diego Open at the Mission Valley Country Club. After two rounds with a relatively hot putter Tony was in fifth place at 135, just two shots back of the leader Mike Souchak. The third round was played in terrible weather and Tony shot himself out of contention for the lead with a 74. He stated sometime later that the record would show that he shot a woeful 79 in the final round, but considering what took place the night before it was a pretty good round of golf.

Tony recalled that he was staying at the nearby Stardust Motel and early Saturday night he received a phone call from a terrific looking model he had met in San Diego the year before. He invited her over for dinner and that was just the beginning of a long and enjoyable evening. He figured that he could play in a golf tournament every week, but it wasn't every week that he could have a heavy date with a girl who looked like a Greek goddess. The next morning he recalled that when he got to the first tee he was pretty relaxed and pretty tired. He also admitted that he didn't care whether he shot a 59, 79, or a 199.

Since then Tony said that you could blame several of his bad rounds on extracurricular activities at night. After a golfer has been out on the tour for a while he learns how to handle his social life so that it doesn't interfere with his golf. One of the first rules of life on the tour, back in the day, was no woman chasing after Wednesday. Too many drinks and too many late nights after the tournament was in progress leads to nothing but high scores and missed cuts. So, Saturday night, the eve of the final round, is not the time to participate in promiscuous activities. Sure, he was only human, but it was not surprising that an excess of activity of this nature can have a debilitating effect on a golfer's round the next day. These are lessons that took a while for him to learn. After a few years on the tour. Tony understood that the most important thing to keep, in golf, is a good attitude and a clear mind.

He said that he wished he could have blamed all of his bad rounds in 1959 to overindulgence. But the truth be known, Tony admitted that many more of his bad rounds were due to bad play and a bad temper. He pointed out that relatively unknowns like Wes Ellis, Howie Johnson and Ernie Vossler were winning tournaments and he wasn't even coming close. Something was wrong and stress and anxiety were coming to a breaking point. In the opening round of the St. Petersburg Open at the Lakewood Country Club his putts were dropping like stocks in the midst of a bear market. After his round of 66, he was tied for the lead with the long hitting George Bayer. This was unusual for Tony because Florida courses were difficult for a Californian until he got used to the Bermuda grass and the elevated greens built up on mounded plateaus. Missing a green meant you had a tricky little uphill pitch shot and more often than not, the lie was off a bare, sandy soil or nestled down in the two or three inch Bermuda grass. It wasn't the type of shot Tony was accustomed to, having learned to play in northern California.

Throughout his second and third rounds, his putting was ice cold and he ballooned to a pair of 76's. By the time his final round came along he said he simply didn't give a damn. He was paired with Chick Harbert, a veteran player he had become pretty friendly with, and another player. Tony described what happened on the back nine. "I actually started to hit the ball pretty well," he recalled. "On the 12th or 13th hole, I've forgotten exactly which one, but I know it was a real tough par four that can only be reached with two long wood shots. My second shot was a beauty and stopped about 15 feet from the hole. The first putt ran about a foot and a half past the hole. Then I missed it coming back. I was so enraged that I just reached out with my putter and began jabbing the ball back and forth as if I was playing polo. It finally popped in and I snarled to Chick, 'Give me a 12 on the hole.'

" 'No, goddammit,' he said with a laugh as we walked off the green. 'You made it in 11, but I lost a lot of cash on you. I bet Walter here you'd get down in 10.'

"Chick was trying to pass the incident off with a little humor, but I didn't think it was particularly funny. Neither, really, did Chick. He gave me a short lecture on the way to the next tee. 'Look,' he said, 'if you're not going to try then don't bother to come out here and drive yourself crazy. Some days you are just going to have to work very hard to shoot a 74 or 75. If you're not willing to put up with it then you're in the wrong business.' "

That was excellent advice for Tony and the timing was appropriate. When young golfers come out on the tour, they are all fired up and their interest in their game is sky-high. After playing well for quite some time, suddenly the player's game falters a bit here or there. They lose confidence, get discouraged and quit giving it their best effort. The result is a total letdown and it takes a lot for the golfer to get back in the groove of thinking and playing to their potential. When Ken Venturi came out on the tour, he had the best rookie year of any pro in history (before Jack Nicklaus) and he took Tony aside and gave him some words of advice to counteract this kind of emotional letdown.

"Play as hard as you can," Ken told Tony, "so that when you walk off the course with a 75 or 76 you can honestly say to yourself that that was absolutely the best score you could turn in that day. Not every day can you shoot a 66 or a 67."

Tony said years later that this was advice that yielded dividends in 1962 and '63 when he finally began to heed it in earnest. But back in the tough years of 1959 and '60, it simply did not register. The week after St. Petersburg, at the Azalea Open, Tony shot 79–75–80–79– for a 313, one of his worst ever in a 72-hole event. For months following, he never came close to having a strong tournament. At the Gleneagles Open in Chicago in June, he missed a 36-hole cut for first time that year. After that, he missed the cut at three consecutive tournaments— the rich Buick Open in Flint, the prestigious Western Open in Pittsburgh and the Insurance City Open in Hartford. In several tournaments, he would post one, two or even three good rounds only to have one really bad one that would upset the entire applecart.

In mid-season, the *Chattanooga News-Free Press* ran a story about Tony when he was in Chattanooga, Tennessee getting fitted for clubs with First Flight. Ewing Watkins and the First Flight staff outfitted him with a 'tailor-made' set of clubs. Tony was described as a quiet spoken, articulate young man who chose golf over college—much to the consternation of one brother who is a CPA and another who is a chemical engineer— and is now in his second year on the circuit, he seems to like it more every day.

"That is an understatement," he grins. "I love it—every minute of it. Oh—it's grind, all right—the travel, the frequent adjustments one must make in climate, food and water—and the fast-pace you must keep scooting around from one place to another. But I wouldn't trade places with anyone—even if my brothers do regard me as the 'black sheep' of the family."

Tony was kidding, of course. But looking back, he may have been trying to convince himself and his family back in San Leandro, California that he made the correct decision when he suddenly turned pro in 1955 after completing a two-year enlistment in the Marine Corps. So, behind that warm personality he displayed for friends and the press, Tony was a young athlete absolutely determined to win tournaments on the PGA Tour. But he was going through the turmoil that many consider to be a mandatory learning curve. Whether your name is Hogan, Nicklaus, Palmer or Lema; it comes down to a boiling point and one question only. Are you willing to pay the price it's going to take in order for you to achieve your goals?

Some observers considered Lema one of the most accurate tee shot artists in the game. He had learned the value of placing his drives by watching Ken Venturi and modeling his swing on the same order. Tony described the fundamentals. "It is a sort of squared stance, slightly closed with my hands, feet and club-head pointing directly at the target." Like Venturi, Lema was a staunch advocate of correct primary position. "If you start right, you are almost certain to end up right," he explained. Competitors and fans alike thought he only needed to polish up his putting to forge his way toward the top. "Some days," Tony explained, "I putt very well. On other days, not so well. I'll get better."

The avid golf enthusiast knows that playing competitively in college has not always been the only path to a successful career on the PGA Tour. Ben Hogan, Sam Snead and Byron Nelson, the threesome featured in a wonderful book written by James Dodson entitled *The American Triumvirate*, were living testimony that a tremendous amount of hard work, talent, and perseverance will suffice. It wasn't until the 1950's that college graduates with experience on the university's golf team started making an impact on the Tour. And in the late 50's, most of the golfers on the Tour had collegiate experience, but many of them were also products from the caddie ranks. Tony was sort of a 'hybrid.' He had the municipal golf course background at Lake Chabot, both as a caddy and a player. As an assistant at San Francisco Country Club for 18 months, he acquired the fluency associated with the country club background. Since he joined the professional ranks upon being discharged from the Marine Corps, college golf was never in the cards for Tony. When asked about the impact from a caddie's close-up view, Tony wasted no words giving his opinion. "If I had a son who wanted to play golf," he said, "I think I would advise him to caddy. You can learn so much just by watching others. And I never saw a good caddie who did not have a good golf swing. I picked up most of my golf that way—and from Lucius Bateman in Oakland who helped me, John McMullin and Don Whitt a lot."

Tony also credits a California amateur with giving him a lot of pointers. "He was a policeman (Ralph Hall) before tragically drowning a year ago," Tony said, "and he was one of the finest amateurs I ever saw. He was a great strategist and he taught me to think on a golf course. Thinking, you know, cannot be stressed too much."

Tony was effusive in his praise of the pros that played on the tour. "They are gentlemen," he declared, "and most of them are glad to lend a helping hand to a youngster. I'll never forget the kind treatment I have received from Jay Hebert, Jackie Burke and Jimmy Demaret. Oh—there are many others—but these three went out of their way to help me when I first joined the tour."

Regardless of new First Flight irons, Tony was working on that change he mentioned at the end of the 1958 season. In order to get a higher trajectory and a left-to-right flight pattern, Tony weakened his grip in order to minimize the power of the right hand and assert that the face of the club will be slightly open at impact. The other adjustment was to keep the ball back toward the center of his stance. Consequently, he came down into the ball with his hips and hands way ahead of it. He was making contact with an open clubface, but he was also starting the ball off toward the right. Most of his shots headed right of the target and then faded even farther right. When the ball was traveling from the right to further right he was lucky to keep it on the golf course.

It took quite a few shots on the practice tee to figure it out, but Tony came to the conclusion that the ball must be played more off the left foot, out where the loft of the club can really get it into the air, and a strong effort made to stay down on each shot. This means keeping the right shoulder underneath the head as the club goes through the ball and moving the hands out towards the target for as long a distance as possible. It not only produces a higher trajectory, but also a good firm shot. "Once a player has started to experiment with his game as I was doing," he explained, "it becomes almost impossible to get back on an even keel. It's like trying to cut down and even up the legs of a wobbly table."

Tony had more than his share of "out of the ordinary" occurrences on the golf course. Nelson Cullenward recalled an amusing faux pas in the 1963 March issue of *Golf Digest*. It seems that Tony was playing in the 1958 Lafayette (LA) Open and he actually putted a ball backwards off the green and into a bunker. His ball rested on a slope that ran sharply downhill, away from the hole. As he moved the putter-head over the ball, he accidentally made contact. The ball rolled backwards right into the trap, and an accident became an incident. "Only I could do something like that!" Tony said in retrospect.

While playing in the Eastern Open in July of 1960 at the Pine Ridge Golf Course outside of Baltimore, Tony wound up putting with his driver for the last 17 holes of his third round. *The Baltimore American* reported that when Tony was leaving the first green his putter suffered an unfortunate fate and became unusable. After the round, Tony was immediately on the defensive, but in a pleasant way he recounted what had taken place.

"I didn't break the putter in a fit of rage even though I had just three-putted the first green," he explained. "While Jerry Magee and Ernie Vossler were putting out I was leaning heavily on the club and bent the shaft. When we walked off the green I tried to straighten it and the thing just snapped."

Tony was faced with the prospect of adjusting to the situation, realizing he would have to finish the round with only the clubs he had when the round began. When you break a club during the round, you can't send the caddy into the pro shop to bring you a replacement. The rules state that you must make do with the remaining clubs that you have in your golf bag.

"Freddie Haas once told me," Tony said, "that if you ever crack your putter, forget all you have ever heard about using an iron and go to the driver."

As if that wasn't bad enough, players are not allowed to practice putts on the putting surface during competition. The first time you putt with any substitute club, it counts. Tony was well aware of the rules. "If you want to give it a work out on the tee or the fairway there are no objections, but it cost you two strokes if you practice on the green. I can't really say that the driver cost me more than one or two strokes when I used it as a putter. The clover around a couple of cups gave me more to worry about than the driver."

Tony had only two three-putt greens after the first hole,

numbers 8 and 17, both par threes. "If I had hit better tee shots, I might have gotten those down in two," he added. "But I must have been 50 feet away both times and I deserved bogeys after those iron shots to the greens. You just can't get any feel putting with the driver from that distance. I'll tell you one thing, I can give this crowd a lesson in lagging them up to the stick, after my experience. You never saw so many commercial stabs!"

On another occasion, Tony broke his putter and it paid dividends. He was playing in the Colonial National Invitation in Fort Worth, Texas when he became disgusted after he bogeyed the 12th hole to go 4-over par. He had 3-putted the green and as he walked off the green he tapped his toe with the putter in his exasperation. The putter snapped in two.

"All we can do now, you know, is to tap our toe with the club so we won't be throwing it," he apologized. "I was mad at myself, so I tapped my toe." At that time, there was a $100 fine imposed on any player who broke his putter during the round. Once again, Tony used his driver on the last six greens and played those holes one-under par, making two birdies, three pars and one bogey. He ended up with a respectable 73 for the round.

At the tail end of 1958, another event happened that had a major impact on Tony's game for nearly a year. In December he went over to Sun Valley where he had made quite a few friends in his days at Elko, for a short holiday. Despite the cold weather, Tony had his clubs with him and before he knew it he was giving an impromptu driving exhibition on the first tee. The head ski instructor at Sun Valley at that time was Sigi Engl; he was to the ski industry what Ben Hogan was to golf. He and his staff were avid golfers so they crowded around and watched Tony belt drive after drive toward the first green covered with snow about 310 yards away. The driver in Tony's hands was absolutely his favorite club. In those days, many tour players, such as Sam Snead, used the same driver for as many as 10 years or more. Many players had drivers, putters, wedges or sets of clubs they formed almost a human attachment to because those clubs meant so much to their livelihood.

Before too long, Tony smashed a long one that reached the front of the green. When he bent over to tee up another ball he took a close look at the clubhead. The wood had shattered completely, right at the neck of the club. Tony was devastated. Afterwards, he said he felt like a little boy who had just seen his dog run over by a car. Not only that, it was more than a year before he got another driver that satisfied him.

The trials and tribulations of trying so hard to accomplish something, yet fall short, happens to every golfer. Whether an amateur is trying desperately to break 80 or 90, or a golfer at the university is trying to win his first intercollegiate tournament, both are goal oriented and nothing short of reaching victory will satisfy their intense passion. From 1958-1962 Tony Lema was absolutely dialed in on one goal and one goal only. He wanted to win that first tournament on the PGA Tour and he wasn't afraid to admit it.

At the Houston Classic in 1960, Boo Odem of *The Houston Chronicle* sat down with Tony after he fired a 69 in the first round and had a real heart to heart talk about capturing that first victory. "I just want to win one tournament, that's all I want," Tony said, shaking his fist. And Tony had the right to make that wish. He had never put four good, solid rounds together for a first-place finish. "You have no idea," he continued, "what the feeling is to go day after day, week after week, and practice, practice, practice and never win a tournament." Odem said the 26-year old golfer had youthful frustration written all over his face.

"A win would make a world of difference in my attitude and my game. It would relieve a lot of pressure, which has built up inside of me. For me to win would be like trying to climb Mount Everest with greasy-soled shoes. I'm very passé about the 69 I shot today. It means nothing to me except it puts me in a good disposition for a couple of hours. Honestly, I am not overjoyed about it."

Bill Collins persevered and won the Houston Classic that year with a 66-71-68-75—280. He won in a sudden-death playoff with Arnold Palmer. Arnold didn't lose too many playoffs in those days! Tony followed his opening round of 69 with 74-73-74—290 and a tie for 24th worth $450.

His pessimistic reasoning was easy to verify if you looked at some of his tournaments in 1960. At Yorba Linda he tied the competitive course record in the opening round with a smoking hot 66 and then went 75-74-73—288 to finish in a tie for twenty-fifth. He opened with a 67 at Palm Springs. On the 90th hole he had to sink a 15-foot birdie putt to get last place money of $139. At Tucson earlier in the year he opened with an eye-popping 66. His next three rounds were 71-72-77 and when it ended on Sunday he wasn't even close to getting a check. Later at Baton Rouge he started with a 71, followed that with 76-73-75—295 and had to hang on to finish in a tie for 21st. It could have been said that Tony was snake bit, but whatever it was he refused to give up. He just kept grinding like a boxer; both looked forward to the next round.

"I have played in every tournament, except the Masters, and that's one I can't fit into my schedule," he said facetiously. "The only thing that keeps me going is the $27,000 (that's official and unofficial combined) I won the first two years. I still think I can become a steady player, but a bad disposition has held me back. I haven't shown it outwardly, but it is eating my insides out. When I first started I went five or six weeks without making the cut. Boy, that digs deep. I don't care if you are living in a plush motel room, you think you are in a padded cell. If you can't win $1,200 a month in this game, it is time to quit and go home."

At the time he made that comment, Tony was way under that figure in earnings. He was not listed in the top 50 money winners during the 1960 season. At that time, Tony's best finish ever was the tie for second at the 1958 Greensboro Open. "I tied with Snead, Finsterwald, Wall and January. They were in fast company," Tony said with a big chuckle. "That earned me $1,100. My biggest check was $1,600 at the Havana Invitational in November 1958. Those four-numbered checks are the greatest. It takes several weeks to spend them and boy do I live it up! I feast on filets, T-bones and sirloins. Then I go back to my hamburgers, ham steaks and chicken fried steaks…and coffee. I always pick restaurants that serve coffee free with meals," he said with a wink.

While Tony was playing in his third Greensboro Open in the spring of 1960, his winnings thus far amounted to $2,200. "It looks like I have been going downhill," he said, "but it's just that I played in more tournaments my first year on the tour. I'm getting a lot of good experience—and I believe I am improving all the while. For a spell there, I was in a slump, more or less. But now, with my putting stroke regaining focus, I think I'm on the way."

Tony had pointed out that the new pros fall into three categories:

1. Those who strive to survive the cut.
2. Those who hope to finish in the money.
3. Those who, like him, are working so hard for that first big break—that first big victory.

"I believe I have licked the first two categories," he said. "I usually survive the cut at the halfway mark and I have been finishing in the money in most of the tournaments. But getting that first win—that's becoming an obsession with me."

After about five months on the tour in 1960, Tony returned home to San Leandro, and decided to give lessons and clinics and work on his own game for about a month until he headed back out to Flint, Michigan. Actually, he was filling in for an old friend of his, Ralph Longo, who was hospitalized with a heart attack. His winnings at that point were around $3,000 and he wasn't satisfied with his progress or his swing. While he was in the Bay Area, he ran into Ray Haywood of the *Oakland Tribune* and told him what he was working on while home on the west coast.

"I've been striking the ball better but my scoring has remained about the same. While working at Golden Gate Fields, I'll make two changes in my game, one mental, the other physical."

His mental change was going to be in the manner of attacking the golf course. "I've been too conservative in the past," he said. "Instead of playing the percentages, I'm going after the birdies like Arnold Palmer—shoot for the pin regardless of hazards."

His second change seemed to reflect a trend that was current at that time which was to abandon the cut shot which fades to the right, popularized in the 50's by Ben Hogan, who was always fighting a quick-breaking hook most of his career.

"I am going to work on my swing it until I draw the shots," Tony said. "Not exactly a hook, but just a slight draw to the left at the end of the trajectory. With the small hook you get more power and distance. That power is worth extra money when the wind blows."

As the 1960 season came to a close, Tony's third on the tour, he was barely hanging on, but his financial backer, Jim Malarkey, referred to him with pride as "another Walter Hagen."

"Tony has the smoothest swing of anyone, including Ken Venturi," insisted Malarkey who continued to commute between Portland, OR and Sun Valley, ID. He had come down to San Francisco to watch Tony play in the Lucky International at Harding Park. "I believe in him—and while I don't regard this as a business investment, I'm going to make money on him."

And of course that would be fine with Tony, who had actually netted his sponsor a profit during the three years despite a tie for second place in the Greensboro Open as a rookie in 1958 having been his best performance to date. According to Malarkey, he showed about a $6,000 profit the first season, broke even the second, down about $3,000 in the third year.

It was obvious to Tony that his inconsistencies were keeping him from recording good scores and picking up good checks. After quite some time, he looked in the mirror and he didn't like what he saw. He admitted to himself that it was his continual lousy mental attitude that was keeping him from playing the kind of golf that he knew he was capable of playing. He'd play in the pro-ams loose and relaxed. Little bad breaks along the way wouldn't bother him. Once the tournament started, he'd tighten up and if the slightest thing went wrong, he would blow up sky high. As a result, his scores would go up and down like an elevator, only more up than down. He missed the 36-hole cut about as often as he made it and after a while he said the only cut he really wanted to make was in the vicinity of his neck with a razor. He was moody, mad and miserable from the time he got up until he went to bed. Not much was going right in his daily life. He wasn't sleeping or eating well. He was getting half-tanked more often than not. He was chasing after women, but he felt this was a false and insecure way of trying to keep himself at an even keel. For the first time, he understood what it meant and how it happened that people in other walks of life had nervous breakdowns. He was trying desperately hard to play winning golf, but not achieving the results he wanted. He felt as though he had lost all sense of values: both on and off the golf course.

As one might imagine, his confidence hardly existed at all. Two-foot putts became a real challenge. Finding the fairways off the tee was a matter of chance. Instead of *knowing* that he could knock a five-iron stiff to the pin, he was thinking, "What if I don't do it?" If a putt fell into the cup, his first thought was, "Boy, I was lucky." He was fined three times by the PGA for throwing clubs. Finally, some of the other players began to talk with him. Ken Venturi, Chick Harbert, Don January all took him aside and tried to calm him down, straighten him out. But Tony was having none of that. He assumed he was in a prolonged slump and that he would eventually play out of it. Another fear that ran through his mind was he felt he didn't know anything but golf. Then what would happen?

Much later Tony let it be known that a real gentleman on the tour made an impact on his attitude and behavior. "Finally one evening in St. Paul," Tony explained, "things had gotten so bad that Dow Finsterwald asked me to come by his room for a fight talk. No player on tour likes to take another aside and lecture him on his behavior, so it is easy to guess what bad shape I was in. I dropped by his room at the St. Paul Hotel, he poured me out a scotch and then laid it on the line. 'Look,' he said, 'don't you think you could give it a better try out here if you got hold of yourself, all the way down the line? Cut out the nonsensical drinking, you can't belt down half a bottle of scotch at night and expect to play halfway decently the next day. Don't go out on the golf course all pissed off at the world. You can't play well then, either. Develop a more cheerful and hopeful mental attitude or you will never be able to play well again.'

"Some of these talks began to sink in. I guess I was lucky that people cared enough about me to deliver them. I never tried to do anything underhanded to anyone else out on the tour. I just liked to have a good time, to play around, have a few laughs, tell a few jokes, buy everyone a drink or let them buy me one. It was inevitable that Pott, Jacobs and Ferree began to drift out of my immediate circle altogether. Jacobs and Pott both had gotten married in 1959 and John finally won his first tournament, the Dallas Open in 1960."

Not long after that high-spirited conversation with Dow Finsterwald, Tony got a rather inspiring capsule definition of a winning attitude by none other than Arnold Palmer. And Palmer was hotter than a firecracker in 1960. He edged Ken Venturi in the Masters by finishing birdie-birdie. He had won the Palm Springs Desert Classic with a 66 and a 65 over the last two rounds. He captured the U.S. Open at Cherry Hills in Denver with that spectacular 65 in the final round. In addition, he had won at the Texas Open, at Baton Rouge and at Pensacola. In November, he captured the Mobile Open with a final round 65. The dazzling Palmer finish was becoming routine on the PGA Tour.

After the Mobile tournament, Tony and Arnold were picked up by some mutual friends and flown down to New Orleans in their Twin Cessna. They spent the night in New Orleans, went to a cocktail party the following afternoon and spent their last night, prior to flying over to West Palm Beach for the tournament, on the host's yacht. He and Palmer were bunked together on a double-decker and both had a little trouble getting to sleep. The lights had been out for a while and Tony called out and asked Arnold if he was asleep. He wasn't so Tony and Arnold talked and smoked a few cigarettes before dropping off. It turns out Tony felt he just had to ask Palmer a question that was on the mind of every player on the tour.

"Do you realize what you have really done this year?" Tony asked.

"What do you mean, 'what I've really done'?" Palmer returned.

"Well, winning what you have the way you have," Tony, replied. "Finishing birdie-birdie to win the Masters. Shooting a 65 on the last round to win the Open. It seems so fantastic, so superhuman to have done these things in that way."

"I've never thought of it in those terms," Arnold said. "I just kind of see what it is I have to do, and I just make up my mind that I'm going to do it. If I have a long putt to make, I just think about making that putt. I shut from my mind the thought of missing it or all the other stuff that would come from my missing it."

Despite those positive thoughts fresh in his mind, Tony

finished out the year in atypical fashion. At West Palm Beach, he tied for first in the pro-am with a 67 and then missed the cut. In the last tournament of the year, at Coral Gables, he won the pro-am with a 65 and finished the tournament out of the money. On the way home, he realized that in almost every tournament throughout the season, he had had at least one very good round.

"There was something there," Tony said later, "that at least gave me the idea that doggone it, somewhere, somehow, by some sort of means, I could make a success of professional golf. Getting to the end of 1960 had been like getting to the end of the high wire during a circus act. That alone had taken something. I was beginning to believe at last that golf involved something more than just hitting a golf ball. The year just passed had been one of self-persecution. Very few people know the mental hell a player on the tour can go through. But I thought I would give the tour just one more year, that was all. I thought, I've suffered enough with this goddamn game. I'm going out there one more time and put myself through that ordeal just one more time. Then I will quit for good. I will have given it a fling whether I gave my best or not. I have tried it. I don't want that kind of life. To sit looking at the four walls of my motel room, nothing to do for the next three days until I can try to qualify for the next tournament, worrying about shooting 78 or 79 and being embarrassed to have my scores put up on the scoreboard with those of other players, with those of my close friends. I had had it. I'd played the act. I had played the bit as a playboy. I was even getting tired of that. You can only drink so many bottles of scotch and go to so many nightclubs. There isn't any excitement in that after a while."

Towards the end of 1960 Tony Lema had hit the wall. He was burned out to the point he was no longer having fun. Not only that, he had lost his determination to succeed on the tour and he had lost his desire to play the game he loved so much. He had reached the point where he hated to look at a golf club, a golf ball or a golf course.

Spending Christmas at home with his family in San Leandro in December of 1960 was the best possible therapy for Tony. He saw a lot of his old friends, went out to dinner, had a good time and did not talk about golf. He began to live like a normal human being again and his attitude turned one hundred and eighty degrees. Eight hours of uninterrupted sleep made a big difference and it became easy to enjoy every day. With the next season right around the corner, he made some resolutions to straighten out his "golf attitude" and to control his temper.

In this period, Tony reflected on his conversations with his friends on the tour who had tried to help him. Dow Finsterwald got right down to brass tacks. Tony had served in the Marine Corps and he knew a little bit about self-discipline. His conversation with Arnold Palmer gave him some first hand advice about how to think your way around the golf course. After the holidays, Tony felt that he was close, so close that a change in tactics and a minor adjustment in a swing that basically was as sound as a rock would bring consistency. "They are playing for so much money out there now," he said. "That if a man can play even reasonably well he should win $15,000 a year. I intend to work on my game until I can get my share."

Temper, Temper Go Away

While Tony was playing in the Palm Springs Classic in January of 1961, out of the clear blue sky, he received an invitation at the last minute to participate in the five-week Caribbean circuit. It was a series of golf tournaments that were held in February-March and swung through Panama, Venezuela, Columbia, Puerto Rico, and Jamaica. Tony had heard about it from his traveling companions Johnny Pott, Tommy Jacobs and Jim Ferree. It was comprised of about fifty professional golfers, forty teaching pros and ten tournament pros. It was a good break in the routine for those ten touring pros since it was an opportunity for them to be in contention every week and hopefully come out of the trip with a tidy little profit.

The pros in Tony's group, the players who were on the tour, were being sponsored by a variety of businesses in each city they visited. Basically, all of their expenses including food, lodging, and transportation were taken care of by these sponsors. The ten pros off the tour received a guarantee against prize money of $200 a week and the purse for each tournament was $10,000 so this was an excellent opportunity for Tony and his friends to improve considerably on the guarantee. Along with Tony, other tour regulars on the trip were: Billy Maxwell, who had just won the Palm Springs Classic; Ernie Vossler, a Texan who had made this trip two times before 1961; Don Whitt, a slender Californian who was making the trip for the first time; Tony's friend Jim Ferree; and Dow Finsterwald, who was flying down for just the first tournament.

On the way down in the seven-hour flight from Los Angeles

to Panama City, Tony was feeling pretty good about this adventure. There was no 36-hole cut so he knew he would be able to stick it out for the entire 72-hole tournament at each site. In addition, he was encouraged by the fact that he would have a real chance to practice every day and not have the traffic in the practice area that occurred at most tour events. Not only that, the field would be much smaller and his chances for some high finishes looked favorable.

He found the Panama City golf course exciting but a little ragged. It seems the rainy season had ended a few weeks prior to their arrival and the fairways were baked out with wide cracks in the dry red soil. In order to make the playing conditions as close as possible to normal, the tournament committee put white stakes along the sides of all the fairways, right up to the very edge of the greens. When your ball was found within these stakes it meant that you could roll it around the sparse grass until you found a suitable lie. Any golfer who knocked his ball outside these rows of stakes usually found it in a crack, among rocks, or upon hard clay. There was so much jagged rock and coral adjacent to the fairways, that if a player hit a shot off line it was far better to declare the ball lost and take a two-shot penalty rather than attempt to find the original ball and take several slashes to get the ball back into play. These conditions were tough to get used to, but Tony managed to finish twenty-third and wasn't too unhappy at this stage of the Caribbean circuit. He practiced before and after each round and felt he was solving some hitting problems that had been plaguing him for the last two years.

Throughout this trip and the following year as well, Tony's roommate was Don Whitt, a fine golfer who hadn't done much on the tour after winning the 1959 Memphis and Kentucky Derby Opens back-to-back. He was a great companion for Tony, that rare person who could be very serious about his golf game while out on the course, but could forget about it completely once the last putt had fallen into the cup. They had a very comfortable routine that suited both of them. Since most of the tee times were late in the morning or early in the afternoon, they would have breakfast after rising around eight or nine o'clock. Then they would go downtown and take advantage of the duty free prices for things like perfume, Swiss watches, and other gifts for friends and family back home. After the shopping trip, it was time for a light lunch, 18 holes of golf, and back to the hotel and enjoy some of the liquor that the Seagram Distillers, which co-sponsored the tour, left in every player's suite. After dinner at the resort, they would check out a few nightclubs and find their way back to the hotel around midnight. After three years of the demanding grind on the PGA Tour, it was a relaxing atmosphere that Tony certainly found easy to enjoy.

Tony recalled an interesting night in Panama, after the tournament was over. He had had a few daiquiris and stumbled into bed a little early. "The pre-Lent carnival was going on," he explained, "and the music was so loud that I couldn't sleep so I got up, dressed and went downstairs. A huge crowd had formed on the dance floor and had moved back to clear an area in the center of the floor. There was the beautiful dark-haired, dark-eyed Carnival Queen and she looked dazzling in her white gown and golden crown. She was doing a lively cha-cha with her partner and they looked as capable as the best professional dance teams I had ever seen back in the States. Then I got a closer look at her partner. It was nobody but my good old roomie, Don Whitt. The next moment I could hardly believe my eyes as he hopped up onto the bandstand and began leading the orchestra, shaking a couple of maracas. He was completely engrossed in his merry-making and even looked Latin with his slim build, his deep tan and short, but dark sideburns. Don is such a terrific dancer and mingler with people that if it were ever left to me to pick a golfer to make a goodwill tour abroad he would be one of my first choices. In Panama, they were ready to make him King of the Carnival."

The next day the sleepless and groggy mass of professional golfers made the four-hour flight to Maracaibo, Venezuela. Tony was quite surprised to find a hot, flat, dusty wind-wracked oil town on the shores of the gigantic Lake Maracaibo. From a distance the lake looked cool and beautiful, but close up one could see the lake's surface was covered with a thin oil slick and was as brown as mud. At that time, Maracaibo had a population of about 400,000 and most of the people lived in brightly colored small square houses. The golf course was situated in a vast desert of red clay and cactus about 15 miles outside of town that reminded Tony of West Texas at the worst time of the year. On the way to the course, they had to drive through slums where thousands of people lived in little tin shacks that must have been like ovens during the hot days and nights in this town just north of the equator.

Despite the setting, the golf course had beautiful fairways with huge, elevated and lush green putting surfaces. Word was that the club had to pour a million and a half gallons of water a day on the course or it would have been gone in a week. The course played to 7,000 yards, which was extraordinarily long back in the early '60s. Don Whitt, the dancer, played almost perfect golf en route to a 283 and one-stroke margin over the popular native Venezuelan Roberto De Vicenzo. Tony was in the hunt (70-72-73-79—294) until the final round when his putter failed him and he stumbled into a tenth place tie with Jim Ferree. But overall, he was pleased and felt this atmosphere was an asset to getting his game in shape.

The golfers looked forward to their next stop on the tour, Caracas, except that just days prior to their arrival the manager of the Tamanaco Hotel, where they were scheduled to stay, had received an anonymous threat that the hotel would be blown up. The government of Venezuela had recently undergone the change from dictatorship to a democracy and there was still a great deal of unrest there and a strong anti-American sentiment. Vice President Richard Nixon's riot-marred visit of 1958 was still fresh in the minds of the golf professionals and most of them were determined to stick pretty close to the hotel.

It turned out to be a glorious week with a balmy 75 degrees every day at the Valle Arriba Country Club situated at the 3,500-foot elevation. Don Whitt won the tournament on a course that was in sharp contrast to the one they had played the previous week. It was only 6,200 yards long but its narrow fairways were perched on a hilly slope that overlooked Caracas. Don shot a 272 and his closest competitor was eight strokes back. Tony finished alone in third place, but he had his moment in the sunshine despite the fact that there were out of bounds markers on 17 holes. He played his finest golf of the tour in the third round as he stood six-under par after 15 holes. If he parred the final three holes, he would have broken the course record set by Roberto de Vicenzo just two days earlier. But Tony said that didn't satisfy him, he was out to shoot a 60!

"On the sixteenth hole," he explained, "a narrow par four of 390 yards, I hooked a 4-wood off the tee and the ball was just barely saved from rolling out-of-bounds by a clump of deep grass. I parred the hole. On the seventeenth, a par four of only 270 yards that runs along the bottom of a canyon, I hooked a 4-wood again, but it stayed in bounds by rolling down the slope alongside the canyon. It was deep grass, however, and I had to scrape to make a bogey. On the eighteenth hole again I tore into my tee shot and hit it clear across the fairway. When I got to the ball it was only two feet in bounds. I parred the hole, but what turned out to be a 65 might just as easily have been six shots higher if God hadn't been looking out for me."

In the many facets of a professional golfer's life of traveling in unique locations, the Caracas experience was a good one for Tony. The city was beautiful and the people were most delightful. On this trip, Tony was one of the top pros and it seemed the people he met at each stop were extra nice. Since the touring pros were the top billing everywhere they went, the locals who wanted to associate with the top dogs treated them with class. In addition, the atmosphere was more laid back and absent was the hustle and bustle that touring pros are so accustomed to back in the States. Tony probably didn't realize it at the time, but being treated a little extra special, as a top attraction, was something he would get more used to within a few years. But in February of 1961, he was in South America and it was time to jump on a four-engine Viscount and enjoy the four-hour flight to San Juan, Puerto Rico.

The first thing thrown upon the fifty golf professionals in San Juan was big hotels, lots of tourists and extremely heavy traffic. They were taken to the Berwind Country Club and the local Chamber of Commerce certainly did not script Tony's description. "The golf course," he evaluated, "is what a polite golfer would describe as a 'sporty little lay-out,' meaning, 'My God, what a cow pasture!' The fairways had ditches crisscrossing left, right and dead center. Hopping all over and around the ditches were the biggest toads anywhere, some as large as pigeons. The golfers were constantly interrupted on their backswings by flying toads."

Despite a modern hotel, Tony and Don Whitt only had one bed in their suite so they agreed upon a friendly wager—the man who shot the low round of the day got the bed, the other slept on a fold-out couch. Tony got the good bed the first night of the tournament by shooting a 72 to Don's 73. Don won it back on the second day with a 74 to Tony's 75. Tony shot a 69 and a 74 to hold the bed the last two nights, but he figured he spent more time in the ditches at Berwind Country Club than he did in the bed.

The only way to avoid hitting into the ditches was to calculate the yardages off the tees and deliberately play short of them. So Tony used the driver very sparingly and teed off with the 3-wood or iron depending upon the location of the omnipresent ditch. In one round, his tee shots had scuttled along the dried out fairways and found a ditch on six holes. Tony was working on controlling his temper at that time; he didn't have it completely under wraps at this stage of his career. He described what happened on the eighteenth hole. "I played a perfect 3-wood off the tee and then watched it disappear. By the time I got down to the ditch I was ready to go off like a Roman candle. I took my 3-wood and hurled it down into the ditch on top of the ball. Then I took my bag of clubs from the caddy and dropped it down on top of the ball and 3-wood. Then I turned to see what my caddie thought of that, but his face had turned white and he was backing off across the fairway. *'No, senor, no senor,'* he begged. *'Por favor, por favor.'* "

Tony's sense of humor was a major asset that enabled him to get through the roller coaster life of a professional golfer constantly on the road sans a great degree of security. While in San Juan, he and Don Whitt ran into an old friend and went to the Caribe Hilton for dinner. While waiting for a table, they started talking to two girls from New Jersey and asked if they would like to join them for dinner. Tony said he was just trying to be polite, besides the girls were rather attractive. He started to give the better-looking one a rush to see if there were any possibilities. It soon became obvious that nothing was going to come of it so when she asked Tony what he did for a living; he let his imagination run wild.

"I'm Sam Lema," he told her. "I've been down here for fifteen years and run a chain of shoe stores. Lema Shoes."

The girl seemed to be a little dubious since his Spanish accent did not come close to that of a fifteen year resident. Meanwhile, Don Whitt was staring at Tony a little dumbfounded and when she asked him what he did for a living he was caught nearly speechless. He didn't know whether to play along with the gag or just tell her he was a professional golfer. Finally, he decided he might as well play along.

"I'm a.., I'm a.., I'm a..," he began stammering. "I'm an international playboy." Tony and his friend broke out laughing, but the poor girls couldn't figure out what kind of nuts they had met.

It turns out; Don was a little peeved that Tony had put him on the spot. "What the heck were you trying to pull?" he asked Tony. "Oh hell," Tony replied. "They didn't want to hear about us being pro golfers. Who would be interested in that?"

"What the hell is wrong with being a pro golfer?' asked the man who had just won two tournaments in a row.

Tony had learned some lessons and eventually passed some good advice along to any player about to go on the Caribbean tour. "I tell a player who has never gone on this tour," he explained, "that he is going to get tired, that the heat and the banging around trying vainly to understand foreign customs and a foreign language are going to jar his nerves, but that he should keep himself under control nonetheless. He is on foreign soil, after all, and should never do anything or say anything, no matter how furious or indignant he may feel, that he could conceivably regret later."

Billy Maxwell avoided the ditches and won the tournament in San Juan by seven shots over Roberto De Vicenzo with a very respectable 273. The caravan's final stop was Kingston, Jamaica and another of Tony's good friends, Jim Ferree, won by six strokes. In addition, Tony felt as though his game was coming around. He wound up finishing eighth as he played consistent golf, shooting 70-73-69-73—285 and winning $550. He had gone back to the fundamental grip he had used in 1958 instead of the fading grip that had fouled him up so badly in 1959 and 1960.

Although he did not win a tournament on the Caribbean tour, he had practiced quite a bit, played some noteworthy rounds, and gained a great deal of experience. He felt if he couldn't start now living up to the promise he had shown in 1958, well, maybe he never would.

But Tony had one more trick up his sleeve before the group of fifty packed their bags for the last time and headed back to Miami. It seems that after the final round at Kingston, the players went from the lounge back out to the driving range and improvised a special clinic for the gallery that remained. With cocktails flowing, the clinic was more a comedy routine than explaining to the amateurs how to hit golf shots. Tony said he tried to demonstrate how to hit a 2-iron, but after three shots the yardage would not add up to a good wedge shot. So a handful of players kidded and tricked each other with good humor as the sole intention of this escapade.

"All of the players were pretty worn out after the tournament and headed for bed early," Tony said sometime later. "I was full of beans, however, and stayed out partying until 4:30 a.m. When I got back to our motel, the Courtleigh Manor, I was in just the right mood to have a little joke at the expense of my pooped-out fellow pros. I slipped a couple of pounds into the hand of the night desk clerk and persuaded him to ring up each room, telling the players that he was instructed to get them up at 5 a.m. to make the flight back to Miami. Well the plane didn't leave until late in the morning and the screaming and shouting could be heard all the way to the Kingston docks. People were still grousing about the motel's inefficiency as we boarded the plane and made our departure from the Caribbean. I had to join the chorus too. If anyone had suspected my role in this prank I would have been flung through the emergency exit."

Upon his return to the States, Tony's first tournament was the St. Petersburg Open. It had been two years since his flameout at the Lakewood Country Club when he hastily but intentionally nine-putted a green that lead to an 84 and stern reprimand from playing partner Chick Harbert. But things were different in 1961. At 27, not only had Tony matured as a young man, but he also had two more years of tournament toughness under his belt. In addition to trying to turn over a new leaf, there was another change that he no doubt appreciated. The tournament was being played on a different golf course in St. Petersburg, the Pasadena Golf Club. It was in immaculate condition, but similar to the courses on the Caribbean tour, there had been very little rain in recent weeks, subsequently the fairways were hard and the ball rolled quite a long way. The alterations he made on the South American trip were paying off as was driving the ball accurately. He started the tournament with a mediocre round of even par-71, but followed that with three rounds he considered the best he had ever shot in a tour event up to that time. He fired a 66 in the second round, followed by a 68 on moving day and finished with another 66 on Sunday. Those solid rounds put him into a tie for thirteenth place and a check for $590. Considering the abysmal state he was in prior to the Christmas holidays, Tony was encouraged by his play in St. Petersburg.

So he headed for Miami Beach and the Sunshine Open with intentions to play well. But Tony ran into the nemesis that caused him to lose focus faster than the speed of light. He had checked into the Miami Racquet Club late at night and the next morning upon waking up he could hear "the sounds of girlish laughter and the splash of dainty bodies leaping into the water." He peeked through the curtains and there in front of him were "four or five extremely lush little feminine morsels." He also admitted that at that very moment he knew it was going to be a very good week and that had absolutely nothing to do with any activities from the first tee to the eighteenth green. His agenda was to have breakfast by the pool, rush over to the golf course and get the business of playing golf over with as quickly as possible, and then return to the Racquet Club in time to begin the afternoon's drinking and sunbathing by the pool. He enjoyed dinner in the dining room, by the pool or on one of the yachts moored at the club's harbor. He took some tennis lessons in order to get better acquainted with the attractive girl who was the instructor. Tony summed up his tennis game rather appropriately, "I never learned much about tennis from the pro, but she was a terrific dancer."

In his book, Tony went so far as to categorize the four types of girls that can be seen around tournaments. The first are the girls who simply want to be seen with a sports celebrity because they figure some of the attention being lavished on him will wash off on her. She is a celebrity hound that wants to bask in his fame and thinks by doing so she becomes a big deal herself. Tony's advice on this type was to plead a headache and take her home early. The second category is the golf-nutty girls. Some are pleasant and really want to learn more about the game, but others just wanted to talk golf, golf and more golf when Tony had other things on his mind. The third and largest category was the well-bred women who saw these tour players not as a golfer or a celebrity but as a man. They were moderately interested in golf, but it didn't make that much of an impression upon them. The final category includes the impulsive, aggressive types who were not afraid to let it be known they were out to have a good time and they figured a touring pro was a strong candidate. Those were the ones that always seemed to dress colorfully on the golf course and would casually bump into the pro of their choice between the green and tee or at the water fountain. If for some reason a woman in this group does not make contact with a specific golfer, Tony said the following scenario would take place.

In his bachelor days, Tony would be stretched out on the bed in his room watching television and the telephone would ring. Tony would answer with, "Hello."

"Hello, Tony," a girl's voice would say, "My name is so-and-so and I was in your gallery today. Do you remember? I was wearing a bright blue dress with a yellow sweater and you said hello to my on your way to the twelfth tee."

"Oh, yes," Tony might reply, sometimes recalling the girl or the incident and sometimes not.

"Well, I was just here in the bar downstairs," the girl would say, "and I thought I'd give you a call and say hello. What are you doing?"

"I'm watching television."

"Good program?"

"Yes, I think you'd like it."

"Well, that's nice."

"Why don't you come up and watch it with me."

"Okay."

That sort of thing happened on occasion but Tony added, that as a bachelor, life on the pro tour could be a pretty lonely business. He was single on the tour for five years and he knew the liveliest spots were Miami, Dallas, Phoenix, Los Angeles, Chicago, New York, New Orleans and San Francisco.

Tony had been given an unwarranted tag of "playboy" by some who did not know him really well. A bachelor, tall and handsome, Tony had plenty of feminine companionship wherever he went. He didn't have to look for the girls; they sought him out.

"But, that playboy angle is overworked," he explained to Nelson Cullenward. "Golf is my business and that comes first. Sure, I like girls. I also like to dance and have an occasional drink. But golf comes first. My erratic performances of the past have been more due to anxiety and a poor mental outlook on the golf course then nightlife. Now I have discovered how to have a winning mental outlook and my scoring has improved."

Hal Wood, the *United Press International* golf writer told one story on Tony that occurred while he was playing in Arizona. "Tony had been going out with a cute little chick every night and came up with the 65 in the first round. I told him that he had better forget the girls and get some sleep," says Wood. "He had decided to eat dinner and go straight to bed, canceling his date. The next day he shot 84."

"That's the end of that," groused Tony. "From now on I'm going to lead my normal life."

As the 1961 season progressed, Tony was struggling hard to stay in the top fifty on the official money list, but he was participating in the Wednesday pro-ams and picking up checks to offset traveling expenses. Out of nowhere, he suddenly developed a severe case of putting jitters. Many think that sort of thing is impossible for a 27-year old in his fourth year on the tour, but it happens to a great percentage and there is no warning. Tony felt that holing four-footers was a major challenge and once again, his confidence had eroded to ground zero. He was taking anywhere between 38 and 40 putts per round and normally that included five or six three-putt greens. Most tour players feel that 32 putts per round is tolerable in order to maintain consistency, but when a player is taking a handful more per round that can lead to frustration and missed cuts. Once again, Tony was having negative thoughts and leaving the tour seemed like the logical solution. He was determined that something like the putting jitters was not going to ruin his entire life. He would quit golf before he would let that happen.

Tony did not qualify for the 1961 U. S. Open, won by Gene Littler at Oakland Hills Country Club in Bloomfield Hills, Michigan. Following the Memphis Open, he went up to Detroit and borrowed a car from a friend, Ed Addis. He drove over to Belmont, just north of Grand Rapids, to play in the Western Open. Once again, the combination of not playing well and an ice-cold putter prevented him from making the cut. He headed back to Detroit planning to drop the car off at Addis's house and then head for the airport and fly back to San Leandro. Ed was not home so while he was waiting for his friend to return, Tony suddenly remembered that Detroit was the home of Horton Smith, the head pro at Detroit Country Club. Smith, the winner of the first Masters tournament in 1934, the year Tony was born, was considered one of golf's greatest putters. Tony had met him a few years prior and decided he would give him a call, see if Smith remembered him, and perhaps help him straighten out the sad state of affairs with his putting stroke. So Tony called the Country Club and soon Horton Smith was on the line.

"Hello, Mr. Smith," he said. "This is Tony Lema. Do you remember that we met a couple of years ago?"

"Sure, I remember, Tony," he said. "How are you?"

"Well, I'm not too good," Tony replied. "My putting is shot to pieces, and unless it gets put together again I am just going to have to quit the tour. I was hoping that you might be able to help me."

"Absolutely," Smith said. "You come right on over. I'm sure all you lost is your confidence, but you come over and will get that confidence back again for you and get you back to a good putting stroke."

Tony said later that almost as soon as he put the telephone down he felt better. He drove over to Smith's club and for an hour they practiced on the putting green. Horton told him what a putting stroke should be and what he could do about smoothing out his putting stroke. Tony said he could feel the confidence coming back as he listened attentively. Horton explained that putting was almost entirely a right–handed stroke and that the left hand was there only to help keep the blade on line. He demonstrated a drill and Tony used it for the remainder of his career. Smith told him to hold the putter with nothing but his right hand and hit the ball at the hole from two feet, then four feet, then six and finally 10 feet. Tony said his stroke and confidence came back almost immediately. He was so eager after that lesson that he jumped into Addis's car and drove to Flint, Michigan, where the Buick Open was to be held the following week. He didn't score considerably well, but he was able to survive the cut and at least get a check. More importantly, he felt better with his putting and knew he could eventually become a very good putter. Much later, Tony spoke about that spontaneous visit with Horton Smith.

"Horton couldn't have been more considerate," Tony recalled. "I can never thank him enough for what he did. It was the greatest hour or two I ever spent in my life and an experience I can never forget. It was a Dutch uncle session and I came away from it with a completely new attitude, a fresh shot of confidence. It was a turning point in my golfing career. His sudden death in 1963 was a tragic loss to golf. He was the only man I know who ever put more into the game of golf then he took out of it. My debt to Horton Smith goes beyond the invaluable putting lesson that day in Detroit. I am the richer for a few memories of him. I recall vividly my match with Peter Alliss in the 1963 Ryder Cup singles competition in Atlanta when Alliss had me dormie—two down with two to play. I took the 17th with a birdie, but I was trapped at the 18th and Peter was over the green. He chipped out about 15 feet away and missed the putt. I blasted out about five feet short and, as I knelt to sight the line on the putt, I looked beyond the hole and saw Horton in the gallery, watching me gravely. His eyes were talking to me and I got the message, clear and strong. I took my stance, locked my head in position and banged the ball into the cup to halve the match. As I walked off the green, Horton greeted me and smiled broadly. 'It couldn't go any place else, could it?' "

The tour headed to St. Paul, Minnesota and Tony's game started showing signs of sharpening as he had three fair rounds and one very good one. He finished in a tie for fifteenth and received a check for $670. On Sunday evening Tony was so pleased with the turnaround in his game he gave a party in his suite on the twelfth floor at the St. Paul Hotel. A large group of the players were scheduled to take a late train that night to Winnipeg where they would play in the Canadian Open. His roommate from the Caribbean trip, Don Whitt described that evening in an article in *Sports Illustrated* written in 1963 by Gwilym S. Brown.

"Tony really gave a wild party after the 1961 St. Paul Open," Don recalled. "You know him. Well, he'd rented a suite at the St. Paul Hotel and he invited a crowd up after the last round. We all got a little loose and wound up driving golf balls through the window and out onto Market Street."

One might wonder if the effects of partying hearty had an affect on his golf game when he'd teed it up in the first round of the Canadian Open. Yes, and as a matter of fact, it was all good. Tony fired a seven-under par 65 at the Niakwa Country Club and took a one-shot lead over the eventual winner, Jackie Cupit. But Tony played well, finished at 11-under par and tied for seventh and won a check of $1,250.

The next tournament was the Milwaukee Open and Tony learned another valuable lesson on the importance of maintaining an even keel in the department of emotional control. Tony started the last round in eighteenth place tied with Ken Venturi and a few others. They were all at 209, eight shots behind the leader Bruce Crampton. After ten holes, Tony was three-under par in the final round and was within three or four shots of Crampton. At that point, he felt he had a chance to catch him. In a blink of an eye, Tony bogeyed the eleventh, twelfth and thirteenth holes, right in a row, and thought for sure that he had thrown his round right out the window.

"Goddammit," he said to himself. "What are you doing now? You're always blowing up like this."

On the fourteenth green, Tony knocked his approach shot within four feet of the cup and had a great opportunity to get a stroke back. He proceeded to miss the short birdie putt. He was just about ready to whirl around towards the clubhouse and put his putter into orbit, but he checked himself just in time. He tried to convince himself that it wasn't the putter's fault and on the way to the fifteenth tee he had a little talk with himself.

"Tony," he said to himself, "wait until you have played the last four holes before you get mad. Then when you get into the clubhouse break all your clubs, smash them, twist them into metal pretzels. Do anything you want. But while you're out here, see what you can salvage. You only have four holes to play and it will only take an hour."

Well, it must have been a good talking to as Tony finished with four straight birdies, jumped back into a tie for sixth place and picked up a check for $1,300. He really got a kick out of the birdie on the last hole and described it later on.

"The eighteenth was particularly memorable," he said. "It was a par five that could be reached with two good shots, but I hit my tee shot into deep grass. Trying to really smash the second shot and get it onto the green I succeeded only in knocking it to the right and under a tree about 80 yards short of the green. I was partially stymied by the tree trunk, and a low branch force me to play the ball low. I choked up on a five-iron and cut across the ball on the shot, sending a low slice out toward the green. The ball hit with a great deal of slicing spin on it, ran toward the green, bounced right around a sand trap and up to eight feet from the hole."

It was Tony's fourth year on the tour and he was learning that a touring pro absolutely must keep his temper under control in order to play consistent golf. In every round, whether we are talking about a touring pro or an amateur, golfers are faced with bad bounces, bad lies and putts that are dead in line with inches to go but fail to fall into the cup. A touring pro's livelihood is at stake, but he must learn that misfortunes happen and they must be accepted without losing his temper. Pros have other issues they must deal with during a round. There are the spectators, some of whom simply do not know the proper etiquette expected of them. Then there are the photographers who are determined to get the classic picture (golfer at impact), but fail to follow the number one rule that no shutters are allowed to "click" until the ball has left the clubface. Tony hit the nail on the head one time when he said, "the sport of golf is definitely one for an unruffled composure." Amen, Tony.

Shortly after Tony came out on the PGA Tour, Don January told him about a trigger-tempered pro named Ivan Gantz who had just quit tournament golf. "I had been on the tour just a short time when I first laid eyes on Ivan," January recalled. "I was walking down one fairway and looked over into another and there was this fellow with blood pouring out of a big gash in his forehead. It was Gantz and he had gone and hit himself on the head with his putter. The pros used to tell about how, after missing short putts, Gantz would dive into creeks or sand traps, hit himself over the head with a rock, or roll around in the grass like a dog trying to scrape off fleas."

Tony was aware that no one on tour was immune to losing his temper. There are hundreds of stories and Tommy Bolt was not the only one in the era of the '60's who had tempestuous outbreaks. But Tony came to the realization that the right idea was not only never to lose his temper while playing golf, but also not even to *feel* like losing it. He knew that was an impossible goal to achieve but the closer a golfer can get to it, the more effective a player he will be. The more he displayed this kind of attitude, the more his name began to show up at the top of the leaderboard. Very interesting!

As the fall tournaments rolled around in 1961, Tony consistently finished in the top ten or fifteen week after week. He won the 36-hole Hesperia Open in California (71-67—138) and following a few weeks off he went down to Mexico City and won the Mexican Open, a paycheck amounting to $2,500. He took the lead in the first round and never was behind as he steadily built up a comfortable cushion and won by six shots. When he was handed the Seagram Cup by Mexican Golf Association President Alfonzo Estrada, Tony said, "This is the first time in my professional career that I went ahead in the opening round and stayed there to the finish." Tony wound up at eight-under par 280 but there were some notables in the field, including, Phil Rodgers (291), George Knudson (293), and Chi Chi Rodriguez (294).

Earlier Tony said that golf was 70 percent mental and 30

percent a physical occupation. Even though the Hesperia and the Mexican Opens were not huge tournaments with elite fields, those victories helped Tony understand and appreciate the advantage of playing with confidence.

"You can never let up," he explained, "You've always got to keep that psychological thing in mind. You go along and play pretty good for couple of weeks and you think: This is the easiest way in the world to make a living, and then you get to playing bad for a while and if you don't watch out you lose all the confidence that you've built up. This has happened to me. Confidence is the hardest thing to get along without. You can get so that you haven't even got confidence in a wide-open pitch shot."

He caught back up with the Tour in December and finished eleventh at West Palm Beach and also finished in the money in the Coral Gables Open—the last event of the year—which enabled him to qualify for the 1962 Los Angeles Open. Since the summer visit with Horton Smith, Tony's putting had become sound, his temperament was under control and he felt his first win in a big tournament was right around the corner. His official earnings for 1961 amounted to $11,505 but combining pro-ams and the Caribbean tour his total income was well over $20,000.

Tony's confidence had risen to the point where he felt he no longer needed to keep the sponsorship agreement he had with Jim Malarkey. Jim had promised Tony that the agreement could terminate whenever Tony felt the time was right. So Tony made that request with only the stipulation that he would pay back the $11,000 debt that had accrued during his rough years. And perhaps, the most encouraging aspect of Tony's life on the tour was that his disposition and mental attitude were so positive, he no longer needed lectures or pep talks from his friends. Tony was certain his goal was in sight. He was determined that he was going to win a tournament on the PGA Tour in 1962.

If I Win Tomorrow

Finally in 1962, Tony started getting the results in golf tournaments he always knew he was capable of achieving. It was his breakout year. Fans and fellow competitors alike had been waiting for Tony to put the numbers on the scoreboard they felt were long overdue. Naturally, everyone wanted to know how he suddenly was able to take his game to another level. He said that he was asked a thousand times by the press and the fans. "Tony, what changes have you made in your game?" "Tony, how do you account for it?" He heard it so many times, he finally settled on the explanation that was the simplest one he could think of. "I guess I'm just lucky," he replied, and the fans and press seemed to accept that form of reasoning.

But Tony knew that it wasn't by luck alone that he began to reach the potential that had been in site but out of grasp for such a long time. He simply matured as a professional golfer on the tour, but he felt that seed had been planted by a friendship that began in the winter of 1960. He was playing in the Palm Springs Desert Classic in February and the format was unique. First, it was a 90-hole event played over four courses in Palm Springs. In each of the first four rounds, the pros were paired with a different team of three amateurs and of course quite a few Hollywood celebrities were part of the amateur cast. It wasn't until the final round when the amateurs were all behind the ropes and the professionals were going at it in routine fashion. Well, 1960 was the first year of the Palm Springs Desert Classic, which was changed to the Bob Hope Chrysler Classic the very next year. Not only was Bob Hope the primary drawing card, but also Bing Crosby, Kirk Douglas and even former President Eisenhower played in the tournament in the wonderful setting of Palm Springs. One of Tony's partners in the inaugural event was Danny Arnold, a producer, comedian, actor and director. Some of his better work included the production of *Barney Miller*, *That Girl* and *Bewitched*. Arnold was a member of the Tamarisk Country Club in Palm Springs and was a fairly decent golfer with a 10-handicap. He had moved out to the west coast from New York about ten years prior and he and Tony hit if off from the very start. In that first round Tony fired a 67 and was tied for the lead with Arnold Palmer, Bob Goalby and Mason Rudolph.

"After our round together," Tony said later, "Danny invited me to stay with him and his wife Donna while I was in Palm Springs. The Arnolds were just about the warmest, friendliest couple I have ever met. We did a lot of talking that week and I guess we got to know each other pretty well. I had a lot of problems and needed someone to talk to. Danny was a great listener, but he was also a pretty good talker as well."

"He was a very likeable guy with a great talent as a golfer," said Arnold. "Donna and I found out he was emotional about his game, but not very serious about it. He wasn't much different than any young kid. But we got to know his problems. He needed someone to talk to and someone to talk to him."

"One of the things Danny Arnold spotted about me pretty quickly," Tony explained, "was the fact that, while I was overemotional about my golf, I did not have a proper attitude about it. These were the dog days in the golfing life of Tony Lema and I needed some straightforward advice about my attitude toward the game. The first thing Danny tried to do was build up my confidence. The greatest golfer in the world is nothing without confidence, while with it a usually mediocre player can be awfully hard to beat. He started out by telling me what a fine swing he thought I had and what a basically fine player I was. One round of golf was all anyone needed in those days to see what kind of temper I had. Danny started trying to convince me that temper tantrums never would work for me, only against me. I wasn't really hard to convince, it was simply that I didn't have the self-control to discipline myself. After I missed a short putt I knew it was wrong to do so, but I would often step to the next tee and almost deliberately try to rifle my drive out of bounds. I was only punishing myself, of course, but I guess that was the purpose. I had missed a short putt, now I wish to be punished for missing it. Simple, yet foolish.

"Danny would talk to me by the hour," Tony continued. "He built up my confidence in myself and my game. He was like a psychiatrist. He convinced me that bad putts and bad shots weren't necessarily caused by an unjust fate or a weakness in me, that if I stayed calm and kept the ball in play, the breaks would come my way too. It began to work. Every golfer has rounds when he's not playing well, but I found I could now shoot 71 or 72 on those days instead of 76 or 78."

Since these bad habits had been so deeply engrained in Tony's disposition on the golf course, he knew it would take more than a few days of talking with Danny to wash the slate completely clean. Whenever Tony was in the southern California area, he would always get together with the Arnolds. In between visits, Tony would call Danny and discuss how things were going and what adjustments were necessary in order for Tony to play with a peaceful mindset.

Since Danny was well known in the movie and television industry, he often had very interesting guests from the entertainment world. During one of his visits, Tony had the opportunity to have a thought provoking conversation with Danny Kaye. It turns out Kaye was as smooth with a golf club in his hand as he was on stage. He was a 70's shooter and had the reputation of playing just as well under pressure in a big pro-am as he did just fooling around with friends. Tony made the remark at dinner that being an actor must be one of the easiest professions around. "That's right," Danny Kaye said. "If you have the guts for it."

The first thing that came to Tony's mind was that he could become half the golfer that Danny Kaye was a showman if he could just get the courage to control his temper. Tony asked Kaye how he prepared himself before he went on stage beneath the bright lights. As a professional golfer, Tony was fully aware there was much more involved in playing tour events than just teeing it up when your group was summoned to the first tee. Kaye told him there were many obstacles to overcome in every show and his first step was to make up his mind that he was going to clear all of them. He would always arrive at the theatre or nightclub early, get a feel for the environment, and just walk around before it was his time to take the stage. He would also go to the site when it was completely empty and reassure himself that everything would go fine a few hours later when the auditorium was packed. The more people from show business that Tony met in the early 60's the more he realized the similarities between actors and tour golfers. They were both performers putting on a show for an audience (gallery) and it was imperative to maintain your cool whether you missed a line on stage or missed a three-foot putt on the back nine Sunday afternoon.

Tony got off to a solid start in 1962 when he finished at 279 and a tie for fifth in the Los Angeles Open. The $1,900 was a decent check but Phil Rodgers ran away from the field at 268, an impressive 16-under par. Tony tied for 32nd at the Bing Crosby and then headed back home for the Lucky International played at Harding Park Golf Club in San Francisco. During this tournament, Ed Schoenfeld, golf editor for the *Oakland Tribune* sat down with Tony and asked him if he wanted to reach the top tier of the PGA Tour and be considered Mr. Golf.

"Sure, there is a fabulous amount of money and a lot of fame attached to being top man, but it's too demanding," Tony declared. "A man like Palmer is not left alone. People are always hounding him, disregarding his privacy and imposing on him. It's a living that can't be consistent. A man can't go along that way very long. Palmer looks very, very tired, worn-out, and I think it has to be affecting his performance. (At that point in early 1962, Palmer was 22nd in earnings with $1,650). Through all of this Arnold has stayed one of the greatest guys on the tour. And, without a doubt, he's the greatest thing to happen to golf in 15 years. In spite of this, I wouldn't want to be Mr. Golf. I want to become one of the leading players on the tour, and I don't believe I'm sluffing off on my goal. I know my capabilities and I'm going to try and succeed by reaching one helluva high goal for Tony Lema, of San Leandro."

In four years, he had earned nearly $60,000 on the PGA

Tour and some of his touring colleagues had said that Tony's on the launch pad headed for big things. With his fifth season under way, Tony reflected about his past and talked about his expectations.

"I feel very good now," he said. "I've been playing much better the past year or so. From my first year on the tour to the end of the third I got progressively worse. I was changing my game, starting to do things mechanically without thinking them out, and things like that. Now I have more confidence then ever. Winning two tournaments, the Mexican Open and the Hesperia, last year, did it."

Tony got off to a solid performance at Harding Park and after three rounds he was in fifth place at 208, six shots behind the leader, Gene Littler. He was in the final pairing with two veterans from San Diego, Littler, the current U.S. Open champion and 1959 Open champion Billy Casper. After warming up on the practice tee, Tony strolled over to the putting green and hit some putts while talking with Ray Haywood of the *Oakland Tribune*. Somehow, the topic of conversation became the amount of money available on the PGA Tour.

"The purses are so large now—$1.5 million this year—that if you play adequately you can make a good living," Tony said. "I know that every week I am getting closer to being a better than adequate player. If a man had shot even par in 1961 he would have won the Open, missed the money only 10 times and had official earnings of more than $45,000. It is enough to keep you out there as long as you think you have a chance."

Tony was quick to point out that par golf obviously isn't always possible under some weather conditions and on some courses, but that generally speaking it isn't an impossible goal.

"I learned a lot," he continued, "but I still have a lot to learn, particularly about putting and thinking. By thinking I don't mean the positive thought business, although that helps, but eliminating mental errors which hurt more than the ones of execution which everyone has to make occasionally. Many of us out here reach a stage where we all hit the ball about as well. The money winners are the ones who know how to manage, who make the right decisions, who always keep their poise and play it smart."

Haywood noted that Tony had become stronger and filled out to 180 pounds compared to the slender rookie he was five years ago when he weighed 164. "I'm 15 yards longer now," Tony told Ray, "without swinging harder, which helps with every club, except the putter."

Tony went on to explain that his biggest problem had been a bad round, either the second or third, as a rule. "That's bad thinking too. I get to trying too hard and forget to play one shot at a time, forget that this is a game of patience. You win a tournament with four steady rounds. I don't have those bad rounds because I go out on the town, or anything like that. Bachelors always get that kind of a reputation if they are seen out after midnight. Actually, if being home early meant winning, I'd be the greatest."

Following that conversation with Ray Haywood, Tony was summoned to the first tee in the final group of the day. Littler drove long down the middle. Casper worked his characteristic long fade shot well into play. Tony delighted the huge gallery by smashing his drive 20 yards past both. Perhaps this would be the tournament without the bad round. If so there was a chance Tony could catch Casper for second money, which would mean the difference between $4,600 and $3,000, since there didn't seem much prospect that either could catch Littler. Despite hitting the best drive, Tony was long with his approach and chipped back to within five feet to save par. He pulled the putt and in exasperation, irritation and nervousness, Tony attempted to backhand the four-incher—and missed. He should have made four but because of a mental error had taken a double bogey six. A mechanical error caused another double bogey on the eighth and Tony made the turn in 40, four-over par. He settled down and played the back nine patiently, one shot at a time, one over par, for a 76 and a 284 total, which tied him for 22nd place and earned $625. That backhand shot had cost Tony $325. You lose strokes and money fast in this game.

Gene Littler hung on to win first prize by shooting a 73 in the final round for a total of 274, two strokes ahead of the hard-charging George Knudson of Canada. Tony headed down to play in the Palm Springs Desert Classic but finished out of the money in the five-round event. Undoubtedly he stayed with Danny Arnold, had a good time and listened attentively to Danny's advice about staying in the present tense and forgetting about bad shots immediately. In other words, professor Danny Arnold schooled Tony a little more on the subject of *Positive Mental Attitude 101.*

When the tour hit Miami in March of 1962 Tony felt his temperament was finally under control and his second trip on the Caribbean Tour had been successful. In the five tournaments on the tour his worst finish was a tie for eighth in the Panama Open. In Jamaica, he placed seventh, tied for fifth in Maracaibo and Caracas, and was runner-up in the last tournament of the tour in Puerto Rico. Doral Country Club hosted the inaugural Doral Open for the first time on the infamous "Blue Monster" and Tony considered this layout one of the toughest on the entire tour. His first round in the tournament certainly proved that point. "I fired a big, fat 82," he said. "Ordinarily a first round score like that would have finished me for the week. Not only because I would have had trouble making the 36-hole cut, but also because I would have been too mad or too depressed to bother playing well after that. At Doral, however, I stuck to my guns, played three good rounds (71-72-73) and, while 82's aren't ever going to put you in contention for the lead in a tournament, I managed to squeeze into the money. I felt quite proud on that occasion."

Billy Casper demonstrated his ability to finish strong on the back nine at Doral. He was down by four shots with eight holes to play and he edged Paul Bondeson by one. That victory was capped off with a 60-foot putt on the 72nd hole. Four years later in the U.S. Open at Olympic CC in San Francisco, Casper roared back on the final nine to tie Arnold Palmer and eventually win the following day in the 18-hole play-off.

As the season rolled along, Tony's game continued to improve. Not only was he playing more consistently, but also he was taking to heart the advice Danny Arnold had shared with him about remaining cool when bad luck came out of nowhere. He played in his first U.S. Open since 1956, but he was driving poorly at Oakmont and failed to make the cut. The following week at Baltimore, in the Eastern Open, he fought back from a first–round 75 and finished third, just two shots

behind the winner Doug Ford. Two weeks later at the Buick
Open, Tony was on the receiving end of a bad break that was
at the top of the all-time list. After three rounds at the Warwick
Hills Country Club in Flint, MI, Tony was tied for the lead at
212 with Pete Cooper, a friend from the Caribbean Tour and
Bill Collins, the big, blond long-hitter from Baltimore. Tony
described exactly what happened in the early stages of that
final round in the Buick Open.

"I was paired with Pete Cooper and Jim Ferree," Tony
recalled, "in the very last threesome on the course, with Bill
Collins just out in front of us. The second hole at Warwick Hills
is a par five that bends around trees to the right. It is possible,
by cutting the corner on one's second shot, to land right in front
of the green and thus give yourself a great chance for a birdie
four. In this final-round I had put my drive in perfect position to
fly my second shot over the trees and up near the green. In an
attempt to do so I hit what I thought was a truly fine five-iron
shot. I looked up in time to see the ball soaring toward the top
of a tree right at the corner. I figured that even if it nicked the
tree I wouldn't have any trouble because the branches were
extremely thin way up there. Suddenly the ball hit something
that must have been as solid as a brick wall. It caromed straight
left, high across the fairway, and went clear out of bounds on
the opposite side. I was shocked and heartbroken.

" 'Son,' said Pete, who was as surprised as I was at the turn
of events, 'that's the worst piece of luck I have ever seen a man
have on the golf course.'

"That was something I didn't need to be told. I was now
two over par on a golf course that eats players alive. A year
earlier a break like that would have had me throwing clubs and
hitting shots in all directions. This time I decided just to work
as hard as I could for the next 16 holes and hope that something
good will come of it. I finished two over par in that stretch for
a 76 and an eventual tie for sixth, but I felt a strong sense of
satisfaction and picked up a check for $1,825 as well. Danny's
constant encouragement had paid off, if not with a tournament
victory, at least with the promise of one."

Midway through the season, it seemed to many people that
Tony Lema was on the crest of a beautiful wave in the Pacific

Ocean and he was about to go for the ride of his life. No, he wasn't on a surfboard preparing to disappear into a pipeline and suddenly come rocketing out the other end. But he possessed all the ingredients to become a superstar in the world of golf and many knew it was just a matter of time. He had caddied, practiced, competed, and been down the long road it takes to acquire *talent*. He had paid his dues. Family members, fans, and golf writers in the Bay Area could just feel it in the air that Tony was so close. The combination of his charming personality, his sense of humor, the camaraderie he had developed with the press, and his sheer ability to play golf had won the hearts of many people in and around San Leandro. Here was this tall, handsome, 28 year-old golfer who traveled around the country and was the city's most notable ambassador of goodwill.

Authorized and sponsored by the city officials of San Leandro, Tony Lema Appreciation Day was held on Thursday, May 17, 1962. There was an official groundbreaking of a 9-hole golf course south of First Avenue with representatives from the state parks commission and the San Leandro Chamber of Commerce. That evening the Tony Lema Appreciation Dinner was held at the Sequoyah Country Club. Frank King and Augie Benites, members of the Chamber played a major role in the event while Nelson Cullenward, golf editor of the *San Francisco News-Call Bulletin* and president of the Northern California Golf Writers Association was the speaker for the event. In addition to being presented the key to the city and a city council resolution, Tony was named the Chamber's Athlete-of-the-Year. Benites felt this was a full scale, all-out showing of San Leandro's recognition of the job Tony was doing.

A number of local celebrities were introduced during the course of the evening, but perhaps the one who received the most laughter was Mickey Anselmo. He had been the caddie master at Sequoyah Country Club and it turns out that he fired Tony. He did what? He fired Tony Lema as a caddy! He never thought Tony would be a good caddy, let alone a champion golfer.

But Tony combined humor and sincerity during his acceptance speech. He was presented a tape recorder and quickly remarked; "Now I can get the tape and listen to HOW

TO PLAY GOLF." Later his comments turned more serious when he was showing his appreciation of the entire event. "I thank God for this," he said, "never thought it would happen to me...there is one person missing...my Dad...but I'm sure he is looking down on all of this."

Obviously, many people were invited to the event but could not attend due to previous commitments. Despite the fact that Tony had not won on the tour, the following telegrams were a sample of the respect that Tony was receiving from his colleagues:

> SORRY I CAN'T BE THERE WITH YOU. YOU ARE VERY
> DESERVING OF THIS HONOR AND YOU WILL ALWAYS
> BE A CHAMPION IN MY BOOK YOUR FRIEND
>   -KEN VENTURI

> PLEASE EXTEND MY SINCERE REGRETS AT NOT
> BEING ABLE TO BE PRESENT THIS EVENING TO HONOR
> YOUR OUTSTANDING CITIZEN TONY LEMA WHO I
> CONSIDER NOT ONLY TO BE A FINE GOLF PLAYER BUT
> A GREAT GENTLEMAN AND GOOD FRIEND.
>   -ARNOLD PALMER

> I WOULD LIKE TO EXTEND MY SINCERE REGRETS AT
> NOT BEING ABLE TO BE WITH YOU THIS EVENING TO
> HONOR TONY LEMA. TONY IS A TRUE GENTLEMAN AS
> WELL AS A FINE GOLFER AND IS WELL DESERVING
> OF THE HONOR BEING BESTOWED UPON HIM.
>   -GARY PLAYER

Tony loved his hometown and was proud of it. When introduced at any tournament or associated event, he insisted that he be listed not just Tony Lema but in the full treatment: "Tony Lema of San Leandro."

Ray Haywood, sports columnist with the *Oakland Tribune*, had followed Tony since he won the Oakland City Championship in 1953. Haywood knew not only what Tony had done up until then, but what he was capable of doing in the future.

"One who has brought honor to his home community, and will bring more, has returned briefly from the many lush fields where he labors. And, because he has brought honor to his home, his people in return honor him. Although he has played well in most tournaments during his five years as a pro, Lema has won only a comparative few. But, very few do even that. The manner of his winning, his attitude toward the game and its migratory life, indicates he can win many."

While Tony continued the process of sharpening all the areas of his game throughout the summer of 1962, there were many events happening around the world. Some appeared in newspaper headlines while others were significant in their own way. The NASA program reported that Ranger IV was the first USA space capsule to land on the moon. Also in space news, a civilian NASA pilot by the name of Neil A. Armstrong took the X-15 to an altitude of 39 miles. Elsewhere, the Rolling Stones performed for the first time at the Marquee Club in London and the late Nelson Mandela was captured by the South African police. In August, Marilyn Monroe was found dead in her Los Angeles home. The Beatles replaced drummer Pete Best with a chap named Ringo Starr and in October, Johnny Carson replaced Jack Parr as the host of NBC's Tonight Show.

But exciting events took place in the world of golf. A 22-year old from Columbus, OH had defeated Arnold Palmer in the U.S. Open at Oakmont and continued to play well into the fall season. The records will show that Jack Nicklaus won the $35,000 Seattle Open with a very strong performance of 67-65-65-68—265 en route to being named PGA Rookie-of-the-Year in 1962. The records will also show that after three rounds over the Broadmoor Country Club that Jack Nicklaus (197) held a two-shot lead over Gary Player (199). Tony trailed Nicklaus by seven strokes when play commenced on Sunday. After a dismal 72 in the opening round, Tony played well and put together a pair of 66's to put him at 204.

"I was ready to go home after the first round," Tony said to the *Seattle Post-Intelligencer* on Sunday evening, "but it became a matter of pride and self confidence. After the two

66's I felt I was playing well enough and might come in with a 64 or 65 today."

About the time that Jack Nicklaus was heading for the first tee in that final round, a whisper began sweeping across the golf course:

"Lema's five-under par after four holes."

Who?"

"Lema, you know, Tony Lema."

The gallery following Tony's blazing start grew steadily with each hole. After he knocked in an 18-footer for an eagle on the first hole, Tony backed that up with birdies on the second and third holes—both were from 18 feet. With a grin, he said later, "I never make a putt more than 18 feet!" He made a two-footer for a birdie on number four and a 12-foot birdie putt curled in on the eighth hole.

Within a few minutes, another message from the official's scoring table hard by the 18th green intoned softly: "Ladies and gentlemen—on the first nine, Tony Lema, 28." The gasp from the hillside was collective and one spectator remarked: "They had better water that nine. Tony's just burned it up!"

After nine holes, Tony's was six-under par and he wasn't finished making birdies. "I was charging all the way," he said. "I knew I had to if I was going to catch up. Sixty could have been broken out there today. I made a lot of good shots but you forget those. The ones you missed are the ones you remember."

He birdied the 14th hole to go seven-under for the round and followed with a par on the 15. On the 16th, his approach shot finished six feet from the cup and he had the chance to go eight-under par and move into a tie with Nicklaus. But the six-footer didn't fall. Afterwards, Tony explained what happened. "If I'd been able to sink that birdie putt I think I would've had a good chance to win, but I pushed it past the right edge and it didn't drop. That may have been the turning point."

The end for Tony happened abruptly on the 17th hole when he attempted to cut a six-iron into the flag, but the ball stayed left, bounced off a spectator leaving him a tricky, uphill third shot. He ran it 15 feet beyond the pin and two-putted for his only bogey of the day.

At the same time, Nicklaus was standing in the 15th fairway,

240 yards from the hole and decided to play it safe and hit an iron into the green instead of a fairway wood. On the par-5 hole he laced a 1-iron shot within five feet and made his eagle to all but secure the victory. "I didn't know I could get that much distance with that club," Nicklaus said later.

On the par-five 18th, Tony reached the green in two and two-putted from 45 feet for a birdie to finish 28-35—63. "On that last putt today," he explained, "I was a little surprised when it stopped short. I hit it real hard because I was gambling and was willing to risk going past the cup." He gave it a good whack but it stopped three feet short. After he made the short birdie putt the huge gallery around the 18th green gave Tony the biggest ovation of the tournament. The first thing he said walking off the green was: "I was very lucky. It was fun today."

Moments later Tony sat down with a few members of the press. "Subconsciously, that 28 round may have hurt me," he said. "What do you do for an encore after something like that? I got a little excited I think." About that time, Nicklaus still had a few holes to play and a member of the media asked Tony, "Are you hoping Jack breaks a leg, Tony?"

"Oh no," Tony replied. "I don't want him to break a leg. A sprain would be enough."

"We might have even taken a little of Arnie's Army away today," Tony smiled afterwards. "I hope he's not mad at me. Really, though, the people were wonderful. The gallery was quiet and orderly all the time."

In the locker room afterwards, Nicklaus was asked if Tony's charge had an affect on his round. "No, Lema's 28 didn't frighten me. First I heard about Tony's round was at the ninth tee and I didn't think too much about it. Seven strokes is a long way to come and I felt I had some birdies in front of me. Later, I did get a bit of a scare. When I was on the 17th, I thought I had a three-stroke lead over Lema. When I walked off the green, someone told me that Lema had shot a 61. That would make it real tight. Then I found out it was a 63 and I could have killed the fellow with the 61 story."

Once Tony heard about Jack's eagle on the 15th, he shrugged and told the press, "Well, that takes care of that." The 1962 Seattle Open was over, but he received a check for $3,000 and had won the hearts of many fans in Seattle.

After that burst of a pair of 66's and a 63, Tony figured there was nothing he couldn't do and that his first tournament win must be one lucky break away. The next stop on the tour was Portland, Oregon and Tony started out with a 65 in the first round, one shot off the leader. And who might that be? You guessed it, Jack Nicklaus. Tony faded back into the field and finished (65-71-70-71—277) in a tie for fourteenth. Nicklaus had finished his second round with a 67 but the PGA's tournament supervisor Joe Black decided he had become a little bit too deliberate. It took quite a bit of courage on Black's part, but he enforced the slow play rule on Jack so his 67 became a 69. As it turned out, it didn't matter as Nicklaus pulled away from the field and won his second tournament in a row.

Perhaps the most important thing that happened to Tony at the Portland Open was the meeting of a caddy named Wally Heron. Wally was about fifty-five, gray-haired, and presented himself in a neat and orderly fashion. When he asked if he could carry his bag, Tony immediately took him on. Tony knew that Wally possessed the one thing that all the tour caddies had in common—an intense love of the game of golf. Wally eventually caddied for Tony throughout the fall season and they developed a close working relationship. Wally felt that if Tony won a tournament, so did he. Since this was Tony's fifth year on the tour, he knew what to expect from a caddy and he wasn't afraid to tell him what he wanted him to do and what he wanted him not to do. In those days, the PGA had a rule that no caddy could work for the same golfer more than two weeks in a row. In addition, each tournament had its own regulations so some weeks it was difficult to get a caddy the player had hired previously. Sometimes, it became a game and the golfers would keep firing the caddy assigned to them by the caddy master until he finally allowed the player to have the caddy he wanted all along. Eventually, caddies were allowed to work full-time for the same golfer until the partnership dissolved for one reason or another.

"Wally Heron's main job when he was caddying for me," Tony explained, "was not necessarily to tell me which club to use. His main talent was that he knew how to keep me relaxed even when I was getting into a fit of nervousness or anger. He had a way of sensing when this was about to happen, and he knew what to do to snap me out of the mood before it began to ruin my play. Often he would ball me out for falling asleep on a simple shot. At other times he would tell a joke to relax me, or rub me on the back or bang me on the shoe with the putter just to let me know that he was there and that he knew what was up. Often, he would try to explain just how fortunate I was even to be in contention, that I had received good breaks along with the bad and would get more breaks if I kept working hard. It was an immense comfort to have him there.

"One of the great assets these caddies have is that they are completely trustworthy. You can trust them with your money, your golf clubs and even your car. Wally would take my clubs home to clean them, or shellac the woods. He was always utterly dependable. If I told him I would meet him by the practice tee at 8 o'clock the next morning, he would be there, without fail, even if I didn't get there until 10. The touring caddies are available for running errands. They take clothes to the laundry or dry cleaner or drive your car to the next tournament if you have decided to fly."

Chances are Wally Heron was a lucky charm besides being an experienced caddy that knew how to keep Tony relaxed on a golf course. And when you arrive in Las Vegas, there is nothing like having your lucky charm along for the ride. So in the last week of September in 1962, Tony and Wally hit town to play in the fifth annual Hotel Sahara Invitational. The tournament was considered to be an "unofficial" event because all 93 pros were paired with amateurs for the first two rounds. Since there were 279 amateurs involved, the competition took place over two golf courses, the Paradise Valley Country Club and the Municipal Golf Club. Because of that stipulation, money earned in the Sahara would not count on the official money list, it would not entitle the winner to play in the Tournament of Champions and would not count in points toward the Ryder Cup team. But as Tony had mentioned many times before, he considered all checks he received as "official money in his pocket."

Tony's first round was scheduled early in the day at Paradise Valley and he simply could not get comfortable over the ball.

It was one of those rounds where nothing went right and he struggled home with a 75. He saw where several players had fired 65's and he summed up his thoughts in one short sentence, "Well, there's another tournament shot." He decided to go back to the hotel and catch a nap so he could be ready to spend the evening gambling and dancing.

Later in the afternoon, a friend called Tony with some news bordering the unbelievable, "Gee, you're lucky," his friend said. "It rained so hard over at Paradise Valley that the first round has been postponed." Tony found that hard to believe so he went downstairs to the hotel lobby to check out the news. As he peered outside, the skies were still blue and there were no signs of the storm. Suddenly, golfers got out of their cars from outside the hotel and we're so wet it looked like they had come out of the hotel swimming pool. It turns out there had been a massive cloudburst at Paradise Valley and several holes had become unplayable. According to the tournament rules, all scores for the first round had become null and void. Talk about a mulligan! Tony's entire round had suddenly been erased from the scoreboard and the next day he had the opportunity to start all over again.

When opportunity knocks, open the door! That's exactly what Tony did the next day as he arrived at the golf course extra early and practiced long and hard prior to his tee time. He went out and shot a 69, six strokes better than the washed out round. The following day Tony fired a 67, which put him at 136 and in third place, one-stroke behind Billy Casper and Jon Gustin. Due to the rain on Thursday, the pros were scheduled to play 36-holes on Sunday with a $1,000 bonus going to the player who shoots the lowest score in each of the final rounds. Tony wasted no time as he went out and shot a 66 in the third round, assuring himself of the $1,000 bonus regardless of what happened in the afternoon round. He continued to play well in the day's second round and reached the eighteenth tee knowing that a par on the final hole would result in his winning the tournament. But he also knew that a birdie would give him a 68 and a good chance for his second $1,000 bonus of the day for low score in the final round.

According to George King of the *Las Vegas Sun*, Tony's

second shot on the 72nd hole stopped 15 feet from the cup and he rammed it home for a birdie three which gave him a 15-under par 270 and a three-stroke victory over Don January and six over Billy Casper. His 68 was the lowest score of the final round so he won another bonus of $1,000. In addition to the $2,800 for first place, Tony collected $645 more in the pro-amateur division. His total jackpot for three sunny days of golf in Las Vegas and one gully-washer of a rainstorm amounted to $5,445. When asked by the press to sum up what accounted for his victory, Tony told them nothing but the truth. "My big break in this tournament was having my first round 75 washed out Thursday."

It was Tony's first really important victory on the tour. The fact that his winnings did not count as official money earned can be construed in two ways. First, it's only a technicality because there was some really fine golfers in that field. Tony played four rounds of pretty solid golf amounting to 270. As noted, Billy Casper finished at 276, six shots behind Tony. Julius Boros wound up at 278, tied with Jacky Cupit, Jay Hebert, and Charlie Sifford. Also in the field were George Bayer (281), Phil Rodgers (283), Al Geiberger (283), and Bob Rosburg (285). Tony himself said later that the fact that it was unofficial "kept me from tasting true, sweet success." Secondly, it proved that Tony had the game to win a tournament with a strong field. Granted, Jack Nicklaus, Arnold Palmer and Gary Player were not in Las Vegas that week but that wasn't Tony's fault. So Tony and his caddy, Wally Heron, left tinsel town with a great deal of confidence, but there was one question on his mind. Recalling his conversation with Danny Kaye, Tony asked himself, "Do I have the guts?"

After a week off, the tour resumed at the Bakersfield Open and Tony picked up right where he left off in Las Vegas. After three rounds, he was tied for the lead at 205 with Billy Casper, both 11-under par. But in the final round, Casper played extremely well as he fired a 67 to capture victory on the Bakersfield Country Club course. Tony shot a 71 and finished in second place and a check for $3,600. As the tour moved on to Ontario, CA Tony was the hottest golfer on the fall tour. In less than a month he had won nearly $13,000 and his earnings since the U.S. Open in June was nearly $21,000.

While he was in Ontario, Tony sat down with a reporter from the *Hayward Daily Review* and talked about his game and what he thought was making a difference. "I'm enjoying the best year I've ever had. I attribute it to my better mental attitude towards the game. It's all a matter of my approach to the sport, the way I think. I have forced myself into accepting the good with the bad and not becoming either too enthusiastic when I play well or too depressed when things go wrong. You've seen golfers curse, beat their clubs and act like kids when they make a particularly bad shot, I know, I used to do the same thing myself. But not too long ago I decided that blowing my top hurt my game. So I set out to change my mental attitude. I schooled myself not to become too concerned about a bad shot. Instead, I turned my thoughts to salvaging whatever I could from a bad situation. If the bad shot cost me a birdie, I started figuring how to get a par.

"Golf is a waiting game and a game of misses. I try to realize that and keep from missing too badly. I just work a little harder and don't keep charging. There is a time to be bold and a time to be cautious. And if I control myself, keep thinking and watching, I can capitalize on my good shots. I let the good and the bad average out."

Tony said that since he adopted that philosophical attitude not only had his game improved, but also he was enjoying it a lot more. He stressed that he wasn't taking his work lightly. He made it a habit to study every situation on the course and apply all the skill and knowledge he possessed. But once the shot was made, he felt that was the end of that. In other words, after many conversations with Danny Arnold and listening to some of his constituents, Tony developed the habit of staying in the present tense and not re-thinking about what had just happened. In addition, he began to appreciate how fortunate he was to be playing golf for a living and finally getting paid well. And the more pleasure he got out of it, the better his game became.

Going into the Ontario Open, Tony was the leader on the western fall tour in points for one of the two invitations to the Masters Tournament at Augusta, Georgia in 1963. The desire to have the opportunity to compete in the Masters had Tony on the golf course early every day. "I'd give my right arm to compete at Augusta," he said. "I've got the chance and I'll do anything I can to keep from losing it."

So it came as no surprise to anyone that Tony came out of the blocks and lead the field at Ontario after two rounds with 69-66—135. Unfortunately, he cooled off in the third round with a 74 and eventually finished in a tie for seventh, two shots behind the winner, Al Geiberger. Tony told reporters that he was getting a little worn out, but he was playing well and decided to go on over to Costa Mesa and play in the Orange County Open, besides it was only about 33 miles down the highway from Ontario. After that, he was going to take a nice, long vacation and recharge the batteries for 1963.

The word *omen* originated from Latin late in the 16th century and it is defined as an event regarded as a portent of good or evil. One might ask how is that translated in the language used by golfers? Let's give it a try. Tony fired a sizzling six-under par 65 and won the pro-am section of the Orange County Open at the popular Mesa Verde Country Club in Costa Mesa, CA. Tony's message to the field could have been summed up in three words. "Watch out, fellas!" The translation is simple. That 65 was an omen that Tony Lema's time had came to capture his first official victory on the PGA Tour and nothing was going to prevent him from doing so. Tony had made over $13,500 in the last five tournaments and started the round in the pro-am by birding four of the first five holes.

After the round Tony said he played perhaps his best round ever on the tour as he accepted $250 for the low pro score of the day and $62.50 when his team finished in a tie for third place. "My round might even had been better," he confided, "but I had several putts which rimmed the hole or bounced back out on the back nine."

The Orange County Open got under way and despite a three-under par 68 in the first round, Tony found himself three shots off the lead. In the second round, he improved with a 66 but at the halfway point he remained three shots back. On Saturday's round, often referred to as "moving day" on the tour, Tony did more than just move. He rocketed to the top of the leaderboard. After making a nice putt for a birdie on the par-4 eighth hole, Tony knocked in a full 8-iron on the ninth for an eagle 2. He remained aggressive on the back nine, continued to make birdies and finished with a sensational seven-under par 64. After three rounds, Tony had a one-shot lead and was summoned to talk to the press.

Doc Giffin, who has served as Arnold Palmer's secretary for decades, was then press secretary for the PGA Tour. Giffin had set up press headquarters in a small card room of the Mesa Verde Country Club. "The press corps was so small, the room wasn't even crowded," Giffin recalled. "We had a portable cooler of beer in there, and I can still visualize Tony holding up a near-empty can of beer after his interview following the third round and saying, 'Fellows, if I win this tournament tomorrow, there'll be no more of this stuff. It'll be champagne for everyone.' A West Coast free-lance photographer, Lester Nehamkin, told the club manager to be sure to have champagne on ice."

In a conversation with Ben Wright, which was printed in *Links Magazine*, Tony picked up the story at that point. "I was still not convinced I could win—why should I be? But I spoke to my great friend Danny Arnold, the TV producer, that Saturday night and immediately felt good when he told me he was coming up to see my last round on Sunday. Danny had been instrumental in bringing about my change of attitude to life.

"Well, I started right enough—birdie, birdie, par, par—but at the fifth hole I knocked my second through the green. That was bad enough, but worse was to come. I went to tap in a tiny putt and missed it, and chalked up a double bogey. My world seemed to be crumbling again. Anything could have happened. But I looked up and there was Danny. He looked at me and I looked at him, and it may sound mushy, but right then I knew things were going to be all right. Thank goodness Danny was there. He walked beside me, talking, talking, and talking. Under the *Rules of Golf* he was not permitted to give me any advice or information, but he was allowed to keep me calm enough to stay on course. I played well enough for a 69, but Bob Rosburg caught and tied me with birdies at 16 and 17. Out we went for the first tee and sudden death."

The first hole at Mesa Verde Country Club is a par-five that doglegs to the right. Rosburg hit two beautiful shots that left him right in front of the green. Tony yanked his tee shot way left on the first hole, sliced his second shot 40 yards to the right of the green, and fortunately pitched his third within three feet of the cup. Bob chipped close to the pin and both made their birdie putts. Afterwards Tony described the first hole. "I thought I had blown the match on the first hole when I hooked into the rough. But then I recovered and that gave me enough confidence to carry me through."

The second hole is a relatively short, 365-yard par four and the green is elevated so the golfers cannot see the bottom of the flagstick from the fairway. Rosburg hit a nice wedge in there and from the crowd's reaction Tony assumed it was fairly close to the pin. Now with the pressure squarely upon his shoulders, Tony hit a poor wedge shot that went to the back of the green. He was faced with a long downhill putt while Rosburg's ball was about six feet from the cup. Tony rolled his putt down the slope within a foot and a half of the cup and made the short putt for a par. Rosburg had an uphill straight putt for victory and Tony was prepared to walk across the green and congratulate Bob when his birdie putt fell into the cup. To everyone's amazement, Rosburg hit it too softly and the ball broke wide of the hole to the left. One can only imagine the sigh of relief that Tony felt as he turned quickly and headed for the 177-yard par-three third hole.

When asked later, Tony described exactly what happened and what he was thinking as the sudden-death match continued. "The green was elevated and the cup was cut into the left side. The proper shot would be a hook that started toward the right side of the green, safely away from danger, and then turn in toward the flag. Bob hit exactly that shot and his ball stopped no more than 10 feet from hole. I had been having trouble trying to hook the ball so I decided to take a chance, fading the ball out to the left of the green and hoping it would come back in near the pin. I hit exactly that shot and the ball stopped no more than 10 ½ feet from hole.

"I was away and it was therefore my turn to putt first. As I got over the ball I suddenly felt certain that I was going to make the putt. I could almost see the exact line to the hole as if the greens keeper had painted it there. I was equally certain that if I made the putt I would win the playoff. My confidence was supreme and I struck the ball straight into the hole. Then I stood by the edge of the green, unable to control my fidgeting, and watch while Rosburg's putt hit the back of the cup and bounced out. Bob was inconsolable. Since his last victory, at the Bing Crosby pro am in January 1961, he had finished second six times. On three of those occasions he had been defeated in a sudden death play-off. 'I guess I'm just a loser,' he sighed. Bob, of course, isn't a loser. He has won six tournaments on the tour, including the 1959 PGA championship, and it was of particular significance to me that I had been able to beat a player of his immense abilities. When Rosburg missed that putt and when I finally came back to earth I was so exhilarated that I think I kissed Danny and shook hands with his wife."

Of course, Tony made good on his promise to serve champagne to the members of the press who were covering the event. He also decided it was something he would do henceforth, at every tournament he won. When Tony was answering questions from the media in that small card room that served as press headquarters, his relief of finally winning an official tour event was evident.

"I've been on the pro golf tour for just about five years and I still was trying for my first official tournament win," he explained. "But I just couldn't get that first one which means so much to a player on the tour, and I had to fight an uphill battle all the way to finish in a tie and then win on the third extra hole."

The win gave Tony a total of 110.67 points and the lead on the fall tour for one of two spots in the 1963 Masters Tournament; it put him ninth on the Ryder Cup team standings and 18th on the official money list with earnings of $26,232. The Orange County Open win was worth $2,800 to Tony and Rosburg received $1,900 for his runner-up finish.

Doc Giffin, the PGA's press secretary, made a point in a *Golf Digest* article written by Nick Seitz in August of 1967 about the aftermath of that "first" champagne celebration. "The late Charley Curtis of the *Los Angeles Times*, for one," Giffin said, "and I believe at least one of the wire-service reporters used the

'Champagne Tony' tag in their stories. I told it many times in the next few months and it caught on nationally."

From then on he was known as Champagne Tony Lema, a nickname as colorful, if not as fitting as "Slammin' Sam," "Bantam Ben," and "Lord Byron." Sports aficionados still consider "Champagne Tony" to be one of the most popular and colorful nicknames ever given to a sports celebrity.

Sometime after the victory, Tony told Ben Wright just what it meant to finally become a winner on the Tour. "Let no one tell you different," Tony said. "That first win gives you maturity and poise. I can't describe how important it was to me as a person and to my career as a golfer."

Nearly thirty years after Tony's victory at the Orange County Open, Bob Rosburg was doing some television work for ABC at the Western Open in Chicago. A few men came up, asked if he had a moment, and then asked him if he remembered the playoff he had with Tony Lema at the Orange County Open at Mesa Verde. Rosburg said, "Sure, I remember that tournament." One of the men said he was in the Marine Corps at the time, at Camp Pendleton, and had gone out with friends to watch the final round. Of course, they knew that Tony had served in the Marine Corps so they were rooting for him. The man asked Rosburg if he remembered Tony's tee shot on the first hole of the playoff that had gone way left. Rosburg said, "I remember that, we thought it might have gone out of bounds so Tony hit a provisional ball." The ex-Marine told Bob Rosburg that it had gone out of bounds by a foot or so and he kicked it back in. More or less, one Marine helping out another. When hearing this, Rosburg laughed begrudgingly but felt he had to tell the fella what was on his mind. "It would have been nice to win," he said, "and I don't regret anything Tony did after that. Tony was a friend of mine. But Tony had told me that very morning that if he didn't win the Orange County Open, he had had enough, and that he was going to leave the Tour and take a job as a club pro." So Rosburg looked right at the ex-Marine and added, "If you hadn't kicked that golf ball back in bounds, Tony would be alive today." No doubt there was shock all over the face of the ex-Marine. Rosburg noted that, "It was a cruel thing to say but it was the truth." After that comment, Rosburg said he walked away.

Earlier in the fall of 1962, Tony had been in one of his darker moments of despair. He was talking with his sister Bernice and she told him that she felt sure that he was about to win, and once he had done so, she just knew he was going to win several times quickly. Within a matter of weeks, her prediction came true. But later Tony admitted that he was on the verge of quitting when everything worked out as she had forecast.

Despite the fact that he had planned to rest his weary bones, Tony had a couple of incentives to stay out on the tour in November. First, he knew he was on a hot streak and he had heard from many pros on the tour that when things are going well, just keep playing. Secondly, he was in pretty good shape concerning the two available invitations for the Masters, but he didn't want to take a chance of missing out because someone else came of out nowhere to pass him in points. He was also wanted to continue and move up on the board regarding making the 1963 Ryder Cup team.

While he was home after the victory at the Orange County Open, he played in a pro-am in Stockton, CA and told Nelson Cullenward of the *San Francisco News-Call Bulletin* about his plans for the remainder of the year. "I want that Masters spot and I intend to earn it," he explained in a determined tone of voice. "I'm leaving again Monday for Lafayette, LA to get in a couple practice rounds for the Cajun Classic next week. Then I'm going to play in the Mobile Open and the Carling Open at Orlando, FL. If I continue my hot streak and win enough points, the money is incidental, I'll come home. If not, I'll stay with the tour through the first week of December before coming home."

So after a short rest in San Leandro, he headed down to Lafayette, LA to play in the Cajun Classic Open at the Oakbourne Country Club. A few unique things happened that week, but none of them involved Tony Lema. John Barnum, a 51-year-old veteran from Michigan won his only tour event with a consistent 68-70-63-69—270. His six-stroke victory over runner-up Gay Brewer was the first time a winner of a tour event had used a

Ping putter. Needless to say, there were literally hundreds more winners of tour events in the horizon with Ping putters in their golf bag. Tony played less than stellar golf as he finished at 286, tied for 19th, won $256 but he moved up to 17th position on the money list. John Barnum was a playing partner with Tony back in that final round at the Tucson Open in 1958 when Tony got real nervous for the first time on the tour and faded back in the pack with a 75. After that ordeal, Tony may not have recognized Barnum but on the other hand, he knew how special it was for John to win his first tournament on the tour.

The following week at the Mobile Sertoma Open, Tony fired four straight sub-par rounds, ignored cold winds on Sunday's final round, and cruised home with a seven-stroke victory over Georgia native Doug Sanders. As he strolled down the 18th fairway, Tony had an eight-shot cushion and said he felt he could relax for the first time. The gallery was shouting at Tony, asking him if he thought he was safe. He shouted back, "Yes!" When asked about his state of mind during the Mobile Open, Tony said, "I was playing so well I dreamed about it at night." His 15-under par 273 earned him a first-place check of $2,000.

Tony played one more tournament in the United States that year. The Carling Open was held in late November at the Rio Pinar Country Club in Orlando. Bo Wininger won the tournament and a tired Tony Lema finished in a tie for 23rd, received a check for $435, and brought his 1962 total official earnings to $28,924. At the end of the year, Tony wound up 15th on the money earnings list. He spent a couple of weeks in San Leandro in December before heading for the Mexican Open in Mexico City. As defending champion, he felt he owed it to the sponsors. "It's the only tournament for me all month," he explained. "I won it last year and feel obligated to attend, otherwise I'd skip it. Playing week in and week out—it's made me stale."

He went down and successfully defended his Mexican Open title with a four-round total of 281. His total earnings for 1962, counting official and unofficial, came to about $48,000. After it became certain that he would receive an invitation to compete in the Masters for the first time, Tony could not hold back his excitement.

"You might say it was my burning ambition to be invited to the Masters. It used to drive me wild to see Rosburg and Venturi in the field, while I could never make it. That's why I kept right on the tour through some of December's Florida events. When I came close to qualifying in the fall, I decided to just keep on playing until there wasn't the barest mathematical possibility of my being nosed out. Now, THERE'S a tournament any pro looks forward to playing in. I'm going to start getting ready for that one right after the first of the year."

Augusta

The avid golfer who attentively followed the PGA Tour had to be impressed with the way Tony Lema played throughout the fall of 1962. Even though his victories were not telecast around the country, his reputation as a fine golfer with an upbeat personality was catching on. In the spring of 1963, national magazines such as *Golf, Golf Digest, and Sports Illustrated* were featuring stories about "Champagne Tony" and they had every reason to do so. Many considered Tony to be an "up and coming golfer" with a great potential to win often on the Tour. Despite the fact that Jack Nicklaus had made a huge impact on the tour in 1962, the catch phrase circulating the world of golf in those days were things like; "Keep an eye on Tony Lema this year" or "Did you hear about that golfer who served the press champagne after he won out in California?"

As is the case in many circumstances, other people in the same environment can see the potential in their peers long before it becomes evident to the public. In an article in *Sports Illustrated*, Johnny Pott, a longtime companion of Tony's, spoke about his golf and his lifestyle.

"He was a wonderful guy and a great player when he first came out," Pott explained. "We all wondered why he didn't start winning sooner. But he liked to do things first class all the way, even then. You know, wine with his meals, late hours—the whole deal. He didn't want to make the sacrifices that have to be made if you want to win. Now he does"

"I don't think that's entirely it," Tony responded. "I think that everything just fell into place at once. I have always known my game was very good, and I have always known how to get the most out of myself physically. I know I have to get away after a tournament, visit friends, and lie on the beach. I fly, instead of driving like a lot of other guys, because I figure it saves me 60 days a year. No, my difficulty has been that I couldn't control my temper. That, plus the fact, that winning my first tournament became a big obsession with me. If I got a bad break or missed a short putt, I blew my top and began to expect bad breaks. It was a form of self-persecution that made it very hard to play consistently. Now I've learned that missing a short putt doesn't mean I have to hit my next drive out of bounds."

In that story, Tony updated golfers everywhere about what was going through his mind as he faced Bob Rosburg in the sudden-death playoff at the Orange County Open. "I was in a pretty agitated state. For the first two holes Rosburg played super golf while I scrambled all over the place, but I managed to halve. Then on the third hole, a par-three, I thought he had me for sure. The pin was on the left side of the green, and Rosburg hit a beautiful five-iron that hooked gently in toward the hole and stopped 10 feet away. I was having trouble hooking that day, so I decided to fade my five-iron shot. It was a good one, too, 10'6" away. I liked the looks of that putt of mine. I thought I could make it, and I did. As I stood at the edge of the green waiting for Rosburg to putt I was so nervous I could hardly keep still. His putt hit the back of the hole, jumped into the air and stayed out. I had won! I don't remember it, but people say I jumped three feet into the air and threw my ball all the way back to the tee. Later I bought champagne for the press, but all the sportswriters there couldn't have drunk as much as I did that night."

Without a doubt, the biggest win, or should we say, the toughest win for a touring pro is his first triumph in an official PGA sanctioned event. To some, it might be equivalent to reaching the summit on Mt. Everest, having an Olympic gold medal placed around your neck, or receiving a diamond-studded ring because your team won the Super Bowl, World Series, NBA, or the Stanley Cup. No matter what sport you compare it to; winning a PGA Tournament is a major accomplishment. As Tony's sister, Bernice, alluded to, once you figure out how to win a championship, watch out, all that hard work is going to pay off in spades. In the May 1963 issue of *Golf Magazine* Tony explained why that first victory meant so much to him. "Until I got that first 'big one,' I always felt a little insufficient, or something like that. I was playing in the big leagues and although I knew that I had made enough money in the past four years to prove to myself that I can play with them, I still needed to win the first PGA event to put a foundation under my morale. I was beginning to think I'd never do it. I was haunted by a feeling that maybe I was a choker, but now I know I can come down to the wire with the best of 'em."

So when the 1963 season got under way, Tony felt reasonably sure that the five years of hard work and experience on the PGA Tour had finally begun to pay dividends. But he wasn't absolutely *positive*. He still felt like to had to keep winning to convince himself he had what it takes to be considered a tour champion.

It didn't take long for him to get right back to the top of the leaderboard. After finishing in a tie for 35th in the Los Angeles Open, Tony headed down to the San Diego Open, held once again at the Stardust Country Club, and now called the Riverwalk Golf Club. After four solid rounds, 271, Tony was sitting in the pressroom listening to a broadcast of the tournament on the radio. Gary Player stood over a 20-foot putt for a par on the 72nd hole. If he makes that putt, Player wins the tournament. Tony was preparing himself to get ready for another sudden-death episode, but when Player's putt hit the bottom of the cup, it was time to get up and head to Pebble Beach and the Bing Crosby. Winning and losing a golf tournament is cut and dried. No such thing as a slow-motion video replay. The ball either goes into the cup or it doesn't. In this case, Player edged Tony by one-stroke after 72 holes and deservedly became the San Diego Open champion for 1963. As runner-up, Tony gladly accepted a check for $2,300, which put him 6th on the money list after two tournaments.

That year the Bing Crosby National Pro-am, often referred to as the Crosby Clambake, was held at three fantastic golf courses. Two rounds, one of which was the final, were on the beautiful Pebble Beach Golf Links. The other courses in the rotation in 1963 were the magnificent Cypress Point Club and the Monterey Peninsula Country Club. Billy Casper won the Crosby with four rounds totaling 285. Tony finished in a tie for 22nd, six shots back at 291. There was a coincidence that happened on Monterey Peninsula that week. Before Tony settled on Wally Heron to be his regular caddy, he had Del Taylor carry his bag in quite a few tournaments. Del had caddied on the tour for several years and had an excellent reputation. He was planning on working for another player that week who, for some reason failed to qualify. It turned out that Billy Casper was shopping around and hired Del Taylor on the spot. The PGA Tour's policy had recently changed and players were allowed to have permanent caddies except for the majors. In addition to getting off to a fantastic start, the twosome worked together for 13 years and Casper said that Del Taylor was a huge asset to his success on the tour.

In the six weeks following the Crosby, Tony played in five tournaments and finished in the top ten in all five of those events. Consistency had become the 15th club in Tony's golf bag. In the Lucky International in San Francisco he finished in a tie for eighth and netted a check for $1,600. It's the closest tournament on the Tour to his hometown of San Leandro and Tony tried his best for the familiar faces he saw in the gallery.

"If I could have only made a putt sometime during the early rounds, I might have pulled this thing out, but nothing would drop for me," he said. "I missed two short putts for birds on the first two holes and then had a three-putt green on the fifth hole for a bogey and that took me out right there. I did manage to sink one on the 13th for a bird, but it was too late and I could not gain any momentum. You know, people who follow a golf tournament are pretty nice and I wanted to say 'hello' to everyone. But playing before a group of friends, or people you know are just pulling for you, makes it difficult. I wanted to win this one in the worst way, just to say 'thanks', but there was just too much tension inside me and I couldn't putt at all today. Perhaps next year I may even win it. Who knows?"

The next week at Palm Springs, he did likewise tying for eighth again. The tour moved south to Phoenix where he improved to a tie for fifth place. The next tournament was

Tucson and he captured ninth position. He took a week off after playing in seven consecutives tournaments and caught back up with the tour in the Greater New Orleans Open. He had a chance to win at Lakewood Country Club, but he tied for second place along with Bob Rosburg, both were three shots behind Bo Wininger. Following that fine finish, Tony took two weeks off before he rejoined the tour for the Doral Open, his last event before heading for Augusta, GA.

After five years on the tour, Tony had finally reached the point where he was able to pick and choose which events he wanted to play in and when he would take some time off to rest and recharge his batteries. "I found out a year ago I was overtaxing myself," he said. "I don't know whether it was too much golf or what. But every time I'd go back on tour in fresh condition I pick up a nice paycheck."

He was asked if he was awed by the sudden recognition attending his breakthrough over the last six months. "Naw, I always knew it was a matter of managing myself," he answered. "The difference now is management and confidence. I have it and it is a big factor."

As reported by the press in early 1963, his name had taken on the magic that denotes a winner. He had suddenly become one of the big attractions on the tour and his name was on thousands of golf clubs manufactured by Fernquest and Johnson. Don Fernquest and Jerry Johnson were golf pals with Tony during his years as a junior golfer. The two young entrepreneurs in the San Francisco area had been manufacturing a growing line of equipment and were marketing the Tony Lema Signature clubs. The clubs had been out for about six months and were selling throughout the West. In his book, *Golfers' Gold*, Tony talked about how life had changed for the better out on the tour.

"In addition to the money I won," he wrote, "I also found that I had reached a high if not exalted station on the tour. Now tournament sponsors would come after me, trying to make sure that I would be playing in their tournaments. All of a sudden people were doing favors for me: making plane and hotel reservations, meeting me at the airport when I arrived in town, seeing to it that a new car was at my disposal while I was there. This is standard treatment for the top players on the pro tour. If we felt so inclined many of us would never have to lift a finger to travel the whole circuit. We are wined, dined, praised, chauffeured, flattered, partied, toasted, served, adored, caressed, coddled, pampered and spoiled. I am impressed by the fact that even once-negligent locker room attendants suddenly have a big, bright smile, and a big, bright clean new locker for me every time I check in at a club."

Tony did not appreciate all of the publicity as more and more stories appeared in national publications. He said that *Golf Digest* painted him as the lover-boy of the tour, a playboy constantly surrounded by beautiful babes. *Sports Illustrated* suggested in a feature article that he was nothing but a playboy who threw rousing champagne parties at which his guests drove golf balls out of hotel windows. This was not the image that Tony had created in his own mind. Malarkey, his financial backer, had insisted that Tony travel the tour first class as part of their arrangement and he had done so. Sure, there had been women, champagne, and a few parties but not to the extreme that Tony was a playboy on the tour and cared little about his occupation. The picture that he saw about himself was a little alarming. He said that few people ever recognize themselves in a story written by another.

"It takes getting used to," he said, "but I began to get used to it. Not because I will ever be convinced that I am a fanatical party lover, but because I began to realize that national acclaim is what I must've had in mind way back in those days at Elko when I was winning tournaments against Walt Harrison and Cliff Whittle, but dreaming about beating Ben Hogan and Sam Snead. Why fight it?"

Despite shooting an opening round 75, Tony had a chance to win at the Doral Open, but ended up finishing in third place, three shots behind winner Dan Sikes and runner-up Sam Snead. He picked up a check for $3,000 in Miami and headed for the Masters in fourth place on the year's money list with $14,831. The three golfers ahead of Tony were golf's so-called Big Three: Gary Player, Arnold Palmer and Jack Nicklaus.

Tony had never taken the drive down Magnolia Lane at the Augusta National Golf Club, but he was excited to be included in the field of 85 for the 27th Masters Tournament. Arnold Palmer had won in three of the last five, in 1958, 1960, and 1962, and was the prohibitive favorite. Gary Player had won his first Masters in 1961 while Jack Nicklaus was the current U.S. Open champion and considered to be a major threat. Tony's name was right there in the mix as one of the favorites.

"They tell me it's Arnie's Alley," Tony said prior to the tournament. "Well, the records bear it out. I'm anxious to play there because I usually do fairly well on Palmer-type courses." And of course the press asked Tony some tough questions. "Is Palmer a mountain or a myth?" Tony handled that one like Cool Hand Luke. "I don't think he's indestructible, but he's the toughest around," Tony said unequivocally. "I'm sure about one thing: Palmer is better than Player and Nicklaus combined."

When asked about who is the greatest golfer, Tony held nothing back. "I think it's going to be impossible," he explained, "in the next few years for anyone to become the greatest golfer—Arnold Palmer has a firm grip on that title. There are so many good players in United States, that I don't think any one will ever again dominate golf like Palmer does now, and Walter Hagan used to. We'd all like to be the best golfer in the world, of course, but while I probably won't achieve that distinction, the PGA tournaments I've won, coupled with the other tournaments I've lucked out in, makes me believe I can win one of the great international events, like the U.S. and British Opens, or the Masters, or the PGA. Anyway, I believe I can, and for the moment that is my immediate ambition."

Palmer thought along the same lines regarding Tony's potential. "He's a wonderful player now—though I suppose that is obvious to everyone," Arnold said. "The thing I like most about Tony is not so much that he treats everyone fair and square, as he certainly does, but that he insists on being treated the same way. I've noticed a lot of people will sacrifice in ways that they shouldn't just to be more popular, Tony won't do this."

Other contemporaries at the time, Billy Maxwell, Dave Hill were some of the many who thought Tony was indeed a top prospect. Their collective opinion was, "He can't miss." "What appeals to me most about Tony," said Gardner Dickinson, "is that all times, all places, he is a gentleman."

As he was rising to the top on the PGA Tour, Tony never forgot to acknowledge that quite a few people had given him invaluable help along the way. "Most of us would like to feel," he said, "that we've done everything mainly on our own, but this is rarely, if ever, true. If you look back, you can see that someone helped you in about every trouble spot. I've been very fortunate; I have had more than my share of help. Jackie Burke, Jimmy Demaret, and Chick Harbert were others who helped me. Chick, especially, is a great teacher and was like a father to me when I first came out on the Tour. I've had more help from him than anyone else. It was from Chick that I got about the best advice on golf that I've ever had. That advice is the foundation of my developed philosophy for playing in tournaments: *'Fight as hard as you can for last money, and then when you get into a position where you might get first money, you'll know how to fight for it.'*

"Ed 'Porky' Oliver was another who took a lot of time and trouble to help me. My first year, I got paired with Porky in the last round of the Louisville Open, as I had been the 36-hole leader. When I started out on that fourth round, I was a little bit nervous and I bogeyed three or four out of the first five or six holes—though they weren't tough holes. Then Ed came over to me and said, 'I just want you to know that all of these people out here are with you—and so am I. So, play as good as you can. Don't be nervous.' I finished with a pretty good round for a piece of the money, and believe me, Porky Oliver is always going to occupy a pretty special place in my golf memories."

During those days, it was well known that some of the players acted so rude and peevish that some gallery members were nervous or literally frightened by some of these touring pros. "However," Tony pointed out, "this situation has greatly improved during the last year. The PGA and some of the sponsors are taking steps to improve some of the contestants' dispositions. When players throw tantrums on the course, especially towards the galleries, the PGA is likely to hand them a good stiff fine. Myself, I like people; I love galleries; by and large, the bigger the gallery the better I play, so that's one problem I don't have to contend with.

"I know how hard it is to keep from getting a little hot-headed out there at times—I don't care how good you're playing, you're always going to miss a few shots that will fire up your temper a little bit. But you can swear under your breath, if you feel you have to, so even better is put the bad shot out of mind by concentrating on the next one. Besides if you stay mad very long, it's going to hurt your scoring."

So who better to ask about Tony's philosophy about keeping one's temper, than Tommy Bolt, dubbed by his contemporaries as "Thunderbolt." "Aside from that being a lot of sissy stuff," Tommy snarled. "I don't think a guy can play well if he goes around with his temper all bottled up inside of him. Of course, some hide their temper while on the course, but I'll guarantee you that if they do, they go home and clout their wife, or somebody."

A Texas pro by the name of Earl Stewart, Jr., was leaning toward what Bolt said. "I have in mind," said Stewart, "what Byron Nelson once told me. 'I never played a decent game of golf,' he said, 'after I became a gentleman golfer!' "

Someone asked Tony how the Tour impressed him after five years? Was it still as glamorous as it seemed when he was a caddy? "Yes, sirree, Jackson. When you read about it as a kid, it looks very, very glamorous," he said. "You savor the thought of playing on the greatest golf courses in the world under sunny skies with the greens cut real good, and everything else pretty smooth, too. But it isn't quite that way. The almost inordinate amount of practice required, which is very boring, and therefore very tiring, is one of the bad things. There is more hard work on the tour than youngsters who haven't played it could ever dream of. However, the practicing and playing gives you a lot of exercise, and you're outdoors, which I like. Makes you feel like a tiger, and makes playing a breeze. There are lots of good times, too, with the people you meet. Also, when you are playing pretty good, your name is in the paper. And if you win quite a few tournaments, you'll have articles about yourself in national magazines, too.

"I try not to waste my days on the Tour. I watch the mechanics of the top players' swings, such of them as are still around. I especially like to watch the way they play trouble shots. They have grooved their swing and mastered all the shots, and that's what I must do. I don't feel that my swing is solid enough now to carry me through any kind of situation, nor have I the consistency, or anywhere near it, that I'd like."

That's an amazing thought that Tony shared with *Golf Magazine*. Here's a man who just turned 29 years old and had spent most of the last 16 years, less the two years in the Marines, either playing in golf tournaments or practicing. Despite those thousands of hours, he still felt that he did not have the consistency that he wanted. At that time, Tony was weeks away from playing in his first Masters, and he still knew that to get to the top of the ladder there was a great deal of work that must be done. If nothing else, Tony's humility was evident as he shared the fact that he felt his swing was not quite solid enough. Nevertheless, he was fourth on the money and after all those top ten finishes so far in 1963, there weren't too many playing better.

"If some young fellow coming on the Tour were to ask my advice on how to act," Tony explained, "I would tell him to keep his mouth closed as much as possible during the first year, anyway, and learn all he can by closely watching the top guys. He would learn more than good golf; he would learn good manners and self-control in front of the public that would be invaluable to him the rest of his life, whether he stayed in professional golf or not."

Doc Giffin, Field Press Secretary for the PGA at the time, said that Tony's invariable courtesy and patience with sports reporters and other press representatives have made him very popular with them. In the spring of '63, Hal Wood, who had been covering the Tour for several years for the *United Press International*, dropped another story about Tony on the ears of the fellows in the pressroom. "Tony has learned some hard lessons," Hal said, "about keeping in condition, and learned them well. 'I don't drink now between tee and green; and all girls must be out of my room by 10:00 P.M.,' Tony told me jokingly not long ago. It is not that Tony ever caroused much, but lately his conduct in this regard could be described as nothing less than exemplary. He won't even drink beer from Tuesday through Sunday."

Speaking of Sunday, Mark Thomas was an assistant PGA

Tournament Supervisor and spoke about a side of Tony that only those very close to him knew about. "Tony laughs it up a lot," Mark said. "You rarely see him without a smile on his face. There are people who think that anyone so merry most of the time, must usually be 'up to something,' but my experience with him shows that deep down he is an unusually decent and straight-thinking young man. For instance, I happen to know that rain or shine, and regardless of his tee time on Sunday— the most important day in any big tournament—Tony never misses going to church. To do this he sometimes has to get up before dawn on Sunday."

After so much anticipation and the sheer joy of finally arriving in Augusta, Georgia on Saturday, March 30, 1963, Tony described his feelings and what he saw. "From the moment I turned off the main highway, and onto the famed Magnolia Lane that leads to the white Southern colonial clubhouse, I felt that I was in the center of old-world Southern plantation life. The main building looks like a tobacco baron's mansion and when a player arrives he's treated like an honored guest, or a visiting diplomat. A doorman seized my clubs and rushed them off to the caddy house. I stepped inside the door, registered at the front desk and was led upstairs to my locker. It was located smack under four pictures of Bob Jones, the club's president, sinking the four winning putts that brought him the Grand Slam of Golf in 1930. Around the clubhouse were framed photographs of past Masters winners; Horton Smith, Gene Sarazen, Craig Wood, Byron Nelson, Snead, Hogan, Palmer and all the others. The atmosphere gave me a tingly feeling because it seemed as if a picture history book of golf had been suddenly brought to life.

"Nor was my first look at the golf course any less exciting. In fact, it is the finest course I have ever seen or played on. The fairways are lush and wide. Every hole is unique and carefully planned as to where the tee shot might be placed, or where the cup might be cut into the green. When you get out on the course you feel you just can't get enough of it. I wanted to lie down and roll around on it, it looked so beautiful. The Masters is played in April each year, and the dogwood, azalea and other shrubbery are in full bloom. The course is a white, red, purple, pink and green paradise."

As Tony became more familiar with Augusta from one practice round to the next, his confidence continued to rise. "I'll probably choke when the bell rings Thursday," he said, making a cutting sign across his throat, "but if I don't, I feel I'm hitting the ball well enough to win. This course, the clubhouse, and even the galleries reek with atmosphere and tradition and the moment I first walked in the gate I could feel it. With the course in such great condition it is a pleasure to play, but, while it doesn't seem too tough, you can't fall asleep for even one shot without being penalized."

The day before the Masters was to get under way, Arnold Palmer singled out Tony Lema as a good bet to become the only golfer in history ever to win the Masters on his first try. "I realize no first-timer ever has won here before," said the three-time winner, "but that doesn't mean it can't happen. And if it does happen, Lema could be the boy to do it. Man, have you seen some of his drives? He hits 'em clear out of sight. I like the rest of his game, too."

While beating a bagful of balls out on the practice tee, Tony apologized to a member of the press. "I'm sorry if I seem preoccupied," he said while reaching for another ball, "but this is my first time here and I'm still trying to get my bearings. I can understand why they say it takes a few years to get the feel of being in the Masters. I'm honored just to have been invited—why, some of the men in this tournament like (Gene) Sarazen and (Byron) Nelson, I only know from reading about. A man who was invited here for the first time and didn't feel the magnitude of this event would have to be numb."

Tony and Ken Venturi teamed together on Tuesday to take on the famed Hebert brothers, Jay and Lionel in a trial run. Tony started right out by knocking the ball stiff for birdies on the first two holes. After the round, Jay Hebert sounded like he was impressed by the way Tony played. "Ordinarily, you have to stick with Palmer," Jay explained, "and some of the boys who have done it in the past. But don't sell a fellow like Lema short. I like the way he's been playing lately and he has the equipment to win here."

Ken Venturi and his wife Connie had invited Tony and Bo Wininger to share the three-bedroom house they had rented near the course for $300. That made it very convenient for Tony to play his practice rounds with Ken. Keep in mind; although he never won the Masters, Ken had some surreal experiences at Augusta National. In 1953, as a member of the Walker Cup, he competed as a 22 year-old amateur and finished a very respectable 16th, tied with notables such as Julius Boros, Jay Hebert and Peter Thomson. In 1956, still an amateur, he had a four-shot lead going into the final round that was played on a very windy day. He was paired with Sam Snead and under those conditions the wind dried out the greens so they were unbelievably slick. Ken staggered home with an 80 and lost to Jack Burke by one shot.

In 1958, Ken Venturi tied for fourth in the Masters, just two shots behind winner Arnold Palmer. Two years later, Ken finished at five-under par 283, after a very fine round of 70 on Sunday afternoon. He was one shot ahead of Dow Finsterwald and Palmer had to birdie the last two holes to win. Ken was being cheered and congratulated as he was escorted to the private office in the clubhouse so he could sit down and watch the last few holes with Cliff Roberts and Bobby Jones. Ken felt deep down that this was finally going to be his year to have the green jacket draped upon his shoulders. On the seventeenth hole, he watched Arnold's approach shot barely reach the green, some 30 feet short of the cup. Then he saw Arnold pour that putt right into the cup so he was tied with Venturi with one hole to play. From the eighteenth fairway, Arnold rifled a 6-iron to within six feet and in his knock-kneed putting style, made that putt for his second victory at Augusta. No one who has not been there could possibly comprehend what it feels like to have played so well on two occasions at the Masters and watch the championship snatched right out of his hands. Tony summed up how his friend Ken Venturi must have felt, not once, but twice.

"Visualize the man dying of thirst in the desert," Tony described, "who dives headlong into a cool stream of water only to find that it is a mirage and you will be pretty close to knowing how Ken felt. He has said that his mental anguish over Palmer's last minute victory was so great that it was days before he could really take in what had happened."

Without question, Tony was most appreciative of all the help Ken unselfishly offered to him in the days leading up to Tony's first Masters. "I played a total of four practice rounds with Kenny. Remember, now, I had never seen Augusta National before and here's a man in the field against me and a guy who almost won two Masters and yet he tells me everything he knows about the layout. Byron Nelson joined us and as we played, Ken and Byron chatted about shots they had hit in past tournaments, where the pins were likely to be placed and what to do on certain holes if the wind was blowing. I kept my eyes and ears open and even though they would be playing against me in the tournament, they answered in accurate detail every question I asked. I learned that you have to be a very gutsy player to score well and win at Augusta. You have to be playing well, but you also have to cut the corners and get as near to the green off the tee as you can. If you play safe you have so many long approach shots and so many long putts that you will have very little chance of winning.

"After my last practice round I asked Nelson what he thought of my swing and how he thought I was playing. He stopped, took a long look at me and said, 'I've watched your swing for three days now. I've observed you pretty carefully and I cannot see a thing wrong. I think you're swinging and hitting the ball beautifully.' This gave me so much confidence and made me feel so good I felt like dancing a jig on the clubhouse veranda. I could hardly wait for the tournament to start."

Despite being a little tense throughout his first round in the Masters, Tony didn't drive it particularly well, but managed a two-over par 74 while playing with Tommy Bolt. Of course, Bolt had the reputation of being hot-tempered, but Tony said that playing golf with Tommy is something he has always enjoyed. By then Tony had developed enough personality to know when to compliment a playing partner's shot and when to say nothing at all.

In the second round, Tony was paired with Sam Snead and received a self-imposed boost of confidence. He shot a 69 to Snead's 73 and actually hit some shots that prompted Samuel

Jackson to say, "Nice shot." For those who know little about Snead, hearing him compliment another player is something that didn't happen too often. He wasn't rude but he just paid attention to his own game. Not much else appealed to Snead while he was playing in a golf tournament. Now, telling off-color jokes or touching the ceiling with his foot, like Mr. Bojangles, during the Master's Tuesday evening Champion's Dinner, that's another story. In this round with Snead, Tony got off to a great start by birdieing the first two holes with putts of 15 and three feet. He bogeyed the par-3 fourth when he missed the green and the fifth with a bad chip. His other birdie on the front came at the eighth when he two-putted the par-5 after reaching the green in two. He parred nine and made the turn at one-under 35. On the back, Tony made eight pars, but his highlight was the par-5 thirteenth hole where after a fine drive, he nailed a four-iron within ten feet and made the putt for an eagle three. After the round, his confidence became evident while talking with the press. "I was thrilled when I was invited here and I was nervous, for what I was doing, playing with all the big boys! Maybe that's why I shot a 74 on the first day. But, then my nerves settled down and I was all right."

The third round was played in wet, cold and rainy conditions and Tony fired a respectable 74. After a bogey on the first hole he got it back right away with a birdie on the par-5 second hole. He bogeyed the short seventh and made the turn at one-over. He bogeyed the tenth hole and ran into trouble on the par-5 thirteenth and carded a six. Once again, he came back with a birdie on the par-5 fifteenth hole to finish with a pair of 37's on a windy day with intermittent rain. "The weather made it real rough," Tony said after the wet and dreary day. The lowest rounds in the entire field that day were 71's recorded by Chen Ching-Po, Julius Boros and Billy Casper. After 54 holes, Jack Nicklaus (74-66-74—214) had a one-shot lead over Ed Furgol (70-71-74—215), a two-shot cushion on Julius Boros (76-69-71—216) and a three-stroke lead over Tony (74-69-74—217) and Sam Snead (70-73-74—217).

Marvin "Bud" Ward was a popular golfer from Washington and was well known throughout the northwest. He won the U.S. Amateur in 1939 and 1941 along with five victories in the

Northwest Open as an amateur and once as a professional. His best performance in a major came in the 1939 U.S. Open when he finished one shot out of a playoff with Byron Nelson, Craig Wood, and Denny Shute. Ward had competed in six Masters and was asked by Bay Area reporter Phil Norman what he thought about Tony's chances in the final round at Augusta National. In a nutshell, Ward gave Tony "a good chance" to win the Masters. He thought Tony must shoot a 68 to win and felt he could do it. "He's been a good finisher lately," Bud told Phil. "Tony doesn't scare. I'd say he's pretty gutsy. With his equipment he can win because three shots can be made up in two holes at Augusta. Palmer and others have shown that sometimes three strokes can be made up in one hole."

An hour or so before the final round, Tony was upstairs in the clubhouse looking at the pairing sheet posted on the bulletin board and checking the comparative scores. Dan Sikes (the lawyer) came up the stairs and stood next to Tony, also studying the list. Dan broke the silence in his Florida drawl, "Tony, you just might be able to win this thing." "Attorney," Tony said, "I feel so charged up I could just walk out the door to the porch over there, walk right through the railing and float straight to the first tee."

Tony thought that if he could play a steady front nine he might be in position to win. He did just that by making the turn at one-under par 35. Jack Nicklaus had a three-stroke advantage over Tony when play began, but after a 37 on the front nine, his lead had shrunk to one. In the meantime, Gary Player, Sam Snead and Julius Boros were all playing well and the top five players were all within two-shots of each other. As the saying goes, 'The Masters starts on the back nine on Sunday,' and the 1963 tournament had all the ingredients of a thrilling finish.

On the tenth hole, a 495-yard downhill par-4 named Camellia; Tony hit a big drive down the left-hand side of the fairway and followed that with a crisp 5-iron within 12 feet for a birdie. The putt was struck perfectly but lipped out at the last second. On the tough eleventh hole, Tony hit his 5-iron approach shot well, but it turned out to be one-club short and ended up barely on the front of the green some 100-feet from the cup. He three-putted for a bogey (his only three-putt all week) and stood one-over par for the tournament. The par-3 twelfth at Augusta is one of the most challenging short holes in all of golf. Depending on where the tees are placed, it plays around 155 yards. Rae's Creek flows right in front of the shallow green that has a depth of no more that 20-25 feet. Oh, and there isn't an avid golfer alive who hasn't heard about the always present swirly wind that is impossible to outguess. In the heart of Amen Corner, the green sits away from the stands that are behind the tee and therefore no spectators surround the green. The golfers walk over the Ben Hogan Bridge to further isolate them and it's the only hole at Augusta National where the golfers are removed from the gallery. Tony hit a superb iron shot in there and had a birdie putt of no more than eight feet. After the bogey on eleven, Tony felt he had to make this putt in order to give himself a chance to win. The putt barely slipped by the cup and Tony could control his temper no longer.

"As I tapped my second putt into the hole," he explained after the round, "and pulled out the ball I barked out a stream of the filthiest language I had used since mustering out of the Marines in 1955. When I straightened up I noticed my playing partner, a Formosan named Chen Ching-Po, who was also having his troubles in the final round, looking at me in a funny way. I walked over to him and apologized for using such vile language in front of a visitor to my country. He smiled and then said in very broken English: 'Is all right. If I knew those words I would use them myself.' That made me feel good again and I hit two good shots on the thirteenth hole and birdied it. This put me back to even par for the tournament and in contention once again."

Tony continued to play solid golf as he made routine pars on the fourteenth, fifteenth, and sixteenth holes while Sam Snead and Gary Player jumped on the bogey train and couldn't get off. Sam bogeyed the par-3 sixteenth and the eighteenth while Gary bogeyed the last two holes. Two holes behind Tony, Jack Nicklaus had bogeyed the twelfth to go to even par for the tournament. Actually it was a stroke saving bogey in the purest form. His tee shot on the par-3 barely cleared Rae's Creek and wound up in the soggy front bunker. He was permitted a lift and drop due to casual water, but his recovery shot carried about twenty-five feet beyond the pin into stubbly rough. He chose to use a putter and it rolled nine feet past the cup. His playing partner, Julius Boros, rolled in a twelve footer for a birdie, to get back to even par. Jack knocked in the nine foot bogey putt to lose only one shot and also be at even par for the tournament. Nicklaus reached the par-5 thirteenth with a driver and a 2-iron, and two putted for a birdie to return to one-under par. So Tony stood on the seventeenth tee even par, one shot behind Jack Nicklaus. If he parred the last two holes, he would be tied with Sam Snead at 288. About the time Tony made a solid par at seventeen, Jack hit a gorgeous, high, soft-falling 6-iron about thirteen feet from the pin that was positioned on the dangerous upper terrace at the back right-hand corner of the sixteenth green. He then proceeded to roll in the putt to go to two-under par. Tony was on the eighteenth tee, two shots back, knowing full well that he had to make a birdie and if Jack ran into trouble on the final two holes—so be it.

The eighteenth at Augusta is a beautiful dogleg right uphill par-4 that measured 420 yards in 1963. On the right side of the fairway are tall, thick- trunked pine trees, while a large bunker is situated on the left of the fairway about where the tee shots land. The green is fairly narrow with three distinct plateaus and there are bunkers on both the right and the left front of the green. The pin was in the middle terrace of the green, toward the right side. Tony hit a great drive past the corner of the dogleg and was about a 4-iron distance from the green. He stood in the eighteenth fairway thinking about what kind of shot he had to hit and what it all meant at the time. Afterwards, he told the press exactly what was going through his mind on the 72nd hole at Augusta.

"It's a helluva a hole to have to make a birdie three on," he recalled, "but I knew I had absolutely no chance to win the tournament if I didn't. If I did so and Nicklaus, behind me, made a bogey on one of the last two holes—certainly a possibility—I might tie or even beat him. At this stage I was very nervous and tense, just as anyone might be, but it was an almost enjoyable kind of tension, a charged up feeling that anything is possible, which focuses your mind down so hard on the shot you have to hit that you were able to shut out everything else... You just go ahead and do the best you can without thinking of the consequences of a bad shot or a good shot... I knew if I landed the ball on the right side of the green it would kick in toward the hole. This meant flirting with the trap on the right side of the green, but I wasn't thinking about the trap. I had a chance to win the tournament, I was passing this way and who knows when I would ever be so close again, so I was just going to take a good, long smell of the flowers. I hit a very firm 4-iron that struck just off the right side and kicked up and onto the green, about 22 feet above the hole."

Once he got to the eighteenth green, Tony and his caddy, Pokey, lined up the putt. The putt had to slide downhill and break two ways. He had to start it about six or eight inches to the left of the hole figuring that it would then break about four or five inches to the right before turning straight at the hole once again. As Alfred Wright wrote in *Sports Illustrated*, "Lema looked over this scary putt with a poise that denied the torment inside him. For all one could tell, he might have been playing a $2 Nassau on Wednesday afternoon back home in San Leandro."

From the moment Tony hit the putt, he knew it had a chance. It started out left then swung toward the right. It held that line for a while then gradually swung back to the left again and headed straight for the hole. Just as Tony leaped into the air, the ball dropped solidly into the middle of the cup. Tony said the exhilaration and relief he felt when the ball disappeared were immeasurable and it was like an explosion inside of him.

The 23-year old Jack Nicklaus was on the seventeenth fairway when an enormous roar from the horseshoe gallery around the eighteenth green thundered across the emerald fairways at Augusta National. In the interview room afterwards, Jack owned up to the fact he was "doggone nervous" and kept looking over his shoulder all day long. "Darn right I was nervous," confessed Jack. "I kept looking at Tony because he was even with par all the way. When he got his birdie on the 18th, I couldn't see him because I was in the middle of the 17th fairway. But I heard a big cheer and I figured he sank a putt."

After Tony signed his scorecard three or four Pinkerton guards led him through the crowd and back into Clifford

Robert's private office in the clubhouse. It was the same room where three years earlier Ken Venturi sat and watched Arnold Palmer make those dramatic birdies on the last two holes and claim his second green jacket. Tony asked to wash his hands and comb his hair. Upon returning, he sat down next to Bobby Jones and shook the hand of this legend. "I'm glad to meet you sir," said Tony.

Over his shoulder, Bowman Milligan, the Jones valet, whispered to Tony, "What size coat do you wear?" As this was Tony's first Masters, he focused on the screen and blurted out, "42 long." A few days later, Tony told a golf writer. "And while they were wondering about my measurements, I saw Nicklaus hit his drive right down the fairway on the final hole and I thought, 'well, I gave it a real good try.'"

On the television, Nicklaus was coming up the 18th fairway, needing a par to beat Tony's 287 by a single stroke. His iron shot from the fairway was long and stopped about 40 feet above the hole. At the time, Tony was thinking that there was absolutely nothing he could do about it either way. He had to sit and watch him win the Masters or watch it end up in a tie after 72 holes. Jack's first putt slid by about four feet and he said later that he was surprised it didn't go in. There were thousands of hushed gasps as Jack bent over the final putt—like a big, frozen polar bear. He nudged it sharply; the ball veered to the left but trickled into the edge of the cup. "Then I was surprised when the second one did," he said. Tony remarked that when he saw Jack's second putt he thought it couldn't go in. "He jerked it a little," said Tony as he got up to leave.

"Don't be disappointed," said Bobby Jones, and Tony replied, "I'm very happy to be here." Outside he drew a deep breath, straightened his slender shoulders and said, "I guess I would have felt much better if he'd three putted it." When it dove from sight into the cup, so did all of Tony's emotions and all of his hopes. On his way to the "outdoor" presentation ceremony, Ken Venturi came over, grabbed Tony, and they stepped into a side room to have a short talk. There were tears in the eyes of both of these men and they staggered around like two blind people trying to regain their composure. Now both of them knew what it felt like to come so close to winning one of the greatest tournaments in the world and then to have it plucked right out of their fingers. They both knew so well how the other had felt. They shook hands and vowed that they would both be back and one day one of them would win the Masters.

Later that evening, Cliff Roberts hosted a dinner for a special group. First time Masters champion Jack Nicklaus was there with his wife, Barbara, along with Arnold and Winnie Palmer, Gary and Vivienne Player, Bill and Shirley Casper and a few others. After dinner, Arnold took Tony aside and told him how well he played in his first Masters. Arnie wanted to be considered a real friend, something that meant a lot to Tony. He told him not to be disappointed about finishing in second place. Once the shock had worn off a bit, Tony did in fact realize how well he played and how well he withstood the pressure packed final holes. It finally sunk in how tremendous that finish was on the 18th hole and he knew he gave it everything he had.

The Augusta National was the big winner that week. Jack Nicklaus' sizzling 66 on Friday was the lowest round of the tournament—by two shots! Gene Littler fired Sunday's best round, a 68, but throughout the tournament there had been only seven other rounds in the 60's. Tony Lema, Julius Boros, Dow Finsterwald, Bo Wininger, Doug Ford, Johnny Pott, and Mike Souchak all had one round of 69 in the tournament.

Needless to say, the press had so many good stories to report following that Masters, there had to be a shortage of ink at every newspaper and magazine publishing house across the country. *New York Herald Tribune*'s Al Laney filed a masterful story that appeared in Tuesday's edition. "When the 1963 Masters is seen in retrospect," he wrote, "these two, Nicklaus and Lema, are seen to be the only two who played what could be called a really good tournament from first to last and their four rounds were remarkably similar. Both opened with 74's that could have been higher but for sound judgment of what can be got out of not quite good play. Both then dropped below 70 on the second day, Nicklaus with 66, Lema with 69, and both came through Saturday's miserable conditions with another carefully played, conservatively conceived 74 that might so easily have been 80 in the day long rain. And then in the fourth round, Lema, playing very fine under pressure golf, just failed to make up Friday's three-stroke deficit.

"Nicklaus at 23 has been National Amateur champion, National Open champion and Masters champion, and you have to go all the way back to Bob Jones and the fabulous twenties to find a parallel. In Nicklaus it is obvious that we have to deal with one of the outstanding performers of golf history. There is no telling what he may do before he is Palmer's age, which is early 30's. It is certainly less obvious that Lema is about to step onto the top level and ask the big three to move over, but there is a strong belief aboard that it will come, largely, though not altogether, because of his play here at his first Masters. Lema is 29 now and although he has not won anything but money so far, he has been well tested by five years on the tournament trail, which he hit after serving with the Marines in Korea. He has all the attributes of a winner; long, accurate tee shots and irons, a smooth putting touch, boldness now tempered by judgment and, above all, golfing style. Lema seems to have that elusive thing called class. It is always a bit foolhardy to make predictions about golfers who have not won important events, but many are saying Lema is the next one and it would be a good thing for competitive golf if the three, who own all the big titles played for in 1962 and so far in 1963, should become four."

As the reporters surrounded the runner-up and peppered him with questions from what his favorite champagne was to what ball he played, Tony insisted on making two points very clear to everyone. "I owe my mental attitude to Danny Arnold," he said. "I have forced myself into accepting the bad with the good. I found blowing my top hurt my game. Danny Arnold talked to me for hours on three things: Stay calm, keep the ball in play, and the breaks will come your way.

"Don't forget, this was my first time at Augusta and anything I knew about this great course I owe to Ken Venturi. He filled me in on every hole. Ken ought to know this place. He was second in 1956 and 1960."

She's Really Helped My Game

A few days later it didn't take Tony long to answer a reporter's question about what would have happened had he actually won the Masters. "We'd have been in the press room all night," Tony admitted. "I can just see myself, lying on that couch (where the top finishers sit for interviews), mike in hand, champagne glass in the other. We'd never have left. If I'd have won, I would have been glad to have blown the whole $20,000 first place money."

As it turned out, Tony had to accept second place money. "Only $12,000 for finishing second, you know," he smiled in obvious disappointment. "I think I have it made," he said, without making it sound like bragging, "even though I finished second. They've already asked me to appear on at least two television matches (*Shell's Wonderful World of Golf*) next year."

"Naturally, I'm elated to finish so high, but there is nothing like being first," admitted Tony, without bitterness, "I don't root against anybody, but I was sure hoping that last putt of Jack's would jump out of the cup. Actually, I felt like I could win it all. Then I began to choke a little on the 15th, 16th and 17th. However, on 18 I just decided to loosen up and let it fly. I'm glad I did. You aren't honest if you say that you are wishing the man well on every shot. But you really learn to live calmly with these things. I had resigned myself to the $12,000 second money and felt that anything beyond that would be surprising."

What if he had won?

"You could have put another "0" on that $20,000," he replied. "That's probably what it would've meant to me. But I'm not crying. When I started out in golf as a caddy in my teens I decided I was going to adopt Walter Hagen's philosophy of life—'Smell the roses along the way.' Well, I've smelled them and I am going to keep on smelling them. I'll probably go out of life as I came in—naked. No regrets ever, and never crying. But let me tell you this. It was a real thrill and I want to pay special tribute to one man—Ken Venturi. Ken is a gentleman. We have been buddies a long time. When I was invited to play at Augusta, Ken invited me to stay with him. On every one of the practice rounds he gave me advice and told me little things you don't get to know about a golf course unless you play it a lot.

"I have a fine family, the best. I never made college, I barely got through high school, but it wasn't my family's fault. They are gods to me. So is Venturi. He's quite a guy."

There was an array of comments from his colleagues about what brought on his sudden success. "He's gotten a little more compact with all of his game," said Arnold Palmer. "He has a more solid putting stroke," said Billy Casper. "His game has just got stronger between the ears," said Billy Maxwell. But Tony agreed mostly with Maxwell. He had finally schooled himself to forget about the bad shots and *immediately* start figuring out how to salvage a par, or in some cases, a bogey.

Lake Chabot head pro Dick Fry recounted the progress Tony had made since he tutored him from wispy boyhood until he became a man. "He came up the hard way. Tony didn't start from the top and work down. When he was a shaver, he didn't have enough money to get to the golf course. My daughter, Marianne and son, John, used to see that he had a ride each way when tournaments were in the city. He hitchhiked around East Bay to courses, and did a lot of walking. In my mind Tony is a better kid because of it. He was modest and came from a very moral, religious family.

"He was born and raised at my course. Until he went into the Marines (1953) he reminded me of an underfed kid. He never had the long game. He had to rely on his chipping and putting to win. Even at that, Tony won the Oakland City championship at the age of 18. He used to battle it out with my boy (John Fry) in most of the tournaments around here. Johnny could hit the ball farther and it gave him some advantage."

Fry said that Tony became a top-grade tour pro because he had improved in every department. "For one thing, he has become a terrific driver. Man, how he hits that ball. I don't know how he ever got that added distance but it's there. He doesn't have to take a back seat to Nicklaus, Palmer or any of them."

We must not overlook the 18 months that Tony spent as an assistant with John Geertsen (1955-56) at the San Francisco Golf Club. Geertsen had a reputation as an excellent teacher and astute judge of potential. "John worked long hours with Tony," recalled Jack Loughman, who also worked at San Francisco Golf Club. "He got him to lengthen his drives by teaching him to move into the ball and improve his timing. While he didn't have the length when he arrived, he did when he left."

Congratulations and comments were coming from every direction, so it was no surprise that Tony's sponsor, Jim Malarkey, made sure golf fans were aware that he played a role in Tony's success. "I've thought all along I've had the potentially greatest golfer of the bunch," Jim said by telephone after watching the Masters finish on TV in his Portland home. At that time Malarkey said the cost of sponsoring Tony was "close to $18,000 per year."

"Many times when I thought I was never going to make it," Tony said, "Malarkey always encouraged me to go on and just wouldn't let me give up. I'll always be grateful to him for giving me this chance."

In most cases, there is usually more than one reason why a sponsor gets involved with a golfer on the tour. He could be a wealthy and generous person who loves golf and sees a tremendous potential in a player. Or maybe he wants to have a sense of participating on the PGA Tour and he knows he certainly cannot rely on his own game. As Tony said one time, it gives the sponsor an opportunity to "have his own horse on the tour." At any time, sponsors can come out, be introduced to a multitude of players, pal around with them, and feel like one of the boys. Simultaneously, the sponsor can go back home, especially after his player has had a good run in several tournaments, and claim bragging rights for the success "his player" has been enjoying on the tour. But, as Tony found out in 1962, Malarkey might have had another motive all along. This was an investment for him and he was darn sure trying to make a profit. As the years went by, and Malarkey must be recognized for his patience, he was also a little shrewd when the contracts were written.

After Tony's rookie year in 1958, Malarkey had a new contract written with a few stipulations. He would receive $14,000 for annual expenses, repay that amount with earnings, and anything over that Tony would keep two-thirds and Malarkey would get one-third. Malarkey included that Tony was to go first-class all the way. Sell the Plymouth, fly from one tournament to the next, stay at the best places, and eat at nice restaurants. Eventually, the basic annual advance was bumped up to $16,000 and although Tony enjoyed the royal treatment, he felt as though it was costing him more to travel on the tour than he wanted to spend. Despite having a good year in 1962, his total earnings were close to $48,000, Tony had little to show since 1959 and 1960 had put him a rather deep deficit. He had signed a three-year contract that contained options extending its life through 1966. In the small print, Malarkey insured that the option was something he could exercise, but Tony could not. But, as Tony said, "I did have reassurances that I could forget the options and end the contract any time I wanted to."

A clause in the contract required that all debts would be carried forward from year to year. So, unless Tony just quit the tour, Malarkey would eventually get his money back. In those tough years of 1959 and 1960, Malarkey called Tony on more than one occasion telling him that he would write off the debt if he would quit the tour. During those two years, Tony earned about $15,000 but spent twice that amount. As the 1961 season began Tony was about $11,000 in debt. His total earnings that year was about $20,000, but by the time he met expenses and gave Malarkey his cut, Tony had virtually nothing left. As the 1962 season continued, Tony came to the realization that it was time to sever the working relationship and go on his own. In July, Tony requested to end the agreement and pay off anything he owed Malarkey. At which time, Malarkey told him, "Okay, I'll have my lawyers draw up the necessary papers and send them along right away."

During the second half of 1962, Tony had gone to Malarkey's

attorney's office when the tour was in Portland and "sat in his lawyer's office while he instructed him to legally end the contract." Despite numerous telephone calls to "get the papers moving" and being reassured that they were on the way, nothing arrived as the season progressed. Tony started making an impact on the tour in Seattle, Las Vegas, Costa Mesa, and Mobile and by the end of 1962; his total winnings amounted to $48,000 while his total liabilities to Malarkey were $49,000. He had erased all debt and was looking forward to flying solo. Tony felt that through it all, Malarkey had gotten his kicks, gotten all his money back and had even made a profit. "Suddenly," Tony said, "it appeared that Malarkey was neither generous nor a sportsman and apparently not even as wealthy as he had led people to believe. He insisted on exercising the options and flatly refused to end the contract."

Tony hired his own attorneys and concentrated on golf in the spring of 1963 as the lawyers wrangled. Since the contract had not been legally broken, a good chunk of all the winnings Tony was making on the tour were ending up in Malarkey's pocket. Tony postponed signing contracts that would have given him quite a bit of "endorsement income" because he knew that only a small percentage of that would find its way to the Lema bank account. Fred Corcoran, one of the most aggressive marketing managers ever in the world of golf, had been talking with Tony for quite some time, but Tony held off until this matter with Malarkey was settled. Later in the 1963 season, this bothered Tony to the point where his golf game suffered and he passed up playing in the British, the Canadian and the Western Open's so he could stay home and consult with his attorneys. Finally, Malarkey agreed to end the contract with Tony, but "the total price came to everything I had made in 1963, less expenses, plus an additional $22,000 to be paid over the following two years. Now I was not only flat broke after having earned $110,000 in eighteen months, but also I was in hock up to my ears. I'm embarrassed to say what I had to pay Malarkey to get out of the contract, but anyone can figure out that it came to a good deal more than $50,000."

Tony said that after five and a half years on the tour, he had nothing to show for it while Malarkey had turned a tidy little profit of over $60,000. He had never made good on the publicity he promised Tony nor had he gotten an agent that he said he would acquire. Tony referred to it as "the school of hard knocks" and had learned a valuable lesson. "I'll never sign another contract," he said, "even if it has been drawn up by my mother, without reading the small print."

Over a year later, Bill Libby wrote in *TRUE The Man's Magazine*, that Tony's sponsor, Jim Malarkey, ran hot and cold. Sometimes he suggested that Tony should quit. "Sometimes, I wanted to quit myself," Tony recalled. "I had some lousy nights thinking about it. But the guy was only buying my time. He couldn't tell me what to do. No one can tell me what to do. So, I kept hacking away."

Looking back, Tony reflected on those tough years when his sponsor was not only getting one-third of his winnings but repayment in full for the advance in traveling expenses. "There's no other way, but there should be," Tony said bitterly. "There's no guarantees you're going to win a dime, and you usually don't, not for a while anyway. The tour's a terrible place when you're not winning. I didn't know anyone or anything. The pros are a good bunch of guys, but they didn't care about me. They had their own troubles. I felt like a little fish in an awful big ocean."

Sure, Tony eased through those rough years with wine, women and song and eventually found himself in debt to the tune of about $11,000. "I didn't think about it much," he said. "I always figured, why suffer today when you can suffer tomorrow? I've always stayed in the best places, ate and drank the best, flown rather than gone the car route. If I'd fallen too deep in the hole, I'd have quit. It's my nature: If I don't live good, I don't play good. I believe in going first class. If not, I'd rather not go."

When all of that hard work began to pay off in the spring of 1963 and Tony was working his way up the money list, he found out that sponsors are not always easy to work with, nor are they easy to slip away from when their services are no longer needed. "I paid him back what he'd spent on me," Tony explained, "and I gave him some of my winnings, but he wanted so much more it was ridiculous. Let's say I paid a very high price for a certain amount of experience. And there is no substitute for experience." Tony didn't make a whole lot of A's at St. Elizabeth's, but he made an A in this class. Only problem, the tuition was high.

There was more going on Tony's life in April of 1963 than a runner-up finish at the Masters and attorneys wrangling over how his arrangement with Jim Malarkey would eventually get settled. It all started aboard an American Airlines non-stop flight from Dallas to San Francisco in 1961. The plane had a scant amount of passengers aboard and a slim, trim, and red-haired, green-eyed, beautiful stewardess by the name of Betty Cline from Oklahoma City met a tall, handsome man (in first-class, of course) who was on his way home to San Leandro. He said many times that it was "love at first flight." "The plane was empty," he recalled. "We played gin rummy. She won my money and my heart. And she married me." "It was," Betty pointed out later, "the only way I could collect." Tony countered that by saying he met an airline stewardess he found he "cared for more than myself."

After dating nearly two years, they had made plans to get married in September of 1963. Whether it was the sudden economic fruition or a couple madly in love, the date was moved up and set for Sunday, April 28. They exchanged wedding vows at St. Leander's Church in San Leandro. On hand to give away the bride was Mrs. Louise Cline of Oklahoma City. Best man for Tony was Jim Malarkey, and among others in attendance were Ken and Connie Venturi. Malarkey's role may seem to be a surprise, but it indicated that Tony and Jim were able to separate personal and business matters when the time came to do so. Speaking of time, it was a real coincidence that while Tony and Betty were standing at the altar at St. Leander's at 3:30, the final round of the Oakland City Championship was winding up at Lake Chabot only a few miles away where Tony had won the event 10 years prior.

Since his victory in the Orange County Open back in October, Tony had been looking forward to his first participation in the Las Vegas Tournament of Champions. Following a brief wedding reception in San Leandro, they flew right down to Las Vegas where a honeymoon suite was waiting for them.

The next day Tony was on the golf course preparing for the tournament. Naturally, he expected to receive his share of gentle joshing from some of his friends on the tour. But he may have not expected the odds-makers to make such a big deal of his role as a newlywed. He was originally listed at 15-1 odds to win the Tournament of Champions. After his second place finish at Augusta the odds dropped to 8-1. When his marriage plans were revealed, Tony ballooned back up to 15-1. A day or so before the tournament, he was seen hitting practice shots with Betty right there at his side and the odds returned to 8-1.

One of the best writers in the business, Jim Murray of the *Los Angeles Times* offered a parody of what might have taken place in the Lema suite on the morning of the first round. "Try to imagine if you will, waking up on the morning of your honeymoon, rolling out of bed and whispering to your bride that you'll see her later, you have a date on the first tee. 'You're what?' she'll scream. 'You're going out to play golf with those bums? Over my dead body! You're married now.'

"Tony Lema teed off. But if he dares to birdie any of the first five holes, he's a better man than most of us. If you can picture him having the nerve to leave the bridal suite with a set of golf clubs in his hand, just get an image of him coming home and admitting he broke 70. His wife will start crying, put in a call to her mother and sob, 'You don't love me anymore, I saw your card.' Tony could win a tournament and lose a wife."

Before going to Las Vegas, Betty had never seen a golf tournament nor had she played golf. "It's just as well," Tony said. "No household is big enough for more than one golfer. I hope she never learns the game." For a while there, Tony attempted to make people believe that living expenses on the tour would be less as a couple than what it cost during his bachelor days. "I figure that married to Betty I can cut my expenses down to $15,000 a year," he said, looking up with a broad smile from a piece of paper that was covered with an ambitious scrawl of numbers. "Not only will marriage be the greatest thing that ever happened to me, I think I can make a profit at it, too." Following that quote, *Sports Illustrated's* Gwilym S. Brown added, "That is Tony Lema's other distinction. He has to be the only golfer on the pro tour who can figure that one can live more expensively than two."

Tony insisted that he would not have considered marriage until there was sufficient cash. "I wouldn't have taken a wife if I couldn't afford to take her with me wherever I go," he explained. "And if we have a kid, he'll go right along with us, in the first-class section. Of course, he'll have to shine shoes…."

It turns out that a year after he made that comment he came up with an appropriate rebuttal. "No way. No way in the world," he laughed. "Unless I stay at the YMCA and she stays at the YW, which is not my idea of a jazzy arrangement. It costs us twice 15 grand. Two can live cheaply as two…maybe…if they're not on the golf tour. The golf tour is a very expensive way to go. My heart goes out to some of the kids, the way they have to live. Fortunately, I am making almost as much as we are spending. In any event, we will never starve."

Shortly after the wedding, Tony discussed just one of the advantages of being married to Betty. "Now I'm the happiest man in captivity," he testified. "Getting serious with Betty has helped me get serious with myself. She's really helped my game." And many of his closer friends, Tommy Jacobs, Jim Ferree, and Johnny Pott have attested to that very fact.

"Marrying Betty helped Tony immensely," said Tommy Jacobs. "He changed a great deal (in the last year he was alive). He was far closer to being content, whereas before he was liable to be sitting in somebody's living room talking to you, and suddenly he would drift off into space. He seemed at times like that to lose touch with reality. Tony was aware of this distance between himself and others, and he definitely wanted to get in step. He wanted to do things for others, particularly for people who had helped him. He just wasn't sure how to go about it. Probably, Tony lacked confidence more than anything else. He never had spent much time with the other golfers. They didn't really like him or dislike him—they didn't understand him."

Perhaps the serious side that Betty brought to Tony was evident long before they tied the knot that Sunday afternoon at St. Leander's Church. After Tony and Betty had been dating for quite some time, the subject of getting married had been discussed on several occasions. According to Tony's sister Bernice, Betty let it be known early on that before she even considered becoming married to Tony, she wanted to meet the entire family in San Leandro.

"It was wonderful," Bernice recounted. "Betty came home with Tony and she made it a point to get to know our family. That was fine with all of us because she was so friendly and easy to get along with. She sat down with everyone; Cleo, Walter, Harry and me. She wasn't scouting us out, but she was about to make a serious decision and I was impressed that it was so important to her to justify the continuity of the entire Lema family. That was neat." Harry married Judi a year later and she and Betty became close friends. "I have nothing but good memories," Judi recalled. "We had some wonderful experiences, whether it was shopping, cooking or just visiting."

Despite all the hoopla concerning the newlywed couple, Tony played well in Las Vegas and finished in a tie for second place. Jack Nicklaus ran away from the field at the Desert Inn Country Club by putting four solid rounds together for a 15-under par of 273. Tony was paired in the final round with veteran Ted Kroll, but when Billy Casper had to withdraw because of a hand injury at the ninth hole, Palmer, playing alone caught up with them on the twelfth hole. "It was a tremendous help, being able to play him face to face instead of wondering how he was doing," Tony said afterwards. "He had me by two shots at that time, but I thought I could catch him." And he did. Tony birdied the twelfth, fifteenth, and seventeenth while Arnie sneaked in a birdie on the fifteenth. They were tied for second with one hole to play and the difference between second and third place was $2,500. That was enough to get the attention of both of these gladiators. On the 445-yard par four eighteenth both hit good tee shots, but Arnold hit first from the fairway and was a little strong as the ball rolled to the back of the green 50 feet beyond the hole. Tony hit less club and put his approach shot 15 feet below the cup. "I had a very makeable birdie putt," Tony recalled, "and Arnie had to hit his down the green and over a rise some 12 feet his side of the hole. His putt was a great one. It came skidding down the green, over the rise and just sort of oozed across the left edge of the cup. I stood there with my mouth wide open and my eyes hanging out. Then I looked up and Arnold was coming across the green, hitching up his pants the way he does when things are going his way, and looking at me. He had a grin as big as a slice of watermelon on his face and it said as clearly as words could have, 'Aha, you s.o.b., I almost got you there, didn't I.' Then he started to laugh at the look of shock still on my face and I laughed too. I just barely missed the putt that would have beaten him for second place. It was worth some brief needling later. We are friends, but there we were on the golf course knifing each other just as hard as we could for that second place finish."

So Tony posted a six-under par 66 against Arnie's 68 and they tied for runners-up at 278. The consolation was $5,300, not a bad payday for the week you're on your honeymoon. At that point, his earnings for the year were $32,496, second place on the tour behind Jack Nicklaus.

Obviously, Tony was making a big impression on quite a few people and one in particular was Fred Corcoran. Born in Cambridge, Massachusetts, Corcoran was an entrepreneur from the word "go." He started in golf as a nine-year-old caddy at Belmont Country Club carrying the bag for Francis Ouimet and at the age of 12 he became the youngest caddie master in the America, collecting five cents from every boy who carried a bag. As a young man he worked for the Massachusetts Golf Association, with Donald Ross at Pinehurst, and as an official scorer for the United States Golf Association. Among his many innovations was the first tournament scoreboard that reflected birdies, pars and bogies in different colors; this method caught on immediately and is used around the world today. In 1936 he became the PGA Tour's tournament manager and the business manager of Sam Snead. During the 1940's he took golf from a minor curiosity to a major business. He later served as the PGA's Promotion Director.

As an idea man and publicist, with a pinch of hustler thrown in, he raised the awareness and business of golf through many avenues. He put together charity matches including Gene Tunney, Babe Ruth, Ty Cobb and he worked for the Red Cross and USO, staging golf exhibitions with the help of Bing Crosby and Bob Hope. He also managed the careers of Babe Zaharias, Ted Williams, and Stan Musial. He managed three United States Ryder Cup teams and was the official scorer at 34 USGA championships.

As he became Tony's business manager, it was a perfect fit for all parties concerned. If Corcoran presented Tony with a product or company to endorse, you could bet your bottom dollar he had checked it out thoroughly. If there was a "Who's Who" in the world of golf, chances are they were good friends with Fred Corcoran. Despite Fred's modest, self-described claim to fame that he had three-putted in 47 counties, he did know what it took to be a golfer (athlete) that was accepted and well liked by the public. Speaking of Tony in the early stages, there was no doubt Fred could see a superstar with charisma in the making. "His swing reminds me of Sam when Snead was young," he said. "And he has the build and certain mannerisms of Ted Williams. He can't miss being great."

The next week the couple took off for the Colonial National Invitational at Fort Worth, TX where Tony finished in a tie for fourth, seven shots behind the winner Julius Boros. Tony was on a pretty nice role. Since the first week of March, his record was the following: second in New Orleans, third at Doral, second at the Masters, 15th at Greensboro, tied for second at the Tournament of Champions, and the tie for fourth at the Colonial. As he explained earlier, it was time to take a week off and recharge those batteries. Next stop—the Memphis Open.

The Colonial Country Club had been the site of the Memphis Open since its inception in 1958. Tony had tied for fifteenth in 1959, for twenty-fifth in 1961 and thirteenth in 1962. Even though his earnings of nearly $36,000 had him in third place on the money list for 1963, Tony had not tasted victory on the PGA Tour since his win at Mobile last November. He knew he was playing well and he had the confidence to believe in his game if he was in position to win on the back nine on Sunday afternoon. After a pair of 67's in the opening rounds, he held a two shot lead. Then it started to rain and rain and rain. The third round scheduled for Saturday was called off after about half the field had teed off. On Sunday, the players didn't even get out of the locker room. The PGA decided that 36-holes would be played on Monday. "When you are playing well and leading a tournament," Tony said later, "you want to get out on the golf course as fast as you can. Well, by the time we teed off on Monday I had been leading the tournament for four days. It's tough to sit on one that long without being able to do something to protect it."

Tony was paired with Tommy Aaron and Jerry Edwards and after the morning round on the 6,500 yard layout, Tommy's 66 was two better than Tony's 68, thereby placing them in a tie for the lead at 202 after 54 holes. In the final round, Aaron played very well and held a two-stroke lead over Tony with two holes to play. "I didn't think I had a chance, really," Tony said. "I had to struggle for pars on 11, 12, 13, and 14, really struggle."

On the 186-yard uphill par-3 seventeenth hole, Tommy Aaron had the honor and nailed a four-iron right on line but twenty feet short of the cup. Tony switched to a three-iron and hit a perfect shot six feet to the left of the hole. Tommy missed his putt while Tony made his cutting the lead to a single shot with one hole to play. The eighteenth is a long par-5 and Tony thought he had chance to get home in two despite the dampened fairways. After a good drive, he smacked a 3-wood that landed in the center of the green about 20 feet to the left of the hole. Tommy was shorter off the tee, hit his second into the rough and reached the green in three about 15 feet. Tony nearly canned the rainbow putt with a huge break, but left it close and tapped in to complete his birdie-birdie finish. Tommy had a birdie putt to win the tournament on the eighteenth green, but it didn't fall and a sudden-death playoff was necessary.

On the first play-off hole both sprayed their tee shots, but Tony followed with an approach that rolled to the fringe about 40 feet from the hole. Tommy hit his iron over the green into a bunker and took three to get down for a bogey five. Tony chipped his third shot to within three feet and made that putt to capture his first win of the 1963 season. As he entered the pressroom following the grueling 37 holes it took on that Monday, "Champagne Tony" lived up to his name and ordered bottles of "the best you've got for the newsmen." The winner's check was for $9,000 and returned Tony to second on the money list with $44,296.

"I'm satisfied with my playing," grinned Tony. "I thought I had a good chance all the way through. It was as if an immense weight had been lifted off my shoulders. I had not only produced two birdies in a row under great pressure, I had won the playoff too."

Tony continued to play well in June as the tour rolled along and made its way through Indianapolis, Flint, MI and Rye, NY before heading for the U.S. Open at The Country Club in Brookline, MA. At the 500 Festival Open at the Speedway Golf Course in Indianapolis, he finished second to Dow Finsterwald and maintained his position on the money list. At the Buick Open at Warwick Hills Golf and Country Club in Grand Blanc, MI Tony finished in a tie for tenth place. He placed 55th in the Thunderbird Classic at Westchester Country Club in Rye, NY the week before the Open saying his body was in New York, but his mind was focused on the upcoming Open at Brookline.

Betty and Tony took a leisurely drove through New England on the Monday before the Open so Tony didn't get a look at the golf course until Tuesday. Only he could put his first impression of Brookline into words that would be accurate. "When I came back to the hotel late that afternoon," Tony said woefully, "I was in a state of shock. I couldn't believe that a course could be so hard. I don't know what I scored, but it must have been in the middle 80's. The next day I began to play a little better, stayed close to par, and so I felt in reasonably good shape for the tournament."

The Country Club possessed the usual Open characteristics such as fast greens, deep rough and narrow fairways, but there were three additional components that contributed to the highest winning score in post World War II history. There were a quite a few mounds, a lot of hills, many bunkers, and small, circular greens. At least twelve holes left golfers with blind or partially blind shots into the greens from the fairway. Sometimes you could see a glimpse of the flag, but depending on the pin location, most players found themselves guessing where they wanted to aim their approach shots. But Tony remained noble and pointed out he did not want to sound like a sore loser complaining of the difficulties. He realized that the course setup was the same for everybody and the player who adjusted best to the conditions would probably prevail as the winner

Boston had been dealt a severe winter and a particularly

dry spring. Hence, the course was not in very good condition. The grass had been re-sown on many of the greens just before the Open and this created very inconsistent putting surfaces. Since the speed varied from green to green, it was a great deal of guesswork on the part of the players. Winterkill, a disease caused by the sun burning through a winter's accumulation of ice and snow had made the fairways extremely ragged. As a result, hitting a fairway did not always assure the player that he would have a lie from which he could hit a dependable shot.

After rounds of 71 and 74, Tony was three behind Jacky Cupit, Arnold Palmer, and Dow Finsterwald and he told writers from the *San Francisco Chronicle Sporting Green* that he didn't think anyone in the Open would shoot even par 284 over the impossible and impassable Country Club course. He felt he was playing extremely well, especially his tee shots, and at the halfway point he was confident that he could win. On Friday night, he went to Fenway Park with Fred Corcoran and watched the Boston Red Sox massacre the New York Yankees. On Saturday morning the players were greeted with a sunny day, but the wind was blowing hard at 40 mph with gusts up to 50. Before his third round, Tony said, "A 280 would win it by a flock of shots. But, anyone who shoots a 280 under these wind conditions and on this layout would have to be cheating." Tony uttered the comment with tongue in cheek, but it was obvious from the astronomical scores in the 1963 Open at Brookline, that these humbled professionals were a pack of honest men.

Tony shot a 74 in the morning round and considering the wind, he was happy. Palmer fired a 77, Finsterwald had a 79, and Jacky Cupit got around in 76, giving him a one-shot lead over Tony after 54 holes. In efforts not to spend too much time and energy grousing about mistakes, Tony had lunch with Betty in the grill and was a little perturbed about bogeying three relatively easy holes—the 420-yard fifteenth, the 175-yard sixteenth, and the 365-yard seventeenth—right in a row. An even par round of 71 would have made the three glasses of milk and meatloaf taste better, but before he knew it, he was summoned to the first tee to start the final round. He said he felt a warm serenity on that first nine as he made eight pars and one bogey. At the turn, he was one shot in back of Cupit, two shots ahead of Palmer and one shot in front of Julius Boros. Tony hit his 6-iron approach on the tenth hole over the green into very deep grass, chipped poorly, missed a 10-footer for par and settled for a bogey five. He maintained his composure and followed that miscue with two solid pars on the eleventh and twelfth holes. On the long par-4 thirteenth hole with the wind at his back, Tony hit a good drive and followed that with an excellent 4-iron that left him 20 feet from the hole. He hit his first putt to within 18 inches of the cup and then asked his playing partner, Walt Burkemo, if it would be all right if he putted out. He stood over the putt, hit it and then watched it horseshoe all the way around the hole and stay out. Later Tony would say that it felt as though Sonny Liston had just punched him in the groin. From that moment on, Tony felt the complexion of the tournament had changed and instead of playing conservatively for the next five holes, he must be the aggressor and get some of those shots back.

On the par-5 fourteenth hole, he was right in front of the green in two shots, chipped up about five feet from the hole and missed the birdie putt. He made a routine par on the fifteenth and had a chance to look at the scoreboard. Tony was nine over, Boros was 11, Cupit was eight, and Palmer, playing right behind Tony, was also nine over par. Tony felt that no one was catching up with Cupit, but he was coming back to the field. As he was standing on the tee at the par-3 sixteenth and trying to figure out what club to hit, an amusing thing happened while the television camera was focused on Tony. He plucked some grass and flipped it into the air to see what direction the wind was going. The grass rose slowly and ascended straight upward. The gallery that surrounded the tee and everyone watching at home got a laugh. Perhaps they could appreciate all around the country the problems the golfers were facing at Brookline. Once again, Tony nailed a 5-iron, ended up nine-feet away and had an excellent opportunity to make a birdie. It would have found the bottom of the cup had he hit it hard enough. At the last moment, it peeled off to the right of the hole. Another birdie opportunity just flew away.

Tony hit another super drive right down the heart of the 17th fairway with about a 7-iron to the green. As he approached his ball, a huge roar erupted from the sixteenth green right behind him. Palmer had obviously knocked in a birdie and moved one stroke ahead of Tony. He hadn't even selected his club when another roar exploded as Cupit had chipped in for a birdie to go two ahead of him and one in front of Arnie. As Tony waited and watched from the middle of the seventeenth fairway, Julius Boros calmly knocked in a 20-foot birdie putt to tie him with Tony. Later, Tony explained exactly what he was thinking.

"I was standing in the seventeenth fairway," he said, "with everyone making birdies around me and the crowds yelling as if they were at a bullfight. I had counted myself out of the tournament and thought that nothing short of a miracle could ever bring me home in front."

Although he figured he had a 7-iron into the green, Tony decided to drop back to a 6-iron, and cut it in toward the hole with a left to right fade. Instead of fading, it went dead straight, took a big hop off the green and high up onto the side of a bunker directly behind the green. As he was standing way above the ball in the bunker, he had to be extremely careful not to slide and cause the ball to move, thereby incurring a two-stroke penalty. He knew it was the end for him. He hit it over the green and chipped it back toward the hole for a tap-in bogey. His drive on eighteen found the rough and he eventually settled for a bogey to finish with a 76 in the final round and 295, eleven over par for the tournament. As Tony looked at the television in the locker room, he watched Palmer miss a short putt to bogey the seventeenth, he saw Cupit hit several bad shots and bad putts to double-bogey the seventeenth, and then he watched both players par the eighteenth to tie Boros for first. All three finished at nine-over par 293. Had Tony made pars on the last two holes he would have been in the play-off too.

As he packed his gear and headed out to the parking lot to meet Betty, Tony was far from being the happiest camper at The Country Club at Brookline. Out of nowhere, a drunk dressed in worn Boston tweeds and a striped tie tottered over.

"Hey, Champagne Tony," he shouted. "What happened to Champagne Tony?"

Later Tony described the scene of events. "Then he clapped me on the back hard enough to break it and ambled off chuckling to himself. I was apoplectic with rage, dropped my bag on the driveway pavement and felt that I was just about to rip his head off. God only knows where I got the strength to hold off."

By the time he and Betty got back to their suite at the Ritz-Carlton in Brookline, Tony had cooled off to the point where he called the desk of The *San Francisco Chronicle Sporting Green* in the pressroom at Brookline and asked, "How did I finish?"

"You wound up tied at 295 with Billy Maxwell and Bruce Crampton."

"What's it worth?"

"You each get $3,170."

"Okay, there's something I want you to do right away. Buy each guy on The Chronicle Sports Department a bottle of the best champagne. Not the cheap stuff. The best. Then send the bill to my home in San Leandro."

At that a tremendous cheer went up from the ink-stained wretches on the sports desk.

"Waitta' minute," Tony said. "How many are there?"

Assured the complement of workers was quite a few men short of an army division, Tony said, "Fine, send for the champagne."

Tony had relaxed and sounded not too disappointed over his closing 76 after starting the final round one behind the leader Jacky Cupit. He spoke with the golf writers about what a challenge Brookline had presented. "You have no idea how tough The Country Club course was for this tournament. The fairways were narrow and the grass high in the rough. Then, the wind, which was bad enough on the first two days, was blowing at least 40 mph on Saturday. This is not a personal alibi, but just look at some of those high scores from fine golfers. I had my chance, but I blew it. I let it get away from me. I know I had a lot of people rooting for me back home. Please tell everybody I'm sorry I let them down."

He compared the wind conditions at The Country Club course with those at Candlestick—"only worse"—and then he added jokingly: "Maybe they weren't so bad. I was only blown down twice."

But he didn't blame the gusts that sometimes hit a velocity

of 40-45 mph throughout the entire day. "I actually played so well that the wind didn't bother me too much," he said. "I had my shots pretty much under control. In fact, I've played pretty damn well. I played the front nines in 70 and the back nines in 80. I couldn't make things go exactly right on the back nine and it wasn't all on the tough holes. I never got into too much trouble. I just missed too many key putts, especially in the last nine this afternoon when I took 18 (putts). You can't get anywhere with 34 and 36 putts."

Tony also blamed himself for a drastic mistake on the seventeenth in the final round. "I tried to slice a 6-iron around a tree to get to the pin rather than just getting to the green," he explained. "The ball hit on the green, bounced and buried itself on the backside hill of a sand trap. Then I blasted it over the green, chipped back stiff and holed it for a bogey."

He said the "wind was out of my sails" on the eighteenth, which he also bogeyed. He drove it into the rough, had a bad lie and couldn't reach the green with his second. "I thought if I ever got into a position to win the Open, I'd fold completely, but it was not the case. This gives me lots of confidence. Now I think for the first time I can add this to my collection of titles eventually. The Open is lost and not won as I and a few others proved today."

With Palmer, Cupit, and Boros set to go in the 18-hole play-off the following day, Tony refused to name a favorite. The word was that the three survivors could look forward to better weather, "and that will be a real break," said Tony. The forecast was for only 15 to 25 mph gusts. Julius Boros built up a three-stroke lead on the first nine and pulled away after Palmer triple-bogeyed the eleventh hole. Boros came up with his best round of the tournament, a one-under par 70, to edge Jacky Cupit's 73 and Palmer's 76. Boros had a reputation for hitting the ball on a very low trajectory, which obviously helped him in the windy conditions. He had won the 1952 U.S. Open played at Northwood Club in Dallas, Texas.

After playing five consecutive weeks on the tour, Tony did what most PGA Tour players do. He flew right on over to Cleveland and prepared to play in the $110,000 Cleveland Open at Beechmont Country Club. First prize was $22,000 and despite all of the work, pressure, traveling fatigue, and disappointment he incurred at The Country Club at Brookline, he was ready to give it another try. He got off to a solid start with a pair of 68's and was cruising along just fine on Saturday until the wheels nearly came off. On the back nine, he had an excellent chance to be the sole leader after 54 holes, but he three-putted the sixteenth and was in a shallow bunker on seventeen where he blasted out long and two-putted for another bogey. A possible 67 turned into a 69 and after three rounds he was tied at 205 with Jack Nicklaus and Arnold Palmer.

In the pressroom after the round he was asked how he felt about those costly bogeys. "I feel just fine," he quipped, "does anybody have a razor?" When reminded his fluffs left him in a tie with Palmer and Nicklaus, Tony replied, "Well, I guess that puts them in pretty good company, doesn't it?" About that time in the interview room, it was reported to Doc Giffin, the energetic PGA press secretary that Gardner Dickinson had withdrawn from Sunday's final round due to heat exhaustion. Griffin scratched his head and wondered out loud what to do since there are 75 money prizes allotted and only 74 players left in the field. "If you don't have any better ideas, Doc," said Tony, "you might give that extra check to the guy who played the 16th and 17th holes the worst on Saturday...and that's ME!"

Tony wasn't the only one who fired out one-liners to the always-hungry golf scribes. "I hit the ball better today than any time since winning the Masters," Jack Nicklaus commented. "By that I mean, the execution. I hit it just the way I wanted to and placed my shots in perfect position. To shoot only 69 the way I hit it is ridiculous. But I guess all the guys are having the same trouble. There should be a lot lower scores on this course. Maybe the guys don't want that $22,000."

"I feel a lot better today," said Palmer. "Those first two rounds of mine (71-68) were horrible. I hit such a bad shot on the 17th hole Friday I almost threw up going down the fairway." Somebody jokingly told Arnie a woman reporter who had interviewed him Friday had written he doesn't wear underwear. "Oh, so that's the reason all those pretty girls were following me today," Arnie cracked.

After a 71 on Saturday, that followed a 66 and 69 on his two previous rounds, Gary Player found himself at 206, one shot behind the leading threesome. He didn't mince words when asked by the press to describe his day on the golf course. "I hit my drives badly, my irons badly, my putts badly and I feel quite badly, thank you."

As reported in the *Cleveland Plain Dealer*, there were innuendos floating around concerning the identity of golf's "Big Three." "The new 'Big Three' is closely followed by a member of the old 'Big Three.' Player is only one stroke off the pace at 206 after hanging up his poorest round so far."

In the fourth round, Tony was paired with Palmer and whether it was butterflies or simply *tournament tension*, Tony said that he felt a little apprehensive about having to beat both of them in the final round. But there was someone else who had the hot putter that Sunday at Beechmont Country Club. Tommy Aaron, who Tony had beaten in a play-off in Memphis about a month earlier, fired a remarkable 66, which included birdies on the last four holes. Tommy was in the clubhouse with at 273 while Jack Nicklaus had fallen back and would eventually finish at 275. As Aaron was signing his scorecard, Tony and Arnie were heading towards the fifteenth tee and noticed on the scoreboard that both of them were currently tied with Aaron. Both needed a birdie on one of the last four holes to pull ahead and win outright. At that point, Arnold turned to Tony and said something that struck him as "an odd thing—odd for a professional golfer, that is, but very nice and typical of Arnie." Palmer said to Tony, "It would almost be fun to tie with you, Tony. We can have such a good match tomorrow. But now let's play just as hard as we can." They did, but neither was able to make the necessary birdie and a three-way 18-hole play-off was scheduled for the next day.

Arnold Palmer got off to a red-hot start in the play-off and pulled away from Tony and Tommy Aaron with a 67 and never looked back. The victory was worth $22,000 to Palmer while the runners-up, who each shot 70, received $8,550. Palmer, who lost in the Open play-off the week before, but had won the Thunderbird Classic the previous week, boosted his three-week take to $54,000 and his 1963 winnings to $85,454. At the presentation ceremony, Palmer said some comforting words about Tony's game. "I watched Tony come along since we roomed together at the Mobile tournament in 1960," Arnie said. "We spent some time on the practice tee together and his driving and putting have really improved. I'll be disappointed if he doesn't keep coming."

Tony countered those words from Arnold in a way that bespoke his opinion of Palmer as a golfer and a friend. "It was a great playoff until we teed off," he cracked to the audience. "I was stiff, tightened and nervous from too much playing and Arnie didn't help things with all those birdies. Arnie and I have one similar distinction—we are both Mobile champions, but after I won it they decided not to have it anymore.

"I would like to say this. The professional golfers, all of them, are indebted to Arnie Palmer for the color he is added to the game, for getting the people to come out and see us, and for the high esteem in which professional golf is held. He is not only a great player, but also he is a great guy and I am glad to have him as my friend."

Tony and Betty stepped off a jet plane in the Bay Area the following day to begin a short vacation in Oakland before rejoining the tour for the PGA Championship at Dallas Country Club in two weeks. He met the local press, revealed that his No.1 goal was to win major championship and he also disclosed that he would play in the British Open in 1964 at St. Andrews, Scotland.

"I was second in the Masters and fifth in the Open, and I could've won one, if not both, with a little luck," Tony said, not immodestly. "The PGA tournament is next and I intend to be ready for it. I hope the rest will help."

For the local media, Tony reiterated a few of the comments that he had made the previous day at the press conference following the Cleveland Open. "All of us who play golf for a living owe an awful lot to Arnie. He brings out the crowds, and that means money. In addition to being a great golfer, he's a great guy. When I started out in this game in 1958 I never dreamed I'd be playing for, and winning, the kind of purses they put up now. Arnie has a lot to do with that. I am grateful to him."

He then predicted, without much fear of being wrong, that Palmer will become the first pro golfer in history to win more than $100,000 in one year. "He's over $85,000 now and needs less than $15,000 to hit six figures. He'll go over the top in no time." When it was suggested that Tony, who was at $60,963 in prize money at that time might also surpass the $100,000 figure, Tony only smiled. "I'm only interested in winning a national championship," he said. "I hope I can do it in the PGA tournament, but if I don't, I'll be back shooting for the first one next year."

Tony got into a little more depth about a new plan he had in mind to prepare for the national championships in 1964. "I'll simply take more time off before the (major) championships to practice," he explained. "If I'm playing well, maybe only a week away from the tour. If I'm not playing so well, I'll take a couple weeks off to get ready. It may work and it may not, but I intend to find out. I feel it's worth a try. Palmer has made it pay it off for him and I hope it will for me."

The local golf writers who really knew Tony well said that he undoubtedly had the greatest personal admiration for Palmer and he also thought highly of Jack Nicklaus and Gary Player, but don't bring up the subject of a "Big Three" in Tony's presence. They wrote that he felt strongly that he could beat any of the three in any tournament he entered. "If I didn't feel this way, I wouldn't play," he snapped, showing the only sign of irritation during the interview. He also took a moment to credit his improvement the last year—an improvement that started in the closing months of 1962—with experience gained on the trials and tribulations of life on the tour. "I also have a better mental attitude, more determination and a tremendous faith in prayer," said Tony. "I don't expound my religion, but I feel everyone should pray, no matter what their faith." He said there was still another reason for his improved play—especially the last several months. At that point he turned to his lovely bride standing beside him and said, "Betty has been a wonderful inspiration for me. I hadn't really lived until I met her."

From Japan to Atlanta

Prior to the PGA Championship, Tony and Betty took a two-week break from tournament golf and attempted to relax in San Leandro. Unfortunately, it wasn't all relaxation as he spent hours meeting with his attorneys and drafting the final documents to end his contractual obligations with Jim Malarkey. Although there was a little heat flying back and forth in those meetings with both sets of lawyers, it was only a precursor to the heat that awaited the competitors of the PGA Championship at the Dallas Athletic Club. For the three practice rounds, the temperature hovered just over 100 degrees in one of the worst heat waves ever during a major. Once the tournament itself got under way, the players had four consecutive days when the thermometer climbed above 110 scorching degrees. As Herbert Warren Wind stated in *The Story of American Golf*, "When his daily round was over, Jack (Nicklaus) hurried to his air-conditioned car and drove to his air-conditioned hotel room, which he never left unless it was to go to dinner at some air-conditioned restaurant."

Considering the oppressive heat, the players put up some real creditable numbers over the 7,046-yard course that stood up valiantly under the conditions. After three rounds, Bruce Crampton (208) held the lead, followed by Dow Finsterwald (210), Jack Nicklaus (211), and Dave Ragan (212). On Sunday, Nicklaus withstood the "oven conditions" one more day and fired a three-under par 68 to finish at 279 and capture the championship by two strokes over Dave Ragan, who had a 69 on the last round. Tony played some solid golf (70-71-77-69—

287), but wound up in a tie for thirteenth. With the victory, the 23 year-old Nicklaus joined Gene Sarazan, Byron Nelson, and Ben Hogan as the only winners of all three American majors: the Masters, the U.S. Open and the PGA Championship.

In August, Tony returned to the east coast where he finished in a tie for 21st in the Insurance City Open and the following week he tied for ninth in the American Golf Classic played at the Firestone Country Club in Akron, OH. His friend, Johnny Pott, took the lead after the first round at Firestone and kept it all the way to edge runner-up Arnold Palmer by four shots. While in Hartford, CT for the Insurance City tournament, Tony took a position on the marketing strategies employed by the PGA Tour. "I think they ought to cut the tour and put up $1 million in prize money and split it three ways," he said. "Everybody, the sponsors, and so on, want Palmer, Player and Nicklaus—they think if they don't have them, they don't have a tournament."

Tony's locker room comment came when he was told that Arnold Palmer, a two-time winner at the Insurance City Open, and Gary Player were elsewhere on the touring circuit, but Jack Nicklaus had signed up. "You take people like Julius Boros," Tony continued, "who won the National Open and three or other fellows like that. When they sign up for a tournament, it doesn't even seem to count." Although Tony did not apparently consider himself among the "Big Three" as a drawing card at the time, he was in third place on the money list behind Arnold Palmer and Jack Nicklaus.

On another occasion, Tony sat down with a Bay Area reporter and tried to clarify his position on this subject. "I begin," he said, "by making it clear that nothing said or written about Arnold Palmer can be interpreted as a knock at him by me. I think he's a great guy and a great golfer. And a fellow of his stature must spread himself thin and travel a lot, which means he must miss many tournaments.

"But what I say here, I say to his face. And that is, that if he competed in all our tournaments, he may not win many more than he does now. No one can keep his game at a razor's edge through the whole circuit. Take the recent Sinatra tournament at Palm Springs. The winning score was 278. If Arnold had played, I don't think the score would have been any lower. It is true that Palmer is a great gallery attraction. When he doesn't play, sponsors are upset, which is really too bad, because there are still an awful lot of fine golfers left in the field."

According to Tony, the astounding popularity Palmer projected in the early 60's had done much toward expediting the growth of golf. "Parents are actually encouraging their sons to become golfers," Tony said, "just as they used to dream of having a boy who played football or baseball. The money is now higher than in most professional sports and the environment is good."

In early September, Tony was getting ready to board a plane for Japan to play against Formosa's Chen Ching-Po (yes, his playing partner in the final round at Augusta) on *Shell's Wonderful World of Golf*. He contacted Nelson Cullenward of the *San Francisco News Call-Bulletin* to let him know that he was starting all over again. The current contract with Malarkey called for the Portland man to get a share of all of Tony's earnings until the end of the year. He also held options to continue the relationship. Just how much Tony paid in cash to end his contract and gain his freedom he wouldn't divulge. "But you can say this. I've earned nearly $65,000 this year and I'm starting out again, broke," said Tony. "I've played all year for nothing." Despite rumors to the contrary, Tony said the severing of the contract was a happy one, and mutual. "But," he added, "I'm free." His fresh start in the pro golf world enabled Tony to keep all of his future purses, plus money gained from testimonials, instructional articles, personal appearances, and any books (*Golfers' Gold and Champagne Tony's Golf Tips*) he might write.

The contract was one of a series that started in 1958 and according to Malarkey, he backed Tony to the extent of as much as $21,000 a year, never less than $16,000, and saw no substantial returns until the end of 1962, when Tony began to justify Malarkey's early vision. "It was a great thing for me," Tony conceded, "knowing that I had his backing. But there comes a time when a fellow wonders whether he is playing for himself or someone else.

"I'm delighted to be on my own, but I'm unhappy about the way I'm hitting the ball," Tony admitted to Cullenward.

"However, I expect to put in some long hours of practice when I come home and I'll be ready for the Ryder Cup matches."

Shortly after Tony's performance in the Masters, the people from Shell contacted him and asked him to appear on *Shell's Wonderful World of Golf*. The concept had started in 1960 and featured the world's leading golfers playing on some of the world's most famous and demanding courses. In addition to the head-to-head competition between two of the game's finest players, the show featured a scenic display of beautiful and challenging golf courses along with an insight of that country's customs and atmosphere. Fred Raphael was the producer and director of the show that assembled some incredible match-ups over ten years.

Tony's match with Chen Ching-Po was played on the Fuji course in Shizuoka, Japan. The club is situated atop high cliffs overlooking the Pacific Ocean and beautiful pine trees and colorful foliage of all sorts separate the fairways. The production in the 60's was extremely thorough and nothing was left to chance except the golf itself. Part of the gallery was hired and they were maneuvered around the course and given instructions where to stand. Each hole took about 45 minutes to film since there were six mobile cameras and they were relocated after each shot. Similar to a movie set, the golfers were told when to proceed from the tee area and walk down the fairway. Once they reached their respective tee shots in the fairways, it was another 15-minute delay while the cameras were situated. The golfers would literally sit on a folding camp chair until the director summoned them to prepare to hit their shot. Then they would mimic a conversation with their caddy despite having made up their minds what club to hit 10 minutes prior. The 18-hole match took two days to film and Tony told friends that despite the constant delays it was a very exciting match. Tony edged Chen 69 to 70 and there is little doubt that after all that fidgeting and waiting and hitting and waiting, he no doubt celebrated afterwards by offering the participants and crew the finest champagne available in Japan.

For the first five years of the production, the commentators were the affable Gene Sarazen, and George Rogers. Rogers left the series and the colorful Jimmy Demaret, with his wit and humor, was along side for the remaining five years. The following dialogue took place between Gene and Jimmy on the first green at the Penina Golf Club during a match between Peter Alliss and Doug Sanders:

> **Sarazen**: "You know, Jimmy, we're here in farm country in Southern Portugal."
>
> **Demaret**: "Yes, Gene, I know we're in farm country. It's lovely isn't it?"
>
> **Sarazen**: "It sure is. How would you know this is farm country Jimmy, you're a city boy from Houston?"
>
> **Demaret**: "Well Gene, it's easy. Why, right over there beyond the fairways used to be rice fields."
>
> **Sarazen**: "Yes, but do you know that those are almond trees just beyond this green?"
>
> **Demaret**: "Of course I know they are almond trees, Gene. Just look at the way their nuts are hanging!"

At that point, Fred Raphael's sound engineer exploded with laughter and he knew they had another clip for their blooper reel since nothing like that could go on-air in those far more restrained days.

Over the next three years, Tony appeared on *Shell's Wonderful of Golf* on three more occasions. He played against Roberto De Vicenzo at the Glyfada Golf Club in Athens, Greece and Raphael had to get a little creative for this match. First of all, the course had just been completed and the clubhouse was barely finished in time for the cocktail party scheduled for the evening before the match between Tony and Roberto. Due to an insufficient watering system, the course was completely burned out and everyone was concerned about how the fairways would look on television because tourism played a huge role in the Greek economy. Fortunately, Raphael met up with a U.S. Air Force colonel who was about to play a round of golf and asked whether he knew of any crop–dusting planes that might be available. He knew a company and they hired the plane and pilot and bought all the green paint they could find and sprayed the fairways. Raphael said in *My Mulligan to Golf* that the place did not come off looking like Augusta National, but no one ever knew or questioned what they did. The match between Tony and Roberto was a great one, with Tony winning by one stroke, 66 to 67.

In 1965, he traveled to the Rungsted Golf Klub in Denmark for his match with Carl Paulson. His final appearance on the show was filmed in May of 1966 at the beautiful Mid Ocean Golf Club on the island of Bermuda. His opponent in that event was Peter Alliss, a gentleman with whom he had some wonderful matches in the Ryder Cup.

Years later, in 1983, I had the opportunity to meet Gene Sarazen. We talked about golf in general for a few minutes and then I asked him his thoughts about Tony Lema. Did he have any particular memories he would like to share? For the longest moment, Gene was silent, he stood there just thinking and slowly his lips began to smile. "Tony…he was a great player and a wonderful man. He had the type of game that would have remained strong throughout a long career. He was the most popular fellow on *Shell's Wonderful World of Golf*. He was a great ambassador for the game."

As Tony and Betty were flying back to the United States, he was looking forward to the Ryder Cup matches with an eagerness he said he hadn't felt in years. Representing your country gives each player a chance to rise above the self-centered existence found on the tour. As promised, he went back to San Leandro and spent a great deal of time tuning his game so it would be in tip-top shape. The day before the event began at East Lake Country Club in Atlanta, GA, Tony was asked about his thoughts of participating in his first Ryder Cup.

"We all will be playing harder and with more inspiration," he said, "because we're not playing for money but for the glory of the United States. It's an honor we can't treat lightly."

At that time, the total amount of tournament winnings for the ten players on the U.S. team was $459,386 and Tony's share of that amount was $64,675.

"Money's nice," Tony grinned while talking to a reporter, "but while some folks might think I'm waving the flag, this is a tremendous honor to all of us and we intend to play harder than ever in our lives." There was another incentive, a growing spirit of friendship strengthened as the week progressed. "You can't quite put your finger on it," Tony said, "but it's a wonderful feeling to have fellows like Palmer and Boros on your side backing you up, instead of running at you like they do the rest of the year."

The 1963 U.S. Ryder Cup team gathered for their first team meeting in Dallas following the PGA Championship. Besides Tony, the U.S. team included Arnold Palmer, who was unanimously elected as the captain, Billy Casper, Julius Boros, Billy Maxwell, Johnny Pott, Bob Goalby, Dow Finsterwald, Dave Ragan, and Gene Littler. At that time, only players with at least five years as a member of the PGA were eligible, so Jack Nicklaus, who had won the Masters and the PGA in 1963, had not yet filled that obligation. Thirty-two matches were played during the three-day event. Each match was worth one point going to the winning country and a tied match yields half a point to each side. Palmer's friendly but competitive attitude was displayed when he had his first meeting with the players prior to the opening ceremony. "Fellows," he said, "wouldn't it be just great if could win this thing 32 to 0?" That was highly unlikely, the British team was too talented and the Americans were extremely tense. It was professional golf's oldest international series, held on a biennial basis between the United States and the British Isles. The event at East Lake CC in Atlanta, Bobby Jones' home course, was the 15th meeting and the U.S. held an 11-3 advantage since the series began in 1927.

The Ryder Cup was established in 1927 by the British Professional Golfers' Association and the PGA of America under a deed of trust from the late Samuel A. Ryder, who was so impressed by an informal match between representatives of the American and British PGAs, held in England in 1926, that he donated a solid gold trophy to stimulate interest in the rivalry.

In Mark H. McCormack's *The Wonderful World of Professional Golf*, he wrote about a comment Palmer made that truly showcased the leadership role that Arnie had accepted and the confidence he had instilled in the United States team. On the eve of the match, at the introductory ceremonies, with the British captain John Fallon listening, Arnie handed out what must have been one of the shrewdest psychological blows ever in the series. When asked to predict the outcome, he declined, saying that he couldn't possibly have any idea how well the British would play. "I'll only say what I have just told my boys in the locker room," he said. "And that is that I don't think there are 10 players in the world who could beat us." The American players went around openly declaring that they couldn't dare lose—"not with Palmer as captain."

Some of the better-known members of Great Britain's team were Peter Alliss, Geoffrey Hunt, Neil Coles, Christy O'Connor, Bernard Hunt, Dave Thomas and George Will. There were some obvious differences in equipment and tactics. The British squad had the option of using the American golf ball, 1.68 inches in diameter, or the British or small ball, that was 1.62 inches in diameter. They chose to use the British ball, not only because they were accustomed to it, but also it had proven to travel farther and it was more workable in the wind. One major problem was its suitability to the texture of grass here in the United States. It seemed to nestle a little deeper in the grass, especially the rough. The difference in tactics was apparent as the British players, with few exceptions, were bouncing approach shots up to, and onto the greens while the Americans went for the flagstick. When the U.S. players got in trouble, they had the short game to save a shot here and there and salvage par. The Brits wound up making bogeys more often than not.

On the morning of the opening matches a large crowd was on hand along with a marching band. The United States flag was hoisted up the flagpole and the band played "The Star-Spangled Banner." Then the British flag was raised to the tune of "God Save the Queen." Tony shared with a reporter what his thoughts were at that time.

"When I heard the music and saw the flags of our two nations," Tony said, "for the first time I felt the full impact of why we were there. Our job was not only to maintain the close and friendly contact that we enjoy with Great Britain, but also to conduct ourselves in a sportsmanlike fashion, and to put on a display of first class, championship golf, and last but not least, to maintain our sense of humor. When you're representing your country, you have to be excited. Old Glory up there makes this more important than any tournament, the Open included."

The first day there was four "foursome" matches in the morning and four more in the afternoon. By "foursome" we mean that each two-man team played one ball against the opponent. One player drove off the odd-numbered tees and his partner off the even-numbered ones. They proceeded to hit alternate shots thereafter. Tony was partnered with Julius Boros for both matches on opening day and they halved the first match against Bernard Hunt and Neil Coles, but they won one-up in the afternoon against Tom Haliburton and Bernard Hunt. At the end of the first day, the United States lead 6-2.

On day two the format was "four-ball" which meant that each player played his own ball throughout the round and the "best-ball" of each team was matched against their opponent. Captain Palmer gave Tony the morning "off" but he was paired with his friend Johnny Pott in the afternoon when they edged Peter Alliss and Bernard Hunt one-up. Palmer partnered with Dow Finsterwald in both rounds winning convincingly in the morning 5 and 4 over Brian Huggett and Dave Thomas and prevailed in the afternoon 3 and 2 over Neil Coles and Christy O'Connor. Maybe Arnie was serious when he said the U.S. team could win all of the matches!

Heading into the third and final day, the Americans held a substantial 12-4 lead, but there were 16 points available as eight single matches were scheduled both in the morning and in the afternoon. When either team attained 16 ½ points, the winner of the Ryder Cup would be determined. Obviously, whenever that occurred, there may be a little celebration but all the matches continued regardless of when the destination of the Cup itself had been decided. Over the years, there has been much discussion as to why the matches are continued when the victorious team has been decided. I suppose the primary reason is that sportsmanship and friendly competition is respected to the end. Just "quitting" is something not found in the lore of golf.

Tony played extremely well in his morning round as he polished off Geoffrey Hunt 5 and 3 to garner one more point for the American team. His opponent in the afternoon was Peter

Alliss, who had defeated Arnold Palmer earlier in the day one-up. At lunchtime the scoreboard showed United States ahead 15 ½ to 8 ½. The British won only six of the thirty-two matches outright, but ten of the remaining matches went to the final hole and sixteen of them at least to the seventeenth green. Tony discussed his preconceived feelings about the opponents and what he learned about them during the Ryder Cup matches.

"I was considerably impressed by the British temperament," explained Tony. "I had always been led to believe that the British were a dry, stiff upper-lip-sort of nation. That perceived notion was thoroughly shattered during my very enjoyable match with Peter Alliss on the afternoon of the final day. At the second hole of a match that we eventually halved, I had a good shot onto the green, fairly close to the cup. Peter had also hit his second shot onto the green, but a good 35 to 40 feet from the hole. Then he stroked his putt into the hole for a birdie three. As he walked across the green to retrieve his ball he rolled his eyes, looked over at me and announced clearly, '*I am sorry.*'

"The crowd that was jammed around the green laughed uproariously and so did I. As far as I was concerned this was the high point of the 1963 Ryder Cup matches."

During another match, Tony was on the tee at East Lake's challenging sixth, a 180-yard par-3 where the small green was guarded by three bunkers and almost encircled by water. He was a split second from beginning his backswing, when suddenly there came the sound of a great crash of glass from the clubhouse several hundred yards away. He stepped back from his ball to regain his concentration, and someone in the gallery cracked, "Tony, there go the champagne glasses." Everyone laughed, including Tony.

So in his first Ryder Cup experience, Tony won three matches, halved two and did not lose a point. The United States went on to 23-9 victory, but Tony had to feel gratified knowing that he was responsible for 4 of the 23 points. Most importantly, for the next two years the Ryder Cup was in the possession of the United States. The next time these teams faced each other was in 1965 when the matches were held at the Royal Birkdale Golf Club in Southport, England.

The 1963 season closed quietly for Tony as he played in

the Whitemarsh Open at Lafayette Hill, PA and finished in 67th place. Two weeks later, he went back to Las Vegas to defend his 1962 title at the Saharha Invitational and finished in a respectable tie for twelfth and received a check for $1,562. His final tournament of the year was a tie for 17th in the one and only Frank Sinatra Open played at the Canyon Club in Palm Springs, CA and won by 24 year-old Frank Beard. Tony ended the year as the fourth highest on the official winnings list with $67,112 while Arnold Palmer maintained number one with seven victories and total earnings amounting to $128,230.

It had been a good year for Tony Lema. His only victory had been at Memphis, but his runner-up finishes in San Diego, New Orleans, Augusta, Indianapolis, and Cleveland had rocketed him to be considered a pre-tournament favorite everywhere he competed. It came as no surprise to anyone when *Golf Digest* announced that Tony had been chosen as the Most Improved Professional on the Tour. Notwithstanding the excitement he created on the 18th green at Augusta National, his marriage to Betty Cline was the most significant event for Tony in 1963. As members of the PGA tour looked forward to 1964 and the more than $2.5 million in prize money, everything seemed to be falling in place for Tony. Fred Corcoran was not asleep at the wheel as Tony's name was attached to pants, jackets, shirts, and underwear, not to mention assorted pieces of golf equipment. Tony had every reason to look forward to 1964. It might just be an exciting and adventurous season.

Try This Putter

Christmas for Mr. and Mrs. Tony Lema must have been a good one for a few obvious reasons. It was their first as a married couple and that's always special. Secondly, Tony certainly did not spend hours and hours away from home on the practice range at Lake Chabot because his golf game was not in top shape for his first tournament in 1964, the Los Angeles Open at the Rancho Park Golf Course. He made the cut but finished at 294, a whopping 10 over-par and 14 strokes behind the winner, Paul Harney, his rival seven years earlier in the playoff at the Imperial Valley Open in El Centro. But it didn't take Tony long to get his game back on track. The following week at the beautiful Rancho Bernardo Country Club (now Rancho Bernardo Inn), Tony finished runner-up for the second year in a row in the San Diego Open. Art Wall, Jr. won with a six-under par 274, while Tony tied with Bob Rosburg for second place two shots back at 276.

The Bing Crosby Pro-Am in 1964 was a great setting to test the finest golfers on the PGA Tour and see who would capture victory in the most challenging circumstances. The weather conditions for the final round proved to be a brutal test for the best players in the game. All the ingredients to determine a real champion were present along the rugged coast of the Monterey Peninsula. Toss in gale winds over 30 mph, a cold, slashing rain and for sound effects, throw in the pounding surf hitting the rocks along the seaside holes of the Pebble Beach Golf Links. Indeed, Mother Nature showed up and shrewdly said to all the pros and their amateur partners, "Hello boys! Can you handle me today? Because I'm here to stay!"

After three rounds, Tony was tied for the lead at 208 with Canada's Al Balding, both eight-under par. No one shot par or better on Sunday but Gay Brewer's 73 was the low round of the day. The wind howled, the rain fell and small-craft warnings went up, but Tony never panicked. No doubt the conditions were costly to Tony as he lost five strokes to par from the seventh tee through the tenth green. But he persevered and won the tournament (284) by three strokes with a hard fought 76. Even in victory Tony wasn't boisterous.

"I'll tell you for 18 holes out there today I was plenty scared," said Tony. "But I knew when I went out to the first tee that if I shot a fairly good score and didn't blow up, I had a good chance. I was driving the ball good, as good as I've ever done here, or as good as you'd have to, to win."

There were many turning points for Tony throughout the round. After hitting his approach shot long on the first hole, he chipped back and the ball rolled 25 feet beyond the cup. He calmly surveyed the putt and ran it in as the gallery roared. He birdied the second hole with a three-foot putt after a great wedge shot. On the par-3 fifth hole, he nailed a four-iron 10 feet from the hole and canned the putt for another birdie and the crowd murmured, "Tony's hot." But the treacherous 7th, 8th, 9th and 10th holes along the blustery edge of the Pacific Ocean awaited. On the short 7th hole, he hit a five-iron right into the teeth of the gale and landed on the green, but three-putted for his first bogey. On the 8th, he tried to run an iron through a bunker but failed, blasted out and two-putted for a double bogey. A bad chip cost him another bogey on the 9th and he went out in 38, two over par.

On the 421-yard 10th hole, Tony seemed to get his game under control until he stepped up to a two-foot par putt—and missed it. "I really felt bad when I started to choke," Tony recalled for the press. "The thing that saved me at that time was my sense of humor. All I could do was laugh after blowing that one. I was so anxious that I really charged the putt and ran it two and a half feet by. I managed to make that one."

After his blunder on the 10th, he missed a six-footer on the 13th but regained some confidence with a great sand shot on

14 and another six-foot birdie putt—he made it this time. He parred 15 and 16 but bogeyed the 17th where the day before he had suffered a double bogey five. As he walked over to the 18th tee, he had the final hole to play with a three shot lead over Bo Wininger and Gay Brewer, both already in the clubhouse.

"I didn't want to hit an iron off the 18th tee because that would have meant I'd had to hit two more irons to the green. And I might have turned over on one and put it in the creek (ocean)." So he smoked a drive off the tee, right through the wind and rain, nearly 250 yards down the middle of the fairway and said to his caddie, "Don't give me another wood until next week."

Tony made his routine par on the 18th and captured the title he had had his eyes on since those rounds many years ago as a junior golfer at Lake Chabot 82 miles north in San Leandro. He said this win was the biggest in his career and the most gratifying. Tony also had high praise for his amateur partner, Father John Durkin, an Air Force Chaplin and a close friend of Bing Crosby. Their 259 total in the pro-am was good for $3,000 second place money behind Mike Fetchick and Charley Seaver.

Tony was most gracious afterwards and said nice things about everybody connected with his win. He even credited the gallery. "I just can't say enough about them. It was wonderful the way they pulled for me and built me up day after day. Father Durkin's influence throughout the tournament was a big help. I only swore once and apologized and he took it like the great guy he is. A couple of other fathers (Father Drone and Father Scannell) were with us too."

At that point, Tony's humble golf beginnings were recent enough for him to fully appreciate the success he was enjoying. It was doubtful he would ever forget what it took to reach this pinnacle. "I'm glad I could accomplish something to make my mother happy," he said as he embraced her after his victory at Pebble Beach. "Goodness knows I caused her enough worry when I was growing up."

One newsman asked Tony if he was representing a golf equipment company and he flashed a sense of humor that helped him through some of the rough spots on the way to his win. "Well, I'll tell you. I've never played with a better set than these *Tony Lema* clubs," he joked. Actually, it was a perfect time for Tony to promote his Fernquest & Johnson irons and he took advantage of the opportunity.

First prize was $5,800 and the pro-am check brought his total for the week to $8,800. It was not considered official PGA tour winnings since it was a pro-am event, but those statistics never bothered Tony in the least. Besides paying his caddy and tending to travel expenses, Tony had one more tab he was more than happy to take care of before he left Pebble Beach. There were quite a few bottles of champagne on ice that Sunday evening and Tony had only one request. "Keep those bottles coming! We've got some celebrating to do!"

As the first half of the season unfolded, Tony played solid golf but nothing out of the ordinary. After the champagne party ended on Monterey Peninsula, (seems as though no historians can pinpoint the exact time) Tony headed up the coast to play in the Lucky International held once again at the Harding Park Golf Club in San Francisco. Chi Chi Rodriguez won his second tournament on the PGA tour with a blistering 65-66 over the weekend and edged Don January in a sudden death playoff. Rodriguez and January both finished at 272, twelve under-par while Tony finished at 283, one-under for the tournament in a tie for 25th. In February, he tied for 44th in the Palm Springs Desert Classic and played better in the Phoenix Open the following week as he tied for 6th at 277, six strokes behind the winner, Jack Nicklaus.

Tony placed a respectable ninth (75-68-74-70—287) in his second appearance in the Masters, but Arnold Palmer was untouchable. He opened with a 69, followed it with a 68 and 69, and had a five-stroke lead going into the final round. Midway through the tournament, Bruce Devlin said, "It looks as if we're all playing to see who will come in second." At one point on Sunday, Dave Marr had reduced Arnie's lead to three, but by the time Palmer reached the 18th tee, his lead was back up to six shots. Marr needed a birdie on 18 to tie Nicklaus for second, and Arnold considerately asked him if there was anything he could do to help, "Yeah," cracked Marr, "shoot 12." Fittingly, Arnie delighted the crowd and TV audience by ramming home a 25-footer for a birdie on the final hole to finish with a 70 and

276 for the tournament. It was his fourth green jacket and completed his run of winning it in the even years of 1958, 1960, 1962, and 1964.

Tony took a few weeks off and caught up with the tour in Las Vegas for the Tournament of Champions. Although Tony's victory at the Bing Crosby in January was not counted as "official" earnings, his victory in the Memphis Open in May of 1963 automatically qualified him for the 1964 Tournament of Champions. He finished in a tie for 24th at 295, sixteen strokes behind Jack Nicklaus, who successfully defended the T of C crown he had worn in 1963. Tony improved the following week as he tied for 17th in the Colonial National Invitational in Fort Worth, TX. He followed that with an 8th place finish in Betty's hometown of Oklahoma City and a tie for 12th upon his return as defending champion at the Memphis Open. Tony wasn't playing poor golf, but he wasn't hitting on all cylinders. He had failed to do anything noteworthy since winning the Crosby and it turns out Betty had supplied him with the correct formula.

"She told me to stick to playing golf and not go home until my form improved," said Tony. "Now I know she was right because it was just a matter of playing myself into form. I had to persevere with my shots until they became consistent."

The Westchester Country Club in Rye, NY was the site for the Thunderbird Open and everyone was delighted with the perfect June weather for the opening round. Canadian Jerry Magee started things off with a sparkling 66, but Tony wasn't far behind with a four-under par 68. In the second round, he closed strong with a birdie-eagle finish and posted a 67 for a halfway total of 135, leading Ken Venturi and Mike Souchak by two. The defending champion, Arnold Palmer, was in sight, only four shots off Tony's lead. The third round was played in a light rain but Tony rolled in a 20-foot eagle putt on the ninth hole to hold off a group of pursuers, He finished with a two-under par 70 and a 54-hole total of 205 to lead Souchak and Bobby Nichols by three shots going into the climatic final round for the $20,000 first prize.

Confidence is a wonderful thing. When Tony was being interviewed after the third round, he warned the press corps. "Bring sleeping bags Sunday. If I win this, it will be a long evening." Referring of course to his role as hosting champagne victory parties.

Sunday at the Thunderbird turned into a two-man duel; Souchak versus Lema, face to face, and the huge gallery watched every shot. Tony's three shot lead improved by two on the very first hole as Souchak struggled for a double bogey. Tony birdied the third hole while the burley former Duke football player made a bogey and Tony's lead stretched to seven strokes. On the short sixth hole, Souchak hit his tee shot over the green into a budding jungle and it looked like the high-stakes match was over. Hold on! Somehow, Mike had an opening and chipped it in for an unbelievable birdie. On the eighth hole, Tony found a bunker, made bogey and his lead was down to five. On the next hole, he had to crawl under a spreading fir tree and scoop the ball out on his hands and knees. He ended up with a bogey six while Souchak reached the green in two and two-putted for a birdie four. At the turn Tony's lead was three strokes.

Tony made a birdie at 12 while Souchak countered with an eagle. Tony's lead was down to two. On the par three 14th, Mike put his tee shot within four feet while Tony hit his into the gallery. "It was a terrible shot," Tony said later. "The chip was bad, and then I three-putted." His lead was gone! Souchak was ahead by one stroke with four holes to play. After they both made pars at 15 and 16, Tony knocked a wedge stone dead on the 17th for a birdie from two feet. They were all square standing on the tee of the 518-yard par-5 eighteenth hole. Neither could get home in two but Souchak's second shot rolled through one bunker ending up on grass just short of another bunker beside the green. Meanwhile, Tony had played his second shot down the left side of the fairway and had 90 yards to the plateau on the green where the pin was cut. He hit a tidy sand wedge eight feet from the cup. Mike could get his chip shot no closer than 25 feet and his first putt stopped four feet short of the pin. While all of this was going on, Tony had spotted Betty standing there in the rain on the 18th hole, walked over and said, "Honey, I sure made this thing interesting, didn't I?"

Tony took long looks from every angle of that eight-foot putt, then he took a few practice strokes, addressed the ball, stood over his putt...and froze. Suddenly, he backed away from the putt and gathered himself. A moment later, he addressed the ball, glanced at the hole and rapped it right into the heart of the cup. Tony had just won the Thunderbird Open and the $20,000 first prize. Second place paid $12,000 so that winning putt was worth $1,000 a foot.

Tony ordered champagne for the press, as was his custom, and promised the newsman, "If I win the U.S. Open, we'll have champagne, and hors d'oeuvres, too." One of the first questions asked in the pressroom was, "Why did you back off the putt on 18?"

"I stepped away from the putt on the 18th hole because I was so choked up, I couldn't bring the club back," he confessed. "I told myself, keep your stupid head still. I almost did. I looked up just in time to see the ball fall in. But when it went in, I knew I had licked it. I hope I never feel that way again. But the night before that final round I was so tense and nervous I couldn't sleep. I kept asking myself whether I was going to blow it. When Mike took the lead at the 14th hole, I think was shocked back to my senses. I knew I had choked, and it made me sore. I relaxed. Back at the ninth hole, when I was under a tree pondering a shot, I was so low, an ant bumped into me head on."

Recovering from what was eventually described as the most exciting finish on tour all season, Tony was numbed by the developments of that final round, which he reviewed for the press. "Winning, especially the way I did, when it looked like I was going to blow it, gave me the kind of lift I needed. It was the biggest thing I have ever done in golf. You just don't realize how it has bolstered my confidence, now I can go into the Open feeling I can win."

Ever the modest man, Tony chalked up credits to the man up above and his mother for enabling him to score such a resounding victory at Westchester Country Club. "Wouldn't have been able to do it without either one of them," chanted a euphoric Tony, as he inserted the $20,000 winner's check into his wallet. "The man on high looks after this little kid, and I only wish my mother could have been here to see me collect this money. She always doubted I could do it."

Then, he felt as though he needed to let the press know

just how indebted he was to his mother's generosity. "She really sacrificed for me when I was a thankless kid," he continued. "But I am filled with appreciation now. I remember when she dipped down into her purse for her last dollar to pay my entry fee in amateur tournaments."

According to *San Francisco Examiner* reporter Phil Norman, Clotilda Lema admitted that she had misgivings about her son Tony in the fruitless fifties. But she said that she is happy now that she had sacrificed and scraped to the bone. "I don't mind telling you I was very upset several times about his golfing," she said from her East Bay home after watching Tony's scorching stretch victory over Mike Souchak on television. "I told him to get out of the business more than once. But he wouldn't listen." Tony proved his mother wrong and she wasn't complaining.

Tony pointed to the 17th hole as the key to victory but refused to call it a turning point. "I had played the 15th hole pretty good and, although I was a stroke behind, I felt confident. It brought out that good feeling in me," he explained subjectively. "By the time we hit the 17th hole I felt the weight shifting from Mike to me. I really don't know how I made those good approach shots (on 17 and 18) unless that man helped me," he said, his finger obviously pointing upward. Tony said he was very aware that at one time his lead was seven strokes. And once again he used a word to describe his actions that few in the world of golf use except Johnny Miller. "I lost all of that lead and one more stroke because I choked. Just say I choked because that is a fact," he confessed. "After that the good man up there took charge."

All the way across the country in the sports department of the *San Francisco Examiner*, columnist Prescott Sullivan was typing his lead for Monday's edition of the newspaper. It was priceless!

"Promptly at 4 p.m. yesterday a case of champagne, iced and ready to serve, was delivered to *The Examiner* sports department, a fact which may or may not account for the mistakes in the first edition. The champagne was from Tony Lema and it arrived within an hour of his victory in the $100,000 Thunderbird Golf Classic at Rye, NY. Now we guess you know why we were pulling so desperately for Tony to sink that eight-foot birdie putt on the 18th green. It meant $20,000 to him and some mighty tasty bubbles to us and the rest of the lads in the office."

Sullivan was a little biased since he had followed Tony when he was making a name for himself in the Bay Area amateur tournaments. In the story, Sullivan explained the combination of Tony's personality and his chosen beverage.

"Tony has made a good thing out of champagne. It has become his trademark and hastened his development as a vivid personality in a game in which there are all too few characters worth remembering. 'Champagne Tony' is an exciting moniker. When its bearer is playing up to it, the galleries desert even the great Arnold Palmer to follow him around the course. You've heard of Arnie's Army. During yesterday's final, placards proclaimed the mobilization of 'Lema's Legion.' "

Tony had developed an engaging manner to go with his distinctive trade name. He was easy to like and the galleries enjoyed cheering for someone with an outgoing friendly personality. Although he was never much for book learning, saying the right thing at the right time was instinctive for him. And he never lied. When the man handed him the check for $20,000, said it was a "pleasure" to give it to him, Tony answered, "Yes, and it's a pleasure for me to accept it, too." You won't find many golfers more forthright than that.

Before he left the pressroom at Westchester Country Club, where the champagne was flowing, Tony said, "After this one, I hope all my friends live it up big. Let them have a drink of champagne on me." Informed that his preferred beverage arrived at *The Examiner* sports department less than an hour after his victory, Tony retorted, "That's just fine. Just keep drinking and hoping. I'd like to win The National Open."

Prior to the U.S. Open, the week after next, Tony had another matter to focus on before his attention was solely on the Congressional Country Club. The Buick Open was being held at Warwick Hills Golf and Country Club just outside of Flint, MI. He and Betty would be staying with close friends, (Mr. and Mrs. Clarence Jones) and it was going to be a good week.

Back in 1958, Clarence Jones had recognized Tony playing with Sam Snead in the Western Open a few weeks before the Buick Open and he could hardly believe his eyes. It was a great reunion and it continued to be just that as Tony always had a "home" to stay in when the tour came to Flint, MI. He got off to a blistering start as he fired a five-under par 67 on Thursday to take a one-stroke lead over Don Essig. HOLD ON! STOP THE PRESS! Later in the afternoon, there was a violent thunderstorm and the first round was wiped out. Tony masked his disappointment with a comment that no doubt had been conjured up by all the tutoring from Danny Arnold. "I won the Memphis Open after it had been postponed twice by rain," he murmured to the press. Forty-eight players did not get a chance to finish their round because of nature's eruptions, but there may have been one other golfer as disenchanted by the storm as much as Tony. Chi Chi Rodriguez had holed out a six-iron on the 507-yard par-five 13th hole for a double eagle two. Talk about an albatross that flew away!

Tony got right back to work the next day on the 7,280 yard Warwick Hills layout by firing a 69, two shots behind his friend Phil Rodgers. His second round 66 gave him a 135 at the halfway mark and a three-stroke lead. Tony made nine birdies in that spectacular round, six in succession and put it in cruise control for the rest of the tournament. His last two rounds were 72-70 and he finished at 277, eleven under-par and a three stroke win over runner-up Dow Finsterwald.

The headlines read "Champagne Kid Biggest Wheel in Buick Open" and "Champagne Flows With Lema in High." It was his second straight victory, his third of the year and pushed him from fifth to fourth in the PGA money standings. Needless to say, Tony was in high spirits as he hosted another champagne party.

"I wouldn't pass up the Buick Open Golf Tournament for the National Open," he said as another $8,177 was deposited in his bank account. "Consider me a lifetime member of this tournament. I'll play in this event no matter when or where it is held—as long as they'll have me." He also earned the use of a new Buick annually for the next five years.

It was hard to believe but even Tony was surprised to

have been able to post back-to-back victories. "It's hard to get charged up two straight weeks," he said. Obviously, the amazing six-birdie binge on consecutive holes of 464, 383, 595, 171, 432, and 410-yards provided the spark in that incredible second round. "It's always been my ambition to get the lead early in the tournament and hold it all the way," he said. Tony had 114 putts, (28-28-29-29) which was his lowest on-the-greens total since he joined the tour. "My short game over the last two weeks has been as good as it ever has been," Tony admitted. "You can't win unless you can get down in two from just off the green or out of traps."

The tournament was telecast nationally on ABC and the commentators were Jim McKay, Bill Fleming, and Paul Christman joined by Jimmy Demaret for that week. The paid attendance for the week was 48,695 fans, which shattered the previous year's record of 33, 904. The final day crowd was 19,041 and there was no surprise that many were part of "Lema's Legions."

In addition to the fantastic golf that Tony was playing in that two-week period, there were two small sidebars that appeared in the *San Francisco News Bulletin* following the Thunderbird Classis and in the *Flint Journal* after Tony's victory in the Buick Open. In the first one, Nelson Cullenward noted that Ken Venturi's third place tie in the Thunderbird and a check for $6,225 "looms as the most important golf news of the year." He said that Ken had been fading in the final round, generally finishing far down the money list. Many thought his nerves and confidence were gone but Cullenward felt "this ought to prove to everyone, especially Venturi, that he still has the golf game and can come back to the top."

Following the Buick Open, Doug Mintline reported in the *Flint Journal*, that Joe Black, the PGA tournament supervisor, says that everybody on the tour is pulling for Ken Venturi in one of golf's most gallant comebacks. "His struggle to get back on top has been a lonely one," Black explained. "After a highly publicized start as an amateur and young pro, Venturi practically dropped out of sight. But he hasn't complained." Mintline said that in 1963, Venturi reached a stunning low when he earned only $3,848 for 94th place among the pro money winners. His take in the Buick Open was $2,344 for sixth place and a total of $8,679 for the two tournaments leading up to the U.S. Open. Very interesting!

All eyes turned toward the nation's capital, the site of the 1964 U.S. Open, and in the sweltering heat the hottest topic was not Arnold Palmer or Jack Nicklaus, but Champagne Tony Lema. No one was more impressed with Tony's current winning streak than Palmer, the Master's champion who was looking forward to capturing the second link of golf's Grand Slam.

"I gave him my putter (a black Tommy Armour model) earlier this year in Oklahoma City. He was having trouble on the greens and I said, 'Here, try this putter.' He did, and he's been going great guns ever since. I should make him give it back, but I am no Indian giver."

So the conversation circling Congressional Country Club was: Can Lema ride his present impetus to a third tournament victory in a row in the pressure-packed Open or will he run out of steam? "He'll have his work cut out for him," predicted 1959 Open champion Billy Casper. "It seems only natural he may suffer a letdown."

Palmer disagreed.

"As long as Tony keeps putting the way he is, he will be hard to beat," said the general of Arnie's Army. "Sometimes when you get rolling you keep right on going. I remember back in 1958 when I won three tournaments in a row, the Texas Open, Baton Rouge and St. Petersburg, lost in a play-off in the Wilmington Open, and then won the Masters. Lema has a game to win here. He hits the ball long and straight. His confidence is booming. It's just a question of whether he can stay hot."

Someone asked Tony, point blank, 'Can you win three in a row?' "If I can put the ball in the cup, I might," he exclaimed. "I was just out there looking around. It's the first time I've ever seen the course. I can tell you I wasn't driving well at all. I mean it. If I keep this up I'll have no chance at all. There are too many good driving holes out there. If you hit the ball well, fine, if you don't, well…" He was asked what he thought it might take to win. "It's hard to say. We'll just have to wait and see where they stick the pins every day. I saw some dandy places out there today where they'll be nothing but trouble for everyone."

The Congressional Country Club in the Maryland suburbs of Washington was a long course, at 7,053 yards the longest ever for the Open. Until the week of the tournament it had vicious rough, wiry, and clumpy bluegrass, tall and thick. When the season began the automatic sprinklers had been turned on almost constantly, for the Eastern seaboard was parched by a lingering drought. The rough was still healthy a week before the Open, but on Sunday it began to weaken, on Monday it began to wilt and by Thursday it had just lain over and died. There was simply no thick U.S. Open rough and shots that went off line would not be penalized, as they would have been in cooler weather.

Still, Congressional was no pushover and Arnold Palmer's 68 in the first round was the only score below the par of 70. In the second round, Arnold came back with a 69 and his 137 nearly placed him at the top of the leader board. Tommy Jacobs, following a 72 in the opening round, fired a blistering six-under par 64 in the second round, highlighted by a 60-foot putt on the 18th hole to be the sole leader at 136. Tommy had been one of Tony's close friends for many years and he was no doubt happy to see an old traveling buddy at the top of the scoreboard midway through the Open. Tony's rounds of 71-72—143 put him seven shots off the lead so he still had a chance if he could put something in the 66,67 range together in Saturday's 36-hole test. It was going to be tough no matter what as the weatherman predicted it to be a hot and humid day with the temperatures hovering around 100 degrees.

Ken Venturi played steadily in the first two rounds, shooting a 70-72—142, six strokes behind Jacobs and five behind Palmer. Most fans were aware of how close he had come to winning the Masters in 1956 as an amateur and the two losses to Arnold Palmer in 1958 and 1960. But in that third round Saturday morning Ken Venturi started *in the zone* and stayed there. On the first hole, his ten-foot birdie putt sat on the lip of the cup for quite some time but finally fell. He made another birdie from 15 feet on the fourth hole, still another on the sixth, and then he knocked in a 25-footer on the eighth. While he was strolling down the fairway of the par-5 ninth hole, he was told a scoreboard was nearby if he wanted to look at it, for by then he had passed both Arnold Palmer and Tommy Jacobs. "No," he said. "I can't change what's up there, and I can't control what the other guys are doing. One shot at a time, that's all that interests me."

His next shot was a deft pitch over a chasm and onto the green where it stopped 10 feet above the hole. That slick, curling putt found the bottom of the cup and Venturi had played the first nine in 30. He picked up another birdie on the back nine, but the heat in Washington was becoming unbearable. The temperature was climbing to 100 degrees, the humidity was high and Ken was feeling the effects. Near the end of his round he wavered discernibly, missing a putt of eighteen inches on the seventeenth and one of thirty inches on the eighteenth, both for pars. His 66 put him at 206, in second position two shots behind Tommy Jacobs who had shot an even par 70 in the morning round. During the fifty-minute lunch break, Venturi was showing signs of dehydration and he drank lots of fluids along with salt tablets. An on-site doctor told him to withdraw. To play in the searing heat in the afternoon, the doctor said, was risking a heat stroke. But he insisted on playing, trying to keep cool by using cold compresses and ice packs.

Before he headed back to the first tee, Ken had a visitor as he lay near exhaustion in the clubhouse. The pro came by and sat with him for just a moment. "You can do it. Ken, you can still win this tournament." Having said that, Tony got up and headed to the first tee. He had his own work to take care of on that hot afternoon.

A few moments later, it was time for Ken to start his final round. Drawn and pale, Venturi was walking slowly on stiff old man's legs, but he was hitting the ball with astonishing sharpness. After parring seven of the first eight holes, he came to the ninth, the 599-yard Ravine Hole, still tied for the lead with Jacobs. Once again, he engineered a delicate pitch shot but left himself a speedy nine-foot downhill putt for birdie. He played it just right, the ball caught the corner of the cup, fell in for a birdie and he had regained the undisputed lead. He wound up shooting a 70 in the final round making par after par on the back nine while Jacobs could do no better than 76. Venturi won the Open by four strokes and the scene on the 18th hole was a magnificent moment in U.S. Open history. As he walked slowly down the fairway, with Joe Dey, who was refereeing on one side of him and Hord Hardin, a USGA Vice-President on the other, he was being applauded all the way. He blocked his 5-iron approach to the right, away from the water and the ball ended up in a bunker about 40 yards from the pin. With several strokes to spare, he played a daring floating wedge shot that sat down ten feet from the cup. The applause from the 20,000 fans started again and slowly grew into a tumultuous ovation. As his 10-foot par putt dropped into the cup, the crowd roared, and Venturi raised his arms. A television cameraman got the perfect angle for the world to read Ken's lips when the ball fell out of sight. "My God, I've won the Open."

Tony shot a pair of 75's on that boiling hot Saturday to finish in 20th place at 293, fifteen strokes behind his friend Ken Venturi. He simply did not get his "A" game going and those things happen. But Tony did something that showed nothing but class. Venturi was busy with the USGA officials, the ceremonial presentation of the trophy, and ultimately the press conference. Upon completion, Venturi received a telephone call from someone who wanted to offer his congratulations. Was it President Johnson calling from the nearby White House? No, of course not. It was Tony Lema, his Bay Area friend who wanted to be the first fellow golfer to extend his congratulatory message to someone who deserved to be known forever more as Ken Venturi, the 1964 U.S. Open champion.

The tour moved on to Cleveland and Arnold Palmer was there to defend the championship he had won a year earlier in the playoff with Tony and Tommy Aaron. There were a couple of changes from the previous year. The tournament would be held on the Highland Park Municipal Golf Course instead of the Beechmont Country Club. Secondly, the putter that had belonged to Arnold a year ago was safely stashed away in Tony Lema's golf bag. Remember, Arnold said he wasn't an Indian giver.

Before the tournament began, there was a proposal being bantered around that the 36-hole, one-day wrap-up of the U.S. Open should be abandoned and the final 36 holes should be played over the weekend like every other tournament on the tour. Tony disagreed unequivocally.

"I think we should keep it at 36," Tony declared. "It is the National Open. If a fellow is capable of walking 36 holes he should be able to play. And if he isn't, he shouldn't be in the Open. The combination of the long course and the heat in Washington made conditions as difficult as we'll probably ever encounter." Tony was never afraid to say exactly what was on his mind and take a stance on several issues.

Tony got off to a good start at the Cleveland Open with a six-under par 65 in the first round, one shot behind the leader, Al Geiberger. Talking to the press afterwards, Tony had words of consolation for the Highland Park officials or players who felt bad about the many low scores recorded on the first day. "It's a compliment to the course," Tony explained. "On some of the rat traps we play, you never know where the ball will squirt. That's not the case here."

They must have toughened up the pin placements, as Tony could do no better than a pair of 70's in the next two rounds. After 54 holes, he was three shots behind co-leaders Arnold Palmer and Jack Nicklaus, who were deadlocked at 202, eleven under par. Nicklaus fell out of it on the first hole of the final round, taking a bogey to Palmer's birdie, and never coming close to making up the two shots. Meanwhile, Tony began waving his "new" putter like a magic wand as he canned putts of 15, 15, 8, 5, and 18 feet for five consecutive birdies starting on the fifth hole. At the turn, he was tied for the lead with Palmer who was playing two groups behind him. Tony kept his foot on the accelerator as he drilled home a 40-footer for a birdie on the 14th hole and got down in two from 45-feet for another birdie on the par-five 16th hole. He was one ahead of Arnie when his approach shot stopped six feet from the cup on the 18th green. He needed that putt for an eight-under par course-record 63 and would force Palmer to finish birdie-birdie for a tie. The first putt slid by about 18 inches and despite the fact that Tony took his time, he missed the short putt and had to settle for a 65 and a fourteen under-par total of 270. Palmer needed to par the last two holes to tie Tony and he did just that—despite the fact that his putt on 18 hit the back of the cup but stayed out. Tony birdied the first extra hole with a 15-footer, giving him the verdict and reversing the previous year's decision in the same tournament when Arnie beat him 67 to 70 in the 18-hole playoff. For the third time in four weeks, Champagne Tony Lema was serving Moet et Chandon, a beautiful French vintage, to the press corps and everybody loved it. His money earnings jumped up another $20,000 and he was just over $60,000 for the year (not counting the unofficial $8,800 at the Crosby) and in second position on the money list. Life was good.

Left: The Lema children posed on the family car in 1936. That's Walter on the left, Bernice in the center, and Harry on the right. Two-year old Tony managed to climb to the top.

Above: Tony Lema (L) and John Fry (R) faced each other in the 1952 Oakland City Amateur Championship. Tony held on to win 3-1.

Above: A portrait of the Lema family. Row 1: Tony, Walter; Row 2: Bernice, Clotilda, and Harry. Fiv beautiful smiles!

Above: In his teens before he joined the Marine Corps upon graduating from St. Elizabeth's High School, Tony often had a golf club in his hands.

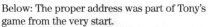
Below: The proper address was part of Tony's game from the very start.

Above: The "caddie dip" and an aggressive lower body was present in Tony's swing when he was a teenager.

Below: Tony and James Garner discuss the virtues of a mallet head putter. *Lester Nehamkin*

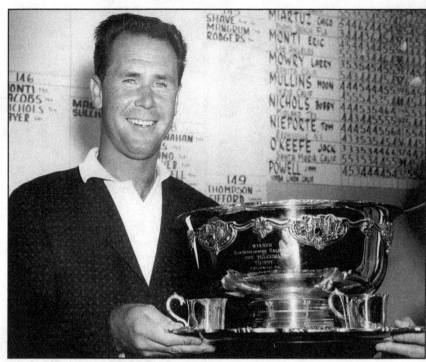

Above: Although it wasn't an official PGA Tour event, Tony's victory in the 1961 Hesperia Open in California helped rev up his confidence.

Above: Tony met Pope Paul VI at the Vatican in 1964. *Felici, Pontifigia*

Above: Tony gives President Nixon a putting lesson in February of 1966.

Above: Tony and Jack Nicklaus were undoubtedly deep into a golf conversation. *Lester Nehamkin*

Above: Tony, Sam Snead, and Phil Rodgers make a pretty good threesome.

Above: Bobby Nichols and Tony knew how to have a good time; on and off the golf course. *Lester Nehamkin*

Above: Father John Durkin, Bing Crosby and Tony braved the cold and windy conditions on the Monterey Peninsula during the 1964 Crosby Clambake.

Above: After his opening round of 75 was washed out because of a thunderstorm, Tony turned the tables at Las Vegas and won the 1962 Hotel Sahara Invitational with a 15-under par 270. His take amounted to $5,445. Tournament officials were almost as pleased as Tony. *Las Vegas News Bureau*

Above: Throughout his career, there was one thing that came quite natural to Tony Lema—the ability to laugh! And many times, it was humor that got him through the rough times on the PGA Tour. He was never afraid to laugh at somebody very close hand—himself! *Lester Nehamkin*

Above: The cold temperature and high winds made the final round at the 1964 Bing Crosby very challenging. Tony's victory was extra special!

Above: Tony doffs his cap on th final green at Pebble Beach in 1964. Despite a final round 76 i horrendous conditions, Tony w by three shots over Bo Wininge and Gay Brewer.

Above: Following their wedding ceremony at St. Leander's Catholic Church on April 28, 1963 in San Leandro,
CA. Tony Lema and Betty (Cline) Lema are driven to the
reception.

Above: Following a tournament victory, Tony
was always delighted to have Betty assist in
the opening of another bottle of Moet & Chandon champagne. *Lester Nehamkin*

Above: Tony and Betty took some time off the tour and
dined occasionally at the Blue Fox Restaurant in San
Francisco. Of course, champagne was served. *Fred
Lyon*

Above: Following his victory in the 1964
British Open, Tony and Betty flew to the headquarters of Moet & Chandon in France where
they celebrated his recent victory and the
extension of his contract.

Above: Tony rips through a drive in his *Shell's Wonderful World of Golf* match in Bermuda against his formable opponent, Peter Alliss, in 1966.

Above: Bunker shots were something Tony became familiar with as far back as 1957 while at the San Francisco Golf Club. The course had 200 traps.

Above: As his career blossomed from 1962-66, Tony never forgot the fundamentals of putting he was taught by Horton Smith in 1961.

Above: Tony reacts to the 22-foot birdie putt he made on the final hole of the 1963 Masters where he lost to Jack Nicklaus by a single shot. *James Drake*

Left: The four winners of the 1964 Majors gathered at Firestone Country Club for the World Series of Golf. From left: Bobby Nichols (PGA), Ken Venturi (U.S. Open), Tony Lema (British Open) and Arnold Palmer (The Masters). Tony won the $50,000 first prize with a 138.

Right: Tony played an exciting *Shell's Wonderful World of Golf* match against Roberto De Vicenzo (L) while the noted Gene Sarazen provided the commentary. Tony came out the victor as he edged Roberto 66-67 at the Glyfada Golf Club in Athens, Greece.

Above: The 1965 Ryder Cup Team captained by Byron Nelson defeated the British team 19 ½ — 12 ½. The players from left to right are: Arnold Palmer, Tommy Jacobs, Gene Littler, Dave Marr, Tony Lema, Byron Nelson, Julius Boros, Don January, Johnny Pott, Ken Venturi, and Billy Casper.

As a native of the Bay Area since birth, Tony loved his hometown and was proud of it. When introduced at any tournament or event, he insisted that he be listed not just as Tony Lema, but "Tony Lema of San Leandro." Friends and fans will always remember "Champagne Tony."

Tip at Just the Right Time

Fred Corcoran, Tony's manager, had pleaded with him to skip the Whitemarsh Open, outside of Philadelphia, and go on over to St. Andrews and get in as much practice as possible before the start of the British Open. Tony had never played "links golf" before and Fred thought it is so different over there and takes so much practice to adapt to a completely different way of playing the game. Tony refused to go early. He played at the Whitemarsh Valley Country Club, shot a very respectable 280, finished in a tie for sixth place and earned a nice little check of $3,917. As they were flying over the Atlantic Ocean, Fred was trying his best "to describe the demons that lie in wait on that windswept Scottish links." He explained "the special mischief of the wind that whirls and dances around the course, switching direction abruptly and erratically and changing the entire nature of the course with it.

"Let me tell you about St. Andrews," Fred said as the plane hummed along. "The course has been there since Mary Queen of Scots and men are still trying to learn how to play it. You haven't got a chance. You needed a week's practice, at least. Men have disappeared in Hell Bunker and have never been found. You can spend a summer in the Principal's Nose (bunker) or the Valley of Sin."

Corcoran recalled that Tony, jackknifed in his seat, turned those keen eyes on him. "Fred," he interrupted, "I don't want to hear any more about it. Just let me tee up the ball out there, that's all I ask. I let them build the courses. I play 'em…"

The plane droned on. "Mr. Corcoran," Tony said, "Do you

mind if I have a couple more drinks?"

A year later in his book *Unplayable Lies*, Corcoran described how he interpreted Tony's conversation on that plane ride. "His answer was characteristic. It closed the discussion with a flat assertion of self-assurance. There was no false bravado about it. It's just the nature of the man to approach the game with a world of confidence. He has jauntiness without cockiness that has led some observers to compare him with Walter Hagan. I think this is unfair to both Hagen and Lema. True, both have a sparkling zest for living and a tremendous flair for moving to the center of the stage. But you can't fit one personality into a mold shaped by another. Lema, in his own right, is a fresh and dramatic sports personality and his gesture of cracking a jeroboam of Moet for the writers when he wins a tournament is just a natural impulse which recalls the princely extravagance of Sir Walter."

Tony and Fred arrived in London in the early hours Monday morning, and from there to Edinburgh, arriving in St. Andrews in a chauffeur-driven car. In those days, the tournament started on Wednesday, with the final two rounds being played on Friday. As Ben Wright noted in his story for *LINKS, The Best of Golf*, many of the British club professionals who played in the Open in the 60's had to return to their hometowns by Saturday morning in order to open their pro shops promptly. A few years later it became a four-day event, similar to the U.S. Open, but it began on Wednesday with a Saturday finish. In the early 80's, the Open changed to the Thursday-Sunday format that is used today.

Tony's road to victory at St. Andrews was actually paved weeks before the tournament by none other than Arnold Palmer. Tony spoke with Arnold and declared his intentions of making his first appearance in "the Open" across the pond. Despite his tremendous victories at Royal Birkdale in 1961 and Troon in 1962, Arnold was disappointed with his play at Lytham St. Anne's in 1963 (won by Bob Charles) and decided to forego the 1964 British Open.

"Tony and I were pretty close friends," Arnold recalled. "After I decided not to play in the British Open that year I told Tony, 'Well, I can fix you up so you'll win.' He got inquisitive as he did all the time when I said something to him. So I arranged through IMG (International Management Group) for Tip Anderson (Palmer's faithful Scottish caddy) to caddy for him."

Within a month or so of his trip to Scotland, it seems that Tony was not certain he wanted to play at St. Andrews. He had announced publicly that he was going, but privately he was vacillating. "First he is going and then he isn't," his wife Betty complained. "I don't know and, believe me, neither does he. Tell me, are other golfers like normal people?" Only after his friend and idol, Arnold Palmer, convinced him that if he skipped the British Open he would be "missing one of the greatest thrills of your life" did Tony acquiesce. At the same time, Palmer felt it would be all but impossible to win at St. Andrews, because of the long flight and the Wednesday starting time would give U.S. golfers only two practice rounds in which to get acclimated to the much different conditions of Scottish golf.

After his last round in the Whitemarsh Open late Sunday afternoon, Tony said, "I just want to see how they operate things over there," and then he and Corcoran began the mad dash for St. Andrews. "Believe me, " he said before he left, "I'll take a close look at the course on Monday and Tuesday. I may even take notes." Tony was not a note taker. "If I had to carry a notebook I would quit the game," he had said. And as his friends learned over the years, Tony was not an advocate of repeated practice rounds, even before major tournaments. "One reason," he said, "is that I have very good depth perception. I can usually tell how far I am from a target even if I have never played the course before."

The Scots were flabbergasted that an American would actually attempt to play in the Open at St. Andrews without many, many rounds of practice. And that point may be well taken. By all rights, since the Old Course takes so long to get to know, Tony should have floundered around misreading the enormous greens, playing havoc with the frightening bunkers and spend a little time in the gorse for good measure. After playing 10 practice holes on the Old Course on Monday afternoon he was able to get in a full round on Tuesday. That was a real learning experience for Tony. He played more than one ball (it must be OK with the R & A) as Tip Anderson taught him where he could and could not hit the ball from the tees to set up the correct angles for the approach shots. Anderson's first advice was to forget the pitching wedge—heartbreaking news for the wedge specialist. A high-flying golf ball is no match for the gusting winds that whip in from the Eden estuary and wide open St. Andrews Bay. Anderson then suggested Tony use the smaller British ball, to cut through the wind. After one round, Tony said he would have preferred something smaller yet—like a marble.

According to Australian golf writer Tom Ramsey and a few San Leandro sources, Tip Anderson gave Tony some notes on a piece of paper. His first advice was, "Think left. This is a driver's course. Here are your lines from the tees:

"1st Hole: 20 percent left of the flag, 3-wood. 2nd: 25 yards right of Cheape's bunker, on left. 3rd: Slightly to the right of bunker nearest tee. 4th: Straight on flag. 5th: Aim for hill coming from bunkers to left. 6th: Aim left, on building in distance.

"7th: Skirt whins (bushes) on right, land right of hill. 8th: Short hole, don't run off. 9th: Line on flag, directly over left of two bunkers. 10th: Aim for white flag of 8th hole. 11th: Short hole, slopes towards you. 12th: Keep left. Aim to stop on flattish hill.

"13th: Drive tight on whins to right, playing hole narrow dogleg to left. 14th: Sight on church spire to right of town. 15th: Just to right of large bunker on right. Direction church spire. 16th: Bear to left of bunker group, playing hole as dogleg. Don't attempt straight line between bunker and railway (now fences). 17th: Care needed. Only tackle short cut over corner if driver's really working. 18th: Straight on monument, back right of clubhouse. A big one puts you on apron."

Tony learned in a hurry that he was not going to have to worry about taking notes. Tip Anderson, right alongside, proved to be the walking, talking encyclopedia for the Old Course at St. Andrews. Meanwhile, Jack Nicklaus was also a newcomer to the course and he had been following his usual practice of pacing off distances and writing down landmarks, eventually realizing that he could not carry enough scorecards to mark down all the bunkers. The Old Course at St. Andrews is not actually difficult. Cranky is a good word for it and as with anything temperamental, it can wreak havoc on occasion—and the occasion is often. It presents an enigma which the players who are attracted to it from all over the world never quite fathom. The course is shaped like the upper body and head of a serpent. It stretches out from the first tee right beneath the shadow of the awe inspiring Royal and Ancient clubhouse and the bleak gray town of St. Andrews. The first six holes go away from the sea—but never far—and then toward it again. The fairways are pockmarked with the most obscure and vicious bunkers and are all flanked with tough whin and rough grass. There are seven enormous double greens that roll with swells like an ocean as a storm subsides. They are so large that a group that is going out and putting on No. 5 may not even be aware that another group is coming in and putting on No.13, and they're all on the same green! Whether it's a coincidence or designed by the architects centuries ago, all seven of these double greens add up to 18. For example, hole number 2 and 16 share a green, 3 and 15 do the same, 4 and 14 and so on. Only four greens serve only one hole; they are numbers 1, 9, 17, and 18.

There are other hazards, too, including a railway line running alongside a large part of the course. Diesel and steam engines clatter and toot all day, and jet aircraft from the nearby Royal Air Force Station at Leuchars thunder across the sky above. But the biggest challenge to skill and forbearance at St. Andrews is something else—the wind. When it comes shrieking ashore from the North Sea, golfers who expect to shoot 72 are glad to get 82s."The great difference between St. Andrews and a U.S. course," said Jack Nicklaus on the eve of the tournament, "is that a large portion of the game here depends on luck. If you play a good shot in the States, you are rewarded. Here it doesn't necessarily happen that way. But who is to say? This is where the game started. Maybe we changed it."

Ken Bowden, the long-time biographer of Jack Nicklaus, was the first editor of the British glossy monthly magazine *Golf World* and Ben Wright was one of its regular contributors. The entire staff would attend the British Open, to which a minimum of 20 pages was devoted for the next issue, and they would meet beforehand and draw lots to see which golfer each of the writers would follow for the entire tournament. Of course, someone would cover the noted Americans such as Jack Nicklaus, other notables assigned were Australian Peter Thomson and South African Bobby Locke, then each a four-time winner of the event. Turns out that Ben Wright "won" the last pick and was none too happy to find that he was assigned to follow Tony Lema every footstep of the way.

He wrote that the local pundits scoffed at Tony's chances of success in the event, repeating that no stranger could master the Old Course at such short notice. Hadn't even the great Bobby Jones found that out, they asked? (In his first visit to St. Andrews in the 1921 Open, Jones withdrew after 11 holes in the third round when he failed to complete the hole and tore up his scorecard.) According to Wright, Lema arrived hung over, unshaven and hardly having slept in 36 hours. Yet he was on the course by mid-afternoon on Monday and played with Doug Sanders, with whom he was sharing a house, Phil Rodgers and New Zealander Bob Charles. Nevertheless, Wright's first impression of Tony Lema was a far cry from what he had expected.

"One could not fail to be impressed immediately by the sheer feline grace of the man, his wiry toughness and his enormous ability. Although his method was one obviously impossible for most ordinary mortals to imitate, it was remarkable for his fluency and perfection of timing. Lema's driving was then, as always, a joy to behold, even though he was plainly exhausted, and bent only on loosening aching limbs while making a cursory examination of the course.

"His pivot was immensely deep—the shoulders turning so fully—that only a superb athlete could achieve it. The left arm was as straight as a ramrod. The takeaway was very much on the inside, but a loop at the top took the hands high. The tremendously swift drop of the wrist on the downswing produced a very late hit. The knees were bent in their flex and they slid forward as Lema's long arms drove on and up through the ball to a very high finish in the accepted American manner.

"But even more impressive than his driving on this occasion was Lema's wedge play. He hit the hole three times during the casual round, with full wedge shots. The Scottish locals were still not impressed, however, complaining that no one who hits the ball so high could master the Old Course. How wrong they were!"

Despite watching Tony hit those high, floating wedge shots that were deadly accurate during the practice round, Phil Rodgers took Tony aside and gave him some stern advice. "Just listen to your caddy," Phil said briefly, "and do exactly what he tells you."

After all of the pre-tournament practice sessions were over, Tony pronounced himself ready for the Wednesday start. This somewhat cavalier approach was misinterpreted by the Scottish press as a forecast of victory. The next day a local newspaper headlined that sentiment and a horrified Tony Lema complained to Fred Corcoran, "I never said I'd win." Replied Corcoran, "Well, you have now." Stepping up to the very first tee, Tony paused to pick up a coin he spotted in the grass. "Look at this," he addressed the gallery, holding the coin aloft. "I'm already the leading money winner in the British Open." Thereafter, Champagne Tony became known by the Scots as, "the Jolly Yank."

According to an article filed by John Lovesey for *Sports Illustrated*, three significant things happened during the first round on Wednesday. First, Tony drew an early tee time and with the assistance of Tip Anderson, he carved out a 73 in the first round when it blew a "calm" 30 mph wind. Second, at the urging of his caddie, he played without his wedge, deciding to hit low pitch-and-run shots into the greens. No one knows what psychological torment it cost Tony to take Tip's advice, but he managed to shoot a solid one-over par round. And third, about the time Tony was signing his scorecard, Nicklaus was teeing off and the wind changed from a gale to a near hurricane.

Ben Wright said, "Lema's first round was a revelation to anyone who had watched him in practice. Now he was really working. His tee shots were rifled solidly and accurately through the strong wind. If one could have found a weakness in his game, it was the low chip or pitch-and-run shots that he attempted from around the greens with little success. Lema's 73, however, was the reward for utterly professional golf."

Nicklaus went out in the afternoon, when the winds were

twice the strength, and shot 76. With gusts up to 65 mph, Nicklaus drove the 381-yard 18th hole but all was not pleasant. "I putted awful," he said. "My eyes kept watering. The sand kept getting in my eyes, and the wind kept blowing me over."

The course was hard and fast. Fortunately, the tournament committee was careful to see that the greens were not cut too short. "If we had had them cut down," said Committee Chairman Gerald Micklem, "it would have been impossible." Equally impossible in these conditions would have been the American ball, and the American players turned gratefully to the smaller British one. "If we had played with the big ball," exclaimed Nicklaus, "I doubt we would have finished."

On the second day, conditions weren't much better but Tony played the Old Course as if he had grown up on it. "The 68 I shot today was one of the finest rounds of golf I've ever played," he said, "but I still don't feel confident. This is the most challenging golf course I've ever been on. You don't dare go to sleep for one moment. And to finish second won't mean a thing. In the year 2064, when people pick up that record book, this is the kind of championship they will look up. You'll be remembered only if you win.

"Look," he asked as he savored the tournament's 36-hole lead, "do you want to know what I really feel about St. Andrews? I feel like I'm back visiting an old grandmother. She's crotchety and eccentric, but also elegant and anyone who doesn't fall in love with her has no imagination. This is the shrine of golf and I've always wanted to play it." Then he sat down to a supper of corn on the cob, salmon with mayonnaise, curried chicken and pears with chocolate sauce.

At the midway point of the tournament, Tony (73-68—141) had a two-stroke lead over England's Harry Weetman (72-71—143) and a three-shot cushion over Australia's Bruce Devlin (72-72—144) and Christy O'Connor Sr. (71-73—144) of Ireland. Jack Nicklaus finished his second round with a 74, which was not bad, considering the wind and that 40 of those shots were on the putting green. It was the most putts Nicklaus had taken in a round since he turned professional. So that put Nicklaus (76-74—150) nine shots behind Tony and he spent two hours practicing his putting in the late afternoon.

Tony was inspired after two rounds and he openly admitted that he felt at St. Andrews like a new boy at school, one who was not sure he belonged. But the spectators were warming up to him, and the spectators in Scotland don't warm easily. For the Scots, golf is a national pastime. They are silent watchers, often signifying their approval with only the barest ripple of handclapping. But when a difficult shot has been executed with perfection, no one appreciates and understands the accomplishment better than the knowledgeable fans in Scotland. By 1964, they had taken to only two Americans since the days of Bobby Jones and his Grand Slam triumph in 1930—Ben Hogan for the perfection he displayed in 1953 at Carnoustie and Arnold Palmer for the boldness he exhibited at Royal Birkdale in 1961 and Troon in 1962.

"You don't have to get in really close to the hole to win their approval with a shot," Tony explained. "They know a difficult shot and appreciate it. And they know golfers." One of the first indications of the undercurrent of emotion that he evoked in the crowd came at the 12th hole in his second round, when he drove the green on the par-4 and knocked in a 30-foot putt for an eagle 2. "They seemed to loosen up then," he noted, "and it made me feel good." By the time he reached the 18th green and posted his 68, Tony Lema had captured the gallery.

The last 36 holes of the tournament were played on a lovely fresh day, with the worst of the wind gone and the sun shining. Jack Nicklaus, who trailed Tony by nine shots, was off on his morning round an hour and a quarter before Tony. As he came down the thirteenth fairway, he stood at five-under par for the round. Tony was going out the parallel sixth at the same time and gazed across the fairway at Nicklaus' scoreboard. As they passed each other, Nicklaus going south and Tony going north, Nicklaus squinted at Tony's scoreboard and saw that he was three-over for the first five holes. In other words, Nicklaus had made up eight strokes of his nine-stroke deficit. The two players stopped momentarily to stare at each other across the joint fairway and take stock of the situation. Nicklaus looked fiercely confident. Tony admitted later, "I didn't feel so good."

Tony promptly parred the sixth hole, and then went on a streak of making five straight 3's—three of them birdies—on holes seven through eleven. Let's clarify. He birdied the par-4 seventh, parred the par-3 eighth, birdied the par-4 ninth, birdied the par-4 tenth and parred the par-3 eleventh hole. So, when he met Nicklaus while he was in the sixth fairway, he was three-over par for the round. By the time he got to the 12th tee, he was even for the day and three-under for the tournament. Jack finished with a birdie on the home hole for a 66. The sight of Nicklaus' scoreboard was just the spur Tony needed to wake up and get going. From that point on, he made seven birdies and never once went over par. On the 18th, Tony holed a 20-footer for a birdie and a third-round score of 68. A Scot in the gallery was heard saying to a friend, "That slams the door, eh." His companion replied, "It locks it, mon." After 54 holes, Tony was seven-under par, at 209. His closest rival was Nicklaus at 76-74-66—216. Instead of the slim one-stroke lead he had when he and Nicklaus had passed each other, he was in front by seven full strokes.

The lead that Tony held was too much even for Nicklaus, who went around in another remarkable 68 though he knew the battle had been finished when his morning attack was successfully met. Tony calmly stuck to his own game as he coasted around the course in the late afternoon in 70 to win with a 279, five strokes ahead of Nicklaus and six in front of Roberto De Vicenzo. Tony was paired with the French champion, Jean Garaialde, in the final group and as they stood on the 18th tee, the crowd of more than 13,000 massed behind them. Tony's drive put him about 50 yards from the pin and he faced the deep "Valley of Sin" that lies in the front part of the last green on the Old Course.

"Maybe it wasn't the most important shot of the tournament," Tony recalled in the pressroom, "for I had a big lead by then, but the most dramatic was a run-up I made on the very last hole, a 381-yard par-4. It was a seven-iron that stopped two feet from the hole on the big green and gave me a finishing birdie."

He had barely swung at the shot before the gallery engulfed him. "I got hit four times before I finished my follow through," he said. For a long time he did not appear. Finally, he extricated himself from the gallery, arriving on the green like an actor late for a cue. He staggered out of the gallery onto the green wiping sweat from his brow with one hand and clasping his putter with the other. He knocked in the two-foot putt for a birdie, picked the ball out of the cup and threw it high into the massive gallery.

In *Great Moments in Sport: Golf* (1974), Michael McDonnell devoted a full chapter to Tony's glorious conquest of St. Andrews in 1964. McDonnell recounted how Tony birdied the last hole with a splendid pitch-and-run 7-iron second shot that rolled precisely through the Valley of Sin, his ball stopping two feet from the flagstick:

"It had been the perfect stroke for St. Andrews, and it demonstrated that Tony Lema possessed not only the instinct but also the comprehensive skill to adjust to whatever special demands a golf course presented. That made him a rare man, and his courtly manner, added to a personal magnetism, gave him a public appeal, which perhaps only Palmer of that generation of American golfers exceeded. That is the lingering memory…"

"All my life, "Tony said, "I had heard about the terrible weather conditions you can encounter at Scotland's seaside courses. Mix gale force winds, they said, with hard greens that won't hold a shot and you have trouble with a capital 'T.' I found out firsthand how right they were.

"It was nice during the practice round at St. Andrews, but somebody turned on the fan once the tournament proper started. Some sage advice I took from my caddy, Tip Anderson, gave me a big boost. Tip advised me to use the run-up approach when I could. He reasoned that the wind might blow higher shots off line and that the hard greens might not hold shots. I didn't even carry a wedge during the tournament."

At the 1978 British Open, won by Jack Nicklaus at St. Andrews, this writer visited with Tip Anderson at a pub in the storied Ol' Grey Toon. As he sipped on a stout lager, I asked what he thought was the most significant part of Tony's superlative play in the 1964 British Open.

"Oh, but the lad plyed so well," Tip eagerly recalled. "I con't sa' enuff aboot tha' accuracy of his drives. Outstandin'. I dare sa' he missed one drive in tha' entire Open. He asked me which steeple or spire to aim for and he was always on target. Yeah, I have fond memories of Tony. Wha' a mon, wha' a mon he was.

"It's thanks to Tony that I can tell Arnie—and I do tell him, as often as possible—You won two Open Championships, but I won three.' "

After receiving the Claret Jug, with his named already engraved upon it, Champagne Tony hosted his best victory party ever. He joined Denny Shute, Sam Snead and Ben Hogan as Open champions who won in their first attempt. At the press conference, Tony referred to Tip Anderson many times and said, "I couldn't have done it without him. He made me play the course right and gave me the right clubs to play it with, and when he handed me those clubs it was as if he was saying on every shot, 'You can do it.' "

Upon receiving the winner's check of $4,200 (1,500 pounds), Tony paid full credit and $1,000 to his caddie. "Tip did it," he echoed more than once. "He was at least 50 per cent of this team and I reckon to say 51 per cent would not be far wrong. He put the right club in my hand and somehow knew how I was going to hit it."

Tony's quick humor with the British press was reported in the August/September 1964 issue of *RX Golf and Travel*. "In burlesque of the inevitable and monotonously phrased questions that characterize such meetings with the press, Lema took the mike and without waiting for the probing, declared, 'I thought the course played very short; the pin positions were very unfair; and the wind was never a factor as it was blowing from all directions at once!' The press corps broke up as Tony continued his monologue with a discussion of the comparison of the small British ball and the American ball."

Perhaps the most noteworthy one-liner of the entire Open occurred shortly after Tony's cork-popping party had subsided. He was approached by another avid golfer, the Duke of Windsor, who, proffering him a glass, said, "I understand you enjoy a spot of champagne."

Sometime, between the moment Tony picked up that coin on the first tee on opening day and when his golf ball rolled through the Valley of Sin towards the cup on the 18th green at the Old Course in St. Andrews, something very special happened. Of course, he won the British Open and his name and memory will always be associated with the Open Championship of 1964. But Dave Marr recalled that Tony won more than the tournament. "Tony Lema," he said, "won the hearts and minds of the Scottish people!"

Besides all the fun and joking around that was part of the Tony Lema mystique and his unique characteristics, there was a serious competitive golfer who made goals and had the confidence to achieve them. The day before he flew off to the British Open, he was talking to a group of golf writers and prophesied. "Now I want to win a major championship. It is on my schedule of things to do, and I am going to do it." He didn't even wait a week. Mission accomplished.

Before Tony headed back to the United States, there was a little business matter that he needed to take care of while he was near the vineyards in France. Along with Fred Corcoran, he flew over to Paris and signed another contract with the distributors of Moet et Chandon. What began for Tony as a casual remark in the cramped pressroom at the Mesa Verde Country Club in Costa Mesa, CA had parlayed into a profitable fringe business with a company that produces 26,000,000 bottles of champagne annually. Somewhere in those classrooms at St. Elizabeth's High School in Oakland, CA Tony must have heard at least one teacher say, "When opportunity knocks, open the door!" He didn't skip class that day!

Fred Corcoran was uncanny in telling stories. He could sit at Toots Shor's in Manhattan and go non-stop reciting Ted Williams' stories, Sam Snead tales and of course, Tony Lema adventures. Two interesting events happened within days of Tony's return to New York. One of the first things he did was to telephone Arnold Palmer whose gift of a putter had started Tony's chain of victories.

"Arnie," he said, "first I borrowed your putter and won three tournaments, and last week I borrowed your caddie at St. Andrews and won the Open. What else have you got I can borrow?" Then, while Arnold was thinking it over, he went on, "...like, maybe, your bank book?"

For a guy who dispenses dollars like he was the Chase Manhattan Bank, Tony could have been kidding on the square. His classic comment has a strong Hagenesque flavor. He said of himself, "I don't want to be a millionaire; I just want to live like one."

While in New York, Tony received a telephone call from a young lady who handles the assignment of lining up guest stars for the television show, "What's My Line." She invited Tony to be the mystery guest on the show for the following week and Tony agreed although, measuring the fee against the inconvenience involved, it was hardly worth his while.

Meanwhile, the PGA Championship was being played that week in Columbus and won subsequently by Bobby Nichols. Back in New York, Tony had another call from the young lady at the network.

"You know, Mr. Lema," she said haltingly, "we try to keep very current on our show..." She started to go on and on about selecting guests but Tony cut in on her.

"What you're coming to," he said helpfully, "is that you don't want me on the show after all. Isn't that it?"

"Well," said the young lady gratefully, "we *do* try to be current, you know, and after all, you *didn't* win this week..."

"Gee, I'm sorry," exclaimed Tony, his eyes lighting up mischievously. "But you didn't tell me I had to win this week. I won four of the last six tournaments, including the British Open, but I slipped up last week. So now I suppose you've got Bobby Nichols?"

The girl confessed this was the case. She explained one more time they liked to be current on the show.

"Maybe we can have you on some other time," she said in a mollifying tone, "after you win *another* tournament."

Tony said that sounded like a square deal if he ever heard one.

"Tell you what," he said suddenly. "Why don't you set it up for a time that will be convenient for *your people* to have me on the show. Then let me know and I'll arrange to win the tournament that week for you. Or, better still...I'll win three in a row. How would that be?"

"Oh, Mr. Lema! Would you *really*?"

Considering the travel from Scotland to France to the United States and all the interviews and notoriety thrust upon him, Tony continued to play some pretty solid golf. At the PGA Championship at Columbus Country Club in Ohio, Tony arrived and his never-ending sense of humor had the golf writers in stitches with a running series of gags about his recent triumphant in Scotland. "You American people are very cordial to us for foreigners. But it's difficult to understand your accent," Tony quipped.

Doc Giffin reported in the September 1964 issue of *Professional Golfer*, that Tony was telling the U.S. reporters about the press conferences at St. Andrews and, pointing out that he had trouble remembering all the holes on the course as he was recapping his round, said that he kept forgetting one hole on the course. "Oh, so that's how you won the tournament," someone remarked. When Tony was talking with scribes, it was always a two-way street.

He tied for ninth place (71-68-72-71—282) but nobody could catch Bobby Nichols. Simply put, Bobby never ran out of miracles. It has been called the most unbelievable performance ever in the PGA Championship as he rescued himself out of trouble over and over again with remarkable pitches and putts and breezed to a nine-under par 271 and a 3-shot victory over Palmer and Nicklaus. A highlight reel would cause anyone to say, "Play that over again, I can't believe he got up and down from there." In the first round, Bobby made eight birdies and putted only 13 times on the back nine. En route to becoming the first wire-to-wire winner of the PGA, Bobby took only 119 putts, 15 fewer than Nicklaus took in capturing the title the year before in Dallas. What was Bobby Nichols secret? A week before the tournament he attended a party at the Owl Creek Country Club near his home in Louisville and found a used putter in a barrel in the pro shop that he liked. The price tag: $5. He bought it and seven days later everybody was convinced it was a magic wand.

Years later, Nichols recalled who his playing partner was in that fourth round at Columbus C.C. "It was quite an honor," Bobby remembered, "In the final round of the 1964 PGA I played with Mr. Hogan. I had worked at Midland, TX while I was going to Texas A & M in 1954-58. The man that I worked for at Midland Country Club was on the Hogan staff and would take me to Fort Worth and I played with Mr. Hogan a few times.

So he knew who I was and of course, I knew him. Later, when I got in his way near the clubhouse before a practice round, he would say, 'Go get a partner, let's go play.' "

August was another good month for Tony as he finished in a tie for sixth in the Western Open played at the Tam O'Shanter Country Club in Niles, IL. His friend Chi Chi Rodriguez won with four strong rounds for a 268, while Tony finished ten strokes behind at 278. Two weeks later Tony placed fifth in the American Golf Classic on the Firestone Country Club in Akron, OH where Ken Venturi won with a 275 and a five-shot margin over Mason Rudolph. It was Venturi's third win of the year (he won at Hartford in addition to the U.S. Open) and it meant a lot to him. "I proved to myself that the National Open victory was not a fluke," he said. "I backed it up now."

There was a return engagement at Firestone Country Club in September and Tony was more than happy to appear. It was the 36-hole World Series of Golf where the only participants were the champions of the four majors for that year. The field included Arnold Palmer, Ken Venturi, Bobby Nichols, and of course, Tony Lema. Tony played lights out with two strong rounds, 70-68—138, and he coasted home with a five-stroke victory. The winner's paycheck was the biggest in golf at that time—a whopping $50,000. After that landed in his bank account, it boosted his combined official and unofficial earnings of 1964 to $122,555, ranking him ahead of the two top "official" money winners, Arnold Palmer at $110,743 and Jack Nicklaus with $101,917. Needless to say, corks from bottles of Moet et Chandon were popping for the fifth time that year. No matter what the reports from the vineyards in France may have indicated, trust me, 1964 was a very good year!

It seemed like wherever Tony went he was piling up honors and cash and carving an ever-widening niche in the world of golf. A week after his win at the World Series of Golf, Tony returned to the site of his first "job" to receive the acclaim from a distinguished group of San Francisco Golf Club members. Tony was so humble you'd think he was still caddying at Lake Chabot instead of wearing the coveted British Open crown. He said to that special group, the two greatest days of his life were "the day I first stepped on a golf course and the day I first came through the gates of this club."

Club president Leroy Spencer presented Tony with a scroll proclaiming him "honorary professional of San Francisco Golf Club with privileges of the clubhouse and golf course." He also extolled Tony with these words: "He not only will be the greatest golfer but the most admired and respected." Tony's modesty and personality shone through his appreciative response.

He disclosed that the "darkest period of my career" was last year when he suffered an attack of tendinitis at the base of his left thumb and forefinger.

"It got worse and I was beginning to despair," he said. "That's when I came here to see Dr. Joseph Meherin and he cured me." Dr. Meherin was in attendance at the luncheon. Tony also recalled that when he was 12 or 13 years old, he came to the San Francisco Golf Club to see a PGA sectional qualifying.

"It was the first time I realized that courses had trees and sand traps," he said. "Then there was the time in 1955 when I was a brash young man out of the Marines. A policeman told me there was a job opening with John Geertsen as assistant pro. He hired me. What he saw in me, I'll never know."

With reference to Geertsen's broad shoulders, Tony noted: "I must have been hard to handle. But once I saw John with his shirt off, I gained new respect. Or maybe it was fear."

He said contact with the members at San Francisco Golf Club "gave me my first idea there was something better in the world then sneaking around and getting what I could." He paid tribute to friends who had guided him away from the "pitfalls of life" and hoped they would realize their contributions "when you see me playing." Tony said he intended to "rest and relax" until the first of the year, playing in only two or three tournaments.

A little while later, after the luncheon, he was teeing off in a foursome. He and National Junior Champion Johnny Miller played against Geertsen and long time friend John Fennelly. With more than 100 following the foursome, Tony shot a three-under par 68 as he and Johnny Miller won, 3 and 2. Geertsen and Miller had 73s and Fennelly a 75.

At the luncheon, Johnny Miller was presented a trophy for being named the nation's outstanding teen-age athlete of the year by *Sports Illustrated*, first golfer to be so honored.

At age 30, Tony had become one of the five or six best golfers in the world. From the fall of 1962 until the fall of 1964, his achievements had been bordering on fantastic. In 1963, he played in 25 tournaments, averaged 70.85 strokes per round and wound up fourth on the money list. In 1964, he played in 21 events, his scoring average was 70.89, and once again he finished fourth on the money list. He played superbly on the 1963 Ryder Cup team and was in good position to make the team for the 1965 matches. Without a doubt, Tony Lema had "arrived." On top of all those statistics was an important attribute in his favor that cannot be calculated. He was still having a good time. Golf was a game and he was enjoying it to the fullest. For a couple of years he had been contradicting his critics by scoring steadily with his personal philosophy.

"I'm considered a carefree sort," he explained. "But people don't realize that carefree guys can have hot temperaments, too, which I do. I used to get plenty hot. I couldn't forgive myself for a bad shot or bad round. I'd blow myself out of the money time after time. It's the easiest game in the world to replay. You say to yourself, if I hit the better shot here, or taken a four instead of five there, or play the way I should have played yesterday, everything would be great now. We have brooders on the tour who are useless because of this. There's a lot riding on every shot, but you can't let it get to you or you'd go out of your mind."

These are faults that all golfers have whether you're playing for a beer, a $2 Nassau or something a whole lot more. What applied to Tony on the tour, applies to all golfers.

"I still get plenty hot, but I've learned to throw it away. It doesn't stick with me. The next stroke counts as much as the last one, and missing a short putt doesn't mean I have to drive the next ball out of bounds. I came to see that today is a brand-new day, as important as yesterday.

"So, I am not the perfect golfer. There is no such animal. It is almost guaranteed that I will hit a few bad shots in every round, and play some bad rounds. But I can cancel these out with good shots and good rounds. If I can't win, it's not the end of the world. Maybe I can finish second. Maybe I'll win next week.

"They used to say I couldn't win because I cut up too much, but that's why I do win. You can't take your self too seriously, you know. It's supposed to be a fun game, but for most guys, even those on the public courses, it's not. When it's not fun for me anymore, I'll get the hell away from it. After you reach a certain point in ability, golf is mostly mental. There are guys who play to 70 percent of their ability, and others who play to 130 per cent."

Some interesting statistics concerning the growing popularity of golf surfaced in 1964. Twenty years earlier, in 1944, there were less than a million golfers playing on a regular basis and they spent $38 million on golf equipment. In 1964, there were 10 million golfers who spent $250 million on equipment and another $380 million on booze in the clubhouse bars annually. In that 20-year period, the number of fans attending PGA events and exhibitions had grown from 300,000 annually to 1,320,000 and with the television exposure spurned by Arnold Palmer; many non-golfers were becoming attached to the game. The purses for PGA events had escalated to $1,360,000 yearly.

In 1950, the leading money winner on the tour earned around $30,000. By 1963, twenty golfers made more than $30,000 and sixty made at least $10,000. In 1963, Jack Nicklaus earned $152,000, Arnold Palmer $135,000, Julius Boros $98,000, while Tony had banked $67,000. By mid-season of 1964, before his British Open triumph, Tony had pulled in nearly $65,000, almost equaling his earnings for 1963.

Obviously, Tony was climbing up the celebrity ladder, as well. A few wins after his initial champagne party at the Orange County Open, he substituted imported champagne for "that domestic kid stuff." The new tradition lured bigger crowds of freeloading writers. After one of his victories that summer, Tony was looking at a full house in the pressroom. "I've counted heads," he said. "Will you fellows settle for soft drinks?" They wouldn't, so an attendant was waved in with a case of the bubbly.

After one hot round, the locker room man presented Tony with champagne. In a few events, Tony served champagne upon his arrival. "You fellows created a fine image for me with this 'Champagne Tony' bit and I'd like to keep it alive," he told a group of journalists. "I shouldn't limit the champagne to my first-place finishes. If I hit a dry spell, we all will."

In his article for *TRUE, The Man's Magazine*, Bill Libby recorded from Tony some ideas on how to enjoy golf but not take it so seriously.

Tony's Tips to Make You a Carefree Golfer

1. Get a girl friend or get married. Soft words and soft lips can make you forget a bad round quicker then anything else. But keep her off the course. If she's not worrying about her game, she can help you forget yours. There's room for only one golfer in the family. Except if you have a son, encourage him to play. There's so much loot in the game these days, he may make enough so you won't have to bother.
2. Don't take advice from anyone you can beat. If you do take advice, don't take much. Quit looking for some secret to the game. There's no secret. There's only practicing and playing. Quit fooling around with your game. Most golfers experiment so much, they remind me of the fellow who keeps sawing legs of the table: it's never going to come out level.
3. Play for a little money. The only way to really improve is to put yourself under pressure. But never play for so much it'll hurt you to lose. And never bet with someone you can't beat. And if it's someone you can beat, always offer him one-stroke less handicap than he needs.
4. Don't try to bear down from the first hole to the 18th green. No one's nerves can take it. Relax between shots. Talk with the other players as you walk around the course. And don't talk golf. If they're grouchy, find someone else to play with. Save your concentration for the shots themselves. Learn to turn it on and turn it off.
5. Get so you're as proficient at playing the 19th hole, as you are the other 18. A good golfer can hold his liquor. A carefree golfer leaves his golf on the course. If golf gets to be your whole life, give up the game. There are other things in life besides golf. Go out and look for them. And if you find them, let me know. Maybe there's something I've missed.

While relaxing that fall, the subject came up about his teenage years when he was running around, boozing it up, and hanging out with a tough gang. "We'd booze it up," he recalled. "It gave us a lot of false courage. We'd look for trouble. I'm lucky I was never caught."

A laugh broke up his pixie face. "I'm only kidding," he said. "It was bad, but not that bad. I caddied. I worked in canneries, shipyards, drug stores, grocery stores, and gas stations. I usually worked nights so I could be on the golf course days. I learned from anyone who would teach me anything. When I got good, I hustled—I even hustled pros. I could pick up a few bucks on the putting greens, maybe $25 or $30 on a round out on the course.

"You know, when you're playing tournaments and you blow $1,000, it's $1,000 you never had. When you're hustling, you can blow the money in your own pocket...if you have any. I bet lots of times without a buck to back me up. It's a funny thing though, when I couldn't afford to lose, I never lost."

In sharp contrast to someone like Ben Hogan, Tony has always been considered outgoing with the press, playing partners, the fans. his caddies, and of course Betty, his wife.

"Lots of times I don't talk golf, which is why I like to have my wife follow me around. We can talk about what we're going to do that evening and so forth and it relaxes me. The fans are fine, but they're not part of me, if you know what I mean. I can't walk a whole round with my tail between my legs. Concentration is the most important thing in golf, but it is not possible to concentrate from the first tee to the 18th green. I save it for my shots and relax in-between. You have to be able to be focused one hundred per cent for each shot."

More articles in national magazines continued to appear as his popularity soared. His galleries continued to grow and soon diehard fans called themselves "Lema's Legions" in comparison to "Arnie's Army." Of course, his followers did not match Palmer's in size, but many times he would be paired with unknowns and as his starting time got closer, the area around the first tee would become 'standing room only.' Betty told close friends that his gallery is so much larger than last year she feels lucky if she gets to see half of his shots. She learned some hard lessons in fan psychology. In an interview with Bill Libby, she shook her head, frowned, and complained. "I keep hearing things like, 'What happened to Palmer? How come he only finished second?' Once I heard one fan say, 'Make way, here comes Tony Lema, the playboy of the western world.' The other day, I heard one say, 'The way Lema's playing, he must still be drunk from all the champagne he put away last night.' I wanted to punch him."

Tony overheard Betty and just smiled. "We play under some bad conditions sometimes, and we are only human," he added. "No one cares whether you are well or sick or tired, maybe worried about something, they just expect you to play well and play your best. It's very hard sometimes, even for me."

Tommy Jacobs, one of Tony's traveling partners back in 1958 and 1959, often saw both sides of his friend. "Tony had his down side; he could be cantankerous," Jacobs said, "but he was basically a good person underneath. Like Chi Chi Rodriguez, he went out of his way to be nice to kids."

He also had a sense of humor. Jacobs told of the time Tony hit his approach shot over a green, the ball coming to a rest in a women's lap. "Tony walked up and solemnly looked the situation over," Jacobs recalled, "then he took out his sand wedge. He made a couple of practice swings, taking a big divot each time—all still with a straight face. Then he turned to the woman and said, 'Brace yourself, lady. This may smart a little.' "

In a reflective mood, Tony talked about the doors that opened because of his accomplishments in golf. "We're lucky, Betty and I, that our job is one we like. A lot of things come through golf. Last week we were down in Hollywood doing some filming for the "Hazel" show, (directed by Danny Arnold). Earlier this year we had a first class all-expense paid trip to London when I played in the British Open. We were met by a chauffeured limousine, taken to all the best places, shown everything. I even had a lesson in a game called Chemin de Fer, based on the same principles as Baccarat.

"It just happens that what I do for a living gets me in the papers and leads to other things. But if there is one thing golf has taught me, it is respect for a professional in any field. The man who parks cars, the guy who runs an elevator, public relations people—everybody has his chosen job to do, and I know it takes working his fanny off 12 hours a day to do it well. The boy who caddied for me today in the Almaden was just as professional as I will ever be."

In that interview, Betty nodded her agreement at his "job" comment, admitted that her stint as an American Airlines hostess before marriage prepared her for keeping his appointments, commitments and disposition in order, and said, "Experience helps."

After they met on the flight from Dallas to San Francisco, they had dinner together but they didn't see each other again until three months later when he flew back to Dallas and she was on his flight. "Then I started going to golf tournaments," she said happily, "and here I am!"

Through Fred Corcoran's connections, Tony had become affiliated with *Palm Beach* and *Jockey* clothing and he really appreciated good fashion. "I throw out anything that's not good; everyone should," he said. "A man needs to like everything he wears. I really like these things with my champagne glass emblem on them." The *Palm Beach* clothing line was scheduled to come out with the "Tony Lema" attire around the first of the year in 1965. "They're light, comfortable and very good looking."

As the season was winding down, Betty talked about the attention Tony received from both the press and the public. "We have no privacy," she sighed. "I am not used to being the wife of a celebrity. I don't know how to handle it. I'm embarrassed by it."

"She's learning," Tony said. "For myself, I eat it up. I never wanted to be a 'who's he?' and I admit it. Oh, I don't like holding long conversations with total strangers, but I enjoy hearing them say they're my fans. I don't like giving up my free time for interviews, especially when reporters misquote me, but you find out who plays dirty pool quick enough, and for the most part, the reporters are real considerate guys, and to a certain extent they've made me what I am today.

"There are many things that enter into it, of course. I had to begin playing good golf or it wouldn't have come to anything. I had to begin at the right place at the right time: The Masters on TV was a dull show last year until I sank that tricky putt that almost beat Nicklaus. I lost, but I stole the show. There are a lot of good golfers, but I stand out. In some tourneys, I'm billed only as 'Champagne Tony,' no last name or anything. The writers did that and I'm grateful."

Tony felt that his public image was changing. "I'm the same guy I always was, but there are exceptions," he explains, "I'm older and more mature. I'm married now. And I'm an important athlete now. People watch me. Kids copy me. I'd be blind not to see that I have new responsibilities now. And I'm willing to meet them. My philosophy of life has changed, but I do have to go about things a bit differently. I need a different publicity, not that cheap theatrical stuff.

"Actually, I've never been in any scandals and I never want to be. I don't dig those characters that go in for sensation. I'm as honest as I can be about the kind of guy I am, but I'm not looking to show off in public. If I ran around on my wife, I wouldn't broadcast it."

Betty Lema made a face, so he leaned over and kissed her. "Not that I'd ever do such a thing," he grinned.

Tony and Betty lived in a plush two-bedroom apartment overlooking a lagoon in San Leandro, but spent only a few months there each year. And of course that was divided into a few days here and a few days there. Tony played in 21 official events in 1964, but after the unofficial events (the Crosby, etc.) in this country, plus another five or six weeks of tournaments overseas, and another five or six weeks of exhibitions and TV matches, he was continuously on the road.

"The money's so big, it's getting harder and harder to pass anything up," he admitted. "It kills you to play without letup, but you're afraid the one you pass up might be the hot one for you. You take the TV stuff seriously, too, because the loot is large there, too."

Betty wanted to express her feelings about life on the road. Remember, she was accustomed to traveling as an airline stewardess. "We have a lot of fun. Life with Lema has to be fun," she said, "but there are a lot of small inconveniences on tour. Living out of the suitcase is hard. We are always leaving things behind. We are always having trouble with our laundry.

But the worst thing is just not having a feeling of permanence."

"We're gypsies," Tony said. "There are two or three towns we play when we have good friends to stay with, where we can relax and feel at home. We stay with friends in L.A., for example. They have this bathtub as big as the pool. They could see we wanted to bathe in it, so they cleared out one night and gave us the run of the place. Unfortunately, there's not many like that."

During this particular interview, Tony was driving in San Diego on the way to a restaurant. The lights of San Diego loomed ahead. "I'm hungry," he said. "In fact, I'm starving. No one thinks of feeding the golf pro during his round, but everyone's feeding their faces around him. My wife had hot dogs in her mouth all day. One of the bad things for me is not being able to go to the icebox when I'm hungry at night. Most of the motels don't have room service. Aw, hell, it's all in what you get used to. There was a time I would have settled for two meals a day."

While at the restaurant, Tony had some down to earth comments about his life. "If I hadn't made it," he explained, "I'd have still had fun. Making it was even more fun. I enjoy being a celebrity; I enjoy leading a good life. I'd enjoy it more if I weren't so suspicious of people. It's very sad. Now that I'm doing well, all sorts of people want to be friends with me. But, I know their friendship depends on my doing well, so I don't want to be friendly with them. We have a saying on tour: 'Last week they drove me home to their house for dinner. This week I can't even get a ride into town.' Sadly, there's a lot of truth to it.

"When I first went home, no one would have anything to do with me. All right, I was a wild kid, but I never hurt anyone. I found out people who won't forgive or forget...until you make it big. Then, suddenly, it's different. But, why? I'm the same person I was. I'll be honest: I think I'm better than the average person, but because of my intelligence, my speech, my manners, my way of life, not because of my golf. I am a good golfer, but what does that prove? I love golf, but it's not my whole life. Is it so wrong to want people to like me for myself, with all my virtues and vices, honest and above board, not just for my golf?"

He sipped his coffee and then he leaned back. The old smile began to erase the regret on his face. "Well, what the hell," he said. "I can't complain. I think my mother, my family, my friends are proud of me. I have a wonderful wife and I think she's proud of me. I've done well and I've got a chance to do better. For the rest of it, well, there's nothing I can do about it, is there? I'll just have to take it as it comes and enjoy it while I can. If I don't have fun now, it may be too late later."

Honey, You're Not That Good

Before we focus on the highlights of Tony's 1965 PGA season, let's take one more look at 1964. All Tony did was win more money on the golf course than anyone else. His official earnings amounted to $74,130; unofficial (Crosby, British Open, World Series of Golf exhibition) was $63,959, for a total of $138,089. In the official earnings list, he finished fourth, behind Jack Nicklaus ($113,284), Arnold Palmer ($113,203), and Billy Casper ($90,653). The final standings for the Vardon Trophy (lowest stroke average) was Palmer at 70.010, Casper second at 70.359, Venturi third at 70.942, and Tony finishing sixth at 71.170. In the Ryder Cup standings, from July 23, 1963 through December 31, 1964, Arnold Palmer was at the top of that list followed by Casper, Venturi, Lema, Jacobs, Souchak, Boros, Hebert, McGowan and Gay Brewer. Jack Nicklaus had not yet been a PGA cardholder for the mandatory five years.

Despite histrionics by a host of great players, notably Tony Lema for winning six tournaments and Jack Nicklaus for winning four, Ken Venturi won the Golfer of the Year from the PGA and he was also named *Sports Illustrated's* Sportsman of the Year. Because of his dramatic clawing from the bottom to the top, Venturi's heroic efforts in the sweltering heat at Congressional in the U.S. Open, caused Nicklaus and Lema to have been forgotten men. Had Venturi collapsed in the heat and U.S. Open pressure at Congressional, Tony would have been the logical choice.

Two years earlier, during the Florida swing of the 1963 season, Fred Corcoran was talking with one of the leading professionals; a former PGA and Masters champion, and asked him a most interesting question. "If you had to pick the 10 most promising young golf professionals, whom would you name?"

The veteran said he would give it some thought and, a few days later, he handed a list to Fred who carried it around in his pocket for a few weeks. One day, during the Doral Open in Miami, Fred showed the list to Chick Harbert and asked him for a candid appraisal. Chick was one of the most articulate and tough-minded men in the business. He skimmed the names quickly and handed the list back to Corcoran.

"It's a good list," he said crisply, "but there's one man missing. I'll take him and you can have the other ten."

"Who's that?" Fred asked.

"Tony Lema," Harbert replied. " He's got 'winner' written all over him. He's got every shot in the bag and I think he's got the temperament to win, and that's important. Why don't you go out and take a look at him?"

Corcoran took Chick at his word and trailed the slender 29 year-old from San Leandro, California, for the last four holes of his round that afternoon. And he liked what he saw. "The young man was good," Corcoran said, "and more than that. There was something there that struck sparks. He was a maverick type, and I like them. In a strange way, he reminded me vaguely of Ted Williams. It was the way he handled himself, the way he stood off and surveyed the crowd with quiet amusement. It was there in his loose-gaited walk. Prospectors must get the same charge when they see yellow glint in the face of the canyon wall."

Corcoran explained that he wasn't asking questions and following players on the Doral Blue Course out of idle curiosity. In his own way, he was prospecting without really being aware of it. His business had been making money for upcoming sports headliners. But he had become so preoccupied with other things—the promotion of international golf tournaments—that he was literally out of business. He had used up his inventory. So, in 1963 he was on the hunt at Doral and Harbert was his guide. Chick pointed Fred towards Tony then basically flushed the young tiger in Fred's direction.

Tony was not riding high when he invited Corcoran to

handle his business negotiations. Sure, he had won the Orange County Open a few months earlier, but Fred really became excited after Tony came ever so close to having a Green Jacket placed on his shoulders at Augusta. But it did not take him long to prove his ability. In the June/July streak of 1964 when Tony captured four tournament wins in six successive weeks, Fred knew he had a winner. Those victories created a lot of cork popping when you're in the habit of springing for a magnum in the press tent, and this was a delightful custom Tony had introduced.

So, Fred Corcoran was at Tony's side when, climaxing this string of victories, he found himself in the *cone of contention* as soon as he met Tip Anderson at St. Andrews, and went on to win the hallowed British Open championship. While Tony was still in the press tent at St. Andrews talking to the reporters from around the world, he received a telephone call from the United States and they passed him the phone. It was none other than the present U. S. Open champion Ken Venturi, offering his congratulations to his friend from the Bay Area. Tony, in an aside to the British golf writers, cracked, "It's from the lad who won that *other* Open championship." That, of course, endeared him to the British press, since according to their beliefs; there is only one Open championship. We all know there are the United States Open, the French Open, the German and Italian Opens. But "The Open" to these journalists, who call the United Kingdom home, is it's annual tournament governed by the Royal and Ancient Golf Club of St. Andrews.

No two persons could be more dissimilar than Tony Lema and Ken Venturi. Champagne Tony bristled with that indefinable thing called color. However Ken Venturi attracted a great personal following of loyal fans that stormed over the course at his heels. But no flashy bon mot (good word) would ever spring from his lips. An extravagant gesture would only embarrass him.

Corcoran believed that both of these former caddies who came out of the San Francisco greenhouse of golf were solid bets to wind up in Golf's Hall of Fame (Venturi made it in 2013). Taking into account all of the exposure Tony received throughout the last two seasons, 1965 promised to be another chapter in which he would ride the wave of success it took so long to build. Conversely, adversary made Venturi a popular champion that all golfers could relate to except his hurdles were observed by golf fans around the world. Corcoran considered it a wonderful experience to know both of these men and a rare privilege to represent them in the world of pubic relations and marketing.

Tony played well in January of 1965, finishing in a tie for 4th at the Los Angeles Open, and a tie for 13th in San Diego Open at the Stardust C.C. As the defending champion in the Bing Crosby National Pro-Amateur at Pebble Beach, Tony's 287 was runner-up to Australian Bruce Crampton, who won by three shots. There's a little sidebar to what happened at the Monterey Peninsula. After two rounds, Tony had fired a 71-65—136 while Crampton opened with 75-67—142. Hence, Tony had a six-shot cushion over the eventual winner at the halfway point. In round three, Crampton posted a 73 while Tony skyrocketed to a 79, putting both at 215 with one round to play. On the final round at Pebble Beach, Tony was simply outplayed as Crampton fired a three-under par 69 against Tony's even par round of 72. Tony's third round cost him the tournament and you can bet your bottom dollar that at least one case of Moet & Chandon's finest champagne was iced down and ready to be cracked. Only one problem—corks didn't fly when Tony shot 79.

Throughout February, he made the cuts at the Bob Hope Desert Classic, the Phoenix and Tucson Opens but finished far back at 40th, 25th, and 21st respectfully. According to a report in *Golf World*, Tony had run into an attack of nerves because of a two-month layoff from smoking and told the reporters "I can't putt a lick." Shortly after his 31st birthday on February 25th, Tony took a swipe at the USGA and his good friend, Arnold Palmer.

"I think the USGA made a mistake in cutting out the double round on the final day of the U. S. Open," Tony opined with a small gathering of friends at a New York City Hotel. "The 36 holes on Saturday was the one feature that distinguished the Open from the other tournaments. The others now are as rich or richer. Some of them like the Masters are gaining great prestige. Now they're all played alike."

The current British Open champion also maintained his stance that there should be more PGA tournaments scheduled, not a lesser amount designed to attract the big drawing cards.

"Arnold says the pro tour should be reduced to 30 tournaments," Tony said. "If Palmer wants to play in just 30 tournaments, or just 15, that's his business. I plan to cut down my tournament schedule. But my opinion is that there should be more tournaments, not less—one every week. Give the other guys a chance."

Not only did Tony remember the steep climb it took to reach the high echelon of the PGA tour, he never forgot about the many talented golfers who seemed to be stuck in a category labeled *mediocre*. Even in the 1960's, there were many extremely good players who simply could not lace four sure-fire rounds together and capture a tour championship. Tony felt there was nothing wrong with having tournaments where the top players may skip, but the local fans and the national television audience were still entertained by some super golf. Let's face reality, in their early years, players like Tom Watson, Johnny Miller, Greg Norman, and Payne Stewart were all no-names who did not begin their careers with victories right out of the gate. Tony felt that young and upcoming golfers not lonely deserved the chance to have tournaments to play in, but the audience (both galleries on site and viewers at home) would get their monies worth. Without a doubt, Tony never forgot where he came from and what it meant for him to be part of a tournament field back in the 1958-62 era. So while he was riding high from 1963-1966, he wanted other fine golfers to at least have a chance while some top names took a week off here and there.

Around the first week in March, Tony was in San Leandro for the baptism of a nephew, Roger, and he discussed a variety of topics with Ed Schoenfeld, a reporter with the *Oakland Tribune*. "Bill Casper is playing like heck," Tony said. "He is off to a flying start and I think he'll have a great year." He also predicted that Doug Sanders, who had recently won the Pensacola Open in a playoff with Jack Nicklaus, was ready for a big year. When asked about himself, Tony wasn't exactly full of the confidence he displayed back in the summer of 1964.

"I like to do something before I talk about it," he replied. "I think my game will be all right. But I am not playing real good now. I'm not putting good enough. I am still not smoking and I feel good. I've gained about 12 pounds and I'm up to 190. I think it will be a good playing weight for me."

In the previous year, *Sports Illustrated* reported that he had given up smoking in the spring and was playing badly. He gave up smoking again in 1965 and had the same results on the golf course. So why does he stop? "I feel better when I'm not smoking," he said. "Eventually, I think I'll be able to play better, too." A noticeable drawback was the excess weight, which would not ordinarily hurt, but might have slowed down his fast pivot, which was a strength of his game. He dropped off the tour for a month saying, "If you are playing badly, why play at all?"

In another interview around the middle of March, Tony was a little cantankerous. "I quit cigarettes about two months ago, at the insistence of Arnold Palmer and I'm having one heck of a time. I've put on a dozen pounds, most of it around my waist. I can't sleep. I'm short-tempered. I'm nasty to myself on the golf course. Until I can get adjusted to the change, my golf is bound to suffer. But I expect to have it whipped within another month. I should be okay for the Masters. I want to work on my game, and I want to kick this smoking habit. I don't see any point in going around buying lung cancer."

Tony prepped for the Masters with a 21st place finish in the Jacksonville Open played the third week of March, but he improved two weeks later in the Greater Greensboro Open by finishing sixth at 280, seven shots behind the winner Sam Snead. In the span of 27 years, from 1938-1965, it was the 52 year-old Slammin' Sam's eighth and final victory at Greensboro.

By 1965, it was clear that the Big Three were dominating The Masters at Augusta National. Arnie had won it in the even years of 1958, 1960, 1962, and 1964. Gary Player won it in 1961, and of course, Jack Nicklaus had clipped Tony by a stroke in 1963. During that period, Palmer had also tied for second (1961), as did Nicklaus (1964) and Player had lost in a playoff (1962). The South African, dressed in his usual black attire, got off to an incredible start by firing a seven-under par 65 on

Thursday. Gary let it be known that he had been reading Norman Vincent Peale's *Power of Positive Thinking* and he was willing to tell the world, "I'm playing so well I can't believe it." But there was a strong group of players at 67, which included Tony Lema, Tommy Aaron, Dan Sikes, Jack Nicklaus, Frank Beard, Doug Sanders, Wes Ellis, Tommy Bolt, Ray Floyd and George Bayer. As Mark McCormack wrote in *The Wonderful World of Professional Golf*, "The Masters was a birdie festival."

Player was asked after his round, who was he worried about the most in that group of players two shots back. He quickly replied, "Jack Nicklaus." Why? "There is no such thing as a par five on this course for Jack. He can reach any green in two. Not only that, he has a great touch. I predict that if the weather is good, Jack will break the tournament record." At that time, Ben Hogan's fourteen-under par 274, he had shot in 1953, was the 72-hole record.

When the players arrived for the second round, they found some changes had been made, namely, the tee markers had been moved back and the pin positions toughened. A bulletin, issued by Bobby Jones and Clifford Roberts stated, "Officials will follow our established procedures with respect to pin positions and tee markers. We anticipate and hope for more low-scoring today." To boot, there was considerable breeze in the air. Actually, the players were wise enough to know the interpretation of the memo could well have been, "Fellas, you cut our course to ribbons yesterday. Lots of luck today."

The second round scores reflected the changes in a heartbeat. Ray Floyd went from 69 to 83 and missed the cut. Frank Beard followed his 68 with a 77. Some others were: Tommy Aaron 67,74; Tommy Bolt 69,78; and Tony followed his 67 with a 73. Gary Player posted a 73, Nicklaus a 71, tying them for the lead at 138. And Arnold Palmer was right there with them, firing a brilliant 68, the only sub-70 round of the day. Among the top 14 finishers, Arnie was the only player to have improved his first round score.

Rounds one and two may have belonged to Player and Palmer, but round three belonged solely to Jack Nicklaus. After a par at one, he birdied the second hole, parred the third and then reeled off four consecutive birdies en route to a five-under

par 31 on the front. On the back, he birdied both of the par
5s, canned an 8-foot birdie putt on 16, parred the rest to post
a dazzling eight-under par 64 and take a five shot lead. Player
summed up the situation rather bluntly. "To shoot 69 on this
course and lose five shots is incredible."

Nicklaus played a solid round on Sunday, posted a 69, good
for 271, which broke Ben Hogan's record of 274 by three shots.
Palmer and Player tied for second at 280, a score that would
have won all but five of the previous Masters, but in 1965 they
were nine strokes behind Nicklaus. Bobby Jones summed up
Nicklaus' performance as only he could. "Palmer and Player
played superbly," said the legend. "As for Nicklaus, he plays a
game with which I am not familiar."

Jack's record of 271 remained at the top of the record book
until Ray Floyd tied it with his seventeen-under performance
in 1976. For over twenty years, Nicklaus and Floyd shared the
honor of posting the lowest 72-hole score at Augusta. In 1997,
Tiger Woods, playing in his first Masters as a professional, fired
four brilliant rounds totaling 270 to post the tournament record
which remains the lowest as of this writing.

Although Tony was only two shots back after 36 holes, he
never got it going on the weekend. He posted a 77 and a 74 to
finish at 291 placing him in a tie for 21st. At the green jacket
ceremony, it was defending champion Arnold Palmer who
placed the coat upon Jack's shoulders; same participants as the
post-round ritual in 1963. As a matter of fact, from 1962 through
1965, Jack and Arnie each won it every other year.

After the Masters, Tony was in 17th place on the money list
with earnings of $10,164. He finished 15th in the Tournament of
Champions to fall down to 24th, but his third place finish the
following week at the Colonial got him back to 16th position.
He withdrew from the Greater New Orleans Open due to back
pain, but two weeks later he tied for 12th at Indianapolis, which
put him at 21st on the money list. Back in January, Tony told
Nelson Cullenward of the *San Francisco News Call-Bulletin*
that he was going to work up to a peak around June, then he
hoped to make his move.

"I think it will take that long for my system or constitution,
or whatever you call it, to get accustomed to my not smoking

anymore," he said. "I'm still a little nervous, but I'll get over it. I want to play well in the Masters, then work my way up to the tournaments I'll be defending (Buick and Cleveland). Then I hope my game is at its peak for the National Open."

By the time June rolled around, it was time to head for Michigan and tee it up in the Buick Open. Tony was back on a course he loved, the 7,280-yard Warwick Hills, and stayed once again with his close friends, Mr. and Mrs. Clarence Jones. His game rose to the occasion, as he displayed a high level of consistency and accuracy all week and successfully defended the title he won a year earlier. Champagne Tony had rounds of 71-70-69-70—280, eight-under par and two ahead of runner-up Johnny Pott. The $20,000 first prize (a vast improvement over the previous year's check of $8,177) vaulted him from 21st on the money list to fourth with a total of $37,164. Not only that, he was paired with Jack Nicklaus in the final round and watched his four-stroke lead melt in the 90-degree heat to a single shot as they stood on the 18th tee. The recent Masters champion had the honor on the last tee, as a result of a birdie on the 604-yard par five 16th hole. Jack wanted to pulverize that last drive and put his approach stiff for at least a tie, but something out of the ordinary happened. Jack Nicklaus hooked it out of bounds, something rarely done by the 25-year-old from Ohio who worked it from left-to-right throughout his career. Nicklaus re-teed it, drove into the rough, hit an approach into a bunker and finished with a triple bogey and a fourth place finish worth $5,000.

Tony's reaction to Nicklaus' fate on the final tee was noteworthy: "I was stunned momentarily when I saw Jack's ball drift over some television trucks. I knew there were some high weeds in the area. At a time like that when a match is that close you never wish an opponent any hard luck, and I was sorry to see Jack in trouble."

As the corks popped in the press tent heralding a champagne celebration, Tony told the press what was on his mind. "It's been a long time since I've heard that sound," he noted with a winner's grin on his face. "I'd almost forgotten what the stuff tasted like."

As the press conference got underway, you could tell

exactly how he felt about Betty because she was one of the first topics of conversation.

"My only regret," he said, "is that she isn't here to share this victory with me. I have a great wife, really," he went on, opening a bottle of champagne and paying no attention when some of the contents accidentally spilled onto his olive green trousers. "She set me straight on all of my outside activities. You know what I mean. Taking care of my business commitments, making television appearances, speeches and the like. I was hopping all over the landscape and neglecting my real bread and butter—golf. She said, 'Honey, you're not that good. You can't go running around the country all the time and show up in a tournament the first day and expect to do well.' "

Tony hadn't won a tournament since the previous September when he captured the $50,000 first prize in the World Series of Golf at Firestone C.C. so he decided to do it her way. He put his outside interests aside and showed up two days early for the Buick Open. That enabled him to play in the Pro-Am, which ordinarily doesn't mean much, but enabled him to become more familiar with the extra long and difficult Warwick Hills course.

Whether smoking was a big issue regarding his putting, we'll never know. Cullenward reported that he was "back on the weed" and Tony said in the press tent that he was starting to feel better over his putts. "I felt I've been hitting the ball OK most of the year, but I haven't been able to get down many birdie putts. I've got a little confidence now and maybe I can keep it going for a couple of weeks anyway."

The next stop on the tour was the Cleveland Open and it didn't take Tony long to bring some good memories to mind. Two years earlier when the inaugural Cleveland Open was held at Beechmont Country Club, Tony was deadlocked with Arnold Palmer and Tommy Aaron after 72 holes; Palmer won the 18-hole playoff by three shots. In 1964, at Highland Park Golf Course, Tony missed an 18-inch putt on the final hole of regulation play to permit Palmer to tie him at 270. On the first extra hole of a sudden-death playoff, Tony knocked in a long birdie putt to capture his first Cleveland Open title.

As the defending champ, Tony jumped into first place in the opening round with a four-under-par 67, tied only by Billy

Casper. The next two rounds, a 70 and a 66, kept him atop the leaderboard going into the final round. Those rounds were more impressive as Tony was fighting a heavy cold throughout the tournament. He played in a heavy sweater despite 80-degree weather and was racing back to the motel after each round for a hot bath and bed. After 11 holes on Sunday, Tony was tied for the lead with another of his good friends, Dan Sikes, the attorney from Florida. They both birdied the twelfth and parred the thirteenth to remain tied at 11-under par, but Tony regained the lead on the 14th when his 15-foot birdie putt found the cup. On the very next hole, Tony's eight-iron approach fell short of the green where he chipped 12-feet past the pin, and ultimately two-putted for a bogey. The tie remained going into the final hole where Sikes' approach was on the edge of the green 35 feet from the hole. Tony missed the green and found the gallery, coming to rest on the lap of a girl spectator seated on a campstool. She remained seated with the ball on her lap until a PGA official ruled Tony could have a free drop. No doubt, this was the occasion when Tony, while waiting for an official, took those two full practice swings and told her "it might smart a little." Soon she realized that he was just kidding and the ball was dropped and officially in play. Tony chipped to within four feet of the cup. Meanwhile, Dan Sikes surveyed his situation, his ball on the clipped fringe, and it seemed almost a certainty that he and Tony would be heading for a sudden-death playoff. After it was all over, Sikes explained what happened: "On a putt like mine, you just try to get it up close. When I looked up I saw it was right on line. When it hit the cup, I thought it might spin out. I nearly fainted when it dropped in."

The attorney's exciting putt on the last hole gave him a 12-under par total of 272 while Tony made that four-footer and finished one stroke back at 273. While Sikes accepted the winner's check of $25,000, Tony was a little dejected but remained a gentleman in defeat. "It was a succession of missed shots," Tony said as he signed his card for a final round 35-35—70 and was presented a check for $13,000. No doubt Tony was referring to his tee shot on the par-3 fifteenth where he left it short of the green, chipped it 12-feet by the pin and two-putted for a bogey. Someone asked Tony what ran through his mind as Dan Sikes' putt on the last hole disappeared into the cup. "Someone knocked a putt in on me, that's all," Tony replied. "I've done it to a few people." Perhaps, no one explained the situation better than Dan Sikes when he was talking to the press and told them he was just trying to get it close from 35 feet. "I guess I had to make it. Who wants to go into a playoff with Tony Lema?" Despite losing a close one that comment had to make Tony feel respected when he read it the next morning in the *Cleveland Plain Dealer*. Not only that, he ascended to number two on the money list as all eyes focused on the national championship.

For the first time, the U.S. Open Golf Championship, played at the Bellerive Country Club in St. Louis, MO, was extended over four days, instead of the final 36 holes played on the third day. Many competitors, including Tony Lema, felt as though the most exciting and demanding day in golf competition was gone. Many thought one element of the uniqueness of the U.S. Open was stripped away from the aura of what it took to prevail as the champion. Why did the USGA make this change? Many thought it was to accommodate television—Saturday and Sunday broadcasts instead of just Saturday, and to collect more money in "rights and fees." Mark McCormack said the USGA gave a feeble excuse like the threat of bad weather, a possible postponement or the exceedingly hot weather the entire field withstood the previous year at Congressional.

Some of the major attractions in a major, such as Arnold Palmer, got off to a horrible start. Arnie shot a pair of 76's and did not make the 36-hole cut. Jack Nicklaus shot 78-72 and was never in contention. The defending champion, Ken Ventui, had 40 putts in the first round and stumbled in with an 81, followed by a 79. On the bright side, Gary Player was at 140 after 36-holes and had a one shot lead over Australian Kel Nagle and Mason Rudolph. In the third round, Player shot a 71 and lengthened his lead to two over Nagle. Player had the championship in hand with three holes to play after Nagle had made a double-bogey 6 on the par-4 fifteenth. On the 218-yard par-3 sixteenth hole, Player hit his tee shot into a massive bunker and blasted to within 15-feet of the pin. His first putt rolled three-past the cup and he rimmed out his next putt, settling for a double-bogey. At the same moment, Nagle holed a birdie putt on the 606-yard par 5 seventeenth hole. The three-stroke swing left them tied for the lead. Nagle made his par on the eighteenth hole while Gary Player also parred his final two holes putting them in a deadlock at 282. The playoff was between two foreigners and a foreigner had not won the U.S. Open since Ted Ray's victory in 1920. On the next day, Gary Player won the championship outscoring Kel Nagle 71 to 74. In 1962, Player had said that if ever won the U.S. Open he would not take the prize money. He was a man of his word as he donated $5,000 to cancer research and the other $20,000 to the USGA to promote junior golf. Throughout all of this, Tony played fairly well as he shot 72-74-73-70—289 and finished in a tie for eighth winning a check of $2,500.

The Western Open was played at George S. May's popular Tam O'Shanter Country Club in Niles, IL just northwest of Chicago and the tournament was held from July 1-4, 1965. The first round of the British Open which took place at Royal Birkdale in Southport, England commenced on Wednesday July 7. That gave participants in the Western Open less than 60 hours or two-and-a-half days to make the trip from Chicago to Liverpool (via London), become acclimated after a six-hour time change, recover from the jet lag and oh, one more thing—learn the nuances of a British golf course that many had never seen. It goes without saying that Tony Lema, the defending champion of the "Open" Championship stuck to his guns and shunned the idea of getting there early for additional practice. Sooner or later, critics and/or many of his fans that were part of Lema's Legions, came to the realization, "Leave him alone, he knows what he's doing."

After finishing a very mediocre 23rd the previous week in the St. Paul Open, Tony once again combined consistency with accuracy as he posted his best ever scores at the Western Open (69-69-68-69—275). He tied for 4th place, five shots behind winner Billy Casper, who fired a sizzling seven-under par 64 in the final round. Tony had to feel confident about his game as he climbed aboard a plane at O'Hare and had one thing in mind—play well at Royal Birkdale and successfully defend the championship he won at St. Andrews a year earlier.

Tony arrived in Southport, England on Monday afternoon for his first practice round and brazenly turned his championship trophy over to the Royal and Ancient (R & A) authorities with the admonition, "Please keep it for me for four days—I'll pick it up on Friday."

Late in the afternoon on Tuesday, the eve of the championship, Tony sat down with the media. "I played two rounds here this week," he said regarding his preparation. "I only played 27 holes in St. Louis before our own Open. I've always felt that two days is enough for me. I can tell in that time where the trouble is. I'm not a good enough golfer to always put the ball where I want it, but at least I feel I know how to play this golf course."

Having started his career in golf years ago as a caddie, Tony oftentimes relied heavily on the advice and judgment of his caddie. That was his way and it certainly proved to successful a year earlier at St. Andrews. He put complicit trust in Tip Anderson and it paid off handsomely when you see his name engraved on the Claret Jug. At Royal Birkdale, Arnold Palmer was competing and Tip Anderson was carrying his bag. No Tip for Tony this time around. In Michael McDonnell's *Great Moments in Sport: Golf*, the British journalist picked up a classic conversation between Tony and his new caddie. The first time Tony was on the 184-yard par-3 twelfth hole, he surveyed the situation and said to his caddie. "I shall put my hand out and you put the right club in it." Willie Aitchison replied, "I'll put the right club there. Just you hit it right." Tony drilled the golf ball through the stiff breeze coming off the Irish Sea and it settled a few feet from the flag. How's that for golfer and caddie being on the same page?

After the first round of the 1965 British Open Championship, newspapers around the world, especially in the United States, carried a banner headline that said it all—**Lema Fires 68 to Take Lead in British Open**. His five-under par round set a course record and put him one stroke ahead of Ireland's Christy O'Connor, who's 69 had been the record for just a few hours. Playing spectacularly Tony made six birdies in his round, starting with one on the first and ending with another on the eighteenth. From the seventh through the fourteenth, he was only two shots over threes. It was very similar to the way he played so exceptional in the third round at St. Andrews after he passed Nicklaus on the sixth fairway. Once again, the galleries were amazed this tall, lanky Californian could play so well despite precious little practice. It was as though his scant preparation gave him insufficient time to notice the perils of Birkdale. But they would get to him before the week was out.

Tony's game cooled off a little in his second and third rounds as he posted 72 on Thursday and a 75 in Friday's morning round. Peter Thomson, the Australian who had won the "Open" in 1954, 1955, 1956, and 1958 had opened with a 74, but followed that with a 68-72 to place him at 214 with one round to go. He was one shot ahead of Tony and they were playing in the same group. After eleven holes, Thomson was playing a crisis-free round and held a three-shot lead over Tony. After a wayward tee shot on the short twelfth, Peter took three putts to complete the hole. An indecisive tee shot on the thirteenth left him in the long grass where he could salvage no better than a bogey and his lead diminished to one stroke. Meanwhile, Tony's short game was stellar and he his confidence was high as he was in the midst of the hunt with five holes to go.

Michael McDonnell, a true golf journalist, had left the pressroom and was standing on the fourteenth tee as Tony and Peter Thomson prepared to play the par-three hole. He captured the turning point of the Open and described in his book exactly what happened as the wind swept over the fairways at Royal Birkdale.

"As they stepped to the fourteenth tee, Thomson knew that he had to stop this swing of fortune before it became irretrievable. He peered down this short hole towards the green and suddenly sensed that something was different about it. The wind had changed so imperceptibly that Lema had not noticed it, and Thomson had almost missed it. They were protected on the leeward side of a sand hill, but the flag in the distance was fluttering at a slightly different angle than in the morning round.

"It needed more club, and Thomson drilled his ball into that distant green. Lema with only his notebook for an ally had missed the green. This was the difference between Thomson's outlook and that of the new breed.

"He had an instinct, a feel for the way a course should be played. His eyes, indeed all his senses, worked for him all the time he played his golf and he had no need of notebooks and yardage charts. And his ability to act on the evidence of his senses won him the British Open, since it halted any further advance by Lema, who wasted strokes on that hole."

Tony faltered in the final holes as Thomson birdied the seventeenth and finished at 285, two shots ahead of Brian Huggett and Christy O'Connor, Sr. "Two things killed me," Tony surmised. "I wasn't driving too well, and my putting wasn't too sharp. I still thought I had a chance, however, up to the 71st hole." On the next-to-last-hole, Tony hit both his drive and second shot into the rough. His 74 placed him in a tie for fifth at 289. "I really wanted to win this," he said later, "but what really makes me mad is finishing like a bum." Tony was referring to three-putting the final green before one of the largest galleries in Open history. To make matters worse, as defending champion, he had to go right back out to the 18th green to face the crowd again for the presentation ceremony. "I will be back next year," Tony told everyone. "This is too good a championship to miss."

Upon returning to the United States, Tony took about three weeks off and basically chilled. In an eleven-week span that started with his appearance in the Tournament of Champions on April 29, Tony had competed in ten tournaments through the conclusion of the British Open on July 9, 1965. That's a lot of travel and constantly packing and unpacking one's luggage. Not to mention the general environment that changes from week to week, the accommodations that vary from city to city, the restaurants that offer altogether different entrees, and of course the weather and playing conditions found at the assortment of venues. Perhaps no one appreciates the comforts of home more than the professional golfers on the PGA Tour. Suffice it to say, the motel and hotel accommodations in the mid 60's were probably not as home spun as they are in the twenty-first century. In that nearly three-month duration, Tony cashed checks totaling $49,272, so the sacrifices he made on the road undoubtedly paid off in the long run.

Tony rejoined the tour in August where he defended his

title at the Thunderbird Classic. He finished in a tie for 35th but sharpened his game the following week in the Philadelphia Golf Classic with a 281 and a tie for fifth place. The PGA Championship was held in Arnold Palmer's back yard at the Laurel Valley Golf Club in Ligonier, PA the following week where Dave Marr played the best golf of his career en route to a two-shot victory over Jack Nicklaus and Billy Casper. Marr's 72-hole total of 280 was four-under par, but things didn't fall in place for Tony Lema. He struggled throughout the tournament, 71-76-75-80—302, and finished in a tie for 61st.

The $200,000 Carling World Open held at Pleasant Valley Country Club in Sutton, MA was the world's richest tournament at the time with a first prize of $35,000. After 54-holes Tony was tied for the lead with Homero Blancas at 209, but Arnold Palmer was in sight in Tony's rear view mirror at 212. Tony built a five-stroke lead midway through the final round, but Palmer unleashed one of his patented comeback charges. He proceeded to put together a run of four birdies including one on the 11th hole which Tony bogeyed to cut the margin to one stroke. Both players parred the next three holes, but Palmer canned an 18-foot birdie putt on the 15th green to draw even. The pair were deadlocked at five-under par when Arnie's missed the green with his four-iron tee shot on the 183-yard 16th, chipped 12 feet long and two-putted for a bogey. On the tricky 402-yard par-4 seventeenth hole, Arnie pulled his two-iron tee shot into the left rough, made a fine recovery from a tough lie to carry the water guarding the green, but three-putted from 40 feet to give Tony a two-shot cushion. Meanwhile Tony cooly parred the last seven holes to finish with a one-under par round of 70 and capture his second tournament win in 1965 (he won the Buick Open in June) and his eleventh title on the tour. His four-round total of five-under par 279 netted him a check for $35,000 which pushed his earnings for the year to $98,016 and his career earnings to just over $300,000.

As usual, Tony dispensed champagne to the press corps and casually remarked, "I was going to skip this tournament because I wasn't playing too well. I drink champagne on a beer budget...now I can afford it." Bright red Carling beer cups replaced the usual champagne glasses, however, the bubbling

Tony explained that "beer and champagne can get along very nicely."

He told the writers he wasn't as calm as he appeared. "I was loose enough 'til I hit the greens," he said. "Then I could feel the pressure." He said he was concerned until he heard that Palmer, playing in a threesome just ahead of him, had bogeyed the 17th hole. "I told myself then, 'You're a fool if you blow it now.' "

Tony played it cautiously and two-putted from 25 feet on the par-3 sixteenth hole. He got a lucky break on the next hole when his second shot was too long, but hit into the gallery and bounced back on the green about 30 feet from the cup. "Now I'll go down to the American Golf Classic in Akron and let golf get even with me," Tony chuckled.

The 1965 Ryder Cup Matches were played at the Royal Birkdale Golf Club, Southport, Lancashire, England on October 7-9. Three months after Tony's rather disappointing fifth place finish in the British Open, he had the opportunity to seek some sort of revenge on the course that humbled him. The United States was represented by a fine blend of youth and experience. Besides Arnold Palmer and Tony, qualifiers for the team included recent PGA champion Dave Marr, Julius Boros, Billy Casper, Gene Littler, Ken Venturi, Don January and Tony's traveling friends from the late '50's Tommy Jacobs and Johnny Pott. The well-respected Hall of Famer Byron Nelson captained the U.S. team. Upon being appointed captain, Lord Byron wrote each of them a letter saying how glad he was to have them on his team, and later he sent each one a handsome alligator wallet to demonstrate his point. Byron Nelson knew how to get the respect and determination from all of his players. One of them said to him late in the week, "If we played this hard in the tournaments back home, we'd all be millionaires." Back in the mid '60's, it took a considerable number of victories to come anywhere near becoming a millionaire.

Because the summer had been extremely wet, the narrow fairways were emerald-green ribbons winding through the 40 and 50 foot high sand dunes that overlooked the Irish Sea and the 16,000 members of the partisan gallery were serenaded by waves crashing upon the beaches. The greens were smooth and because of the moisture they would hold any well-hit approach shot, a definite advantage to the Americans who were accustomed to hitting iron shots much higher than their adversaries. Nonetheless, the Brits were on their home soil and they were known to be formidable and stubborn opponents.

On the first day with foursome matches (alternate-shot), the American pairing of Arnold Palmer and Dave Marr met the British team of Dave Thomas and George Will. Palmer and Marr could do nothing right, failed to win a hole and were beaten soundly 6 and 5. However, Palmer spent his lunch break on the practice tee and played some astonishing golf in the afternoon round. He and Dave Marr started with a birdie on the first hole, then made six straight 3s for an outgoing 30, which was five under par. Four holes later, Palmer-Marr returned the favor by defeating Thomas-Will by the same margin they had lost in the morning, 6 and 5. The most fortuitous pairing for the U.S. on the opening day was Tony Lema and Julius Boros. In the morning, they shot three-under par 70 as Tony holed a tough putt on the final green to beat Lionel Platts and Peter Butler one-up. In the afternoon, Tony and Julius played superbly and buried Jimmy Hitchcock and J. Martin 5 and 4. At the end of the first day, the score was a standoff, 4-4, and Captain Nelson was relieved because he knew the British team was much better at foursome golf than the Americans.

The four-ball matches (best-ball of each two-man team) were played on the second day as Arnold Palmer and Dave Marr were paired again, fired a best-ball 33 on the first nine and crunched Peter Alliss and Christy O'Connor 6 and 4. Tony and Julius Boros were also teamed together again and matched Neil Coles and Bernard Hunt on the front nine with three-under par 32s. Lema-Boros lost the tenth hole and were unable to gain ground as they lost the match one-down. In the afternoon, Tony teamed with fellow Bay Area native Ken Venturi and they gained revenge from Hunt and Coles by winning one-up in a grueling match. By the time sunset rolled around, the U.S. team held a 9-7 leading going into the final day where there were 16 singles matches scheduled, eight in the morning and eight in the afternoon.

On the final day of the 1965 Ryder Cup matches, Tony played some magnificent golf. In the morning match against Peter Butler, it was a nail-biter all the way until Tony slapped a pitch shot from 90 yards out to within four feet of the 18th hole to win the match one-up. In the afternoon, he birdied seven of the 14 holes he played as he routed Christy O'Connor 6 and 4. Tony's second victory of the day clinched at least a tie for the United States. Just moments later, Tony's partner from earlier in the cup matches, Julius Boros, had the honor of officially securing the cup with a 2 and 1 win over Jimmy Hitchcock, also his second triumph of the day. The U.S. won 10 of the 16 matches on the final day and brought the Ryder Cup home, by a margin of 19½–12½. Personally, Tony had to feel better leaving Royal Birkdale in October than he did in July. The United States had captured the Ryder Cup for the 13th time in 16 meetings. Tony won five of the six points attainable. In the 1963 event in Atlanta, Tony had won three matches and halved two. Cumulatively, in the two Ryder Cup events that Tony participated in, he played in 11 matches; he won eight, halved two, and lost one. Out of a possible 11 points, Tony had won nine for the United States.

The Piccadilly World Match Play Championship was founded by Mark McCormack in 1964 and was won by Arnold Palmer, who was McCormack's first client. The tournament had an eight-man field from 1964 through 1976, as the event consisted of 36-hole matches played in a single day and for years was held at the Wentworth Club, in Virginia Water, Surrey on the southwest fringes of London, not far from the Windsor Castle.

For its first 40 years the tournament was an unofficial one, highly regarded by golf fans in Britain and many other countries outside the United States. It was popular with players, and happily coexisting with the European tour, at whose home course it was played, but winnings were not considered as earnings on the official tour money list. The introduction in 1999 of the 64 Man WGC–Accenture Match Play Championship, which selected it's field on the basis of the world rankings, was a blow to the prestige of the older event, whose exhibition aspects, with a small invited field was emphasized by contrast.

Shortly after the Ryder Cup victory, Tony went to London and participated in the 1965 Piccadilly World Match Play tournament. In his book, *Peter Alliss' Most Memorable Golf*, Peter did a wonderful job setting up the semi-final match between Tony and Gary Player. In the opening round, Gary had defeated Neil Coles and Tony had won his match over Peter Alliss.

"For a start the pair were opposites," Peter recalled. "Player, as he is only too willing to admit, was a bit of a bore with his talk of no alcohol, coffee or tea, plenty of nuts, bananas and raisins, the virtues for a golfer of supreme fitness and the benefits of religion. If his body was manufactured, so was his swing. Tony Lema, on the other hand, had a relaxed, flailing, elegant swing of rare beauty. But on the course he always seemed tense and nervous, rather like Bobby Jones, but had much the same grace under pressure. He could use tension, not be destroyed by it. Off the golf course he had a very relaxed image, much enhanced when he bought champagne for the press after a tournament victory.

"Lema's victory in the 1964 Open Championship, together with his US Tour wins, had made him a star. Gary Player felt that Tony resented the 'Big Three' Status of Palmer, Nicklaus and himself and knew that Lema believed he was entitled to membership of that exclusive group. Lema had been saying there was really a 'Big Four.' There was also the matter of an important endorsement contract with Slazengers UK. They had dropped Gary and signed Lema instead. The semi-final match which followed was the most enthralling I have ever seen. It has been called the greatest match ever."

The account of what happened that memorable day is based on the story written by Michael McDonnell in his book, *Great Moments in Sports: Golf*. After disposing of their opponents in the opening round, Tony and Gary Player faced each other in the semi-final round. Player had already established the reputation as a golfer who was unbelievably determined to succeed and totally immersed himself in the task at hand. But on this day, Tony was cruising along playing solid golf and found himself with a comfortable five-hole lead as they prepared to play the last nine holes. He probably felt that even if he failed here or there, Gary would be running out of holes to mount a serious comeback. On the short tenth hole, Tony missed the green with his approach shot, failed to get up and down and lost the hole. Player hit two fantastic shots on the eleventh hole, which led to a birdie, and suddenly Tony found himself three up with seven holes left. They halved the twelfth but on the next tee, Tony snapped his drive far left where the ball came to rest surrounded by twigs and tall grass midst a forest of trees. While Tony tried to figure out an escape route, Gary Player stood quietly beside his ball in the middle of the fairway. Tony advanced his ball only a few yards to the fairway, but Player was in no hurry to hit his approach to the green. He wanted Tony to emerge from the woods and see his next shot. Player hit a terrific mid-iron to the green, leaving himself a ten-footer for a birdie. Meanwhile, Tony's approach to the thirteenth green ended up some 25 feet short of the hole. Tony felt that if he could make this putt for a par, he might just stop the bleeding and bring a halt to Player's momentum. He struck the putt perfectly and both men watched the ball gather the distance to the hole, then, with its last gasp, it disappeared. Tony sighed with relief convinced that he had saved himself. Player had a chance to win the hole, but he knew if he missed, it would restore Tony's flagging confidence. After reading the break carefully, Gary Player drilled that ten-footer into the cup and reduced his deficit to two holes with five to play. Gary had to be thinking at the time, "game on."

Tony kept Player at bay for the next two holes and reached the sixteenth tee two up with three to play. Despite an extremely narrow fairway on the par-4 hole, Player reached for his driver and made sure that Tony noticed. Both had left the driver in the bag during the morning because the margin for error was too fine. Player hit his drive perfectly into the fairway, and waited. At that point, Tony had to be painfully confused. He didn't want to risk hitting his driver nor did he want to allow Player too much advantage of a short and more accurate iron into the green. With all those contradictions swirling about in his mind, Tony chose to hit a three-wood and once again he came over the top and the ball went deep into the woods on the left. Gary won the hole and that left Tony one-up with two to play. On the par-4 seventeenth hole, both hit the green in regulation, but Tony was out and had the opportunity to put the pressure on his opponent. He had to be thinking, "just make this putt" and Gary will have to make his to extend this match to the final hole. Tony stroked his putt into the cup for a birdie. Now it was Gary's turn to feel the pressure and he answered by knocking his putt right into the heart of the cup.

Player had lived with the prospect of failure since he was down all day long, but Tony could not shake off the awful horror of how this disaster had ambushed him. Despite the fact that he was still leading on the eighteenth tee, Tony must have felt like a loser. Both men hit good tee shots on the dogleg, but Tony's approach was not hit crisply and ended up short of the green. Player hit his shot to the right heading for the trees, it disappeared from view and he waited for the sickening sound of the ball crashing into the limbs. But the noise of collision did not come as an obedient arc took over and the ball found its way through the trees onto the green and settled close to the flagstick. Observers said that Tony was so shattered by the turn of events, he left his pitch shot way short and this time there would be no life-saving putt. They were all square after 36-holes and were compelled to play extra holes.

After coming back from a five-hole deficit over the final nine holes, Player knew that no matter how many extra holes it took, he was going to win. Tony hit a poor drive on the first hole and the memory of what he had lost and perhaps the thought of starting again, now suffocated him. He attempted to hit a long approach across a valley to the green, but the ball snaked low and plunged into a bunker far below the green. Player hit an excellent shot onto the green and Tony faced a nearly impossible attempt to get up and down. He two-putted for a bogey while Player made his par and won the match. They shook hands and Player's wife Vivienne rushed forward and they began to walk back down the fairway to the clubhouse. Suddenly, the world went grey. Player weakened and flopped to the ground. He was crying, although he did not know why. He passed out and trembled. A doctor in the crowd rushed to help him. In a few moments, he was better.

After he collected himself, according to *Peter Alliss' Most*

Memorable Golf, Player described what that day meant to him. "All through 1965," Gary said, "in the big events, I played in a state of enchantment, but this day, the day of the Lema match, was one of the most astonishing in my life. I have looked back on it and come to see in it a summation of so much of my character and personality, good and bad, so much of a reflection of the pattern of my life, that it has become for me a strange, unnatural distillation of all it means to be Gary Player, all that Gary Player is. Simply, it contains my whole life story."

Gary Player proceeded to defeat Peter Thomson in the final match, 3-2, to secure his first Piccadilly World Match Play title. He went on to win it four more times, in 1966, 1968, 1971, and 1973. But we know one thing for sure. Until the day he died (less than a year after the match) Tony would wake up in the middle of the night wondering just what went wrong that day at Wentworth.

This Is My Last Hole

The 1966 season got off to a rough start as Tony was suffering from an injured elbow that gave him quite a bit of pain. Actually, his right elbow flared up in November when Tony was scheduled to go on a 31-day round the world trip with amateur golfer Bill Bosshard, who had won a tournament at the Dorado Hilton Hotel course in Puerto Rico sponsored by Hilton Hotels. A calcium deposit in his elbow had prevented him from playing on that trip. A doctor had advised him to let it rest for 30 days. Tony tried to play in India, but after a few hits, he decided to heed the medic's advice. At the season's first tournament, the Los Angeles Open, Tony refused to alibi about his elbow, although it obviously was painful to swing the golf club. Nelson Cullenward, of the *San Francisco News-Call Bulletin* reported (much) later that while in LA he asked Tony—in front of others—if it bothered him.

"Not a thing wrong," he swore. But Nelson said that alone, "he gave us an entirely different answer, swearing us to silence."

Another reporter who had become a good friend with Tony, Doug Mintline of the *Flint Journal*, wrote about a conversation he had with Tony the night before the Buick Open in June. "Tony explained how Butazoldin, a special medicine, had made it possible for him to postpone surgery on a troubled elbow and stay on the tour. Ironically, the surgery would have idled Lema for three months."

Despite the discomfort, Tony struggled through the first three rounds of the Los Angeles Open played once again on the Rancho Park Golf Course with scores of 72, 73, and 70.

On Sunday's final round, Tony put it all together with a five-under par 66 to finish at 281 in a tie for thirteenth position, eight shots behind the winner, Arnold Palmer. Two weeks later, Tony headed north for the Bing Crosby National Pro-Am where he did something meaningful, yet it had absolutely nothing to do with his game. After playing consistently and posting 70-72-72—214 for the first three rounds, Tony was paired in one of the final groups with eventual winner Don Massengale, who had never tasted victory on the tour after six years. The tall Texan overcame a four-stroke deficit heading into the final round and nursed a one-shot lead over the final 10 holes. Coming from behind and orchestrating one of his patent finishes, Arnold Palmer birdied three of the last four holes and made a nice clutch eight-footer to save par on the par-3 seventeenth hole. Massengale displayed considerable class when his third shot on the famous 18th hole at Pebble Beach went through branches of a huge pine tree without touching a twig and ended up four feet from the hole. He made the putt to insure his triumph ahead of the rampaging Palmer. At the press conference, Massengale gave credit to Tony for his victory.

"Tony was extremely helpful as the pressure built up, especially after I three-putted the 14th for a bogey," he said. "He helped calm me down and a couple of times he told me, 'You've got everything under control. Slow down and take it easy. Let them come at you.' I got the message because I know you don't play catch-up on this course. That's why I'm happy I got off to that good start (4-under par 32 on the front nine). Yes, I felt the pressure the whole round. With Palmer behind you, you need all the birdies you can get."

Tony must have felt quite a bit of pain with his right elbow as he soared to a 79 and finished in a tie for 16th place. But somewhere along the way, he had to feel indirectly fulfilled by offering those words of encouragement to Don Massengale who was fighting hard for his first victory. There's no doubt that Tony knew all about the moments of anxiety and the feeling a competitor has when the butterflies (in one's stomach) are flying out of order. The following week Tony had planned on playing in the Lucky International Open at San Francisco near his hometown of San Leandro. He withdrew a few days before the tournament began which was an indication the soreness in his right elbow had flared up again and rest was necessary. Tony did not play on the tour at all during February and his next tournament was the Doral Open in Florida, March 10-13.

Other than his tie for sixth in the Jacksonville Open the last week in March, Tony had a lackluster swing through Florida and the pre-Masters Greater Greensboro Open. He finished in a tie for 59th at Doral, a tie for 28th at Orlando, and a tie for 15th at Greensboro. At Augusta in 1966, Tony had rounds of 74-74-74-76—298 to finish in a tie for 23rd, ten shots behind eventual winner Jack Nicklaus, who defeated Tommy Jacobs and Gay Brewer in an 18-hole playoff. The following week, Tony participated in the Tournament of Champions where he carded a 297 and wound up in a tie for 22nd place, 14 shots behind winner Arnold Palmer. He attempted to play in the Dallas Open Invitational the next week but withdrew after three rounds. But don't give up. Tony certainly didn't. The warm weather in May was about to heat up Tony's game as he went on a streak where his lowest finish in seven consecutive tournaments was a tie for ninth, his highest was his favorite spot on the scoreboard—at the very top!

Before Tony rejoined the tour in May he fulfilled his commitment to *Shell's Wonderful World of Golf* by playing a match against Peter Alliss at the Mid Ocean Golf Club in Bermuda. In addition to playing a worthy opponent in a beautiful setting, there was something else that was special about the event. Months before, Tony was given a few options about where he would like to play his next televised match. When he found out that Bermuda was a possible site, he opted for that in no time. Part of his ancestry had spent time on the island of Bermuda and Tony thought it would be neat to visit Bermuda and do a little research. Shortly after making the decision to play there, Tony decided it would be an excellent setting to bring the entire Lema family. While negotiating with *Shell's Wonderful World of Golf*, Tony had one request. "Instead of paying me," he explained, "can you use that money to take care of the travel and accommodation expenses for my family? If the expenses are more than what I get paid for doing the show, just bill me the difference." Needless to say, the people at Shell Oil were wonderful as the Lema family enjoyed Elbow Beach to the max. Included on the trip were Tony's wife Betty, his mother Clotilda, his brother Harry and his wife Judi, his sister Bernice and her husband Art, and his brother Walter who was not married at the time. Family members said it was the perfect trip to get together and they all had a wonderful time. Looking back, they realized how very special it really was for everyone.

In his hilarious book, *My Mulligan to Golf*, Fred Raphael described what happened at Bermuda before and during the filming of one of Shell's most noteworthy matches.

"Prior to the match," Raphael wrote, "Tony was his usual jovial self and my last memory of him will always be my best. I bought him a bottle of champagne at dinner the night before the match. He matched my generosity. Then someone else did. Boy, were we hung over the next day—including both Tony and Peter.

"The match got off to a fast start with both Tony and Peter making birdies on the second hole, but after making a birdie on the sixth, Tony was one-stroke up. On the par-3 seventh, he ran into big trouble when his tee shot flew over the green and finished on the down slope of a bunker behind the green. It was a very difficult shot, and he couldn't quite pull it off. He left it in the trap. His next shot from the sand was a beauty, but it was too late. He made a bogey and the match was level.

"On the back nine, Alliss had many opportunities to move ahead of Tony, but his putting failed him on at least four consecutive holes (it might have been the champagne) and he missed his chance for birdies. Tony had been on the ropes for most of the back nine, but Peter could not administer the knockout blow. At No. 17, Lema rebounded and made a 15-footer for birdie and took a one-stroke lead with one hole to play. Alliss made his par on the beautiful finishing hole and Tony had only to make a three-footer to win the match. But it was not to be and, fittingly, the match ended in a tie."

The Greater New Orleans Open was played at Lakewood Country Club in mid-May where Frank Beard fired a five-under par 67 in the final round to post a 12-under par 276 and a two-shot victory over Gardner Dickinson. Tony was one-stroke back after playing his best golf of the season with rounds of 68-71-69-71—279. His third place finish resulted in a check for $5,150, but more importantly his elbow was obviously feeling better and his confidence was building as he approached the warm weather he enjoyed so much.

At the Colonial National Invitational in Fort Worth, TX, Tony picked up right where he left off in New Orleans. After four solid rounds, he ended up at 282, just two shots behind winner Bruce Devlin. Tony got within two strokes on the last nine, but barely missed putts on the five finishing holes. But let's not sell Bruce Devlin short—it was the 26th straight tournament that Bruce had finished in the money. For Tony, it was his second third place finish in two weeks and a check for $6,765 had to make the pain in his right elbow disappear for a while.

Memorial Day weekend was special for Tony as he and Betty returned to her hometown of Oklahoma City and his game was reaching an apex. Prior to the opening round, Tony's last ten rounds had been 71 or better and with the help of medical science, the pain in his elbow was tolerable. He held nothing back as he uncorked four superb rounds (69-68-69-65) over the Quail Creek Golf & Country Club and won the first prize of $8,500 at the Oklahoma City Open by six shots with a record-setting 17-under par 271.

"This is a real good course," Tony said after butchering the 7,173-yard par-72 layout. "The scores would be a lot higher with a halfway decent growing season and the usual winds. Under those conditions, I'd be happy to settle with a 284."

But as it was, Tony's iron play was splendid all week and he spoke highly of the course conditions. "The course played excellently," he said enthusiastically. "The greens were terrific throughout, and I never had a bad fairway lie."

It was the best weather the PGA Tour had seen in some time, and it was unusual for the usually gusty plains of Oklahoma. But as it was, the rough was short, the winds were minimal and Tony probably combined four of the finest days of golf he had ever put together. He went 72 holes without a bogey—except for a one-over par caused when a two-stroke penalty wiped out a birdie in the second round. On the fifteenth hole, Tony unknowingly played improperly from a drop area of ground under repair. After the round, he was set to sign his scorecard when playing partner Ernie Vossler said the matter should be discussed with PGA officials. A two-stroke penalty was assessed to Tony's score. Had he signed the card—as it stood it—would have meant disqualification for signing an incorrect card, so instead of a 66 he took a 68.

"It's better to be here at 137 than have a 135 and be on my way home to Dallas," said Tony after having the birdie changed to a bogey. "I don't care what anybody says about that penalty, I played 72 holes without a bogey as far as I'm concerned. I don't believe I've ever heard of that before."

Tony started the final round one stroke behind Tom Weiskop, but quickly gained the lead by holing out a chip for a birdie on the second hole while Weiskopf had bogeyed the first. In a threesome with Kermit Zarley and Nicklaus, Tony felt the turning point came on the par-five eighth hole where he made a four-foot birdie putt while Nicklaus made a dramatic recovery from a water shot but missed a putt inside three feet, settling for a bogey.

"I knew I was in good shape, but I decided to keep playing it all-out," Tony said. "I was worried about Jack. I knew he would have to hump the rest of the way." Nick Seitz reported in a local newspaper "It was all over but the champagne guzzling after Tony birdied Nos. 10, 11 and 13 to go 17-under par. He parred in. Weiskopf trailed by six strokes, Nicklaus by eight as Tony's last round was a solid 32-33—65."

Tony was almost as bubbly after his victory as the champagne he provided for the press. "I'm never coming back to Oklahoma," Tony joked, "because I want to remember it this way—windless." But Tony, who sipped champagne with the press corps after his victory, had every intention of returning. "I haven't had any of this since last August," Tony said in the pressroom. While looking over a scorecard for photographers, Tony was asked to explain his strategy for his wife.

"Get down the fairway, on the green and in the hole as fast as you can," he laughed.

Champagne Tony Lema had faced a head-on combat with Tom Weiskopf and Jack Nicklaus, the Masters Champion in 1965 and 1966. He played superlative golf and won his 12th PGA tour championship. It was perhaps the most gratifying victory in his career. Elbow surgery would be scheduled for later in the year, but Tony looked forward to playing in Memphis, the Buick Open, the U.S. Open at Olympic Golf Club in San Francisco and of course, the British Open at Muirfield in July.

At the Memphis Open the following week, Tony upped his streak of consecutive rounds of 71 or better to 18 in a row as he shot 69-70-69-69—277 and finished in a tie for ninth place. Then it was a return to Grand Blanc, MI and a quest for Tony to win his third straight Buick Open title. The press chided him in a friendly manner when they asked if his mind was on the Buick Open or was he gearing up for the U.S. Open the next week at the Olympic Club in San Francisco.

"That's the one every golfer wants to win," Tony said referring to the Open, "but what's wrong with trying to pick up $20,000 along the way?" He explained the fact that being the defending champion had nothing to do with his decision to play at Warwick Hills. "I don't like to take a week off before the really big one," said Tony. "If I do, I get too charged up thinking about it. This way I concentrate on the job at hand and let next week take care of itself. Of course, I'm thinking about the Open—all golfers do, but I honestly feel I'll have a better chance to win it by playing here."

Tony, along with many others in the 144-man field, used the Buick Open as a final tune-up for the "really big one." "I notice," Tony remarked, "that Arnie is here, too."

Despite Tony's love of the Warwick Hills golf course, his affection for the fans, and his track record, something went wrong in his first round. He stumbled home with a horrendous 78. It would have been easy for him to say, "This just isn't my week" and go through the motions on Friday, miss the cut and head home for some early practice rounds at the Olympic Club. But that wasn't the way Tony Lema played golf. He buckled down in that second round, shot a terrific six-under par 66, followed that with weekend rounds of 70 and 73 to finish in a tie for fourth and pick up a check for $4,650.

Jack Clowser, a golf reporter for the *Cleveland Press* filed a story a few weeks later that no doubt revealed another dimension of the ever-going non-stopping humor that Anthony

David Lema provided for the media. He hadn't been above 71 in 18 tournament rounds prior to his first round 78. After a similar debacle, many players on the tour would have sought to avoid an interview. "Say it's a good thing I'm a multi-millionaire, so I don't need this money," he beamed.

The next day following that magnificent 66, one of the reporters in the pressroom asked, "Could you explain such a complete reversal of form overnight?" Tony replied, "Well, it's like this, fellows. My wife flew up to the tournament yesterday, and we hadn't seen each other for over a week. So we just spent a nice relaxing evening watching television, and I settled down and shot a 66."

A good friend of Tony's, Phil Rodgers, won the tournament at 284 with runners-up Kermit Zarley and Johnny Pott tying for second at 286. Tony's turnaround was a perfect example of how to overcome a terrible day on the golf course and prove to yourself that you can come back and post a high finish. Without all of those disappointments that Tony suffered from 1959-1962, I doubt he would have developed the inner strength and the ability to stay in the present tense and never give up. Somewhere in his mind during the second round, he had to say to himself, "I owe it to these fans here at the Buick Open to show them I appreciate their support and there's no give-up in this golfer."

The Olympic Country Club in San Francisco was an exciting site for the 1966 U.S. Open. The course wasn't particularly long at 6,719 yards, but the rough was wiry and every fairway on the undulating course was flanked by trees. When Ben Hogan and Jack Fleck tied for the 1955 U.S. Open at Olympic, their four-round total was 287. Although Arnold Palmer had finished 10th on the money list in 1965, he was regaining confidence in his putting and had won the Los Angeles Open in January and the Tournament of Champions in April. Since his first Masters victory in 1958, Arnold had captured the "Green Jacket" three more times, the 1960 U.S. Open at Cherry Hills in Denver, two British Open titles in 1961 and 1962 and 42 PGA events. Arnold had been nicknamed "the King" and the end of his reign was nowhere in sight. He was not the Palmer of old, but at age 36 he still possessed the swashbuckling attitude as he "hitched" his trousers when he was pumped up and he rolled putts into the back of the cup as well as anyone.

Following a mediocre first round of 71, Palmer shot a spectacular 66 on the second day as he putted for birdies on every hole except one and was only off the fairway once. But, as Peter Alliss noted in his book, *Peter Alliss' Most Memorable Golf*, "Was it ominous, however, that Arnold had missed short putts on each of the last two greens?"

After 36 holes, Arnold and Billy Casper, who had rounds of 69 and 68, were tied atop the leaderboard at 137. Jack Nicklaus, the man Palmer feared the most, was five strokes behind having had two rounds of 71. Tony got off to an unspectacular start with a 71-74—145, eight shots behind but still in the hunt.

Palmer and Casper were paired in the third round and Arnold started boldly as he pulled away with a four-shot lead after six holes. Errors crept into his game and by the 13th hole, they were deadlocked, but Casper was in the rough seven times and eventually faltered to a 73, whereas Palmer steadied his ship and posted a 70. Tony played well, shot a 70, and remained eight shots behind the leader. Going into the final round, it was a four-horse race: Palmer 207; Casper 210; Nicklaus 211; and Lema at 215.

In the final round, Palmer galloped away on the front nine with a superb 32, establishing a seven-stroke lead on Casper with Jack Nicklaus and Tony nine shots behind. Rick Reilly wrote an exciting article for *Sports Illustrated* some 21 years later entitled "Seven Ahead, Nine to Go, and Then?" In that story, Reilly captured some interesting quotes including something Billy Casper said to Arnold at the turn. "You know Arnie, I'm really going to have to go now to get second place." Other thoughts undoubtedly crept into Palmer's mind. He started the day with hopes of breaking the U.S. Open record of 276, set by Ben Hogan at the Riviera Country Club in 1948. Years later, Palmer said, "I knew what the record was, and I knew I had the British Open record (276 at Troon in 1962), I thought it would be nice to have both." He only needed a round of 68 to do that and it was well within his grasp—a 36 on the final nine and the record belonged to him. Palmer bogeyed the par-4 10th hole with a poor chip and he two-putted from 10 feet. After he bogeyed the par-3 thirteenth hole, he needed to par the last five to break Hogan's record and he had a five-shot cushion on Casper. On the par-3 fifteenth, a 150-yard hole, Palmer went boldly for the flag despite the fact that the pin was well to the right side of the green close to some bunkers. His ball drifted a little too far to the right and ended up in one of those bunkers. Arnie blasted out to within nine feet, watched as Casper drained his birdie putt and then missed his. Suddenly, Casper had cut Palmer's lead to three with three holes to play.

Looking back, Billy Casper recently described what he thought was the turning point. "Really, it happened at 15," he explained. "The flag was cut in the right front part of the green and I hit it about 28-30 feet beyond the hole and Arnold went for the flag and ended up in the trap to the right and came out long. I holed my putt and he missed his and lost two shots. As we walked to the sixteenth tee I thought to myself, 'I can win this tournament' and I think that as he walked to the next tee he was thinking, 'I think I could lose this tournament now.' "

Casper played the 604-yard par-5 sixteenth to perfection. He laced a driver down the center of the fairway, followed with an online two-iron down the fairway and a 5-iron on the green close enough for a makeable birdie putt. On the other hand, Palmer had thoughts of reaching the green in two, but pulled his tee shot and tried to force a three-iron out of the long and sticky rough. The ball traveled about 70 yards and nestled itself into even deeper rough. Following a wedge shot back to the fairway, Palmer attempted to reach the green with a 3-wood on his fourth shot but found a greenside bunker. Miraculously, he got up and down for a bogey and stood one shot ahead of Casper as they headed for the 17th hole. Arnie pulled another tee shot into the rough on the long par-4 and registered another bogey due to poor driving. Casper made a one-putt par and the gentlemen were dead even with one hole to play.

On the short, 330-yards, but devilish 18th hole at Olympic, Palmer attempted to play it safe. Later, he recalled his thoughts as he prepared to hit on the 18th tee. "I'm just thinking, 'Get this son of a bitch in the fairway.' " Once again, he swung too fast and the one-iron shot flew left, into the deep, snarly rough.

Ironically, Palmer's ball was very close to the same spot Hogan played from 11 years earlier. In his book, *Go for Broke*, Arnie described the lie and everything he put into the shot. "My ball was caught deeply in the tangled rough," he explained, "and it would take a high lofted club—the 9-iron—to dig it out of there. And the way the ball was sitting, it figured that I wouldn't hit it much more than halfway to the green with that club. But I put everything I had—every muscle that could be brought to bear—into that nine-iron shot."

Mike Reasor, his caddy who later became a regular player on the tour, described the shot from his vantage point. "I've never seen such an ugly lie. I took a look at it and I said, 'this guy would do well to hit it in the front bunker.' The veins were bulging out of his neck. He took a swath of grass you couldn't believe. The ball barely flew over the lip of that bunker, but it came out with no spin and rolled clear to the back of the green. It was the greatest shot I've ever seen."

Palmer was 30 feet away with a slick downhill putt while Casper was half that distance from the cup putting for a birdie. After his first putt stopped three feet short of the hole, Arnie realized, along with the huge gallery surrounding the green, that he had to putt again, three feet, straight downhill, with the U.S. Open title on the line. At that time, the continuous putting rule was in force. After the fact, Palmer let it be known what his thoughts were at the time. "I remember looking at that putt and thinking, 'Everything is on the line here. My pride. My business. My livelihood.' And there I was making it even harder." He then rammed the ball into the hole. Casper two-putted for his par and they tied for first place at 278. Nicklaus finished third, seven shots back at 285. Tony shot a 71 in the final round and wound up in fourth place at 286. As Arnie headed for the press conference following that debacle, he recalled later, "All I could think was, 'I've just lost a 7-shot lead in the U.S. Open, and now I've got to tell the press exactly how I did it.' "

Casper summed up the fourth round very succinctly when he said, "The only way that all could have happened was that I had to play extremely well and he had to play a mediocre round on the back nine. It was interesting!"

In the 18-hole playoff the next day, Palmer surged ahead

with a 33 on the front nine while Casper settled for a 35. But Casper showed his never-say-die attitude by canning a 40-foot birdie putt on the eleventh hole and a 50-footer on number thirteen. Coincidentally, Palmer made errors similar to the day before, including butchering the par-5 sixteenth again, this time a double-bogey seven. The final score: Casper 69; Palmer 73. As Rick Reilly noted in his article, "For the back nine on the last two days, Casper shot 66, Palmer 79."

It's amazing how the touring pros in the 1960's would come off such a grueling tournament as the U.S. Open and play the very next week halfway across the country. That's exactly what Tony did as well as the newly crowned U.S. Open champion. Not only that, Casper's playoff victory over Palmer was on Monday so three days later it was time for Casper to put the peg in the ground at the Western Open at Medinah C.C. in Chicago. And let's not forget, Casper had won the 1965 Western Open at Tam O'Shanter so it was only fitting that he would return and defend his championship. Medinah C.C. #3 proved to be a noteworthy venue as Casper was the only golfer in the field to shoot under-par as he collected another tour championship with a one-under par 283.

For the third week in a row, Tony played solid golf (71-71-75-71—288) and finished in a tie for fifth place. So, from the middle of May until the end of June, Tony had really put some impressive numbers on the scoreboard: a T3 at New Orleans; another T3 at the Colonial; a win at Oklahoma City; a T9 at Memphis; a T4 at the Buick; a T4 at the U.S. Open; and a T5 at the Western Open. The last round of the Western was played on June 26, so Tony and the other competitors had until Wednesday July 6 to prepare for the 95th Open Championship at Muirfield Golf Links in Gullane, East Lothian, Scotland.

After the first round at Muirfield Golf Links, Tony's one-under par 71 was one shot behind the leader, Jack Nicklaus. At that point, Nicklaus and a group of golfers who had the knack for links golf pulled away. Tony shot 76, 76, and a 75 to finish at 298 in a tie for 30th place. In the meantime, Nicklaus fired a 67 to take the half-way lead which he lost to Phil Rodgers after a third round 75. He followed that with a two-under par 70 to finish at 282 and a one-stroke victory over the colorful

Doug Sanders and Dave Thomas of Wales. Third-rounder leader Phil Rodgers stumbled home with a 76, but had nothing to be ashamed of with a fourth-place finish. It was Nicklaus' first Open Championship, (he would eventually capture two more, both at St. Andrews, in 1970 and 1978) and he proclaimed Muirfield to be "the best golf course in Britain."

The exact day is not certain, but sometime between the final round of the Open Championship and the beginning of the PGA Championship at Firestone C.C., Tony sat down with Howard Cosell at Westchester C.C. in Rye, NY. They recorded an interview entitled *Tony Lema: Champagne on the Green* that was filmed by Howard Cosell Productions in association with WABC-TV in New York. Cosell was known for his unabashed manner of firing "tough to answer questions" that were preceded by quite a bit of thought and research. Here are the highlights of that conversation:

Howard Cosell: Tony, right here on the 18th green at Westchester Country Club, you made an 8-foot birdie putt to capture the 1964 Thunderbird Classic and a one-shot victory over Mike Souchak. I recall that you backed away from the putt, gathered yourself and then knocked it right into the hole. Tell me, were you nervous as you stood over that putt for the second time?

Tony Lema: I was so nervous I could hardly hold the club. You have no idea of the tension in professional golf. That putt was the most important putt to me in professional golf.

Howard Cosell: You say it was the most important putt of your professional golfing career. Why?

Tony Lema: That's right Howard, I would hate to think what would've happened had that putt not gone in the hole. You know I had a pretty big lead there in the tournament. I think it was almost as high as seven strokes with 11 holes to go. I started to deteriorate a little bit. Mike Souchak actually picked up eight strokes on me and went one shot ahead and I birdied the next to last hole to draw even with him. He had made a five on this par-five 18th hole and I had that 8-foot putt for a four. So I was quite nervous as I stood up to it and as you saw there, I couldn't take the putter back the first time. I had to back off and collect myself, and thank God I went up, hit it and it went into the hole.

Howard Cosell: Yes, but the essential point is, it was the most important putt you said of your golfing life. Why? Because of what might've happened to you if you had missed it?

Tony Lema: Right, I think it would've done so much to knock my confidence down, to have a big lead and then lose the tournament. But as it was, I had a big lead, lost it and then finished birdie–birdie to win it. So nobody can say Tony Lema choked—at least not then.

Howard Cosell: I wonder if people really do understand the enormous pressure of competitive golf, which you also hinted at, at the top of the show.

Tony Lema: I don't really think anybody can, unless they actually do play it themselves under tournament conditions. A player like Ben Hogan and Sam Snead right now, even though they are in their early 50's can hit the ball as well now as they ever could. But on the short and important chip shots and putts, their nerves just aren't good enough to carry them through. I know, I'm 32 years old now and I must have nerves of about an 80 year-old. They're shot. They are, yeah.

Howard Cosell: It never changes, from tournament to tournament, you're ready to crack up.

Tony Lema: That's right. I think the thing that makes a winner in golf, is not only the best player, but the one who can keep control of his nerves better than the next guy.

Howard Cosell: How do you do it?

Tony Lema: Talk to myself, concentration, prayer, many things. Whatever way you feel that you can do it, that's the way to go ahead and do it.

Howard Cosell: Tony, in 1962, you really started to connect. Up until then, you were going nowhere as I remember, as a pro golfer.

Tony Lema: That's right Howard, I went for almost five full years on the PGA Tour before I won my first major golf championship. And it happened out in Orange County, California in 1962. That's also where I got the nickname, "Champagne Tony." I was leading after three rounds and I was in the press tent, drinking a cold beer, pretty hot day and I was quite elated about the fact that I was winning. And I told the boys, well, if were in here tomorrow we're going to celebrate with champagne. So I lucked out, won the tournament, we celebrated with champagne and ever since then it's been "Champagne Tony."

Howard Cosell: And you represent a company?

Tony Lema: That's right, Moet & Chandon.

Howard Cosell: And you indulge?

Tony Lema: I do. I imbibe a little bit.

Howard Cosell: Yes, it's been "Champagne Tony" ever since and it's Champagne Tony who pours it on the green. But up until you won that tournament you had been seriously flirting with the idea of quitting professional golf, hadn't you?

Tony Lema: Yes, that's right Howard. I was going to make sure that before I got married and things like that, I wanted to be successful at what I was doing. I fell in love just prior to the fall of 1962. When I won my first two or three tournaments, I think that falling in love with my wife gave me just the edge that I needed, to kind of settle myself down. I think it made a tremendous difference.

Howard Cosell: Stabilize you. Gave you motivation.

Tony Lema: Just goes to show you that love can do anything. Even win golf tournaments.

Howard Cosell: That's right and last year (1965) you won, according to the official purses, $101,816. That's a lot of money in one year.

Tony Lema: I hope there's no taxman around here. (Laughter)

Howard Cosell: And the year before that, you won around $70,000, and before that you won over $60,000. So they say now, "golfers are spoiled." The money is too much and they're getting their hands on it too easily.

Tony Lema: Let me tell you something right there, Howard. I can't agree with you more, but it's wonderful. (Laughter)

Howard Cosell: Tony, you've still got some big ones to win. You've still got a lot of winning to do.

Tony Lema: That's right, Howard. I don't think I would be really happy with myself unless I won one of the three major championships in the United States. You know, there are four major championships in the world; the British Open, the Masters, PGA, and the US Open. I would like to win the American National Open. That would be my big goal in golf.

Howard Cosell: And of course, you have won the British Open.

Tony Lema: Right. And really, I would not be too unhappy if I didn't ever win anything any more. I feel very fortunate that I have won as many as I have. It's been a wonderful surprise to me.

Howard Cosell: Yes it has, but at the same time Tony, in perfect candor, you saw the merging in this country of the so-called "Big Three," Palmer, Player and Nicklaus. You didn't take to this because you know perfectly well that you're a pretty important golfer in this country, and so is Casper and so are well, a lot of others. But you didn't like this "Big Three" development, did you?

Tony Lema: Well, I'm not too crazy about it. I think it's the three of them and I will not deny the fact that they are great players and they've got all the major championships in the world. But every week they go into a tournament, it's the "Big Three." If they're not there, they write about them all week, about not being at the tournament. And if they're there, they write about them all week no matter how they finish in the tournament. They just don't win that many tournaments throughout the year that this constantly has to be shoved down our throats. They're three wonderful guys, great names in the game of golf, but too many times players like Bobby Nichols, Billy Casper and some great young players are not getting a fair shake.

Howard Cosell: Fact of the matter is Tony, and you know this, I'm not going to make you be immodest about it, you've got a kind of personal glamor that at least two of that so called "Big Three" does not have. You're aware of it, aren't you?

Tony Lema: Well, I'm not. I really don't follow you there. I love to play golf and I'm an emotional kind of a character. If things are going badly, I'm liable to frown, but then at the same time I like to laugh at myself. I am fortunate enough so I can do that. And if I'm happy, well, I laugh a little and live it up.

Howard Cosell: I remember one tournament though, the one we talked about earlier, the big one you won, the British Open. That's not a big money tournament Tony, and yet it meant so much to you. Describe your emotions.

Tony Lema: That's right, Howard, the British Open is one of the four prestige championships in the world, and contrary to what you probably believe, when I won it, it was the most humbling experience I've ever had in golf.

Howard Cosell: Why humbling? Why that word?

Tony Lema: Well, the reason I went over in the first place, was to visit St. Andrews, which is the birthplace of golf. And when I won it, I was taken into the room where they make the all the rules of golf, the Royal & Ancient Golf Committee Room. I saw the old golf balls, the old golf clubs, and all these pictures of the old players. It made me realize how it started and what it is all about. I really felt quite humble and fortunate enough to win it.

Howard Cosell: Actually you had a kind of humble demeanor throughout the tournament. For instance, in the next to last round, do you remember that brilliant putt of yours on the 18th green?

Tony Lema: Well, that helped to win. It was a putt of about 30 feet on the 18th hole. The best part about it was, Jack Nicklaus was getting ready to tee off on his fourth round off the first tee and he was watching me putt out. And when I holed that 30-footer, I looked at him, he looked at me, and he just shook his head.

Howard Cosell: He made a charge at you during that tournament, as a matter fact.

Tony Lema: Yes he did, he came from quite a ways back a couple of times there, very close. When Jack is charging at you, you know you've been charged at.

Howard Cosell: And then there was the final day in the final round, the crowd swarming around you after you pitched to the 18th green, the way they always do and you bursting through the crowd, you remember the feeling?

Tony Lema: It was fantastic. The minute I chipped the ball, the crowd closed in on me and I couldn't even see where the ball ended up. They were kind of grabbing, pushing and pulling me. Some were trying to help me get through while others were hanging on. I was lucky I got out with my life, but they're great people.

Howard Cosell: Do you remember the elation as you seized the ball from the cup?

Tony Lema: Well, I was elated when I got through the crowd and found out the ball was two feet from the hole. (Laughter)

Howard Cosell: Tony, are there many rivalries among you pro golfers? How do you really get along? You, personally, with the rest of the guys.

Tony Lema: Well, I'll tell ya. I think you would be very surprised. I have never seen any fights and very few times have there been any harsh words. With all the pressure that we are under, we are constantly on edge. I think everybody respects everybody else's feelings. We're living with each other practically every day and there is a camaraderie that is second to none. I think it's a great bunch of guys.

Howard Cosell: Who are your best friends? Do you have any?

Tony Lema: Oh, Phil Rodgers, Bobby Nichols, quite a few of them. I'd say they're all good friends of mine.

Howard Cosell: In 1964, when you and Bobby Nichols and Ken Venturi had three of the four major titles, didn't you guys plan to form your own "Big Three" of golf to put an end to the Nicklaus, Palmer Player thing?

Tony Lema: Well, I had the idea that if the three of us got together and formed our own "Big Three," or whatever you'd want to call it, we might be able to have something come of it, but nothing happened. Golf is a game of individuals, and that's what we were, three individuals. We just never got together.

Howard Cosell: You know, I talked before about the desperate frustration that comes with double bogeying. Let's hit this one right on the nose. The public wants to know about this. In your opinion, will Arnold Palmer ever get over his collapse in the National Open at Olympic CC in San Francisco here in 1966?

Tony Lema: Well, it's going to be a very difficult question to answer. But I would say that no matter if Arnie wins the U.S. Open 10 straight times he will never forget the fact that he had it locked up and it got away from him. Why or how, I don't think anybody knows and I don't know if Arnold knows. It's just one of those things. You've got to live with it. He's going to have it on his mind...

Howard Cosell: Has it already affected his play? Have you seen it affect his play?

Tony Lema: I don't really think so, I think Arnie has got a lot of good years left, he's not old by any means and he's strong as a bull and I think he is going to be around for a lot of years to come. And he's got the determination that every time he gets a little bit down, that gives him more incentive and he comes back better than ever.

Howard Cosell: Let's put together the perfect golf game, leaving Tony Lema's game out of it for the moment. If you had the ideal driver, I don't mean actual club, I mean golfer, who would you pick?

Tony Lema: I'd like to play Jack Nicklaus' second shots. I really would.

Howard Cosell: All right, who do you think hits the best iron shots?

Tony Lema: There are about three or four that I would like to hit the irons for me. There's Billy Casper, Tom Weiskopf, Frank Beard and Phil Rodgers.

Howard Cosell: And on the green?

Tony Lema: On the green, I'll take to two California boys and you can pick anybody else you want. I'll take Phil Rodgers and Billy Casper and I'll go with my team.

Howard Cosell: Are you running a Billy Casper hour these days?

Tony Lema: Sounds like it but I'll tell ya, the guy is a very underrated player and as far as the mechanics of the game, I don't think there are too many people much better.

Howard Cosell: Do you think he's the greatest all-around player in the game today, leaving you out of it?

Tony Lema: Well, if he's not, he comes darn close to it.

Howard Cosell: Do you think you can be?

Tony Lema: Well, for what I'd have to do to try to get to that position, I don't know if I would like to try it.

Howard Cosell: Let's try this. Let's walk around to the clubhouse, Tony, have a seat at a table, maybe a drink, and talk some more.

Howard Cosell: Tony, a lot of people think this is the life, plush Country Club, the land of soft breezes and beautiful surroundings. This is the way you fellows are generally figured to live, but tell the people how many weeks out of the year you are at home.

Tony Lema: Howard, I'm lucky if I get home six weeks a year and I'm darn lucky if I get to sit on the veranda at a Country Club. We keep a pretty hectic schedule.

Howard Cosell: What's it do to your marriage?

Tony Lema: I take my wife with me, so I don't have that problem. But I don't see how the guys with kids going to school and their wives at home really make it. I think it would be a lousy life.

Howard Cosell: As a matter of fact, one of the principal problems, golfers who are on the trail, who are married, face, is the very fact of worrying about their families and that interferes with their concentration and their play. Is that not so?

Tony Lema: That's for sure. I think that a guy who has a family at home and he's out on the road and he's playing winning golf, I think that's a tribute to his concentration.

Howard Cosell: And yet it's a fact that you want children and that you and Betty will have children.

Tony Lema: I hope so.

Howard Cosell: So this could seriously affect your professional future.

Tony Lema: Well, what I am going to do Howard, and I am no spring chicken, is that when the kids get up to the age when they are at home and going to school, that's the day I'm going to quit playing.

Howard Cosell: How long will that be, do you suppose?

Tony Lema: Well, I hope it won't be much over five or ten years from now. It's a great game and I would like to play it forever, but I want to stay home, too.

Howard Cosell: You say it's a great game Tony, but there's a coterie of sportswriters in this country that says; golf is not a sport, it's a game. A pastime, because there is no offense or defense, there's no potential body contact. That even baseball has contact, leaving basketball and football aside. What's your rejoinder?

Tony Lema: Well, we don't have any physically contact, but we've got everything any other sport has. We have offense and defense on the course and we have plenty of it. And to play good winning golf, you have to be in tremendous physical condition. So, I don't know where they get the idea that we are not athletes. I think we certainly fill that bill without any problem.

Howard Cosell: You really have to be in tremendous condition. For instance, the public knows that Jack Nicklaus and Phil Rodgers are…pudgy.

Tony Lema: A little portly, I'd say. But you see, they're still in very good condition. They're strong, both of them. Just the fact that they like to taste what's on the table a little more then a lot of other people, does not say they are in bad condition. I know a lot of football players that weigh quite a bit and some baseball players have a pretty good pouch on them.

Howard Cosell: And that's right. I was waiting for you to get to that point because it's very, very true. In golf, a man plays basically against himself, doesn't he?

Tony Lema: That's right. It's a game, against your self and within your self.

Howard Cosell: And isn't this perhaps the greatest test of all?

Tony Lema: You can almost find that to be true in any sport, but in golf you don't have to rely on any teammates. (That their attitude will be the same as yours). In golf it's all you, nobody else.

Howard Cosell: As a matter of fact, this is one of the most demanding challenges known to American sport. The individual sport: where a man can't look to another man for help. Koufax (LA Dodger pitcher) gets help from eight other men. No matter how you slice it.

Tony Lema: That's very true in baseball and football games. How many guys are saved by a good catch, or a good block, or a good pass. In golf, you make the breaks. You hit it and where you hit it, you go find it, and hit it again.

Howard Cosell: As you recap your golfing life thus far, Tony, what would you say is your greatest frustration?

Tony Lema: My greatest frustration is the fact that I have to live out of a suitcase, and in hotels and motels. I've hit too many bad shots that meant something to pick out one and I've been quite delighted with quite a few good ones.

Howard Cosell: Wait a minute Tony. You said Palmer would never get over his collapse in the National Open. You said that earlier. And you claim that you can get over missed putts that cost you a lot of money.

Tony Lema: Not really, because they all come back. Whether it be when I'm laying in bed or traveling on an airplane or some conscious moment. A lot these things come back. I don't have anything quite like the burden Arnie has, but he'll live with it.

Howard Cosell: What has been your most rewarding moment apart from the putt right here at Westchester that won you the Thunderbird?

Tony Lema: The putt that I made from about ten feet to win my first official tournament on the Tour. (Orange County Open, 1962) I think that in every pro's life, that very first tournament win was the one that really got the monkey off his back. And it certainly did for me.

Howard Cosell: When you do give up golf, the pro tour at least, how would you like people to remember you? How would you like them to characterize you?

Tony Lema: Well, I really haven't thought of that, Howard. I would just like to play good golf, successful golf as long as I can. If I'm remembered, that's fine.

Howard Cosell: Do you want to be remembered as a great golfer?

Tony Lema: Ah, I don't know, I'd rather be remembered as a decent sort of person and as an athlete.

Howard Cosell: That's exactly the point I was getting to. So it will be enough for you to be thought of as one of the glamour boys in the golden age of golf.

Tony Lema: In the right way, "glamour" yeah.

Howard Cosell: Uh huh, and the glamour includes champagne.

Tony Lema: Would you like some?

Howard Cosell: I'd love some.

(With that, Tony uncorked a bottle of Moet et Chandon and filled two glasses.)

Tony Lema; There's nothing like ending a nice day or a good game of golf with a little taste of the bubbly.

Howard Cosell: Tony, I enjoyed it.

Tony Lema: Cheers.

The last major tournament scheduled in 1966 was the 48th PGA Championship, played July 21-24 on the South Course at Firestone Country Club in Akron, OH. Oddly enough, the 1966 PGA Championship was originally scheduled to be held at Columbine Country Club in Columbine Valley, Colorado, a suburb of south of Denver. A flash flood of the adjacent South

Platte River in June 1965 caused significant damage to the course and forced a postponement. Firestone was scheduled to host in 1967, so the venues swapped years.

A not-so-young but vibrant Sam Snead, at age 54 , shared the first round lead with Al Geiberger, as each fired two-under par 68's. Snead held the lead alone after 36-holes as he shot a 71 on Friday while Geiberger managed a two-over par 72. There was a host of really good players at the top of the leaderboard as play continued into the weekend. Those players included: Dudley Wysong, Billy Casper, Gene Littler, Gary Player, Julius Boros, Jacky Cupit, Arnold Palmer and Doug Sanders. Tony got off to a horrendous start as he shot a 78 in the first round, but came back with a respectable 71 on the second day to make the 36-hole cut by a few shots. On Saturday, Tony shot a 72 and stood at 221, some 13 shots out of the lead as Geiberger came back with a 68 in the third round to take a four-stroke advantage over Dudley Wysong going into the final round.

At breakfast on Sunday morning, Tony was in a hurry. "Betty's eaten and I told her I would be only 15 minutes," he explained, asking the waitress to bring him his check along with his food. He gulped down his juice, bacon and eggs with one hand and signed the check with the other.

"Now don't," he told the waitress, "spend this tip in one place. See you later," he said, when he took off.

"Good luck, Tony," she said as he left.

"Thanks, I'll need it," he said.

The *UPI* reporters said that was the last time they saw Tony smiling, gay and full of life. After all, he was about to meet his lovely wife and go out and play the game he loved, the game that brought fame and fortune. Little did he know it was going to be his last round.

When Tony arrived at Firestone Country Club that Sunday morning, July 24, 1966 a rather awkward conversation took place in the locker room. Tom Place, the popular and always busy golf writer for the *Cleveland Plain Dealer*, had covered many events over the years that Tony had played in. Hence, they became good friends as happens many times among PGA Tour players and golfwriters. While covering the PGA Championship at Firestone C.C., Tom recently shared what happened that

Sunday before and after Tony's round.

"My Dad came over from Pennsylvania to watch the final round of the PGA Championship," Tom recalled. "We were sitting in the press tent, a big tent in the parking lot at that time. I told my Dad, 'I'm going to talk to Tony for a moment because I know he is leaving right after the tournament. He has a chartered flight over to Illinois after his round. I want to go over and say goodbye and make sure everything is OK.' So, Dad and I went over and Tony was sitting on a bench in front of his locker and we chatted about some things. He started to say, where he was going and so forth. Then Tony said, 'I'm playing lousy this week.' I will never forget his exact words that followed. He continued, 'I just wish I could get out of here. I just wish I could get out of here. I'm playing lousy. I just wish I could get out of here.' He said that three times. I have never, ever forgotten that. And he got up and said, 'I guess I'd better get going.' The three of us walked down the staircase at Firestone towards the first tee as he was making his way over to the practice area. Tony said, 'Hey, I'll see you before I leave. I'll stop by the press tent. I think Betty will stop by, too.' "

As Tom and his Dad walked back to the press tent, his Dad said, "I've never heard Tony talk like that." And I said, "I never have either. That's the first time I've ever heard him say something like that. Maybe he just had a premonition that something was going to happen. That he needed to get away from there for some reason and he didn't know what it was."

Tony managed to knock it around in a four-over par 74 to finish the tournament at 295, some 15 shots over par. On his 72nd hole, the long and challenging par-4 at Firestone Country Club, the incident described in the *Prologue* of this book took place. After smashing his tee shot down the fairway, Tony saw the two lads fighting over his tee that had landed at their feet. As a reporter and a golf fan, I can still see Tony reach into his pocket and pour those golden tees into the hands of those youngsters. They scurried away and standing just a few feet away, I said, "That was nice Tony." Although 47 years have passed, I can still hear Tony's words ringing clearly as he began to stroll off the tee. "Hey," he smiled as he looked towards me, "they're only kids. Besides, this is my last hole." I wished him luck and he said, "Thank you." Little did anyone know just how special that gesture was to those two youngsters.

About ten minutes later, *Cleveland Plain Dealer* golf reporter, Tom Place, was standing outside the scorecard signing area and continued his account of what took place.

"He completed his round in midafternoon since he was one of the early starters. He was signing his scorecard and Betty came over and said, 'Well, we're on our way. Where are we going to see you next?' I don't remember where it was but I told her, 'One of these weeks, we'll catch up with you again.'

"A few moments later, Tony walked in and we stood and chatted for a while. Some people wanted to talk with Tony but he replied, 'Hey, I'm talking with Tom here.' So, we just visited and he said, 'I guess I'd better get on my way.' We shook hands and away he went."

After he said "goodbye" to Tom Place, Tony headed for the locker room getting ready to pack up and head for the airport. Due to the airline strike that was going on at the time, Tony had arranged to charter a flight from Akron to Hammond, IL, about 35 miles southeast of Chicago. He was playing in a 36-hole event on Monday and Tuesday in Crete, IL at the Lincolnshire Open. Before he left the locker room, Tony had a rather bitter conversation with Ken Venturi. In 2004 Ken Venturi published an autobiography entitled *Getting Up & Down* and he recalled what took place at Firestone C.C.

"I remember the day vividly," Venturi wrote. "On Sunday afternoon, I confronted my longtime friend, Tony Lema, in the locker room. Lema, I had been told, planned to skip a dinner that was arranged in his honor by a local Italian-American club. I was very disappointed in him.

" 'What are doing?' I said. 'You promised these people you would be there.'

" 'I'm going to an outing in Illinois,' he said. 'They're giving me $2,000. They're flying Betty (his wife) and me up there. I'm going where the money is.'

"I went from disappointment to disgust.

" 'I don't care how much money you're getting,' I argued. 'You gave your word to these people. You can't back out now.'

"My plea did no good.

" 'You will live to regret those words,' I said."

The *UPI* reported that after his round on Sunday, Tony was in a hurry to catch the flight over to Chicago for the Pro-am on Monday. In his haste, he left his golf shoes in the locker room at the Firestone Country Club.

The following information was contained in the report according to the CIVIL AERONAUTICS BOARD Bureau of Safety.

The Beechcraft H-50, N538B had originally departed from Joliet Municipal Airport, Joliet, Illinois, at approximately 1400 CDT, on July 24, 1966. The purpose of the flight was to pick up two charter passengers at Akron, Ohio, and transport them to the Chicago—Hammond Airport, Lansing, Illinois. Attached to this report is a letter explaining the arrangements of this charter operation. The flight to Akron was not reported other than normal.

At the time of departure from Joliet the pilot-in-command was Mrs. Doris Mullen, occupying the left front seat. Dr. George Bard was occupying the right front seat; this was also the seating arrangement at the time of the crash.

According to Mr. Don Rosenson, the General Manager of Mainline Aviation, Inc., of the Joliet Air Charter Service, Inc., Dr. Bard was not acting in the capacity of co-pilot or crew member.

The investigation revealed that fuel was not added, or that any other service was performed on N538B, while in the Akron area.

A completed IFR flight plan, form 398, was found in the aircraft wreckage. This form states a proposed departure time of 1730 EDT, initial cruising altitude of 10,000 feet, estimated time en route two hours and four hours of fuel on board. The above flight plan is made a part of this report.

The attached ATC (Air Traffic Control) package revealed that there were no distress or in-flight problems reported by the pilot of N538B. The above package entails the transcriptions of the recorded conversations of N538B en route Akron, Ohio to Chicago-Hammond Airport, an uncontrolled airport.

The landing at Akron Municipal Airport was uneventful and at 1613 CDT, N538B called the Akron Combined Station Tower on the local field telephone. N538B filed a flight plan from Akron to Hammond, Indiana, and was given en route weather. At 1727 CDT, N538B departed the Akron Airport on an IFR clearance and was identified on radar.

After climbing to 10,000 feet altitude and at 1822 CDT, Cleveland Center gave Chicago Center a radar hand-off on N538B twelve miles east of Antwerp Intersection, maintaining 10,000 feet MSL. At 1832 CDT, the Chicago Center observed N538B to be north of course and advised the pilot. At 1856 CDT, the Chicago Heights radar controller established radio and radar contact with N538B, verified altitude at 10,000 feet MSL and issued altimeter for Chicago area 30.10. At 1901 CDT, N538B was cleared to descend and maintain 7,000 MSL., and the pilot reported leaving 10,000 feet MSL. Three minutes later N538B was cleared to descend and maintain 3,000 feet MSL. Subsequent to descending to 3,000 feet MSL., the pilot of N538B reported in VFR conditions and cancelled the IFR flight plan. At 1920 CDT, Chicago Center broadcasted to N538B that radar service was terminated and the pilot was cleared to leave Center frequency. At approximately 2020 CDT, the Joliet Flight Service Station received a call from the Illinois State Police that an aircraft had crashed on the Lansing Sportsman's Club at Munster, Indiana.

Post-mortem examination of both pilots revealed no evidence of a human factor was causative to this crash.

Pilot Mullen was issued a Commercial Pilot's Certificate on June 4, 1962, and an instrument rating on March 27,

1963. She held a valid commercial pilot's certificate number 1488424, issued on February 2, 1965. According to Dr. Wylie Mullen, Jr., the pilot's husband, she had accumulated approximately 2,000 total flying hours. His estimation of 700 multi-engine hours was made including about 15 hours in this make and model aircraft.

Research of the FAA records revealed that N538B was properly licensed and certified. The airworthiness certificate was issued on October 12, 1959, and the last inspection, a periodic type, was accomplished on April 12, 1966. An approximate total of 1,682 hours had been accumulated on the airframe, as of July 24, 1966

Approximately forty-five people were interviewed concerning this accident. Attached to and made a part of this report are twenty-one numbered witness statements.

According to witness No.1, who was on the seventh tee of the golf course:
"I usually look to the south and watch for skydivers as I did at this time and observed a twin engine aircraft at a low altitude over the Chicago—Hammond Airport East of the hanger. Due to the low altitude at this point I assumed that the plane was taking off from the airport as I have landed and taken off from the airport as a passenger many times in the last 10 years.... The plane continued in an easterly direction approximately an eighth to a quarter mile south of the High Tension Line which runs east to west in this area. As the plane approached the area... it banked toward the north and the pilot gunned the engines as the altitude of the plane was lower than the wires. After clearing the power lines one or possibly both of the engines began to sputter, and the plane banked slightly to a northwesterly direction. The plane at this time was over a populated area and was headed for the southeast corner of the Lansing Sportsman's Clubhouse at approximately 50 to 75 feet above the rooftops.

"The plane continued in this direction until it was over

the fence on the east side of the clubhouse grounds parallel to the railroad tracks. At this time the pilot banked sharply to the left and the plane pancaked directly in front of the seventh green. As it hit the ground there was the sharp sound of impact. The plane bounced approximately four to five feet into the air at which time it was a slight explosion, similar to the touching of the match to gas fumes, the plane caught fire as it fell into the edge of the lake."

According to seventeen (17) witnesses the direction of flight was to the northeast with a left 180° turn over a residential area. Nineteen (19) witnesses also state that the engines or engine was sputtering or not sounding normal.

Louks Campagna, a witness, said the low-flying plane swerved to avoid a group of people standing near the club house, the engines died, then started and died again, and the plane plunged to the ground, digging up a furrow near the seventh green before bursting into flames as it fell into the water. One witness said onlookers heard screams as they rushed from the club house.

"The pilot was a hero," he said. "The plane swerved to the left—if it didn't a lot of people would have been hurt."

A key witness to the events that happened that afternoon was Joanne Parkhill. On a beautiful October afternoon in 2012, Joanne and I visited the scene of the accident and she described exactly what she saw 46 years ago. She was a member of the Lansing Sportsmen's Club walking down the sixth fairway. She looked skyward, saw the low-flying plane and wondered why airplanes were allowed to fly so close to the ground. She commented to her playing partners, "there ought to be a law about planes flying so low." Within seconds she realized an emergency was happening right before her eyes.

"I was playing with Ed Carne and another lady," she recalled. "When it happened, we ran right to the water's edge and you could see the four people. Once the plane hit the water, the front end went into the water and the tail of the plane came up.

When it came down, it just exploded. There was no movement in the plane. Whatever happened, happened quickly and there was no suffering.

"My family is from Akron, OH and my father had been out at Firestone Country Club that very afternoon watching the players in the PGA Championship. When the crash happened, we found out shortly afterwards that it might possibly have been the plane Tony Lema had chartered. I called my Dad from the mid-course phone booth and said, 'Dad, you're not going to believe this, but they just had a plane crash and there's a possibility it was Tony Lema's plane. In fact, they are almost one-hundred percent sure.' He said, 'I can't believe it. I was out there just hours ago watching Tony play at Firestone.' He called WAKR in Akron and told the radio operator what he had heard from me. The radioman said, 'I can't put that on the air. That is unbelievable! Didn't we just see him play a few hours ago?' My Dad said he just could not believe what had happened.

"I was watching television that evening after the plane crash," Joanne explained, "and I heard on the news that Tony Lema's mother-in-law found out about this tragedy on the news. I thought to myself, 'that is a terrible thing, I can't believe the proper authorities did not get in touch with her. And that's how she found out her daughter and son-in-law had died in the crash.' I thought about it and called the information for Oklahoma City and they gave me her name and address. So I wrote her a letter and told her I was out on the sixth fairway when the plane went down. I told her we ran across the bridge and we were by the water's edge and could see there were four people in the plane and nobody was suffering. I told her that it was over so quickly I don't believe the people in the plane knew….they were unconscious and there was no suffering. It simply happened so fast.

"Never thinking I would hear from her again, about a week later, I received a letter from Mrs. Louise Cline. She wrote, 'You know, I don't know who you are, but all I can tell you is that you have to be a Mother. I wasn't able to sleep, worrying about the pain and suffering they must have gone through and your letter meant so much to me because it gave me peace that there was no suffering. And I want to thank you for getting in touch with me and letting me know.' I thought that was very gracious of her to write back and let me know she had received my letter."

The tragic news of the plane crash reached members of the Lema family in a similiar manner through news media that caught everyone off guard. "Harry and I were watching *Voyage to the Bottom of the Sea* on television," Judi Lema vividly recalled, "and I was holding my six-month old son who was asleep in my arms. All of a sudden, the television announcer said, 'We interrupt this program to bring you a bulletin from our West Coast newsroom. Professional golfer Tony Lema and his wife Betty were killed in a light plane crash.' With that, we just started floundering around, not knowing quite what to do. I told Harry that he had to go to his Mother's because she couldn't be alone, you know, when she heard this. So, he left to go to his Mother's and the phone rang. It was Danny Arnold, the Hollywood producer,(from the *Hazel Show* and *Barney Miller*) and he said, 'Hey, This is Danny Arnold.' Well, I don't usually get phone calls from Hollywood producers. He was very calm and said, 'What are you doing?' And then I started crying. I told him that we were watching TV and he asked, 'Have you heard from anybody?' And I said no, we don't even know if it is true. We have no idea what's happening. And he said, 'I'll get back to you.' He called back a few minutes later and said that he talked to a friend of his from the AP (Associated Press) and he said, 'It's true.' And then I don't remember what we said after that. He said that he would be coming up from LA and contact us or something.

"But Harry's Mom had her daughter's mother-in-law and father-in-law there and they were gardening. The phone rang and it was Cleo's hairdresser, and her hairdresser said, 'What are you doing?' She said that we're here working in the garden. The hairdresser said, 'You're not alone.' And Cleo said, 'no.' The hairdresser said, 'Well, sit down I have something I need to tell you.' So, the hairdresser told her. About that time, Harry pulled up and his Mom just came running out of the house.

"Same thing happened with Bernice," Judi continued. "Not sure of the details, but she had taken Marc to the store because Marc had his learner's permit and he wanted to get some ice cream. Any chance to drive a car when you are sixteen. So they were in the car and Bud was home. And when they got back from the store, Bud had heard the news and told them. But NOBODY ever contacted us officially. It was all through the news. Everybody knew Tony was from San Leandro. All they had to do was call the San Leandro Police. The police knew where Cleo lived. We got sympathy cards addressed to, 'Family of Tony Lema, USA' that came from France and all over. So, there was no reason we were not contacted. And the same thing happened to Louise Cline, she was watching TV when she got the news."

Following the conversation that Ken Venturi had with Tony Lema in the men's locker room earlier that day, he had gone out for dinner and included the following information in his book, *Getting Up and Down.*

"I left for dinner. A few hours later, I returned to my hotel. When I walked in to pick up my keys, the clerk at the counter gave me the news.

" 'It's too bad about that golfer who got killed today,' she said.

"She didn't tell me the name and I didn't ask. Somehow I knew."

After *Cleveland Plain Dealer* golf writer Tom Place had said "goodbye" to Tony and Betty Lema, he went back to the pressroom. He had a bit of work to do as the PGA Championship was winding down and a popular Al Geiberger was about to win his first major tournament. Regardless of the peanut butter sandwiches that Al made famous that weekend, it was his sterling golf that really mattered. He finished at even-par 280 and won by four shots over runner-up, Dudley Wysong. The heavyweights tied for third at 286 were Billy Casper, Gene Littler and Gary Player. One-stroke behind them in a tie for sixth were Julius Boros, Jack Cupit, Arnold Palmer, Doug Sanders and Sam Snead. Tom Place filed his story for the newspaper and went home for the evening. Recently, he told me how he found out about the tragic news about Tony Lema.

"Well, at that time I was living in Chagrin Falls," Tom remembered. "I went home after the tournament was over and around 9:00-9:30 that night I got a call from the newspaper office. They said, 'Tony Lema was just killed in a plane crash.' My first response was, 'No. You're kidding, no way.' They said, 'It just came across the wire. And we know you are a good friend of his and we need you to write a piece about him.' I said, 'Wait a minute. There's no way I could write something about ...I just saw the man...We just had a good visit.' The man from the office said, 'We need you to write something. We need it immediately.' So I sat down and wrote a piece about it. I don't remember exactly what I wrote, but I included Tony's quote about, 'I just want to get out of here.' It was as if he knew that something was going to happen. And that was sort of what I wrote and my relationship with Tony and Betty. It was on the front page the next morning and I read it and thought. 'It wasn't so bad after all. I received a lot of comments, but that was the end of that.' "

Fred Corcoran, Tony's business manager learned of Tony's death that Sunday night. "It's a terrible thing. I'm all broken up," Fred remarked when he heard the news. "I was with him at the airport in Akron about 5:30 p.m. I must have been the last person to talk to him before he took off. It's a big loss to the world of sports. He was one of the greatest golfers I've ever seen. He was exciting to watch. I followed him around the course in his last round in the PGA. His putting was off."

Corcoran disclosed that the original plane Lema had chartered "didn't show and Tony told me he had chartered another. He had me paged over the loudspeaker system. He wanted to talk over some business affairs. We sat in an auto waiting for the plane. He told me he was tired and wanted to get home to Dallas. His wife is from there, you know."

In Jim Moriarty's article *Days of Wine & Roses* that appeared in the July 2004 issue of *Golf World*, Johny Pott said that he had gone to Mass earlier that morning with Tony and everything seemed to be going along in normal fashion. According to Johnny Pott, a friend from Akron had dropped Tony and Betty off at the airport and Tony saw the pilot was a woman. He looked at his friend and said, "I really love women. I like to go dancing with them, but I don't want to go flying." It wasn't until he was convinced of her professional record as a pilot and the many hours she had registered in her logbook that he would even get on the plane. When Tony boarded the Twin-Engine Beechcraft Bonanza, he looked at this friend and said, "Wish me luck." The friend replied, "I always wish you luck, Tony." And he said, "No. Wish me luck on this flight."

Fred said that he had to leave to take a private plane to New York and he told Tony: "I'm going to Cooperstown Monday to see Ted Williams inducted into Baseball's Hall of Fame."

Corcoran explained that Tony and Williams were friends. "Tony told me to give Ted my best and tell him I'm proud of him." Corcoran added that Tony was a "very religious person. He went to church Sunday morning before starting his last round in the PGA."

"Tony was one of the real great guys on the tour," Jack Nicklaus said upon learning about Tony's death.

"A shock to us all—a real loss to the game," said Max Elbin, president of the PGA. "Tony had a world of color and he added tremendously to the appeal of golf. He was a great inspiration to the younger players."

"We were like brothers," said Ken Venturi the 1964 U.S. Open champion. "I have known Tony for 20 years. In fact, my mother gave him his first pair of golf shoes. I just can't believe it."

"He was a man's man, a player's player," said Tommy Jacobs, chairman of the PGA players committee. "Most of us didn't understand Tony when he first joined the tour, But we learned we were just taking him the wrong way. We found he was a great guy."

There was a particular deviation from Tony's normality that fascinated him from the time he was a student. Directly across from St. Elizabeth's on E. 14th Street were the Poor Clare Sisters where nuns were behind curtains and not allowed to be seen by visitors. They took a vow of not seeing people and lived a life of prayer, community and joy. It was a form of "monastic existence" for this particular group of nuns and Tony seemed to have been awed by the fact that you would go in there and behind a window or a curtain you would talk to "a voice." That appealed to his sense of eeriness. He would go to Poor Clare Sisters and discuss things like "I'm having trouble at school" or a multitude of other subjects. He continued these visits well into his career. When Tony started making a few bucks on the Tour he would put cash in an envelope and send it to them. Because they were cloistered, they had no idea he was a famous golfer on the PGA Tour. It wasn't until the plane crashed; they read the front-page of the newspaper and realized who had been sending envelopes of money to them all of those years.

Without a doubt, one of the most interesting golf writers who really kept readers informed about what was happening in the world of golf was Doug Mintline of the *Flint Journal*. He and Tony worked together professionally, but simultaneously they became friends. Doug knew how close Tony was to Clarence and Thelma Jones, the couple Tony befriended in his early days at San Leandro and kept in contact closely after the Jones' moved to Flint. Doug also knew how to coax Tony to unveil his lighter side and initiate stories that were downright funny. Shortly after Tony's tragic death, Doug's column entitled *The Mint Line* contained two stories that showed Tony's wry sense of humor along with his passion for friendship.

"I'll remember Tony in 1962 taking offense to a column about Bo Belinsky's fun-loving fame.

" 'What does Bo do that I don't do?' Lema quizzed. 'I may not be an item in Walter Winchell's column, but I never had to have any publicity to get a date. And you have to agree, my pitching and putting are worth more than Bo's pitching!'

"Lema had a flair for the colorful life.

" 'Females are the spice of life,' he once stated as a bachelor. 'If someone asked me to choose between a round of 63 and a date with a beauty contest winner, I might lean toward the latter.' "

In March of 1966, following the death of Clarence Jones, Tony wrote a letter to Doug Mintline. In his column, Doug shared Tony's letter and his own thoughts with the readers.

"I received a letter on March 18 from Tony in which he talked about losing a close friend in Clarence Jones.

" 'People like Clarence never really die because they usually have such an effect on people that much of them rubs off and is copied,' Tony wrote. 'Thank God he had a chance to see me win the Buick Open. He had much more confidence in me than I did.'

"Lema, too, had a profound effect on people and his happy personality and love of golf will long be remembered by the people of Flint and the nation. No sports fan who ever knew, watched or read about Tony will ever again take a sip of champagne without remembering the excitement Lema created."

Thirty years after the sudden death of Tony Lema, Dean Howe of the *Flint Journal* wrote an article reminding the local readers that Michigan golf fans still held a special feeling for two-time Buick Open winner, Tony Lema.

"His untimely death sent shockwaves throughout the sports world. No person was more devastated than Jerry Rideout, then the chairman and mastermind behind the Buick Open golf tournament.

"It was Rideout who had arranged for Lema to participate in a one-day pro-am tournament in suburban Chicago.

" 'I still think about it today like it was yesterday,' said Rideout. 'I was absolutely devastated when I heard the news. Tony was on his way to being one of the great golfers of all time.'

"In the early years of the Buick, Rideout had formed a special bond with the touring professionals. He was particularly fond of Lema because of the way this young man approached the game.

" 'Tony had a style about him,' said Rideout. 'He was colorful and seemed to be at ease all the time. The fans loved him, the press loved him, everybody loved him.' "

In an article entitled "Last Look at Tony Lema" that appeared in the August 1967 issue of *Golf Digest*, Nick Seitz uncovered something few people knew. In order to repay his fellow pros on the PGA Tour for everything he received, Tony had let it be known that he would like to serve on the Tournament

Committee, an assignment that was not financially rewarding and basically a thankless job. He also began to spend more time in the locker room, getting to know more players and exchange ideas on the practice tee as well as swapping jokes and occasional harmless pranks. Bob Goalby, who edged Tony for Rookie-of-the-Year honors in 1958, let it be known that his Comeback-of-the-Year honors he received in 1966 was partially due to some advice Tony had shared with him less than a week before he died. "I don't let a bad shot bother me now," Goalby says. "I can see the value of keeping calm, and as Tony told me, you have to live a little."

The columnist for the *Oakland Tribune*, Ed Levitt wrote a heart-touching story that appeared in the newspaper on Monday, July 25, 1966 and was undoubtedly seen and read by thousands of locals who knew Tony.

"The corks stopping popping last night. Champagne Tony was dead.

Tony Lema already had become a legend at 32. But how do you deal with a legend?

If you're Tony's mother living in San Leandro, your heart breaks.

If you're just a golf fan, you feel the loss deeply, almost as though a member of your family had passed away.

And if you're a reporter who had known and admired the young man, you fight the sadness inside and try to tell Tony's story.

'If I never win again,' said Lema after his only victory on the PGA Tour this year in the Oklahoma City Open, 'I won't be so disappointed that it will kill me. Golf has been good to me. I've won more than I ever hoped to win. I'd like to give a little bit back to golf because it's been so awfully good to me.'

Tony gave back more than a little bit. He was its colorful, bubbly, ambassador of goodwill. He was a great drawing card, a proven champion and a guy you wanted to be around for the laughs.

But there was another side to Tony—a humble side. Last fall he approached our Ed Schoenfeld, his long time confidant and chronicler, with a proposition. 'Do me a favor,' said Tony.

'I'm going to buy a batch of season tickets for Oakland Raider games and I'd appreciate it if you would pass them out to some poor kids around town.

'I was in their shoes once. I know how it feels. Now that I can do something I'd like to help them out.

'I not only want them to see a football game, I want them to go in style and sit in the best seats.

'But don't mention my name. This is strictly between you and me. Just tell the kids the tickets came from a friend.'

The tickets were distributed to Boys Clubs, Scouts and underprivileged youths here. Nothing was ever written about it. But a scout leader finally let the word leak out. Immediately the appreciative youngsters began to send thank you notes to Tony. Later the tall swinger from San Leandro admitted that hearing from those kids made him feel as though he had accomplished something worthwhile in life.

A few years ago Tony was given a testimonial dinner at the Athens Club here. He was so overwhelmed by the large attendance that he refused to sit down at the head table to eat until he had shaken hands and personally thanked everyone present.

Tony ate a very late and a very cold dinner that night—with but six of the original 400 guests.

About his golf, Tony once explained:

'We're not all born with sunny dispositions. Most of us have to learn not to fight ourselves.

'I had a harder time than others. Probably due to my Portuguese ancestry, I have a quick temper.

'I used to throw clubs. I was too impatient. Friends would say, 'Wait. You'll start playing better.' But I didn't want to wait. I wanted to play better right now. It didn't come suddenly. I worked hard on it.'

He was a celebrity who at times preferred anonymity."

One of the most creative and articulate writers in all of sports was Jim Murray of the *LA Times*. He knew how to shape a story, get his message across and leave the reader with the feeling "nobody could have said it better." That's exactly what he did in his column that appeared in the *LA Times* two days after Tony perished in that horrible plane crash. The title of his article was "Lema Could Smile at a 67, Or 79." Here it is, in it's entirety:

"I have nothing against my good friend Allen Geiberger but I wish today Tony Lema had won the PGA in Akron Sunday.

Winning the PGA, you see does many things for a golfer. It gets him 10 years of exemptions in the Masters, for example. It gets him in some tournaments forever and it gets him innumerable television shows like the World Series of Golf.

But for Tony Lema, it might have saved his life. You can't win much more than that.

Tony bogeyed a plane trip to a small town in Illinois, as you may have read. It was one of the few times old Tony under-clubbed himself. The plane landed in the rough and toppled into a lateral water hazard, a place Tony seldom found himself. The very least history should have done for Tony is let him finish on the green. In birdie position. Had he won at Firestone, he would have been on a trophy stand, not a burning airplane.

The term 'color' is used loosely in sport. Usually, it is applied to a schizophrenic shortstop, a pop-off prize fighter, a fat home run hitter or a half-witted halfback who has learned to score without learning to read.

But Anthony David Lema, who once described his life as a long channel swim fighting the undertow of failure, was one who genuinely and meritoriously deserved the word 'colorful.'

It wasn't the 6 feet 2 inches, the 180 pounds and the swing you could pour on popcorn, but Tony also had a nice eye for a birdie or a beauty and a nice ear for the quotable quote. I remember once at Augusta, at a bull session, someone commented about Billy Casper, 'All he can do is putt.' Tony thought a minute, then answered, 'Well, I guess he has been sinking a lot of 400-yard putts, then, as he has won quite a few tournaments lately.'

I guess history will say the most important tournament Tony ever won was the British Open, but Tony himself knew better. The most important tournament Tony ever won was an off-brand little event called the Orange County Open at Mesa Verde in Costa Mesa, CA in October of 1962. The open itself succumbed to sudden-death, but it had a sudden-death playoff that year between Tony and Bob Rosburg. The night before, sipping a soft drink, Tony looked with distaste at the bottle and its syrupy contents and announced:

'Listen! If I win this thing tomorrow, there'll be no more of this stuff. It'll be champagne for everyone.'

A nickname is the sincerest form of flattery in the sports business. When you're 'The Bambino' or 'The Brown Bomber' or 'The Galloping Ghost,' you've arrived. Anthony David Lema ceased to be just another guy trying to make the cut and became 'Champagne Tony.'

A nickname gives you more than recognition or status. It gives you drive, the urge to excel. You are WATCHED. And a watched man is always more careful how he addresses posterity, as one writer put it. 'Champagne Tony' never allowed himself to hit the slovenly shots A.D. Lema sometimes permitted himself. There have been days when Tony would shoot an 80 on the golf course, but par the bar. Not when he became 'Champagne Tony.'

He became a Ryder Cup player. He won back-to-back tournaments once, a feat left only to the greats of the game. He finished second in his first Masters, barely missed a National Open playoff at Brookline.

Tony was not a back-slapper, a cork-popper. He made his living a tough, grinding way—sinking 10-foot putts. But he could smile at 79 as well as 67. Not many can.

You had to look down in the fine print to find what Tony did at Firestone last weekend. What he did at Lincolnshire made big black headlines. All golf feels it has just driven a ball out of bounds. Off the 18th tee."

Prescott Sullivan was a veteran sportswriter for the *San Francisco Examiner*. In early August of 1966, he wrote a touching and accurate piece that was a real summation of Tony's career. Here, in part, is the article entitled, "Tony Got a Short Count."

"Countless columns have been written about Lema since his demise.

The story of his humble beginnings and the rough road he had to travel to get anywhere has been told and retold many times over.

As an aspiring young golfer, the ex-San Leandro caddy was too poor to buy shoes. As a young pro, he was a nobody for five years. But, there was something he always had. He was born with a touch of class.

It showed up the first time he won anything and had a few bucks in his pocket. Keeping a promise to the boys in the press tent, Lema ordered champagne. The investment, although it was not intended as such, was to reward him with a priceless name.

Champagne Tony. It was a perfect label. If the handsome, free-spending, pleasure loving former Marine needed an assist on his way to becoming the most vivid golfing personality since Walter Hagen, that was it.

Everywhere he went, people warmed up to him. In England, he was the Jolly Yank. London lionized him after he'd won the British Open in 1964. Lema put it on good by donning a bowler, morning coat and trousers and strolling along The Mall with a bumbershoot on his arm.

He returned to the United States puffing grandly on a long stemmed cigarette holder given to him by an admirer—Duke of Windsor. Lema had a way with royalty.

You know all that. Champagne Tony was quite a guy. The obituaries brought out the jolt his death was to golf.

Yet, the full extent of the tragedy can never be measured. The plane crash in Indiana killed a great golfer. But, how much greater would he have been had not death intervened?

Lema was just getting started, so to speak. While he had some big years, they went back only to 1962 and his biggest years, we'll always believe, were still ahead of him.

We know this. He had beaten the best. When he was on his stick, there wasn't anybody he had to fear.

Until he developed a sore arm, they were going to have to do something about the so-called Big Three, comprised of Arnold Palmer, Jack Nicklaus and Gary Player. Lema was banging at the door. They were going to have to let him in even if it meant setting the table for four.

The arm trouble slowed him up. But, it was beginning to respond to treatment. Happily married, and settled down, Champagne Tony was getting back on his game.

Given a few more years, he might have won acclaim as the greatest golfer who ever lived. Time ran out on him much too soon. Fate gave him a short count.

Tony was 32. Only 32. That was the tragedy."

Shortly before this book was sent to press, Tom Place and I talked one more time. After all these years, it dawned on me that Tony Lema was a *real friend* of Tom's. And so was Betty. Champagne Tony was not just another player in the field as Tom traveled from one tournament to another to report for the *Cleveland Plain Dealer*. In that conversation, Tom quietly conveyed to me what he thought about Tony Lema.

"He was a very special man," Tom said, "It's incredible to think what he might have accomplished. He was a talent and everyone knew it. He had a little bit of a temper, maybe, but he had a great personality. People loved him."

When Tony's mother, Clotilda, was told about her son's gesture of giving those tees to the young boys on the last hole, she wasn't surprised. "He did a lot of good for the under privileged children," she said. "He loved children. He thought someday they'd amount to something. Tony loved golf, but he would call me once a week, no matter where in the world he was. On his birthday, he would always send me the number of his age in roses."

There have been many descriptions of Tony Lema and how he lived his short but successful life. But no one said it better than Tony himself. "What I want," he said, "and have always wanted more than anything else, is a place in life, to be a personage. I think there are many opportunities in the world today, and I would like to find my place in it—and not just aim solely at being the greatest golfer who ever lived."

Tony's Swing Thoughts

L ess than a year before his death, Tony teamed with noted golf writer Bud Harvey and wrote a book entitled *Champagne Tony's Golf Tips.* The book was full of swing tips and an assortment of golf knowledge but throughout, Tony made sure the golfer reading his book maintained one goal to apply to his or her game. And that primary thought was how to develop a sound golf swing and how to get the most out of your game. Tony had a wealth of experience and understood the technicalities of the golf swing as well as anyone. At the same time, he realized that whether someone was a beginner or a seasoned veteran, a golfer could not expect to copy Tony's swing or anyone else on the tour, and go out the next day and challenge par. Just as he had learned after thousands of hours of practice at Lake Chabot and Lucius Bateman's Airways Fairways, Tony explained in his teaching articles that golf is a game where you take one step at a time and develop a sound swing and a strong overall game by patiently putting all aspects together like a jigsaw puzzle. In addition to his book, Tony had instructional articles published in *Golf, Golf Digest, Sports Illustrated* and the *Oakland Tribune.* In this chapter, we will take a look at Tony's swing and attempt to pinpoint exactly why it was so rhythmic and effective. More importantly, his tempo was so smooth that it didn't look like he was swinging hard, but he generated enough clubhead speed to be one of the longest hitters off the tee in his era. Rather than make this a highly technical chapter and present you with a thousand swing thoughts, let's have fun. Let's touch upon some key areas that Tony stressed in his teaching articles and allow you to apply whatever you wish, to your own game. Without a doubt, Tony would prefer to have his instructional views taken in this manner.

In an article published in the September 1963 issue of *Golf Magazine*, Tony emphasized the importance of getting your FACTS together: Fundamentals, Attitude, Confidence, Tempo and Simplicity. He stated that when your game has a solid foundation and you don't have to rely on luck, you will make your own breaks. He advised golfers, who wanted to cut strokes off their games, to learn through practice, the mechanics of the game and how the ball reacts under various conditions. He advised golfers to learn how to hook and slice deliberately, how to hit sand shots, how to play the downhill, uphill and sidehill lies, when not to use the putter from off the green, and how to hit the wedge from the rough near an elevated green. These are the shots that cause high scores. They are also the "type of shots" all touring professionals have as part of their arsenal. Make them a part of yours, too, because without this knowledge you are at the mercy of the elements, the layout of the course, your mental attitude and physical condition. With them you can map out your strategy of playing each hole and better your chances of success even if you cannot follow your original plan to the letter.

Tony used the "Vardon" or overlapping grip and he stressed that the golf swing is not a one-hand swing, but that it takes two hands that must work together. "It takes two to tango and two to swing."

Regarding the stance, he was an advocate of pointing his golf shoes at "five minutes to one." He felt the heart of the golf swing is the knee action and if your feet were pointed straight ahead, the right foot will restrict your pivot on the backswing. If the feet are open about 20 degrees, you run into the same problem in reverse—the anchored left foot restrains you on the backswing. He emphasized, "the foot position is determined by the need to pivot the upper part of the body a full 180 degrees."

He stressed the key to a sound stance is balance. "When you're standing up to the ball correctly you should have a strong sense of stability, as if your center of gravity is located in your bottom and your weight is evenly distributed on both legs and solidly supported in the heels." He liked to think of the billiken as a model. The billiken is a round-bottomed figure you can push over from any side and which will rock back erect again. That's because it's weighted in the base and has a dead-level center of gravity.

Tony said your knees should be flexed, but not relaxed. There should be some tension in your legs, springiness. Your body should bend at the waist—but only slightly. He felt the inclination at the waist should be just enough to make the out-thrust rear-end the most prominent feature of your profile as you stand up to the shot.

One thing about Tony Lema you no doubt have learned by now is that his sense of humor was omnipresent. In the introduction of *The Swing* in his *Golf Tips* book he lets the reader know that he understood the interest and complexities of the golf swing. "I suspect," he wrote, "that if anyone wanted to hole up in a public library and run a word count by subject matter on the literature of the 20th century, he would find that the most popular subjects are sex, crime and the golf swing—and not necessarily in that order. Before we go any further, let's have a clear understanding. You're not going to find a golf swing in a book.

"Timing and rhythm mean everything in the golf swing. If you are blessed with muscular coordination, a natural sense of rhythm, you can hit a golf ball right now. Maybe not as far as you might prefer or always in the right direction, but the act of hitting the ball holds no mystery for you. On the other hand, if you were born without that little subconscious tick-tock called timing, no assurance from me is going to keep the golf swing from becoming the most complicated essay in physics since Archimedes sat down to work out the principle of flotation.

"I'm told by those who spend a lot of time studying such things that I have a highly stylized swing. I don't know. Like most golfers who play at the top tournament level, to me, swinging a golf club is something that comes as naturally as breathing. Certain features of my swing have been pointed out to me and sequence photographs I've seen tend to confirm them. One knowledgeable British writer remarked on what he called the 'absolute smoothness' of my swing, and on the fact that the pace of the swing never varies from shot to shot, and from club to club.

"There are other unique features of my own swing which we'll develop in a mechanical breakdown of the golf swing. For instance, my left arm remains inordinately firm and extended throughout the backswing. My wrists don't cock fully until the hands start dragging the club back into the downswing. There is more than the normal amount of knee action in my body pivot, and my head and shoulders recoil like a battery of deck cannons when I hit the ball."

When Tony was executing these swing thoughts on a daily basis and writing about them with Bud Harvey back in 1965-66, the description of "the lag" had not yet become nomenclature in the world of golf. As I know it, lag describes pulling the butt of the club down toward the ball with your left hand and maintaining your cocked-wrists until the very last split second. At impact, you unleash all of that stored up power and the clubhead speed is at its maximum at just the right time. For Tony to have this swing thought perfected and actually be cocking his wrists as he began his downswing, shows us that he was way ahead in the development of the modern day golf swing. Now we know why he was considered both a long and accurate driver of the ball back in his successful years on the tour. Credit for this swing thought and the revision of making it work must go to Tony and those who helped him develop that syrupy swing. So, back in the early 1950's when Tony was hitting ball after ball under the tutelage of Lucius Bateman and Dick Fry in San Leandro, a few years later at San Francisco Golf Club with John Geersten and the late Ken Venturi, who was passing along the swing thoughts he learned from Byron Nelson, Tony put all this together and came up with "his" swing. And it worked.

While developing his swing, Tony felt there were two things that must be kept in mind throughout. First, all golfers want to generate the greatest possible clubhead speed at the instant of impact. Secondly, we must bring the clubhead into the ball squarely along the line of flight. In other words, we want to hit the ball precisely and squarely so it will leave the clubface with no place to go, but away and out. In order for that to happen, Tony said a golfer must develop a mental picture of the path we want the clubhead to follow, from address to the top of the backswing and down again. In order to put the club on this path, we must start by taking it back low and along a perfectly straight line for at least a foot. Why? Because you want to bring the clubhead back along this same track when you hit the ball. He urged golfers to remember those two points as keystones in the structure of the swing. Picture the path of the swing in your mind, and start the club back along that path.

In *Champagne Tony's Golf Tips*, Tony developed the Ten Commandments of the swing—five up, and five down. He told his readers, "Obey them faithfully and you're a cinch to reach golfer's heaven. Some you can violate only under penalty of having your whole game shot to hell." Here they are, word for word, Tony's Ten Commandments of the swing:

1. The Waggle. Upon establishing a good, comfortable stance at address, you hold the club with your fingers and waggle the clubhead a few times, just to acquire a "feel" of he clubhead and sense the weight at the end of he shaft.

2. The Forward Press. It serves a double purpose. It starts the hidden timing clock ticking in the subconscious to initiate the tempo of your swing. Secondly, it gets the hands in motion smoothly and fluidly so the clubhead can start back gracefully and effortlessly.

3. The Drag. Take the clubhead back along a flat plane for a distance of 12 to 18 inches. The worst thing a golfer can do is "pick up" the club. As the club is drawn back, the fingers should experience a strong sense of pulling against some force that is holding the clubhead.

4. Left Arm Thrust. Make a conscious effort to extend the left arm. We really don't draw the club back at all—we sort of push it back along this low plane with the straight left arm. At this point, the right

arm is only playing a supporting role, going along for the ride. As the clubhead continues back along this widest possible arc, the left arm continues firm and extended as far as it will go. The idea is to establish the broadest possible arc for maximum clubhead speed, and to establish a firm radius for the swing. The left shoulder, moving behind the thrust of the arm, rolls under the chin and is aligned with the right shoulder squarely against the target.

5. Wrists are Hinges. There is no rolling of the wrists on the backswing. The left wrist, in fact, is virtually locked in place until it is cocked on the downswing. The right wrist acts like a door hinge and the clubface remains squarely facing the swing path. Barring any complications, the face of the club is going to come down along the swing path in the same position it had going up. In the old days, it was considered the height of elegance to roll the wrists, coming and going. Why, I don't know. All it did was throw the face of the club wide open at the top of the backswing, and rolled it back into position coming down—sometimes.

6. Wrist Cock. When the club reaches a state of suspense at the top of the backswing, the fingers again start dragging it down. This feather-light pressure on the fingers is the signal to bring hand support to them for a firmer grip, and to cock the wrists for the coming whiplash. The little metronome in the brain yells, 'Now! Now it's time to cock the wrists!'

7. The Brace. As we are poised momentarily at the top of the backswing, our weight has to be transferred to the left side, which has to brace to receive it. This is a fluid movement, led by the left knee and followed instantly by the hips and shoulders. The sliding forward of the hips is accompanied by a swivel action, which begins slowly on the downswing, then gathers momentum as we come into the shot. As the clubhead flashes down toward the ball, the

right arm is straightening and the fingers, which have been running the show up to this time, turn to the hands and wrists and say, 'Take over, boys—it's time to turn on the booster.'

8. Cracking the Whip. Just before impact, the left hand and wrist—supported by the braced left side—break to a stop. This sets up a wall of resistance for the right-hand to whiplash the clubhead through the ball. The effect is to cause the head and trunk to recoil and follow in behind the shot. There can be no whip-cracking effect unless the original drawing force comes to an abrupt stop. As we bring the clubhead into the ball, the left arm changes its role from active to passive while the right hand and fingers are snapping the whip–kicking up the force and speed of the clubhead and getting the ultimate ounce of punch out of the stroke. The left side already is braced from the hip down. There is the solid wall of resistance we are hitting against. But there is no way we can anchor the trunk. So what happens? As we snap the clubhead into the ball, our shoulders have to recoil, carrying the head with them. This has the effect of bringing the right shoulder down and under, and bending the body into and behind the shot.

9. Stay Square. At impact, the left wrist is square and solid, bracing against the right-hand as the club whips through the bottom of its arc. For a distance of at least 12 inches beyond, keep the back of the left hand squarely facing the target. The left side is firmly braced from hip to toe. The hips are swiveling and shoulders are turning forward to face the target. Both arms are perfectly straight now. The left is still guiding and controlling the sweep of the club and the right is carrying the flow of force from the larger back muscles to the hands.

10. Strong Left Elbow. Don't let the left elbow collapse as you carry through to a high finish. More shots are ruined by a collapsing left elbow than by 'peeking.'

Keep that left arm firm and extended until it has
to yield naturally to the sweeping arc of the swing.
Then let it go with the flow of force, and always
'finish high.'

In addition to these swing thoughts, Tony emphasized
there's no reason to get the clubhead back in a hurry. He
stated, "The whole point of the backswing is to get the club
into position to use it. Actually, nothing happens until you start
dragging that club down again and cock the trigger. So keep
that backswing slow and silky."

Not only did Tony and Gwilym S. Brown work together
in the production of *Golfers' Gold* in 1964, but also they got
together again and produced a two-part series that appeared in
Sports Illustrated on March 15 and March 22, 1965. The article
was entitled "A New Way to Play Long Irons" and Tony showed
how golf's most difficult clubs could be mastered by combining
rhythm and restraint with some concepts that greatly simplified
the entire swing. The fantastic illustrations drawn by Francis
Golden were presented in such a way it was easy for all golfers
to comprehend the message Tony was trying to convey.

In the present era of golfers using hybrids, low irons are
seldom found in player's golf bags. And why should they be
used? Hybrids are easier to hit, more consistent and allow
golfers of all handicaps to be more accurate from 150 to 225
yards. So, without going into detail about how to hit a one, two,
three or even four iron, let's take a look at Tony's explanation of
how to develop a sound pivot or body turn. Tony said that many
golfers do not have a good pivot because they do not really
know what a good pivot is.

Figure A . As Tony's downswing starts, his hips are coiled and to the right of a vertical line extending from the ball, which is opposite the left heel.

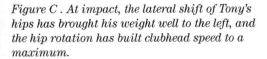

Figure B . As his hands reach the hitting area, his weight comes off his right foot, his hips move as far to the left as they will go and they begin to rotate.

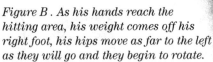

Figure C . At impact, the lateral shift of Tony's hips has brought his weight well to the left, and the hip rotation has built clubhead speed to a maximum.

"The correct pivot," he explained, "combines a lateral shift of the hips to the left with a counterclockwise rotation. Both elements are necessary. The lateral shift moves the body weight off the right foot and quickly over onto the left, thus insuring solid contact down and through the ball. The counterclockwise rotation of the hips builds up clubhead speed through a controlled use of the body rather than by a violent and usually badly timed effort of the hands and arms. It also helps bring the hands far down into the impact area while the wrists are still cocked—which means the wrists really snap through as the ball is hit...Throughout the pivot, the head must be held extremely still. Above all, keep the head from either dipping or rising as you start the downswing. There is one head motion that is permissible. Just before impact, an experienced player's head will shift slightly to the right. This phenomenon is the result of a very fast pivot. My body has generated so much momentum that the head naturally moves to the right. But my weight is well over on my left side, which is where it belongs."

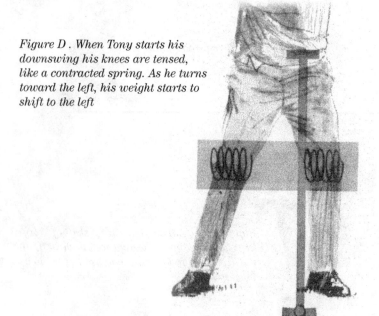

Figure D . When Tony starts his downswing his knees are tensed, like a contracted spring. As he turns toward the left, his weight starts to shift to the left

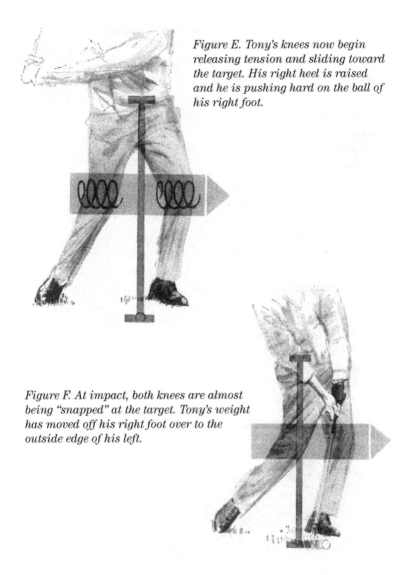

Figure E. Tony's knees now begin releasing tension and sliding toward the target. His right heel is raised and he is pushing hard on the ball of his right foot.

Figure F. At impact, both knees are almost being "snapped" at the target. Tony's weight has moved off his right foot over to the outside edge of his left.

Ever since his caddie days in Oakland, Tony has been an advocate of something known as the "caddie dip." It is a sort of exaggerated knee action often seen in the vigorous swings of teen-agers. The caddie-dip adds up to little more than keeping the knees very mobile throughout the downswing. "I try to imagine," Tony explained in the *Sports Illustrated* article, "as

I come down, that my knees are a single unit and that I am snapping this unit at the target almost like snapping a towel. This action automatically rolls my weight off the right foot and onto the left at the proper time. It also promotes a full pivot and even seems to get the wrists into a more powerful position at impact. This fluid action of the knees becomes an instinctive part of the swing fairly quickly and is a lot easier than trying to concentrate on shifting weight from one foot to the other as you come down."

With so much emphasis and importance directed toward the lower body movement, Tony also presented in the *Sports Illustrated* article the value of incorporating a good shoulder turn. Just before Tony played in his first Masters in 1963 and finished runner-up to Jack Nicklaus, Byron Nelson told him, "You are staying down and under the ball so well, that you just have to play well in the tournament."

Figure G . At the top of his backswing, Tony's left shoulder (black box) is almost directly underneath his right.

Figure H. At impact, the position of the shoulders has reversed, but they are in the same plane as before.

Tony explained that "staying down and under the ball," meant that his right shoulder was low when he came into and through the shot. "It is a fundamental thing to learn," Tony wrote, "yet many golfers never manage it. The common mistake is to let the right shoulder rise during the downswing until it is level with the left, and instead of the shoulders turning together like a wheel pitched as a steep angle, they turn like a wheel lying flat on its side. The correct up-and-down rotation achieves several things. First, it concentrates leverage and force directly behind the ball, the spot where power does the most good. Second, it keeps the clubhead square and moving out toward the target, thus increasing loft and control. Finally, the proper shoulder turn will help the body remain steady— which is going to give you increased consistency, even during a swing that happens to be faster than usual. A good way to get a mental image of the plane the shoulders should be rotating in is to check the position of your left shoulder at the top of the backswing. Now you should attempt to get the right shoulder in that same position at the bottom of the downswing."

Along those same lines, Tony published a Pro-Pointer in *Golf Magazine*'s 1965 Annual edition entitled, "Shoulder turn for more distance." He acknowledged that everyone is constantly searching for some "secret" to help them hit the ball farther. "The best advice I can give," he said, "is to hit that practice tee until you have accomplished a larger shoulder turn and an increased arc." He emphasized that clubhead speed is what determines distance—and a larger shoulder turn with increased arc helps you generate greater clubhead speed.

Throughout his career, Tony created quite a few expressions, one-liners, or simple phrases that made a lot of sense. I don't think anything is more important than his description of the "Cone of Contention." He considered any shot 50 to 75 yards out from the green to be classified as a shot within the "Cone of Contention." Tony estimated that the average amateur golfer plays about 75 per cent of his strokes within 75 yards of the cup. In his book, *Champagne Tony's Golf Tips*, he stressed that golfers have to work at their short game. Whether it be a greenside chip shot, a pitch to an elevated green, a bunker shot, a flop shot, or anything else, Tony said, "You have to get out there and swing the club, for hours, until the feel of these shots is burned indelibly into your muscle memory." He wanted all golfers to know that they can develop an effective short game. Back in the 60's, American golfers were obsessed with the idea that every ball he hits into the green had to be loaded with backspin. "The amateur golfer," he wrote, "seems to have equated a lot of backspin with professional skill, and a mark of golfing distinction to strive for. True, it takes a degree of skill to make a ball spin in when it strikes the green. But every shot to the green doesn't necessarily call for this treatment. You don't have to make every shot to the green a dancer. In fact, as long as you can safely keep the ball running at the pin, you're in scoring position. Don't ever forget that."

Tony urged golfers to consider putting when off the green instead of chipping; provided that you have a smooth surface for the ball to travel rather than bumpy terrain or thick grass. Often times on long chip shots, especially the uphill variety, Tony suggested using mid-irons, sometimes the 4 or 5-iron.

"Our feet are rather close together," he explained, "with the ball lying slightly behind the center-line. We're going to put a lot of wrist and forearm into this shot and we want to anchor the rest of the body except the knees, which act as swivel joints. We bring the club straight back from the ball with the palm of the right hand and the back of the left hand remaining square against the hole all the way. This could almost be called an exaggerated putting stroke. There is little or no arc to the swing. The clubhead hugs the surface except at the very end of an extremely tight little backswing—and again at the very end of a loose and easy follow-through. The ball will be struck with overspin. By calculating the length of our swing, we'll just pop the ball over the rough or fringe and drop it on the cut surface for a good roll at the pin. All you have to do is bring the clubhead squarely into—and through—the shot. Bump the ball, don't scoop it."

Tony developed an excellent wedge game which helped him get many birdies on par-five holes or save par following a bad drive or a mishit second shot on a par-four. He felt the wedge could be used for hitting into the green from any distance up to 100 (or more) yards when you need a high trajectory shot to drop abruptly on the pin. He said the wedge is played from a rather open stance with the ball played back toward the right foot. He felt the club should never be swung with full power— no more than a three-quarter swing or less. As often as not, a wedge shot is "punched"—that is, "played by opening the blade for a fast stop and cocking the wrists immediately as the club is started back, so the hands come into the shot ahead of the blade in a 'chopping' motion. I'll close the face somewhat if I want the ball to roll when it lands. For accuracy, I always remember to keep the back of the left hand squarely facing the hole, and the swing is 'square back, square through.' I always hit down and through the ball."

Realizing there are hundreds of different situations for the wedge to be used, Tony gave all of us a cerebral message.

"Don't use the wedge indiscriminately," he warned, "just

because the shot that comes off its blade is such a beautiful thing to watch. You're not out there on the course to star in a motion picture. I presume you're out there to negotiate the course in the fewest possible number of strokes. So look the situation over. If the circumstances call for the high loft and the quick stop, by all means use the wedge. But if the green is wide open, the terrain smooth and firm, and the green offers plenty of running room to the hole, take my advice and run the ball in there with a medium iron or even a putter.

"The short game consists of three types of basic shots: the chip, the pitch-and-run and the pitch-and-stop. I would strongly urge anyone to build his short game around the pitch-and-run concept. Reserve the loft-and-stop shots with the wedge for the specific conditions that call for them. These high, arching shots are used to lob a ball over danger—whether it's a bunker, a pond or treacherous terrain—and drop it steeply onto the green. Remember, the chip shot is basically an extended putt, played with an exaggerated putting stroke. Why not use the tool best adapted to the shot?"

———————————

Tony's career was definitely strengthened by the visit he had with Horton Smith in the summer of 1961. Sure, it took a year or so for Tony to establish the degree of confidence Horton instilled in him, but once he believed he could make nearly every putt, his entire game improved. Tony's putting philosophy can be expressed with just a few basic laws. He said the putt is essentially a hand-and forearm shot, played with no body movement. The wrists are hinges and the club is swung like a pendulum. The club is brought straight back from the ball and returned to the shot along the same low, flat plane. The blade doesn't open at all. The putt is struck with the right hand. The left hand serves as a control, leading the stroke through and toward the hole. In order to impart overspin on the ball, it must be struck with an upward blow, with the club coming into the shot as the blade passes the bottom of its arc and starts to rise. This will create overspin which is so desirable because it will give the ball a better chance of maintaining the intended line and enough pace to reach the cup. And lastly, Tony believed the head must not come up to follow the track of the ball. He said to keep your head down all the way and listen for the putt to drop.

In the April issue of *Golf Magazine* in 1965, Tony wrote an article entitled "Taming the monsters" which described the importance of mastering the huge and undulating greens at Augusta National. In the first part of the story Tony said, "Last year (1964) I shot a 68 in the second round with just 27 putts. That's the way I like to play golf! And that's the way you have to putt to win at Augusta."

Tony referred to himself as a "feel" putter and said that if he was putting well, he was thinking positively, and that his attitude was good and he had confidence. He explained that he would "feel" distance and it was transferred from his eyes to his fingers. Without consciously putting his finger on any solitary thing, he said that he would "feel" the line and also "feel" the distance.

"I would suggest," he wrote in that article, "that the average player concentrate primarily on putts of about eight feet at the beginning of any practice session. This will build up the "feel" and confidence at the same time. Only after you have started stroking the ball smoothly and geared it to the distance at hand should you start moving back away from the cup. But remember that 'feel' and a smooth stroke is the true secret of putting. You can't get it without practice

"The best putters," Tony described, "are the confident putters, and a confident putter doesn't drift off into a state of suspended animation. He goes about the job efficiently, neither hurrying the shot or dawdling over it. It's a course I earnestly recommend in the interests of faster play and better golf.

"I can't emphasize too strongly this matter of confidence. From observation, I've come to the conclusion that the best putters in the game are the breezy and optimistic people. You show me a good putter and I'll show you a fellow with a cheerful and buoyant attitude toward life. The best advice I can offer is to build confidence in yourself and your ability to run that ball into the hole. And always give it a good run at the cup. The hole is there, waiting. It's large enough to take the ball. All you have to do is give it a chance to go in. That's the closest thing there is to a putting secret."

In Tony Lema's hayday, there were not many articles in golf magazines or books primarily focusing on the mental aspect of winning PGA Tour events. So it came as quite a surprise when Tony wrote an article for *Golf Magazine*'s July 1965 issue entitled, "The killer instinct." The subtitle said it all. "You can have the finest swing in the world, the coolest head and the steadiest nerves, but if you don't have that 'never-say-die' attitude, you'll never be a winner."

Tony said, "The golfing woods are full of tigers (now that's a play on words if I ever heard one!) and it's going to take a man with determination or guts, to dominate the current field or even carry off one of the big ones. It isn't easy, believe me. In the major championships there is so much pressure on every shot that it claws its way right up into your throat and threatens to choke you. The ball gets so that it looks about the size of an aspirin tablet and even a two-foot putt can look about two miles long. That's when, if you're going to be a champion, you have to hitch up your belt, spit in the devil's eye and carry off the shot that seems impossible."

Tony pointed out that Arnold Palmer was the epitome of this willingness to make a hell-for-leather all-out charge on the final nine of a tournament. He also said that the "greatest of them all, for my money, was Sam Snead. He has a total of 115 tournament victories to substantiate my theory." He classified Billy Casper as part of the killer instinct group and pointed out that "although Billy looks quiet, amiable and easy going, you put him on top or within one or two strokes of the lead and you'll think you're looking down the twin tunnels of a double-barreled shotgun.

"I would say that the two major factors which indicate a man has the killer instinct that is so vitally necessary to play winning golf is the chilled steel nerve to charge down the stretch, plus the ability to scramble successfully in the clutch. You have to be this kind of tiger because the game of tournament golf has changed so vastly in the last decade."

In this story, Tony brought to mind two additional major credentials that guys with the killer instinct had going for them: determination and smartness. He said that no matter how hard you try you can't always get your game going all cylinders so you just have to wheel it around in the best manner possible. As the fourth round of a tournament progresses, Tony said that you are trying to stay up with the leaders. But when you are hitting iron shots close to the pin and putts are falling, you know it's time to take that calculated risk and go after it.

"As I have said before," Tony advised, "being foolhardy will get you nowhere. It's just that if you have a chance to carry off a gamble, you weigh the odds pro and con and, if you feel there's a shade the best of it is going for you, you take the risk. The tigers simply feel, more often than the non-killers, that the edge is with them. Meaning, of course, that where some will play for the fat part of the green even in a desperate situation, the divot desperadoes will go for that pin tucked away in a corner. I would have to hold that a poor swinger with guts can develop into a more consistent winner than a great swinger who lacks the killer instinct. But he would have to possess an excellent short game."

Tony brought to mind the importance of a strong short game and determination exemplified by Bobby Nichols.

"Certainly," Tony recalled, "nobody ever showed more determination, or scrambled more mightily, than Bobby Nichols did in winning the PGA Championship in 1964 at Columbus CC. He was missing the greens, but in the clutch he simply was determined that he wasn't going to be beaten—and he wasn't. What it amounted to is that he talked himself into playing better—or at least scoring better—than he would have otherwise. Palmer is the best of all at this and don't ever sell placid-looking Billy Casper short in this department, either."

After the Masters in 1964, where Tony had finished in ninth place, he said he was in a low frame of mind. He went through a process of self- analysis and came to the conclusion that he was guilty of reverse reasoning. On the make or break shot, he was hoping things did not go wrong. He took himself apart and decided that his chief failing was this mental grasp of success. It didn't take Tony long to focus in on how to think positively rather than allow any sort of doubt or fear to creep into his mind during the pre-shot routine. Less than two months after the Masters, Tony charged from the opening hole in the Thunderbird Classic. As described earlier, Tony and Mike

Souchak engaged in one of the classic battles of the year on that Sunday afternoon in Rye, NY. As he and Mike came to the final hole in a driving rain, they were all even. Mike had a poor pitch shot on the par-5 and left himself a 25-foot birdie putt which he ultimately two-putted. Tony had deftly knocked a 90-yard wedge about eight feet below the cup. In this article about the killer instinct, Tony described what was going through his mind.

"I stepped up to that eight-footer," he recalled, "with the water running down my face, crouched over the putt and then was smart enough to step back from it. Just before I was about to stroke the ball, I realized that I was worried about missing the putt. 'Positive thinking,' I lectured myself. 'You're going to hole this baby.' Then I went back and slid it home to win.

"What then, you may ask, happened three weeks later at Cleveland when I missed a short putt on the final hole to wind up in a tie with Palmer—and holed a longer one on the first playoff hole to beat him. It was the same story. You worry about missing and the odds become astronomical against you. Think you're going to knock it in the hole and you slash the odds to ribbons. 'Positive thinking,' I told myself again, 'Let's let the tiger loose.' "

Letters

June 19, 1956

Mr. Tony Lema
San Francisco Golf Club
Ingleside
San Francisco, California

Dear Tony:

You made a significant contribution to sportsmanship and
the best interests of golf by your participation in the
Open Championship at Rochester last week.

For this, you have the sincere thanks of the United States
Golf Association.

Enclosed please find your prize check, along with a list of
the awards. We congratulate you on your performance.

With renewed appreciation and kind regards,

Sincerely,

Joseph C. Dey, Jr.
Executive Director

JCD:rm
Encs.

COMMENDATION FOR

TONY LEMA

SAN LEANDRO CITY COUNCIL RESOLUTION NO. 62-56

Whereas, Tony Lema has emerged as one of the bright stars of the golfing world; and

Whereas, the City of San Leandro is proud of the fact that it may claim Tony Lema as one of its citizens; and

Whereas, Tony Lema by his activities both on and off the links has brought not only fame but honor to himself and to his native City of San Leandro; and

Whereas, Tony has insisted on all occasions that he not be listed as a resident of any adjacent city of the East Bay Area, but that his true home designation be shown as San Leandro, California; and

Whereas, Tony has supplied and continues to supply entertainment for the sports-minded citizens of this City; and

Whereas, Tony exemplifies the highest standards of both sportsmanship and ability:

Now, therefore, the City Council of the City of San Leandro does RESOLVE as follows:

That this City Council does hereby extend its praise and commendation to Tony Lema for his proven ability and conduct both on and off the golf courses of this country and expresses to Tony its pride in being able to refer to him as one of our own.

Introduced by Councilman Cheatham and passed and adopted this 7th day of May, 1962 by the following Councilmen:

Kenneth G. Cheatham   William F. Suarstedt

Valance Gill   William Swift

Alvin W. Kant   Robert J. Taylor

Jack D. Maltester
Mayor of the City of San Leandro

1st letter

REV. GEORGE MONAGHAN

1965

Sept 24 —

START

① Dear Father,

(END) I went to Lake Chabot yesterday but they gave me your letter, I think if you would have put it in a bottle and thrown it in the Ocean, it would have made better time,

I appreciate your writing and also the fact you follow my career.

① God has been very good to me and I am a firm believer in the Power of Prayer. It has always been the 15th club in my bag.

I can be so grateful for my Catholic background, without it I would never have stayed out of jail (TROUBLE)

Please let me know where you are, I would love to visit you.

Sincerely
Tony Lema

TONY LEMA ①
REV. GEORGE MONAGHAN
1848 HAYS STREET
SAN LEANDRO, CALIF. 94577

2nd
Letter

Oct 12 - 65

Rev'd
all
Dear Fr, Monaghan.   all good

② It seems like two hundred
years since you gave me that talking
to at St Louis Bertrand, when I was
still in grade school. An awful lot
of things have happened, both good & bad.
My only wish is that on the final day
the Good will offset the bad and I can
go to where the fairways are lush
and the greens are smooth.

I can say without a doubt that
the greatest thing anyone has in life
is their Religion. So many times I
have felt like saying the Hell with
it all, but after a brief pause I
can realize that those things that
we seek with such determination are
really so unimportant. I have had

2   Oct 13   2nd Letter

TONY LEMA
1848 HAYS STREET
SAN LEANDRO, CALIF. 94577

a certain amount of success in
golf due to the two strongest powers
known to us humans, and that is
Faith in God and Prayer. I have
cut down a few with these two extra
clubs in my bag. I now pray that
with this added success I can become
a better man and a better Catholic, for
you know there are many pit falls
in life and the struggle is unending

I am still the mischievous young
man you knew, so I am not trying
to fool you by any means.
I hope that you will remember us
in your prayers and I will be up to
see you in the early part of Nov. I will
give you a call to see if you are free
for a few hours.

Golfingly
Tony

Tony Lema
1848 Hays st
San Leandro Calif.

ST. REV. GEORGE MONAGHAN
14095 Woodland Drive
GUERNEVILLE, Calif.

May 1 - 1986

Dear Fr.

Thank you for your card. If I just slow my backswing down I think it will help. I am really on a busy schedule now of tournaments. Its a lot of work when you are not playing too good, but a lot of fun when you are,

③ Please keep Betty and (ME) I in your prayers. We can really use the help.

Hope you are getting a chance to play a little golf.

Prayerfully
Tony

TONY LEMA

42st
Letter
1966

May 24

Dear Fr Monaghan

Hope this letter finds you in good
shape and that maybe you are getting a
chance to play a little golf.

④ My game, at least the last two weeks
seems to be a little better, thank God,
it has been a long dry spell and I think
I am losing my taste for champagne.

My congratulations on your up coming Silver Jubilee
as a priest. On Sunday June 12 I will offer
my Mass and Holy Communion in honor of you.

I hope you will have a chance to drop out
to the open at the Olympic Club in SF in June.
It would be nice to see you again

Devotedly,
Tony

Byron Nelson

FAIRWAY RANCH
ROANOKE, TEXAS

June 9, 1966

Mr. Tony Lema
3310 Fairmount
Dallas, Texas

Dear Tony:

I am most grateful to you for your very kind letter
from Memphis. It was so nice of you to say the things you
did about me. All I really did was to tell the truth about
you, and the way you play. I have found over a long period
of years, if you will just be honest and really say what is
the truth about a person, if it's good, it is always proper,
and certainly there is no need to say anything bad about anyone, because no one is perfect.

I have released a couple of stories recently stating I
believe you are the man to beat in the National Open this
year in San Francisco. I feel you are really coming onto
your game again, and that your driving is beautiful.

I will be looking forward to having the opportunity to
talk about you on the telecast again. I have heard many
people say that they thought your play in Oklahoma was some
of the greatest golf that has ever been shot, especially your
friends in Dallas.

Looking forward to seeing you in San Francisco. Good
luck.

Best personal regards,

Byron

Byron Nelson

BN:b

WABC-TV

1330 AVENUE OF THE AMERICAS, NEW YORK, N. Y. 10019 • LJ 1-7777

RICHARD L. BEESEMYER
Vice President &
General Manager

July 21, 1966

Dear Tony,

Mary and I certainly enjoyed having dinner
with you and the Cosells last Sunday evening.

I haven't seen the rushes on the show yet
but I understand everything came out just
fine. I am enclosing a sales promotion
brochure we did on the show and I thought
you would like to have one for your collection.

If there is anything else that I can
personally do for you, please don't hesitate
to pick up the telephone and call me.

Again, Tony, thanks for a most enjoyable
evening and good luck to you on the remainder
of the tour.

Sincerely,

/enc.

Mr. Tony Lema
3310 Fairmont
Dallas, Texas

An Owned Television Station of American Broadcasting Company, Division of American Broadcasting Companies, Inc.

Letter from Tony Lema to Howard Cosell

July 22, 1966

PGA Championship
Firestone Country Club
Akron, OH

Dear Howard and Emmy:

Thank you for a delightful stay the other day. It was very
pleasant. I only wish I could have stayed longer. I feel we
did pretty well on the film. I do hope it turns out the way
I am, the way I think the public knows me. I hope we can
work together again sometime. Sorry, I will be unable to go
to London with you for the Clay-London fight. I have to play
Cleveland that week. Have a ball. Love to the family.

Very Sincerely,

Tony Lema

Moët & Chandon
(founded in 1743)

Épernay France
July 27, 1964

Madam Lena,

It is with profound feeling that
we just learned of the tragic deaths of your
son, Tony, and his wife.

The bonds which God brought
us together through contact with M M. Schieffele
had rapidly assumed such a cordial turn
that your son had truly become a member
of the family of Moët et Chandon.

We do wish you to know how
much we, too, share your deep sorrow in
his untimely death — it will leave in
the hearts of all who knew him, an
emptiness which is impossible to fill.

Words fail us to tell you
how deeply we share your grief. We wish
to assure you, Madam, of the great sincerity of
our feelings of sympathy in this very sad event

(Signature)
Fr Chandon de Briailles

TRANSLATION

August 2, 1966

Dear Sir:

In many sports such as baseball and football there are Halls of Fame dedicated to men who have proven they can stick to their chosen sport and come out on top. I would say that Tony Lema is an idel for young boys and girls who are trying to be the best. With practice that is exactly what Tony Lema did to be among the best golfers in the world.

I would like to make a request that will have a great influence on Tony's admirers and the golfers of today. That instead of having the P.G.A. at Firestone C.C. , have it at some course named after Tony in some way and have it dedicated to a man who gave up his life for golf.

IT MAY SEEM LIKE I AM ASKING ALOT BUT TONY HAS DONE MANY MORE GOOD DEEDS THROUGH HIS LIFE TO DESERVE THIS AND MUCH MORE !

Think it over.

An admirer of

Champene Tony Lema,

Cindy Baker

Age 12
543 N. Jackson St.
Fremont, Ohio
43420

Postmarked Aug 6, 1966

Dear Mrs. Lima

    I have thought of you all week but my heart has been too heavy and my eyes too full to try to write. Our trip home was made as easy as possible. People are really wonderful. We have re-

ceived mail from all over the country. Received a letter - and perhaps you received one also - from a woman who saw the plane crash. Her letter was a big comfort to me. Also a letter from the Priest that married them - from the wives of golfers and from their neighbors in Dallas. I pray that in time your pain will ease as well as my own.

        God Bless You
          Mrs. Baxter

Louise Baxter — Betty's mother
515 S.W. 36
Oklahoma City, OK

(She moved to Guthrie - later)

August 31, 1966

Dear Mrs. Lema:

The thought has often occurred to me that letters of condolence
possibly do not assuage grief, but -- on the contrary --
accentuate it. For that reason I refrained from writing you
when I heard of Tony's untimely death, even though my first
impulse was to let you know how deeply shocked I was. However,
in the weeks that have elapsed since the tragedy, I've come to
feel that you might gather some solace from the experiences I
shared with Tony, whom I considered a special friend.

Tony had thousands of friends, of course, which is to be expected with a public figure known to and popular with millions
of people. But my wife and I lived with Tony -- and Betty --
intimately during all of last November when we toured the world
together, and during that time we came to know Tony in a privileged way -- as a person rather than as a personality.

The irony of Tony's death on a golf course was paralleled by the
superficiality of the epitaphs written by people who knew him
little and who ascribed to him in death any number of virtues
that he -- in life -- would have been the first to deny.

Advertising
GARDNER, STEIN AND FRANK, INC.
Sales Promotion
Marketing

Tony was a <u>real</u> person -- with the strengths and weaknesses,
virtues and faults, foibles and feelings of real people. He
was a sensitive, intelligent, probing person -- conscious of
his potential and grateful for the golfing prowess with which
he was gifted.

Tony resented being used. The selfishness of people angered him,
and he was quick to express his ire. But -- and this he confessed to me one evening in some far-away place -- he never
failed to live over each day before the next day came and casti-
gate himself for all the things he had said that could have been
said nicer or been better left unsaid.

Tony treasured <u>real</u> friendship and was quick to spot the camp
follower, the fair-weather friend. He once described to me the
loneliness of the motel room that followed the tournament
victory, and the joy of a late hour call from a friend thousands
of miles away who was thinking of him. Tony coveted such friend-
ships, and once -- during a day-long automobile trip in Israel
when we were discussing a business matter that had controversial
overtones -- he put his arm around me in an impulsive gesture
and said, "That's a problem for our lawyers, Bob. Let <u>them</u> get
in a hassle -- not us."

Tony was a generous person -- to a fault. He was impressionable
and relied on people whom he trusted. He asked advice of friends,
spoke of a desire to plan for future financial security, expressed
a longing to broaden his outlook and to acquire an appreciation
of art and music. He had a zest for life, and during our trip
he derived obvious pleasure from all the experiences that regale
real people -- for Tony was very much a real person.

Our world trip ended in Hawaii last December, and our group of
eleven people who had lived together for a month spent a farewell
evening together. Gifts were exchanged and vows made to see each
other often. After dinner Tony made a speech, and thanked us --
including Betty -- for "putting up" with him! Never before in my
life had there been such a moment that expressed the warmth and
fraternity that people can feel toward each other and which was
exemplified by your son that evening.

GARDNER, STEIN and FRANK, inc.

It was only a few short days later when my wife and I had
returned home that I received a letter from Tony again thanking
us for making his and Betty's trip enjoyable. This letter, too,
illustrated better than any words I could every write the
generosity of nature that was Tony's.

My wife and I last saw Tony and Betty in Chicago during the
Western Open. It was an all-too-brief reunion, particularly
in view of the calamity which was to occur so shortly afterwards.
We feel his loss deeply and we look back upon the time we spent
with him as a unique and wonderful period in our lives. We
consider ourselves fortunate that we knew Tony Lema, the person.
We hope that the passing of time will bring into perspective
for you the greatness of Tony as a sports figure and help comfort
you in the loss of your son.

                                          Sincerely,

                                          Bob Stein

Mrs. Clotilda Lema
1848 Hays
San Leandro, California

GARDNER, STEIN and FRANK, INC.

SHELL OIL COMPANY
50 WEST 50TH STREET
NEW YORK, N.Y. 10020

October 26, 1966

G. G. BIGGAR
VICE PRESIDENT
PUBLIC RELATIONS

Dear Mrs. Lema:

During the past six years of "Shell's Wonderful World of Golf", we have always sent our golfing stars color prints as a small remembrance of their association with our television series. It was a way of saying "Thank You" beyond our routine business relationship.

I think Tony would have wanted you to have the enclosed album of photographs taken during the filming of our Bermuda match last April. I am also enclosing a few extra color prints for yourself and the family.

Sincerely,

Gordon Biggar

Enclosures

Mrs. C. Lema
1845 Hays Street
San Leandro, California

May 16, 1983

Dear Judy,

     I really enjoyed receiving the matches and bumper stickers. I gave some to my mother and father and we've displayed these rather unusual stickers on our cars.

     I have enclosed the original letters Tony wrote me many years ago. I feel you should have these to display in your golf museum. I have copies for myself to keep.

     The opportunity to write to Tony was a great one for me. For him to reciprocate with letters — that was truly wonderful, a fan's dream. I was one of his biggest fans and will always think highly of him.

     Hope you enjoy the letters and that they are of some value.

                         Cathy Sorrels

Tony Lema

Aug 1st

Dear Kathy

I am glad you liked the pictures and am rather thrilled that you named your China Horse after me even if it is only half.

Please keep rooting for me as I need all the support I can get.

Bye for now.

your friend

Tony

Tony Lema

December 26, 1965

Miss Cathy Hurst
124 Heady Avenue
Louisville, Kentucky 40203

Dear Cathy:

Thank you very much for the Christmas card. It was very
sweet of you and I certainly enjoyed it. I thought that
was a nice picture of you and your brother. He does look
like a little brat like you said, but I can't believe
that he is.

I was not able to play in the P.G.A. 4-ball tournament
in Miami as I have a bad elbow and do not know when I will
be able to play golf again. Please say some prayers for me.
Also, I was not able to film the CBS Golf Classic starting
on Christmas Day, so the only time you will see me on TV
will be either with a live showing of a tournament, or
I will be on on January 8th in Shell's Wonderful World of
Golf. I filmed that earlier this year and it will be
shown on January 8th.

I hope by now you have gotten my book and I hope you enjoyed
it. Take good care of your little brother. It seems like
he needs it. Tell him I am better than Ken Venturi, and
I will try to prove it.

I wish you and your folks a real nice holiday season, and
I always look forward to your letters. Be good, and take
care of yourself.

                                        Sincerely yours,

                                        Tony

                                        Tony Lema

TL/si

1848 Hays
San Leandro, Calif.

Tony Lema

February 28, 1966

Miss Cathy Hurst
124 Heady Avenue
Louisville, Kentucky 40207

Dear Cathy:

It's always nice to receive your letters, although I didn't
get to answer your last one as soon as I would have liked
to.

I have been pretty busy this past month trying to get my
elbow in shape for the big tournaments that are coming up
in the next few months. I still don't know just what is
going to happen, but I hope you will remember me in your
prayers, because I know that will help more than anything
else.

I hope things are going well with you and your folks, and
with your little brother. That new golf course that your
father joined sounds just great. I bet he really enjoys
playing it.

Take care of yourself, and I'll look forward to hearing
from you.

Golfingly,

Tony Lema

TL/si

Tony Lema

March 15

Dear Cathy

Thank you for your very nice card
so far I have been lucky and have not
had an operation. I am taking a new
drug which has helped an awful lot
hopefully I can put the operation off
until late this year.

In case you don't get a chance
to see the shield show I made in Bruce
I shot 67 to Roberto DeVecenzo 68 we
had a real good match and I hope
you still get to see it.

Please keep your fingers crossed for
me so my elbow wont bother me during
these big tournaments.

Thank you again for your concern.

Dutifully yours

Tony Lema

Tony Lema

April 24, 1966

Miss Cathy Hurst
124 Heady Avenue
Louisville, Kentucky 40207

Dear Cathy:

I hope my game in the last few months has not disappointed you. I haven't been playing to well as you can easily see.

My problems healthwise are in pretty good shape, but I am just not playing too good. It is just one of those things.

Soon I hope that I will be back in winning form. Take care of yourself, and do real well in school.

Yours friend,

Tony Lema

TL/si

May 24, 1966

Miss Cathy Hurst
124 Heady Avenue
Louisville,Kentucky

Dear Cathy:

It was so nice to hear from you again.

Sounds like I have a real staunch fan in you.
If I can only hold up to your expectations, all
will go well for the two of us. To say the least,
it sounds as if you never miss reading about your
golf.

I didn't get rained out of my new house during all
the floods, but the Dallas Open was post-poned for
a few days.

I did pretty well in the Ft. Worth Torunament
this past week-end. Tell your Mother to just keep
right on hexing those other Golfers, and you'll
see my name more often.

Haven't much time now, as Betty and I are packing
for the next Tournament. With your fingers crossed
and your best wishes, I am sure to win.

Until next time, love,

Sincerely,

Tony Lema

August 11, 1966

Dear Mrs. Lema,

I would like to offer you my deepest
sympathy for the sudden loss of your son
and daughter-in-law. As popular and famous
as your son was, you have received countless
letters but mine is more of a different
nature.

My 13 year old daughter, Cathy Hurst
has exchanged quite a few letters with
your son in the past year. She became
interested in golf a little before she
was twelve and wanted to get a picture
of a well-known golfer. She wrote to
Mr. Lema. I asked why she picked him
being from Kentucky she had other choices
and really some more famous. This was
her answer. "Mother, he is a gentleman.
He doesn't lose his temper in front of the
camera and throw his clubs and he acts
like he really enjoys being with people.
Also he always has a word of

encouragement for another player if that person gets a little shaky. He is a golfer's golfer and if I write to anyone, I want it to be the best."

Her faith in your son was never shaken. He sent her a picture and wrote her letters. Some of these came just before tournaments when we knew he must be pressed for time and surely tense.

Every day she rushed down the stairs to see how her hero was doing - She bought the book "Golfer's Gold" and wrote him how much she liked it. She suffered his losses and cried with happiness over his victories. I don't think he could have been closer to this family had he been an actual member.

At the news of his loss, our family and friends called to offer Cathy their sympathy.

Her step isn't quite as bouncy these days and her interest in golf is fading. Maybe sometime she will find another hero.

I just wanted you to know that Tony Lema became a perfect example of what I have been trying to teach her in her few short years. Dignity demands respect. Mr. Lema was dignified and he had the respect of all around him.

Again, may I offer my sympathy and also my gratitude, I am grateful you raised such a young man whom my daughter could choose as her hero in this day and age when there are really few people who are worthy of hero-worship from our young children.

Mrs. C. E. Hurst

May 15, 1983

Dear Jude

Cathy and I received the invitations to the opening. Unfortunately we can't attend but will be with you in spirit.

After talking it over we decided Tony's original letters should be with your family. Cathy has the copies and the wonderful memories. I am sure other people reading them will gain an insight to the personal side of Tony Lema. Even his first letter which could very well have been the only one to a little girl shows his very warm feelings and concern for other people. This is lacking in too many of today's celebrities.

Maybe someday we can visit California and look over the golf course, certainly a deserved tribute to your brother. I hope the opening is a great success.

Sincerely,
Alberta Hurst

"I love life and I want to live."

These words describe the career of Tony Lema. Death cut him down at the height of a bright career. His death saddened all of his friends.

If Tony were here this evening, I believe he would have something to say to his friends. His words would be words of gratitude and happiness.

We believe that Tony Lema has achieved his happiness. Happiness means friends that forgave Tony the faults he possessed and granted him forgiveness for any mistakes he may have made in his life--friends who forgave with the same mercy that Almighty God dispenses to each one of us for our mistakes.

Happiness to Tony Lema was marrying a girl like Tony married-- with whom he was completely happy.

Happiness to Tony Lema was being granted time in his life for many achievements--especially amazing feats in his chosen profession of golf.

Happiness to Tony Lema was satisfaction in his accomplishments and the washing away of many frustrations.

Happiness to Tony Lema was pausing for a few brief minutes in his life and saying to Almighty God "If I never win another major tournament I'm grateful to Almighty God for granting me the achievements I have listed up until now. If I never win another tournament or accomplish any other goal, my cup of happiness is filled to over-flowing."

Happiness to Tony Lema was the time to change from a meaningless life to one of genuine worth and usefulness.

Happiness to Tony Lema was meeting each one of you who was truly his friend and cementing with you a bond of genuine friendship and deep regard.

Happiness to Tony Lema was the help he gave to his mother and the members of his family.

And so we toast the memory of Tony Lema; we promise never to forget him and we trust that his blithe and generous soul is happy with a happiness given to no man here below--Tony Lema.

REV. V. I. BREEN
HOLY GHOST CHURCH, 37588 FREMONT Blvd
FREMONT, CA ?

post
office
box
fifty-two
youngstown,
penna.
15696

May 16, 1983

Dear Mrs. Lema:

I have been very pleased to learn of the golf
course project that the City of San Leandro is
dedicating to Tony. Those of us who knew Tony
and played with and against him still remember
him so well and miss him very much. He was,
as you wrote, a special friend of mine, and I
am happy to see San Leandro recognize and pre-
serve his memory in this manner.

I really wish that I could be with you and all
of Tony's friends there in San Leandro next
month, but I am scheduled to be playing in a
seniors tournament in Cleveland at the time
and I'm afraid that commitment rules out a
trip to California that Tuesday.

I send you my best personal good wishes.

                           Sincerely,

AP:cjh

Mrs. Clotilda Lema
c/o The Honorable Valance Gill
Mayor
City of San Leandro
City Hall
San Leandro, CA 94577

Friends Remember Tony

Doug Sanders, PGA Tour

"He was a great friend. We laughed and cut up, drank a little wine and champagne. We traveled together, he was just a nice guy. A good friend and he was loved by all. I never heard Tony say anything bad about anybody and I didn't hear anybody say anything bad about Tony. It was one big family back then. We traveled together; we had a caravan of four or five cars traveling from one tournament to the next. In those days, people didn't criticize as much as they do today.

"I don't think Tony excelled in one particular thing a great deal, he just excelled in all of the areas of his game. He was just a good player all the way around. Of course he loved the night life, but we all did back in those days. That was part of life. In 1961 I won five tournaments, lost U.S. Open by a stroke and lost to Arnold Palmer in a playoff in the Phoenix Open. It was a great time. After a tournament was over, a few couples would sit around the pool, relax a little bit, have a hamburger and a couple beers. Go to bed early that night, get up early the next morning, jump in the car and beat the traffic on the way to the next tournament. That was friendship. Of course, I think I'm a rich man because I measure wealth by friendship, not by dollars and cents.

"Tony was a great friend and I was supposed to be on the plane with him when it went down. It's a blessing. God has a way of telling you when and what to do and what not to do. You just have to be blessed that God was looking over me because I had already gone to get my bags to get on the plane with Tony. I told someone that I couldn't go down to Columbus to play in a tournament that Monday because I had burned my thumb. And so I decided at the last minute I couldn't go play because of the thumb. I remember because it was on my birthday. Things like that happen. I'm glad I'm here. I cannot say enough nice things about Tony.

"He was my house guest in St. Andrews when he won The British Open in 1964. Regarding his win at the British Open, Tony was a very confident person; a good chipper and putter. He was just a real good player, but most of all, a real nice guy and a great friend.

"On the last hole at St. Andrews in 1970, Tony's caddie came up to me, handed me a white tee with Tony's name on it. He said, 'Doug, use this for Tony, on this hole.' Well, a white tee represents 'five' to me. I didn't want to tell him I'm superstitious about white tees, so I went ahead and used it. And of course, I three-putted the green and made five. Things just happen, you know, but some people are superstitious. I am a little, about things like that. It didn't have anything to do with Tony, it was the fact that it was a white tee, but I used it because of Tony, because he was a great friend."

Al Barkow, Golf Magazine (1970-72), Golf Illustrated (1985-90, 1994-96), Currently Golf World

"Tony Lema was someone I really liked and as has everyone who knew him, saw his much-too-early-demise as a very sad event. I didn't get to know him well, only on the *Shell's Wonderful World of Golf* shows in which he played and I worked with the staff. I remember that he was one of the very few American pros of his time who took advantage of the opportunity to visit places in the world—Greece, the Continent—and stay over for a few days to take in the sights/sites, culture, food, etc. Most of the others couldn't wait to get back to the good ole steak and potatoes in the U. S. of A. I think everyone knew Tony liked to have some fun in the evening, and I recall going down to watch him hit some balls before his match with Peter Alliss in

Bermuda. After chunking the first one he remarked with humor in his voice, 'The first one every morning is the toughest one.' Indeed. The expression on Tony's face that I recall spoke of him. He was like a kid with free rein in a candy store. He was onto something he was not so much getting away with, but feeling really lucky. Tony was a good guy. Missed to this day. He enlivened the game in his short time, and had a winner's stuff on and off the course."

Bobby Nichols, PGA Tour

"Speaking of friendship, Tony was interviewed one day and I remember a writer asking him, 'Who are your friends on the Tour?' He answered, 'I have a couple friends that are a little closer than normal and that's Bobby Nichols and Phil Rodgers.' So, yes, we played a lot of rounds together and had some good times. He and I were partners one-year in the CBS Matches and we finished in second place.

"Tony had a knack for cursing, you might say, following a bad shot. He had somewhat of a temper, not a violent temper, but after a bad shot, he would let loose with some choice words. He did this quite often. When we were filming the CBS matches, they taped all the players and their shots. Well, when we got finished, Frank Chirkanian, who ran the show, gave all the players a reel of the show. He gave me a big reel with all the highlights and then he walked over to Tony and said, 'Here Tony, here's your reel' and gave him a strip of tape about a foot long. 'This is all we could save,' Frank said sarcastically, 'the rest of it had to be edited!'

"Oh, we had some good times together. Went out at night and so forth before he and Betty got married. Tony was a lot of fun, he knew how to have a good time."

Billy Casper, PGA Tour

"You know, Tony was a semi-loose cannon when he first came out on the Tour! When Betty came into his life, she calmed him down and he became a really, really fine player. Not only that but a really good guy, too. In my book, *The Big Three and Me*, I have a picture of the Ryder Cup team and Tony's in that picture. When I scroll through the book, I always stop and look at that picture because of him. He was just really rounding himself into becoming a real competitor. He'd won the British Open and he was really playing consistent golf. He really had a good future ahead of him...then the tragedy happened. It was a shock to a lot of us.

"We were talking about Tony recently out in San Francisco. I was sitting with Don January, Gene Littler, and Billy Maxwell. January brought the fact up that some of the major airlines were on strike (United Air Lines) then and Tony had to alter his plans and charter a flight. It was a real shame. He was just moving into his prime and he and I developed a very close relationship. We talked about a lot of the important things in life rather than just golf and casual things that a lot of people would talk about.

"He and I had a great relationship. I miss him. He had changed his life tremendously. He became a real man. He dreamed the important things in life towards the end of his career. Not only did we play, but we talked a little bit about those important things. In January of 1966, my family became members of the LDS Church. Tony and I would often talk about religion...him being a Catholic... that same Father in Heaven that we pray to all the time... so we got extremely close that way. He was probably the only player that I can remember talking to often on the golf course. When we had time to spend together, we could talk about the important things in life."

Regarding religion, faith and belief, Billy Casper talked about the way Tony was before he met Betty and the changes he made afterwards. "Those are the things that he wasted in life and she was the calming influence upon him that helped him see and feel more about life and probably she helped him become a much better player, too."

During the interview, the subject came up concerning the influence Danny Arnold made on Tony regarding maintaining his temperament and remaining in the present tense.

"You can't change things that just happened on the golf

course," Billy explained, "and that's a tough thing to learn. It takes a tremendous amount of discipline for a person who has the ability and skill at playing the game. And I had to discipline myself not to get 'up' or 'down' with good or bad shots. Just take every shot at an even keel and not get excited or get down because when you did that you are using energy that is often needed towards the end of a round. I learned that early in my career, but I am not sure in those days if everyone understood that. I played 21 years on the regular tour and I think the reason I had that longevity was that I controlled my emotions.

"As a rule, I didn't look at scoreboards, but in the fourth round of the 1966 U.S. Open, when I was on the ninth hole and Palmer was so far ahead of me, I looked at the board to see who was behind me. And I remember, it was Jack Nicklaus and Tony Lema. They were two shots behind me. As we left the green, I turned to Arnold and said, 'I want to finish second this week.' The way he was playing, there was no way you were going to catch him. I knew I had to play well because Nicklaus is such a great player in the Open and Tony had developed a reputation of playing extremely good golf. I wanted to finish ahead of them, but as Palmer started slipping, I started gaining. All of a sudden, I caught him. The same way in the playoff, he had a two shot lead at the turn, but I holed a long putt on the eleventh hole which had about an eight foot break to the right but he bogeyed it and we were all even. Then I went ahead and won by four. Yes, I remember it so very distinctly. I looked at the board and there was Tony and Jack Nicklaus and I knew I had to play well on the back nine.

"Tony changed his life completely around and a lot can be attributed to Betty. He was in the Marine Corps and I was in the Navy. Tony served and I have a great admiration for those who have protected our liberties. He was a special man. He was just getting into the real good times of his life when his death occurred. It was really a shame. We lost a great person and a great champion. He changed his life so much that I believe the Father in heaven needed him for a special assignment in the hereafter."

Phil Rodgers, PGA Tour

"The advice I gave Tony just before the 1964 British Open got under way was fairly simple. I knew Arnold Palmer had arranged for Tip Anderson to caddy for Tony, so I told Tony, 'Hit it where he tells you and hit it with the club that he hands you.' He had played only one practice round there at St. Andrews. But over the years, Tony and I spent a lot of time together, especially in the off season. I would go up to San Leandro or he would come down here to San Diego. Of course, I remember when he won his first tournament at the Orange County Open here in Southern California.

"Tony and I were battling it out at the Buick Open in 1966 on that last day when we played 36 holes because of a rain out earlier. I was fortunate enough to win the tournament and Tony came right into the pressroom and said, 'Hey, I've got this Moet and Chandon champagne here and I'm delegating it to Phil so you guys can share it during the interview.' Shortly afterwards, we were trying to get on the same airplane on the way to San Francisco and the U.S. Open. Well, between us, we had four bottles of that champagne and they weren't going to let us on, but the pilot finally said it was OK. Needless to say, it was a most enjoyable flight.

"During the 1966 PGA Championship, there was an airline strike going and it included United Airlines. Tony and I had dinner on Saturday night. He mentioned that he was going over to Chicago on a chartered flight and I gave some thought to fly with him. Changes were made on Sunday since I finished a few hours before Tony. I ended up driving over with a golf representative who worked out of Chicago. I heard about the plane crash on the radio.

"Tony was a fairly 'outward' person until he got married. Once he and Betty became a couple that was his whole life. I remember him as a very good friend, a very nice man and we got along very well, on and off the golf course."

Johnny Pott, PGA Tour

"My first year on tour was 1957 and the third tournament I played in was the Imperial Valley Open, which of course is the tournament that Tony won. That's where I got my first check. From that time on, a foursome that included Tony, Tommy Jacobs, Jim Ferree and myself started traveling together, playing practice rounds, and staying at the same motels and so forth. We formed a friendship. One year we played in the Canadian Open, I believe in Edmonton and then caught a train to Vancouver and shared a cooler of Carling beer on the way. We didn't do anything silly. We were all trying to make enough to pay our bills, paying attention to our games and fortunately we were all playing fairly well and having a good time. It was just a matter of time before we started doing better. I won two tournaments in 1960, Tommy beat me in a playoff in San Diego but we continued to be friends. After Tony won the British Open there was more pressure on him to appear in outings and commercial appearances, which put him in another level. Throughout all of those years we remained good friends.

"I roomed with Tony the week before I got married in 1959. Tony was such a fine player and a little older. He had the experience from his time in the Marine Corps, knew a little more about life and we respected him for that. He had a good time but he didn't do anything bad. We were all young, we dressed well and walking through an airport we were often recognized. Tony never drank too much, we had a good time but we didn't let a 'good time' get in the way of out performance. We talked quite a bit about 'hey guys, if we behave, we can beat those guys that go out and drink every night. If we can beat the guys that were having too much fun, if we can beat the ones that are not trying real hard, and if we can beat the ones because are games are better, hell, we can make a living out here.' We were pretty sensible and we helped one another with our golf games because that's what you did back then. We played practice rounds and noticed if one's swing was off a little bit here or there. We all wanted to beat the other guy but we never resented anyone who had a better week than we did.

"I kept up with Tony and it was such a sad thing the day he

was killed. I had gone to Mass with him that Sunday morning. There was some confusion about the whole thing. My airplane was at the Goodyear Airport, which is right beside the Firestone Country Club. The twin Beechcraft had flown in from the Chicago area and was over at the Akron-Canton Airport. So the courtesy car had driven Tony to the Goodyear Airport but then had had to make the 30-minute drive over to the Akron-Canton Airport. That probably led to Tony's frustration about his insecure feelings concerning the female pilot.

"Later that afternoon, I flew down to Columbus for the pro-am which was held the next day at the Columbus CC. That Sunday night it came across the TV that Tony had been in an airplane accident and eventually they confirmed that all aboard had been killed. That same week, we played in Indianapolis and the fellow that had taken Tony to the airport and Tony had stayed with at Akron came to the tournament and shared what he knew about the accident. It was a humbling week that we had lost one of our players and I had lost a very good friend.

"Tony had a lot of golf left in him. He was doing better, had a great following and no telling how good he could have been. He was a good player, that's all I can say. There's no doubt about the great run he had in 1964. I think all of us started playing better after we got married and had a wife and a partner. He hadn't reached his peak, he had just smoothed out to the point where he was capable of winning every week. He was on a good run. He was winning at a variety of golf courses and he was winning with our best players in the field. No one really knows what he could have done. It was quite a shame, a great loss for the golf world. We needed more people like Tony out there who had a wonderful personality and was very outgoing with the kids. The kids loved him at the Buick Open. He had so many teenagers that rooted for him; it was something to see. Tony should be remembered. For a period of about eight years, he was certainly one of the top players and he's worthy of a book about his career. Tony had a following and he made time for the people and I think everybody respected him as being a worthy champion."

Bruce Devlin, PGA Tour

"He wasn't around very long after I came over here and started playing in 1962. From 1964 through 1966 I got to know him fairly well. Obviously he was a wonderful player. I had actually arranged for he and Betty to come to Australia. We were to meet in San Francisco after that two-day tournament he was scheduled to play in following the PGA and then head to Australia. That's what the plan was, but obviously it didn't happen. You know, enough people have said enough really nice things about Tony Lema, I probably agree with everything that everybody has said. He was a great guy, a fun guy to be around. He was a terrific player. His record, well, once he learned how to win, his whole attitude changed completely as far as a player was concerned. He was in contention pretty much every week after that. "

When asked if he thought Betty had a calming influence on Tony's golf game and his entire life, Bruce answered matter of factly, "Yes, I think it was one of the best things Tony ever did. She was a nice lady. I had taken Jack Nicklaus over to Australia in 1964 and then Bob Murphy and a couple of guys came over as well. My wife Gloria and I were looking so forward to spending some time with Tony and Betty in Australia. But it never did happen."

During the interview, Tony Lema's victory in the 1964 British Open became a topic of conversation and Bruce was quite humble as the weather conditions were addressed. "To be quite honest," Bruce said, "I thought I had the best first two rounds and I was several shots behind Tony." It seems as though Tony played early in the first round and shot a respectable 73 in normal wind conditions. That afternoon, as Jack Nicklaus attested to earlier, the winds blew ferociously. Bruce Devlin fired a solid even-par 72 despite those extreme conditions. On the second day, the winds blew harder in the morning as Bruce shot another solid 72 to sit at 144 halfway through the tournament. The winds became much calmer in the afternoon of the second day and Tony blazed around the Old Course in a smooth four-under par 68. So after two rounds, Tony was three shots ahead of Bruce, but the conditions had a major affect.

"Despite the difference in playing conditions," Bruce added, "He was worthy of a being the British Open Champion. I can tell you that. I didn't really get to spend a lot of time with him except in 1965 and 1966. But he was sorely missed. He was a great asset to our game and we lost a great one when he passed."

Peter Alliss, European and PGA Tour

"My time spent with Tony Lema was very short, but productive and enjoyable. From the day we met we started a warm friendship. He won the Open Championship in 1964 at St Andrews and suddenly I found myself playing a series of exhibition matches as his partner around the UK. We spent several days together and I was taken by his friendliness, his golfing skill, which seemed to come naturally, and his joy of life.

"His death was a tragedy, not only for his family, but for the world of golf. Who knows how far along the golfing road he would have travelled."

Bob Toski, PGA

"There were three golf professionals whom I knew and loved that passed away because of an airplane accident. They were Tony Lema, Davis Love, Jr., and Payne Stewart. Their passing left a void in my heart because of my association with these gentlemen!

"Tony was an extrovert and very outgoing to both the gallery and the press people. He had a way of making you accept him immediately on personal contact. His style of play was welcomed by the British people because he could strike the ball at a low trajectory and play golf the English way, so to speak, and then drink champagne after the round. He was to me a lot of what Walter Hagen was when he went abroad; a personality that won people over immediately, with a different style of play, but very successful.

"My son, Robert, met Tony when he was about ten years

old, and to this day he still talks about it. Tony was one of a kind. He left many great memories to many great people on and off the golf course."

Ken Venturi, PGA Tour & CBS Broadcaster

Note: This quote from Ken Venturi was made shortly after Tony's death as an introduction to the production of Howard Cosell's film entitled Tony Lema: Champagne on the Green.

"When Tony Lema died in a plane crash not long ago, golf lost one of its best and most colorful players. Tony was a player who gave a touch of real class to the game. As someone has said, the golf tour will go on with the meat and potatoes, but the champagne is gone. I knew Tony Lema for 20 years as a friend, pupil and competitor both on and off the golf course. We were from opposite sides of the Bay, he from San Leandro and I was from San Francisco. But golf brought us together, in fact, my mother gave him his first pair of golf shoes. I gave him lessons and he was on my great supporter list and always pushed me. He was always the first on the phone to congratulate me for a win. But we always argued a lot. The kind of an argument that is a 'privilege' of a real friendship. The conversation you are about to see was completed just a few days before Tony and Betty Lema died in a plane crash. I was asked if it should be shown and my answer was, of course. And it pictures Tony as he was and I am sure as he would like to be remembered. This is the Tony I knew; honest, outspoken, humorous and colorful."

Dave Marr, PGA Tour and Golf Broadcaster

Note: As part of the production of Howard Cosell's Tony Lema: Champagne on the Green, Dave Marr made the following comments about Tony Lema.

"Tony and I started together in 1957. As a matter of fact, the first tournament he played in, was also one of my first tournaments. We were kind of 'rabbits together' on the tour and the rabbits grew up and Tony got a little longer fangs than I did. He became a very fine player and a great name in golf. We've covered ten years and played a lot of golf together.

"I was with Tony a week ago Wednesday at the PGA Championship. Tony and I went out to the course in the same courtesy car for a practice round and he was in very good spirits. He was looking forward to a good tournament, but as it turned out it wasn't as good as some of his other tournaments. You just can't imagine that when Susan and I got home on Sunday night after the PGA and heard the news, you don't know what to say. It could have been any one of us. When you lose a star of Tony's magnitude, a person who is colorful, a great player, a fine person, it's just a shame. Golf loses something and I think people lose something, too.

"Tony had great times and played great tournaments, but I don't think he really had a chance to prove if he was 'great' or just 'very good.' We will all miss him and think about him for a long time to come."

Peter Thomson, Five-time British Open Champion

Note: The following comments were taken from a You Tube recording.

"The memories of Tony Lema have been largely forgotten or ignored. After he won The Open Championship at St. Andrews in 1964, he came to play in 1965 and defend his title at Royal Birkdale. He and I played the last two rounds together, in one day I might tell you. Not long after that he lost his life in an air crash. It's sad to say that hardly anybody remembers him now. I played against him, face to face on that occasion, and I reckon he was one of the best players I've ever seen."

Bob Charles, PGA Tour

"Unfortunately I did not know Tony Lema that well. I probably only played two or three rounds of golf with him, but I do recall playing a practise round with him at St. Andrew's in 1964 the day before The Open started. I believe it was his one and only look at the old course before the event due to his late arrival in Scotland.

"I should mention he did get a break by playing early the first day when gale force winds got up to 60 miles per hour after he had played the front nine. His 73 in the morning looked good on the board when all the afternoon players shot in the high 70's and low 80's.

"Having won four tournaments already on the tour in 1964 Tony was considered, next to Jack Nicklaus, the favourite for the event and without Arnold Palmer playing The Open, he had Tip Anderson on the bag.

Sadly his career was cut short, but his few years on the PGA Tour made a big impact with galleries, sponsors and fellow professionals in the years of the Big Three."

Max Jerome Winters, Caddied for Tony

"I began caddying at 14 at Rolling Green C.C. in my hometown of Arlington Heights, IL. In 1962 the Western Open was coming to Medinah, so on Easter Sunday my best friend and I hitchhiked the 15 miles to Medinah. I was 5'10", 145 lbs, but the caddie master gave me a double. I made $8 and I was hooked.

"By mid-June, the excitement was palpable. The Thursday before the tournament, there was a caddie draw, based on seniority. I drew the 17th alternate, and figured I was out of luck.

"On Monday morning, the caddie master told me I would be caddying for some guy named Tony Lema, who nobody had ever heard of. One guy, who claimed he was a Tour caddie, said Tony Lema was a 5'7" Puerto Rican pro.

"He didn't show up on Monday, but about noon on Tuesday, I saw Ken Venturi get out of a courtesy car with his wife, a beautiful dark-haired woman named Connie. Last out was Tony

Lema, 6'2", dark hair combed back, a yellow Jantzen shirt and gray trousers that were a little too short. Somebody told me that was Lema, and I waited nervously for him to come over to the pro shop.

"I introduced myself. He told me he was glad to meet me, and I grabbed this enormous leather bag that must have weighed 80 pounds and had this narrow little strap. About an hour later, Tony came out and said we were going to hit some balls. We waited for a ride out to the range, and as our car pulled up, some guy named Ben Hogan got in the back seat, so I had to sit on the convertible top, which was down.

"I could see Tony was nervous about being near Hogan and they didn't say a word. At the range, I dumped Tony's leather shag bag, and headed out about a hundred yards. They didn't require helmets yet, and I was a little worried, until I saw how straight these guys hit it.

"Except for the reigning U.S. Open Champ, a kid named (Jack) Nicklaus, the Western Open that year was a who's who in golf.

"Tony finished 13th, 73-73-77-69—292 highlighted by a 30 on the back nine on Sunday. He won $1,125 and paid me $40. I used it to buy a bus ticket for my Grandmother's house, which was near Aronimink C.C. outside of Philadelphia, site of the 1962 PGA Championship. I went there and got a job raking sand traps and repairing ball marks on the 16th green. When Tony came through on Thursday, he made a 30-footer for a birdie and told me it was because of the good shape I kept the green in.

"That fall he won the Orange County Open in California and Champagne Tony was born. I started a scrapbook, continued writing and in 1964 I followed him all summer, starting with his Buick Open win. In 1965, I left high school to meet him at the first Bob Hope Desert Classic. I ended up caddying for James Garner that week.

"In June of 1966, I again caddied for Tony at Medinah in the Western Open. This time he finished fifth. As he and his wife, Betty, got ready to head for the airport, he handed me a set of new Slazenger *Tony Lema* irons he had used in practice on Tuesday. He told me to meet him in four weeks at a charity tournament the Monday after the PGA, on the South Side of

Chicago.

"I was in the coffee shop of the Holiday Inn in Lansing on Sunday night at 8:00 on July 24, 1966, when the tournament director said that Tony and his wife Betty had died in a small plane crash on a golf course two miles away."

Note: Jerry became the owner of his own computer consulting company and married Charlene. They became parents of a son named Anthony Lema Winters.

Scott Stephanuik, G.M. & Head Pro at Lansing C.C.

"During the winter of 2010, it came to my mind that nothing had been done here at Lansing Country Club concerning some kind of dedication to Tony Lema. Since the 45th Anniversary was coming up, I thought it would be nice to do something on his behalf. So I sent letters to many of the golf professionals who played with him back in his day, the Golf Channel, CDGA, (Chicago District Golf Association), the PGA, local newspapers, magazines and so forth. We had an in-house dedication for our members and other guests who were interested. On the third Sunday of July around the 24th of the month, we had a nine-hole Scramble. As we teed off, we did a 'champagne toast' as would be appropriate, and during that round, we had champagne available on the seventh hole. We have done it for three years now and will continue this kind of dedication for Tony Lema as long as I am here. We want to carry on the legend of Tony.

"My uncle had been a scratch golfer and a huge fan of Tony Lema's. In 1990, when my parents joined the club, we found out the accident had happened here. I was born in 1980, so I learned all about Tony Lema and his impact on golfers everywhere. Over the years, I had never seen anything here in a form of dedication and thought it was about time."

Dan Jenkins, Sports Illustrated

"I remember very little about Tony. Didn't know him like I knew some of the other stars. I knew Fred Corcoran much better. Fred was responsible for 'Champagne Tony.' I do know this. His death was the worst phone call I ever got from an editor at *Sports Illustrated*. I'd already written my PGA piece, had dinner, drinks with writer pals, and had gone to bed. The call woke me up early, telling me Tony had been killed and the magazine needed an insert. I don't know what I wrote, but it wasn't an easy piece to write."

Jack Berry, Detroit Free-Press

"Tony won successive Buick Opens, 1964-65, and contended in 1966 to the point he had champagne ready and waiting for a celebration with the media. Unfortunately he shot 1-over-par 73 in the final round and fellow Californian Phil Rodgers finished 2 shots ahead of Johnny Pott and Kermit Zarley and 3 ahead of Lema. Tony donated the champagne to Rodgers so he could celebrate with the press. In the half century run of the Buick only one other player won it back-to-back. Vijay Singh... and Vijay didn't pop for champagne.

"It's a shame that Tony died so young and ironically, he was enroute to a Buick dealers outing in suburban Chicago when his plane crashed. I think Tony deserves to be in the World Golf Hall of Fame, but that's a tough nut to crack with his career tragically being relatively short."

Jim Moriarty, Golf World

"I was working once on a story about Tony and called John Miller, who was anxious to talk about him. Miller told me Lema was one of his heroes. He said whenever he wanted to hit the ball straight, he was Johnny Miller. If he wanted to fade it, he was Lee Trevino. Whenever he wanted to draw the ball, he imaged he was Tony Lema. That's a pretty impressive threesome."

Tom Place, Cleveland Plain Dealer & Director of Media Relations for the PGA Tour

"Tony and became quite good friends because of my association with the Cleveland Open. I was at the *Plain Dealer* for 20 years and we used to cover a lot of golf. I'd go to Florida during the Florida swing. I would like to share a story. In 1965 at the Open Championship at Royal Birkdale, Tony came in there as the defending champion. There was a very small press corps in those days. Well, Peter Thomson had just won by two strokes. Tony had shot 68-72-75-74—289 and was four shots back in a tie for fifth. But he came storming into the locker room and Fred Corcoran was there trying to calm him down. Tony was livid. He said, 'I could have kicked the ball around and beat that SOB from Australia.' He was really hot and then a very proper British Open official came into the locker room and said, 'Mr. Lema, we need you at the awards ceremony.' Tony replied, 'I'm not going to the awards ceremony.' The official countered, 'You have to, Mr. Lema, it's very appropriate for the defending champion to be there and present the trophy to the new champion and you are the defending champion, so it's important for you to be there.' Tony said, 'I really don't...' Before he could say another word, the official said, 'And it would be appropriate for you to put on a blazer before you went out to the ceremony.' Tony looked at Fred Corcoran and said, 'Fred, I don't have a blazer.' Well, about then Tony looked at me and I'm about 5'10' compared to his 6'2". Well, I had on a navy blazer with a Golf Writers Association of America emblem on the pocket. He looked at me, then looked at Fred and said, 'You don't need that blazer for a while, do ya? Let me try that on.' So he put it on and here are the sleeves about two inches above his wrists. He walked over to a mirror and said, 'Hey, this is not so bad.' Then he started to laugh and changed the atmosphere immediately. Suddenly, he was like the old Tony Lema. He went out, presented the trophy, and came back in and we chatted for a while. I'll never forget, he said, 'Tom, I'll bet that's the first time in history that a Golf Writer's blazer was part of the awards ceremony at the Open Championship.' "

John Fry, PGA, (Boyhood Friend & Competitor)

"My Dad was the pro at Lake Chabot Golf Course in Oakland, CA. Tony's older brother, Walter, started caddying at Lake Chabot and young Tony found out that Walter was making a couple dollars caddying. He said, 'Gee, I think I'll try that, too.' I'd say Tony was about 12 years old when he started caddying in 1946. He began playing and little by little, he got better and better. Tony and I were friends and adversaries, not necessarily close buddies, but we played against and with each other quite a bit. Through the years, as he became more famous, we kept in touch, but I was not in his inner circle.

"In 1952 we played against each other in the finals of the Oakland City Amateur Championship and he beat me in a 36-hole match. I think we were several under par, I can't remember for sure. After that, we both graduated from high school and soon afterward he joined the Marines and was unable to play in 1953. Fortunately, I won it that year.

"Tony always had a good short game. I could hit the ball a little bit farther with the driver, but his short game was always very good. As the years went by, he got much better with his long game. And with his natural talent with his short shots, it made him become a great golfer.

"One of the unique things about Tony Lema that made him become the golfer and the person that he was, was that he had the ability to learn. At the San Francisco Club, Eddie Lowery was a member of the club as he was the owner of a big automobile dealership in San Francisco. Byron Nelson would come out every year for two or three weeks, buy an updated car from Lowery and spend some time at the Golf Club. There were a lot of good golfers around and Tony did get to play with some of those better players, including Harvie Ward and Ken Venturi on a regular basis. Tony picked up on the way they handled themselves, their demeanor and their style. That rubbed off on Tony and he learned from them. That's why being at San Francisco Club was such an important part of his stepping further up the ladder and becoming a champion golfer. San Francisco was a hotbed of many very good golfers. Lowery would have games set up. I don't know if Tony ever played in these games, but he was around them and as I said, good habits rubbed off on him.

"I think the Tony Lema story is worth telling. Tony Lema's life was short, but it was full. Tony grew up without a lot, but he won only one tournament as an amateur, the Oakland City Championship. He came back from the Marine Corps, had the experience we discussed at the San Francisco Club. He had some initial success on the tour then went into a slump. I had some contact with him during those tough times. Tony was famous for shooting 68 on Friday and 78 on Saturday cause he was out all night on Friday… and there's a lot of truth to that. A fellow named Danny Arnold, a television producer and director became friends with Tony and when Tony stayed at Arnold's house, Danny enforced a curfew rule plain and simple. 'You can stay here Tony, but there is an 11 o'clock curfew.' Danny Arnold was a smart guy.

"In the early 60's, Tony started to shape up physically, mentally and by my angle, he got in shape, spiritually. His mother was a very devout Catholic, as well as the entire family. Tony made some special devotions to the Blessed Virgin Mary. He made a habit of going to Mass on the first Friday of every month in addition to Sundays. In life, the most important thing is 'your story.' Tony's story is that he went from small beginnings, had quite a bit of success, then he went into a slump, then he made a comeback physically, mentally and spiritually. Down deep inside him, he had a strong belief in God. It wasn't long, but he lived a very successful life. At the end of the line it's a terrible thing that he and Betty died in that airplane crash. But he had done what every person would want to do in their life. He made peace with himself and with God."

A Note From the Author

To all the readers who have made it to this page, I certainly hope you enjoyed this biography of Tony Lema. Obviously, you are free to draw your own conclusions on his life, his untimely death and this presentation. There are two prominent issues I have chosen not to include. Tony and Shirley Cozy had a brief marriage that was a well kept-secret on the Tour. They had a son named David Anthony Lema, who was born in 1961. I felt obliged to allow Shirley and David to maintain their private lives. Hence, this is the only place they are mentioned in this book.

Secondly, there was a great deal of debate as to whether it was necessary to present a picture of the plane that carried four people to their deaths on July 24, 1966. I made the decision to omit such a picture. I'd much rather allow the readers of this book to close the last chapter and visualize Tony and Betty Lema smiling, knowing that although their time on earth was short, they lived every moment to its fullest potential.

Appendix A - Tony's Tournaments

* Unofficial Money

Date	Tournament	Position	1st	2nd	3rd	4th	5th	Total Score	Official Money	Total Money	Rank
6/16/56	U.S. Open Championship	50	77	71	79	81		308	200	200	
10/14/56	Western Open	T22	76	71	72	72		291	185	185	
	1956 Totals								**385**	**385**	**147**
1/13/57	* Bing Crosby National Pro-Am	T50	75	75	86			236	*67	67	
1/27/57	* Imperial Valley Open	P1	71	73	67	65		276	*1,000	1,000	
2/3/57	Phoenix Open Invitational	T32	68	74	71	71		284	Out of Money		
11/3/57	San Diego Open	T40	70	73	72	70		285	Out of Money		
11/10/57	* Long Beach Open Invitational	T30	69	73	70			212	Missed Final Cut		
12/15/57	Mayfair Inn Open	T6	73	66	69	67		275	725	725	
	1957 Totals								**725**	**1,792**	**123**
1/6/58	Los Angeles Open	T39	76	70	70	75		291	113	113	
1/12/58	Bing Crosby National Pro-Am	T30	75	69	80	70		294	175	175	
1/20/58	Tijuana Open Invitational	T49	71	73	76	73		293	Out of Money		
1/22/58	* El Centro Pro-Am	T2	70	72				142	*375	375	
1/29/58	Phoenix Open Invitational	T27	79	74	72	70		286	77	77	
2/9/58	Tucson Open Invitational	T14	66	65	70	75		276	327	327	
2/24/58	Houston Open	T18	72	75	72	70		289	570	570	
2/25/58	* Port Arthur Pro-Am	T11							*15	15	
3/2/58	Baton Rouge Open Invitational	T38	76	73	72	74		295	Out of Money		

Date	Tournament	Place	R1	R2	R3	R4	Total		Money
3/11/58	Greater New Orleans Open	T45	75	72	71	75	293	Out of Money	
3/16/58	Pensacola Open Invitational	T44	71	72	77	74	294	Out of Money	
3/23/58	St. Petersburg Open Invitational	T46	76	74	71	72	293	Out of Money	
3/30/58	Azalea Open Invitational	T16	70	72	76	76	294	263	263
4/13/58	Greater Greensboro Open	T2	69	69	70	69	277	1,080	1,080
4/20/58	Kentucky Derby Open	T6	67	67	75	70	279	950	950
4/27/58	* Lafayette Open Invitational	T21	72	71	69	74	286	*180	180
5/4/58	Colonial National Invitational	T36	74	73	77	74	298	Out of Money	
6/1/58	Western Open	T19	71	68	70	75	284	249	249
6/8/58	Dallas Open Invitational	27	66	70	74	72	282	180	180
6/23/58	Buick Open Invitational	T18	75	77	72	70	294	900	900
6/29/58	Pepsi Championship	T37	71	71	75	73	290	150	150
6/30/58	* Apawamis Pro-Am	T12						*30	30
7/6/58	Rubber City Open Invitational	T29	71	70	70	70	281	51	51
7/13/58	Insurance City Open Invitational	T26	70	74	68	68	280	168	168
7/14/58	* Nephrosis Pro-Am	T11						*15	15
7/27/58	Eastern Open Invitational	T54	76	70	74	78	298	Out of Money	
8/11/58	Miller Open Invitational	T26	69	72	69	68	278	345	345
8/17/58	St. Paul Open Invitational	T13	67	74	64	67	272	656	656
8/23/58	Canadian Open	T24	66	67	73	70	276	218	218
9/1/58	Vancouver Open	T13	77	70	66	68	281	950	950
9/8/58	Utah Open Invitational	11	67	68	71	70	276	550	550
9/14/58	Denver Centennial Open	T5	72	69	66	67	274	930	930
9/21/58	Hesperia Open Invitational	T20	71	67	74	73	285	180	180
11/9/58	Carling Open Invitational	T12	69	73	76	74	292	775	775
11/16/58	*Havana International	T6	74	73	72	75	294	*1,600	1,600
11/23/58	West Palm Beach Open Invitational	T13	69	71	66	73	279	425	425
11/30/58	* Havana Pro-Am Invitational	4	70	70	70	72	282	*900	900
12/7/58	* Dorado Beach Invitational	T22	76	71	74	78	299	*392	392

Date	Tournament	Finish	R1	R2	R3	R4	Total	Money	Amount	Events
12/14/58	Mayfair Inn Open	W/D	70	72	77		219			
	1958 Totals							**10,282**	**14,856**	**36**
1/5/59	Los Angeles Open	T17	73	69	73	72	287	680	680	
1/18/59	Bing Crosby National Pro-Am	W/D	74					Out of Money		
2/1/59	San Diego Open Invitational	T53	68	67	74	79	288	108	108	
2/8/59	Phoenix Open Invitational	T26	72	69	71	70	282	Out of Money		
2/15/59	Tucson Open Invitational	T33	70	67	69	71	277	690	690	
2/22/59	Texas Open Invitational	T10	74	71	67	72	284	150	150	
3/9/59	Greater New Orleans Open	T26	73	75	73	69	290	332	332	
3/15/59	Pensacola Open Invitational	T13	75	70	67	71	283	Out of Money		
3/23/59	St. Petersburg Open Invitational	59	66	76	76	84	302	Out of Money		
3/25/59	* Latham-Reed Pro-Am	T35					152	*50	50	
3/30/59	Azalea Open Invitational	T64	79	75	80	79	313	328	328	
4/12/59	Greater Greensboro Open	T14	73	72	75	67	287	50	50	
4/19/59	Houston Classic	T52	71	73	73	76	293	Out of Money		
4/20/59	* Port Arthur Pro-Am	T8	71				71	*44	44	
5/17/59	Arlington Hotel Open	T41	72	73	70	74	289	630	630	
5/25/59	Memphis Open Invitational	T15	72	68	69	70	279	Out of Money		
5/31/59	Kentucky Derby Open Invitational	T31	73	70	71	72	286	160	160	
6/7/59	Eastern Open Invitational	T26	66	73	72	74	285	Out of Money		
6/21/59	Canadian Open	T39	70	77	75	71	293	203	203	
8/23/59	Rubber City Open Invitational	T25	67	71	72	72	282	900	900	
8/30/59	Miller Open Invitational	T12	68	66	67	72	273	33	33	
9/7/59	Kansas City Open Invitational	T30	68	70	71	76	285	Out of Money		
9/14/59	Dallas Open Invitational	T51	73	75	72	73	293	Out of Money		
9/27/59	Golden Gate Championship	T50	74	70	73	72	289	Out of Money		
10/4/59	Portland Centennial Open	T5	65	68	69	73	275	1,000	1,000	
10/11/59	Hesperia Open Invitational	13	72	71	71	68	282	450	450	

10/18/59	Orange County Open Invitational	T34	70	70	72	74		286	Out of Money		
11/22/59	Mobile Sertoma Open Invitational	T31	73	70	75	73		291	Out of Money		
11/29/59	West Palm Beach Open Invitational	T57	72	75	76	81		304	Out of Money		
12/6/59	Coral Gables Open Invitational	T23	69	76	71	70		286	218	218	
	1959 Totals								**5,932**	**6,026**	**55**
1/18/60	Yorba Linda Open Invitational	T25	66	75	74	73		288	113	113	59
1/24/60	Bing Crosby National Pro-Am	T38	78	68	76	79		301	100	100	62
2/7/60	Palm Springs Desert Classic	T53	67	71	72	74	74	358	140	140	72
2/15/60	Phoenix Open Invitational	T17	75	69	70	66		280	480	480	63
2/21/60	Tucson Open Invitational	T50	66	71	72	77		286	Out of Money		68
2/28/60	Texas Open Invitational	T56	74	71	77	77		299	Out of Money		72
3/1/60	* Sherwood Forest Pro-Am	2	71					71	*251	251	72
3/6/60	Baton Rouge Open Invitational	T21	71	76	73	75		295	165	165	65
3/21/60	St. Petersburg Open Invitational	T32	73	75	75	72		295	Out of Money		73
3/27/60	De Soto Open Invitational	T44	75	74	71	75		295	Out of Money		75
4/3/60	Azalea Open Invitational	T33	74	70	75	74		293	Out of Money		76
4/17/60	Greater Greensboro Open	T53	71	77	76	74		298	Out of Money		84
5/2/60	Houston Classic	T24	69	74	73	74		290	450	450	72
5/22/60	Hot Springs Open Invitational	T43	71	74	71	74		290	Out of Money		76
7/4/60	Buick Open Invitational	T53	72	77	74	78		301	Out of Money		86
7/17/60	Western Open	T47	75	67	74	76		292	115	115	85
7/31/60	Eastern Open Invitational	T32	71	71	75	70		287	72	72	87
8/1/60	* Piping Rock Pro-Am	T6	70					70	*93	93	87
8/2/60	* Apawamis Pro-Am	T8	69					69	*96	96	87
8/7/60	Insurance City Open Invitational	T55	69	74	69	76		288	Out of Money		89
9/12/60	Utah Open Invitational	T25	70	68	64	72		274	180	180	93
9/18/60	Carling Open Invitational	T29	72	69	72	70		283	140	140	89
9/25/60	Portland Open Invitational	T15	67	70	71	70		278	510	510	81

Date	Tournament	Finish	R1	R2	R3	R4	R5	Total	Money	Money	
10/3/60	Hesperia Open Invitational	T22	71	75	75	70		291	175	175	77
10/16/60	Orange County Open Invitational	T27	69	75	71	73		288	77	77	78
10/30/60	*Borrego Springs Pro-Am	30	76	71				147	*38	38	78
11/7/60	*Hotel Del Coronado Pro-Am	10	67	73	68	73		281	*300	300	78
11/20/60	Cajun Classic Open Invitational	T23	72	70	72	68		282	150	150	76
11/27/60	Mobile Sertoma Open Invitational	T19	69	73	72	71		285	195	195	76
12/11/60	Coral Gables Open Invitational	T40	70	72	75	71		288	Out of Money		76
	1960 Totals								**3,061**	**3,838**	**77**
1/22/61	Bing Crosby National Pro-Am	T34	72	71	77	72		292	170	170	64
2/5/61	Palm Springs Desert Classic	62	72	71	74	69	80	366	Out of Money		80
2/12/61	*Panama Open Invitational	23	76	73	71	75		295	*100	100	85
2/19/61	*Maracaibo Open Invitational	T10	70	72	73	79		294	*425	425	92
2/26/61	*Caracas Open Invitational	T3	74	71	65	71		281	*763	763	101
3/5/61	*Puerto Rico Open Invitational	22	72	75	69	74		290	*100	100	107
3/12/61	*Jamaica Open Invitational	8	70	73	69	73		285	*550	550	110
3/19/61	St. Petersburg Open Invitational	T13	71	66	68	66		271	590	590	73
4/16/61	Greater Greensboro Open	T28	74	77	75	70		296	147	147	86
4/23/61	Houston Classic	T50	71	74	74	71		290	150	150	86
4/30/61	Texas Open Invitational	T30	70	71	72	67		280	150	150	84
5/7/61	Waco Turner Open Invitational	T7	70	73	71	74		288	802	802	68
5/21/61	Hot Springs Open Invitational	T16	71	72	70	69		282	470	470	63
5/28/61	500 Festival Open Invitational	T44	74	72	69	73		288	110	110	61
6/4/61	Memphis Open Invitational	T25	69	66	74	70		279	290	290	65
6/26/61	*Rheingold Pro-Celebrity Invitational	T21	71					71	*200	200	69
7/2/61	Buick Open Invitational	T34	71	72	75	77		295	200	200	67
7/9/61	St. Paul Open Invitational	T15	71	70	66	71		278	670	670	63
7/15/61	Canadian Open	T7	65	70	72	70		277	1,250	1,250	56
7/23/61	Milwaukee Open Invitational	T6	69	68	72	66		275	1,300	1,300	47

Date	Tournament	Pos	R1	R2	R3	R4	R5	Total	Earnings	Total $	#
7/24/61	* Edgewater Pro-Am	T11	70	72				70	*75	75	47
8/6/61	Eastern Open Invitational	T13	68	72	69	72		281	828	828	48
8/7/61	* Piping Rock Pro-Am	T4	69				69	69	*281	281	48
8/13/61	Insurance City Open Invitational	T30	71	69	68	73		281	106	106	49
8/20/61	Carling Open Invitational	T11	74	69	71	69		283	900	900	45
8/27/61	American Golf Classic	T46	72	73	75	76		296	110	110	44
9/4/61	Dallas Open Invitational	T25	70	72	73	73		288	290	290	46
9/10/61	Denver Open Invitational	T10	70	68	65	70		273	850	850	44
9/17/61	Greater Seattle Open Invitational	T18	67	71	64	72		274	490	490	42
9/24/61	Portland Open Invitational	T14	70	69	70	70		279	653	653	40
10/1/61	Bakersfield Open	T25	74	72	69	71		286	168	168	42
10/8/61	* Hesperia Invitational	1	71	67				138	*1,200	1,200	42
10/15/61	Ontario Open	T44	69	78	73	72		292	Out of Money		42
10/26/61	* Sahara Pro-Am	T4	67	67	72			206	*750	750	42
11/5/61	* Almaden Open Invitational	T17	72	70	74	75		291	*138	138	42
12/3/61	West Palm Beach Open Invitational	11	73	68	70	72		283	710	710	42
12/10/61	Coral Gables Open Invitational	T24	68	74	69	72		283	103	103	43
	1961 Totals								**11,506**	**16,089**	**43**
1/8/62	Los Angeles Open	T5	70	66	73	70		279	1,900	1,900	5
1/22/62	Bing Crosby Pro-Am	T32	71	74	82	71		298	210	210	14
1/28/62	Lucky International Open	T22	68	70	70	76		284	625	625	16
2/4/62	Palm Springs Golf Classic	T53	74	72	68	72	73	359	Out of Money		22
2/11/62	* Panama Open Invitational	T8	73	67	73	71		284	*450	450	30
2/18/62	* Maracaibo Open Invitational	T5	69	75	72	74		290	*700	700	31
2/25/62	* Caracas Open Invitational	T5	71	70	73	71		285	*700	700	35
3/4/62	* Puerto Rico Open Invitational	T2	71	71	70	70		282	*938	938	40
3/11/62	* Jamaica Open Invitational	7	71	73	70	67		281	*600	600	41
3/25/62	Doral Open	T48	82	71	72	73		298	47	47	50

Date	Tournament	Finish					Total	Money	Money	Rank
4/22/62	Houston Classic	T15	70	70	73	72	285	1,075	1,075	52
4/29/62	Texas Open Invitational	T28	67	74	72	69	282	216	216	52
5/6/62	Waco Turner Open Invitational	T18	73	74	72	72	291	390	390	55
5/27/62	500 Festival Open Invitational	T15	68	69	69	67	273	1,050	1,050	50
6/3/62	Memphis Open Invitational	T13	68	67	69	72	276	875	875	44
6/10/62	Thunderbird Classic Invitational	T57	73	73	73	78	293	230	230	50
6/24/62	Eastern Open Invitational	3	75	67	70	69	281	2,200	2,200	41
7/1/62	Western Open	T13	73	73	77	69	292	1,125	1,125	38
7/8/62	Buick Open	T6	71	69	72	76	288	1,825	1,825	34
7/15/62	Motor City Open	T53	70	69	74	73	286	Out of Money		35
7/22/62	PGA Championship	W/D	77	72			149	100	100	35
8/12/62	American Golf Classic	T23	73	77	73	69	292	476	476	40
8/19/62	St. Paul Open Invitational	T15	68	70	71	70	279	775	775	38
8/26/62	Oklahoma City Open Invitational	T4	77	68	70	70	285	1,800	1,800	33
9/3/62	Dallas Open Invitational	T43	75	74	71	75	295	Out of Money		33
9/9/62	Denver Open Invitational	T22	71	71	71	73	286	375	375	33
9/9/62	Seattle World's Faie Open	2	72	66	66	63	267	3,000	3,000	31
9/16/62	Portland Open Invitational	T14	65	71	70	71	277	551	551	31
9/23/62	* Sahara Invitational	1	69	67	66	68	270	*2,800	2,800	31
9/30/62	Bakersfield Open Invitational	2	68	69	68	71	276	3,600	3,600	21
10/14/62	Ontario Open Invitational	T7	69	66	74	69	278	988	988	21
10/21/62	Orange County Open Invitational	P1	68	66	64	69	267	2,800	2,800	18
10/28/62	Cajun Classic Open Invitational	T19	74	73	69	70	286	256	256	17
11/11/62	Mobile Sertoma Open Invitational	1	67	68	68	70	273	2,000	2,000	15
11/18/62	Carling Open Invitational	T23	69	75	69	72	285	435	435	15
11/25/62	**1962 Totals**							**28,924**	**35,111**	**15**
1/7/63	Los Angeles Open	T35	72	70	68	74	284	136	136	35
1/13/63	San Diego Open Invitational	2	65	68	71	67	271	2,300	2,300	6

Date	Tournament	Finish	R1	R2	R3	R4	R5	Total	Money	Money	Rank
1/20/63	Bing Crosby National Pro-Am	T15	74	72	74	71		291	720	720	8
1/27/63	Lucky International Open	T8	73	67	70	72		282	1,600	1,600	7
2/3/63	Palm Springs Golf Classic	T8	72	70	74	67	68	351	1,450	1,450	6
2/12/63	Phoenix Open Invitational	T5	72	71	65	69		277	1,600	1,600	6
2/17/63	Tucson Open Invitational	T9	73	71	69	67		280	975	975	7
3/4/63	Greater New Orleans	T2	72	69	68	73		282	3,050	3,050	5
3/24/63	Doral C.C. Open Invitational	3	75	72	70	69		286	3,000	3,000	4
4/7/63	Masters Tournament	2	74	69	74	70		287	12,000	12,000	3
4/14/63	Greater Greensboro Open	T28	73	69	71	73		286	365	365	3
5/5/63	Tournament of Champions	T2	72	69	71	66		278	5,300	5,300	3
5/12/63	Colonial National Invitational	T4	71	69	73	73		286	2,800	2,800	3
5/27/63	Memphis Open Invitational	1	67	67	68	68		270	9,000	9,000	2
6/3/63	500 Festival Open Invitational	T2	70	64	69	67		270	3,400	3,400	2
6/9/63	Buick Open Invitational	T10	71	74	73	70		288	1,310	1,310	2
6/16/63	Thunderbird Classic Invitational	T55	72	71	74	73		290	240	240	3
6/23/63	U.S. Open Championship	T5	71	74	74	76		295	3,167	3,167	4
7/1/63	Cleveland Open Invitational	P2	68	68	69	68		273	8,550	8,550	4
7/21/63	PGA Championship	T13	70	71	77	69		287	1,550	1,550	4
8/18/63	Insurance City Open Invitational	T21	69	69	72	75		285	532	532	4
8/25/63	American Golf Classic	T9	71	71	70	74		286	1,400	1,400	4
10/6/63	Whitemarsh Open Invitational	T67	74	75	70	83		302	230	230	4
10/13/63	Ryder Cup Matches										4
10/20/63	Sahara Invitational	T12	72	70	71	69		282	1,563	1,563	4
11/10/63	Frank Sinatra Open Invitational	T17	76	71	70	69		286	875	875	4
	1963 Totals								**67,113**	**67,113**	**4**
1/6/64	Los Angeles Open	T57	75	71	71	77		294	Out of Money		10
1/12/64	San Diego Open Invitational	T2	67	70	72	67		276	2,300	2,300	10
1/19/64	*Bing Crosby National Pro-Am	1	70	68	70	76		284	*5,800	5,800	10

Date	Tournament	Finish	R1	R2	R3	R4	R5	Total	Money	Money	Rank
1/28/64	Lucky International Open	T25	66	74	73	70		283	588	588	16
2/2/64	* Palm Springs Golf Classic	T44	72	74	68	69	81	364	Out of Money		16
2/9/64	Phoenix Open Invitational	T6	68	68	71	70		277	2,067	2,067	10
3/30/64	Azalea Open Invitational	T19	70	73	73	76		292	325	325	28
4/12/64	Masters Tournament	T9	75	68	74	70		287	1,700	1,700	21
5/3/64	Tournament of Champions	T24	77	80	70	68		295	1,045	1,045	27
5/10/64	Colonial National Invitational	T17	78	71	71	71		291	1,150	1,150	28
5/18/64	Oklahoma City Invitational	T8	70	72	77	66		285	1,400	1,400	23
5/24/64	Memphis Open Invitational	T12	68	66	69	71		274	1,110	1,110	23
6/7/64	Thunderbird Classic	1	68	67	70	71		276	20,000	20,000	5
6/14/64	Buick Open Invitational	1	69	66	72	70		277	8,177	8,177	4
6/20/64	U.S. Open Championship	20	71	72	75	75		293	700	700	4
6/28/64	Cleveland Open Invitational	P1	65	70	70	65		270	20,000	20,000	2
7/5/64	Whitemarsh Open Invitational	T6	66	72	67	75		280	3,917	3,917	3
7/10/64	* British Open Championship	1	73	68	68	70		279	*4,200	4,200	3
7/19/64	PGA Championship	T9	71	68	72	71		282	2,300	2,300	3
8/9/64	Western Open	T6	70	69	70	69		278	1,960	1,960	3
8/23/64	American Golf Classic	T5	69	71	70	76		286	2,200	2,200	3
8/30/64	Carling World Open	T17	72	71	70	75		288	1,617	1,617	3
10/18/64	Sahara Invitational	T24	73	70	71	71		285	700	700	5
11/1/64	Almaden Open Invitational	T10	70	71	73	72		286	875	875	4
	1964 Totals								**74,130**	**84,130**	**4**
1/11/65	Los Angeles Open	T4	70	71	72	69		282	3,300	3,300	4
1/17/65	San Diego Open Invitational	T13	65	68	73	70		276	825	825	6
1/24/65	* Bing Crosby National Pro-Am	2	71	65	79	72		287	*4,000	4,000	6
2/7/65	* Bob Hope Desert Classic	T40	72	67	77	75	71	362	*299	299	10
2/14/65	Phoenix Open Invitational	T25	73	71	70	70		284	661	661	14
2/21/65	Tucson Open Invitational	T21	68	72	71	73		284	576	576	14

Date	Tournament	Finish	R1	R2	R3	R4	Total	Money	Money	Rank
3/21/65	Jacksonville Open	T21	73	70	75	73	291	703	703	22
4/4/65	Greater Greensboro Open	6	71	74	68	67	280	2,900	2,900	17
4/11/65	Masters Tournament	T21	67	73	77	74	291	1,200	1,200	17
5/2/65	* Tournament of Champions	15	73	71	73	77	294	1,500	1,500	24
5/11/65	Colonial National Invitational	T3	71	69	70	70	280	5,100	5,100	16
5/16/65	Greater New Orleans Open	W/D	73	69			142			19
5/30/65	500 Festival Open Invitational	T12	75	72	69	69	285	1,900	1,900	21
6/6/65	Buick Open Invitational	1	71	70	6	70	280	20,000	20,000	4
6/13/65	Cleveland Open Invitational	2	67	70	66	70	273	13,000	13,000	2
6/20/65	U.S. Open Championship	T8	72	74	73	70	289	2,500	2,500	2
6/27/65	St. Paul Open Invitational	T23	70	70	72	71	283	875	875	2
7/4/65	Western Open	T4	69	69	68	69	275	3,067	3,067	2
7/9/65	* British Open Championship	T5	68	72	75	74	289	*1,330	1,330	2
8/1/65	Thunderbird Classic	T36	70	73	71	71	285	511	511	3
8/8/65	Philadelphia Golf Classic	T5	71	69	67	74	281	5,600	5,600	3
8/15/65	PGA Championship	T61	71	76	75	80	302	300	300	2
8/23/65	Carling World Open	1	71	71	67	70	279	35,000	35,000	5
8/29/65	American Golf Classic	T5	71	73	72	73	289	3,800	3,800	2
10/9/65	* Ryder Cup Matches									2
	1965 Totals							**101,817**	**108,945**	**2**
1/9/66	Los Angeles Open	T13	72	73	70	66	281	1,450	1,450	13
1/23/66	* Bing Crosby National Pro-Am	T16	70	72	72	79	293	*1,200	1,200	26
3/13/66	Doral Open Invitational	T59	74	74	71	76	295	Out of Money		77
3/20/66	Florida Citrus Open Invitational	T28	71	74	71	71	287	756	756	68
3/27/66	Jacksonville Open	T6	74	68	68	69	279	3,250	3,250	41
4/3/66	Greater Greensboro Open	T15	72	68	71	72	283	1,550	1,550	34
4/11/66	Masters Tournament	T23	74	74	74	76	298	1,300	1,300	36
4/18/66	Tournament of Champions	T22	77	75	69	76	297	1,750	1,750	34

Date	Tournament	Finish	R1	R2	R3	R4	Total			
4/26/66	Dallas Open Invitational	W/D	75	70	69		214			37
5/16/66	Greater New Orleans Open	T3	68	71	69	71	279	5,150	5,150	24
5/22/66	Colonial National Invitational	T3	71	71	69	71	282	6,765	6,765	18
5/29/66	Oklahoma City Open Invitational	1	69	68	69	65	271	8,500	8,500	9
6/5/66	Memphis Open Invitational	T9	69	70	69	69	277	2,175	2,175	10
6/12/66	Buick Open Invitational	T4	78	66	70	73	287	4,650	4,650	9
6/20/66	U.S. Open Championship	T4	71	74	70	71	286	6,500	6,500	8
6/26/66	Western Open	T5	71	71	75	71	288	3,650	3,650	8
7/9/66	* British Open Championship	T30	71	76	76	75	298	*286	286	8
7/24/66	PGA Championship	T34	78	71	72	74	295	775	775	9
	1966 Totals							**48,221**	**49,707**	**17**

Appendix B -
Tony's Victories

Year	Victories	Honors
1957	Imperial Valley Open	
	Montana State Open	
1958	Idaho State Open	
1962	Sahara Inv. Open	
	Northern California Open	
	Northern California PGA	
	Mobile Open	
	Orange County Open	
	Mexican Open	
1963	Memphis Open	Second in the Masters
	Northern California PGA	Most Improved Player
		Ryder Cup Team
1964	Bing Crosby Invitational	
	Northern California PGA	Golf All-American Team
	Thunderbird Open	Sport Magazine Award
	Buick Open	
	Cleveland Open	
	British Open	
	World Series of Golf	
1965	Buick Open	Ryder Cup Team
	Carling World Open	Canada Cup Team
		All-American Golf Team
1966	Oklahoma City Open	

Acknowledgments

Throughout this project, I was grateful to have conversations which led to insights with many people who unselfishly sought recollections from their respective memories and assisted me in this endeavor. Without their help, there is absolutely no way I could have gathered this information to present the real story of Tony Lema's wonderful life. I express my gratitude to Harry and Judi Lema, Tony's brother and sister-in-law who shared with me hundreds of newspaper articles, pictures, and hours of their time bringing stories back to life. Harry passed away before publication, but his contributions are deeply appreciated. Bernice, Tony's sister, was invaluable in her recollection of stories and events that took place in Tony's adolescent years. Walter Lema, Tony's brother, also shared memories of the close-knit family.

Special thanks and appreciation are in order for Colin Murray, Director of Communications of the PGA Tour and Meg Briggs, Administrative Assistant in Communications of the PGA Tour. Without their assistance I would have not been able to reach many of the PGA Tour professionals who added so much to the story. I also acknowledge longtime friend and associate Larry Rouse, PGA with tour insight information and Bobby Pollitt, PGA who assisted me with marketing ideas. Another constant source of ideas and encouragement was Rick Fredecker, a friend and proof reader who kept me on course, along with Mark MacDonald, collegiate golfer with insights on tour development. Perhaps the person who encouraged me in the most efficient way was author and friend James Dodson, whose inspiration was concise and to the point, "Great idea Bill, go write it." I would also like to thank Paul Hobart, PGA, who assisted me in detail with selecting the golf tips Tony Lema had published that would best represent his core beliefs of the golf swing. A special note of appreciation to Russell Fink of the Russell Fink Gallery in Virginia for connecting me with Tony Golden, the son of artist Francis Golden, who gave me the family's permission to include the outstanding art

Francis presented in the swing sketches.

I appreciate the precision and detail given to me by Joanne Parkhill of Hammond, IN who witnessed the airplane crash and was so gracious in the way she reached out to Betty Cline's mother. Special thanks to Scott Stephanuik, Head Professional at Lansing Golf Course who has initiated an annual tribute to Tony Lema there at the golf course.

For nearly a year, I requested many books through the Worthington Libraries in Columbus, OH. They were terrific and overly cordial with their cooperation in finding resources from all over the country.

A book cannot get printed and published successfully without the expertise and detail provided by the printing company. In this case, the entire staff of Scorecards Unlimited, particularly Beau Filing and Jacob Samblanet, were extremely helpful throughout the process of publishing this book. And of course, I acknowledge with great appreciation all of the PGA touring professionals and media correspondents for their unselfishness in providing some excellent information for Chapter 16, "Friends Remember Tony."

Bibliography

Allen, Robert J. *Tony Lema: From Out of Nowhere*, Golf Magazine, May 1963

Alliss, Peter with Michael Hobbs *Peter Alliss' Most Memorable Golf* , Stanley Paul 1986

Anderson, Dave *If Lema Had Lived. Golf Digest*, July 1989

Brown, Gwilyn S., *Golfers' Gold*. Little, Brown and Company, Inc. 1964

Brown, Gwilyn S., and Francis Golden (art sketches), *Instructional Article*, Sports Illustrated, March 15 & 22, 1965

Burger, Frederick *A Lingering Memory*, Golf Journal, August 2001

Callow, Nick The Ryder Cup, *The Complete History of Golf's Greatest Competition*, Carlton Books Ltd 2012

Casper, Billy *The Big Three and Me*, Genesis Press, Inc. Columbus, MS 2012

Concannon, Dale. *The Ryder Cup: The Complete History of Golf's Greatest Drama*. London: Arum, 2001

Corcoran, Fred, and Bud Harvey. *Unplayable Lies*. New York: Duell, Sloan & Pearce, 1965

Cosell, Howard. *Tony Lema: Champagne on the Green*. Howard Cosell Productions in association with WABC-TV, New York

Cullenward, Nelson. *Lema Had It*. The National Golfer, Sept. Oct. 1966

Davis, William H. *Looking Back at Lema.* Golf Digest, October, 1966

Dodson, James, *The American Triumvirate*, New York, Alfred A. Knope, 2012

Firmite, Ron. *The Toast of Golf.* SI Vault.Sports Illustrated, 1995

Fried, Ad & Gene Cooney, *He Had Not Had Enough, But He'd Had It All*, Monterey, 1990

Goodner, Ross, *Triumph and Tragedy of 'Champagne Tony'*, Golf Digest, August 1986

We Remember Tony...RX GOLF and TRAVEL

Lema, Tony with Bud Harvey *Champagne Tony's Golf Tips*, McGraw-Hill, New York 1966

Libby, Bill *Champagne Tony Lema: Smooth Swinger in a Rough Game*, TRUE The Man's Magazine, September 1964

Lovesey, John *Victorious Crusade In The Valley*, SI Vault, 1964

McCormack, Mark H. *The Wonderful World of Professional Golf*, Atheneun, New York, 1973

McDonnell, Michael. *Great Moments in Sport: Golf* (1974)

Moriarty, Jim *Days of Wine & Roses*, Golf World, July 2004

Murray, Jim. *Lema Could Smile At a 67, Or 79*, LA Times, July 26, 1966

Palmer, Arnold with William Barry Furlong, *Go for Broke!* Simon and Schuster, New York 1973

Raphael, Fred with Don Wade, *My Mulligan to Golf*, The American Golfer, Inc., 2011

Reilly, Rick *Seven Ahead, Nine to Go, and Then?*, Sports Illustrated, June 15, 1987

Roessing, Walt. *California Builder of Champions*. Golf Digest, January 1965

Seitz, Nick. *Last Look at Tony Lema*. Golf Digest, August 1967

Sullivan, Prescott. *Tony Got a Short Count*, San Francisco Examiner, August 1966

Venturi, Ken with Michael Arkush. *Getting Up & Down*. Chicago: Triumph Books, 2004

Wind, Herbert Warren, *The Story of American Golf*

Wright, Ben *Heroes of American Golf—Tony Lema*, Links, July/August 1995

Additional Sources and References

The newspaper and magazine clippings made available by Harry and Judi Lema provided me with a great deal of information I never would have been able to accumulate. Clotilda Lema, Tony's mother, started the collection, but Harry and Judi maintained the information over the years. I would also like to express my thanks to the late George Marks, a USGA Rules official out of Salt Lake City. The following is a list of known newspapers and periodicals that provided assistance as I gathered information to produce this book.

The San Francisco News, The San Francisco Chronicle Sporting Green, The San Francisco Examiner, Oakland Tribune, The Arizona Daily Star, Arizona Republic, Baltimore American, The Flint Journal, Chattanooga News-Free Press, The Houston Chronicle, The Seattle Times, The Seattle Post-Intelligencer, Las Vegas Sun, Hayward Daily Review, Orange County Register, The Dallas Morning News, The Chicago Daily News, The Chicago Tribune, New York Herald Tribune, Newsweek, The Cleveland Plain Dealer, The Los Angeles Times, Sports Illustrated, Golf Digest, Golf Magazine, The Greensboro Record, The Cleveland Press, The Oklahoma Journal.

Photographic Credits

First and foremost, most of the pictures came from the Lema family archives. I am extremely grateful. To all of the photographers, we thank you and appreciate your professional work.

Front Cover: Tony celebrating after his victory in the 1964 Bing Crosby
Back cover: Associated Newspapers LTD

Index

CPSIA information can be obtained
at www.ICGtesting.com
Printed in the USA
LVHW090911310721
694223LV00004B/67